P9-DTM-415

DATE DUE

DEMCO 38-230

About Island Press

Island Press is the only nonprofit organization in the United States whose principal purpose is the publication of books on environmental issues and natural resource management. We provide solutions-oriented information to professionals, public officials, business and community leaders, and concerned citizens who are shaping responses to environmental problems.

In 1994, Island Press celebrated its tenth anniversary as the leading provider of timely and practical books that take a multidisciplinary approach to critical environmental concerns. Our growing list of titles reflects our commitment to bringing the best of an expanding body of literature to the environmental community throughout North America and the world.

Support for Island Press is provided by The Geraldine R. Dodge Foundation, The Energy Foundation, The Ford Foundation, William and Flora Hewlett Foundation, The James Irvine Foundation, The John D. and Catherine T. MacArthur Foundation, The Andrew W. Mellon Foundation, The Pew Charitable Trusts, The Rockefeller Brothers Fund, The Tides Foundation, Turner Foundation, Inc., The Rockefeller Philanthropic Collaborative, Inc., and individual donors.

About The Global Development And Environment Institute

The Global Development And Environment Institute (G-DAE) was founded in 1993 to combine research and curricular development activities of two ongoing programs at Tufts University: the Program for the Study of Sustainable Change and Development in the School of Arts and Sciences, and the International Environment and Resource Policy Program at the Fletcher School of Law and Diplomacy. The combination creates a center of expertise in economics, policy, science, and technology.

G-DAE works toward understanding actual and possible past and future trajectories of economic development, emphasizing the relation between social and economic well-being on the one hand, and ecological health on the other. It develops an improved theoretic understanding of economic systems as they are embedded in the physical contexts of technology and the natural world, and in the social/psychological contexts of history, politics, ethics, culture, institutions, and human motivations and goals. Finally, it assists the public and private sectors of nations at different stages of development to develop policies that promote sustainability. G-DAE pursues its goals through research, publication projects, curriculum development, networking, and policy work.

A SURVEY OF
ECOLOGICAL
ECONOMICS

FRONTIER ISSUES IN ECONOMIC THOUGHT
VOLUME 1
NEVA R. GOODWIN, SERIES EDITOR

A SURVEY OF ECOLOGICAL ECONOMICS

EDITED BY RAJARAM KRISHNAN,
JONATHAN M. HARRIS, AND NEVA R. GOODWIN

A Research and Publication Project
of the Program for the Study of
Sustainable Change and Development

The Global Development
and Environment Institute
Tufts University

ISLAND PRESS

Washington, D.C. ■ Covelo, California

Riverside Community College
Library
4800 Magnolia Avenue
Riverside, California 92506

DEC   '96

HD 75.6 .S855 1995

A survey of ecological
  economics

Copyright © 1995 by Island Press

All rights reserved under International and Pan-American Copyright Conventions.
No part of this book may be reproduced in any form or by any means without per-
mission in writing from the publisher: Island Press, 1718 Connecticut Avenue,
N.W., Suite 300, Washington, DC 20009.

ISLAND PRESS is a trademark of The Center for Resource Economics.

Library of Congress Cataloging-in-Publication Data

A survey of ecological economics / edited by Rajaram Krishnan,
    Jonathan M. Harris and Neva Goodwin.
        p.   cm.
    "A research and publication project of he Program for he Study
of Sustainable Change and Development. The Global Development and
Environment Institute, Tufts University."
    Includes bibliographical reference and index.
    ISBN 1-55963-410-3. — ISBN 1-55963-411-1 (pbk.)
    1. Economic development—Environmental aspects. 2. Sustainable
development. 3. Ecology—Economic aspects. I. Krishnan, Rajaram.
II. Harris, Johnathan M. III. Goodwin, Neva R.
HD75.6.S855   1995
338.9—dc20   95-9315
                                                          CIP

Printed on recycled, acid-free paper ✪

Manufactured in the United States of America

10 9 8 7 6 5 4 3 2 1

To Nicholas Georgescu-Roegen
1906-1994

He showed the way for ecological economics.

Contents

PART II
Definition, Scope, and Interdisciplinary Issues

PART III
Theoretical Frameworks and Techniques

PART IV
Energy and Resource Flow Analysis

PART V
Accounting and Evaluation

PART VI
International Economic Relations, Development, and the Environment

PART VII
Ethical and Institutional Issues in Ecological Economics

Authors of Original Articles

B.R. *ALLENBY* AT&T Bell Laboratories, Princeton, New Jersey

MIGUEL A. *ALTIERI* Division of Biological Control, University of California, Berkeley

JESSE H. *AUSUBEL* Program for the Human Environment, Rockefeller University, New York, New York

ROBERT U. *AYRES* INSEAD, Fontainebleau, France

JAYANTA *BANDYOPADHYAY* Research Foundation for Science and Ecology, Dehradun, India

EDWARD B. *BARBIER* Dept. of Environmental Economics and Environmental Management, University of York, United Kingdom

BRIAN *BARRY* Dept. of Government, London School of Economics, United Kingdom

R. STEPHEN *BERRY* Dept. of Chemistry, University of Chicago, Illinois

JAGDISH *BHAGWATI* Dept. of Economics, Columbia University, New York, New York

KENNETH E. *BOULDING* formerly Dept. of Economics, University of Colorado, Boulder (deceased)

JEFFREY H. *BOUTWELL* American Academy of Arts and Sciences, Cambridge, Massachusetts

STUART *BURNESS* Dept. of Economics, University of New Mexico, Albuquerque

J. BAIRD *CALLICOTT* Dept. of Philosophy, University of Wisconsin, Stevens Point

P.F. *CHAPMAN* Open University, Milton Keynes, United Kingdom

PAUL P. *CHRISTENSEN* Dept. of Economics, Hofstra University, Hempstead, New York

MARY E. *CLARK* formerly Institute for Conflict Analysis and Resolution, George Mason University, Fairfax, Virginia and Dept. of Biology, San Diego State University, California (retired)

CUTLER J. *CLEVELAND* Center for Energy and Environmental Studies, Boston University, Massachusetts

MICK *COMMON* Centre for Resource and Environmental Studies, Australian National University, Canberra

ROBERT *COSTANZA* Maryland International Institute for Ecological Economics, Solomons, Maryland

RONALD *CUMMINGS* Dept. of Economics, Georgia State University, Atlanta

HERMAN E. *DALY* School of Public Affairs, University of Maryland, College Park

JOHN A. DIXON   Environment Dept., The World Bank, Washington, D.C.

FAYE DUCHIN   Institute for Economic Analysis, New York University, New York,

TRANS HUU DUNG   Dept. of Economics, Wright State University, Dayton, Ohio

PAUL EKINS   Dept. of Economics, University of London, United Kingdom

SALAH EL SERAFY   Consultant, The World Bank, Washington, D.C.

P.S. ELDER   Dept. of Environmental Design, University of Calgary, Canada

J. RONALD ENGEL   Professor of Social Ethics, Meadville/Lombard Theological
     School, Chicago; and Lecture, Divinity School, University of Chicago,
     Illinois

MALTE FABER   Alfred Weber Institute, University of Heidelberg, Germany

LOUISE A. FALLON   Environment Dept., The World Bank, Washington, D.C.

GEORGE FOY   Economist, Oakton, Virginia

SILVIO O. FUNTOWICZ   CEC-Joint Research Centre, Institute for Systems
     Engineering and Informatics, Ispra, Italy

NICHOLAS GEORGESCU-ROEGEN   formerly Dept. of Economics, Vanderbilt
     University, Nashville, Tennessee (deceased)

ROBERT GOODLAND   Environment Dept., The World Bank, Washington, D.C.

NEVA R. GOODWIN   Global Development and Environment Institute, Tufts
     University, Medford, Massachusetts

T.E. GRAEDEL   AT&T Bell Laboratories, Murray Hill, New Jersey

RAMACHANDRA GUHA   Center for Ecological Sciences, Indian Institute of
     Science, Bangalore, India

CHARLES A.S. HALL   College of Environmental Science and Forestry, State
     University of New York, Syracuse

BRUCE HANNON   Dept. of Geography, University of Illinois, Urbana

JONATHAN M. HARRIS   Global Development and Environment Institute, Tufts
     University, Medford, Massachusetts

PAUL HARRISON   Institute of Community Studies, London, United Kingdom

JOHAN HOLMBERG   Swedish Agency for Research Cooperation with Developing
     Countries, Stockholm

THOMAS F. HOMER-DIXON   Peace and Conflict Studies Program, University of
     Toronto, Canada

RICHARD HOWARTH   Environmental Studies Board, University of California,
     Santa Cruz

ROFIE HUETING   Central Bureau of Statistics, Voorburg, The Netherlands

PER-OLOV JOHANSSON   Stockholm School of Economics, Sweden

D.H. JUDSON   Bureau of Business and Economic Research, University of
     Nevada, Reno

ROBERT KAUFMAN   Center for Energy and Environmental Studies, Boston
     University, Massachusetts

PAUL G. KING   Dept. of Economics, Denison University, Granville, Ohio

DAVID C. KORTEN   People-Centered Development Forum, New York, New York

RAJARAM KRISHNAN Global Development and Environment Institute, Tufts University, Medford, Massachusetts

JOHN V. KRUTILLA formerly Resources for the Future, Washington, D.C. (retired)

GLENN-MARIE LANGE Institute for Economic Analysis, New York University, New York

SHARACHCHANDRA M. LÉLÉ Harvard Institute for International Development, Cambridge, Massachusetts

MARTIN W. LEWIS Dept. of Geography, University of Wisconsin, Madison

P.B. LINHART AT&T Bell Laboratories, Murray Hill, New Jersey

ERNST LUTZ Environment Dept., The World Bank, Washington, D.C.

ANIL MARKANDYA Harvard Institute for International Development, Cambridge, Massachusetts

JUAN MARTINEZ-ALIER Dept. de'Economia y, de'Historia Economica, Universidad Autònoma, Barcelona, Spain

OMAR MASERA Energy and Resources Group, University of California, Berkeley

PHILIP MIROWSKI Dept. of Economics, University of Notre Dame, Indiana

GLENN MORRIS

INDIRA NAIR Dept. of Engineering and Public Policy, Carnegie Mellon University, Pittsburgh, Pennsylvania

RICHARD B. NORGAARD Dept. of Energy and Resources and Dept. of Agricultural and Resource Economics, University of California, Berkeley

CLIFFORD NOWELL Dept. of Economics, Weber State University, Ogden, Utah

ELIZABETH ODUM Dept. of Natural Sciences, Sante Fe Community College, Gainesville, Florida

HOWARD ODUM Environmental Engineering Sciences, University of Florida, Gainesville

TALBOT PAGE Dept. of Economics, Brown University, Providence, Rhode Island

INJA PAIK

DAVID PEARCE Dept. of Economics, University College, London, United Kingdom

JOHN PEET Dept. of Chemical and Process Engineering, University of Canterbury, Christchurch, New Zealand

CHARLES PERRINGS Dept. of Environmental Economics and Environmental Management, University of York, United Kingdom

HENRY M. PESKIN Edgevale Associates, Inc., Silver Spring, Maryland

JOHN L.R. PROOPS Dept. of Economics and Management Science, University of Keele, Staffordshire, United Kingdom

GEORGE W. RATHJENS Dept. of Political Science, Massachusetts Institute of Technology, Cambridge

JEROME R. RAVETZ Research Methods Consultancy Ltd., London, United Kingdom

J.F. RICHARDS   Dept. of History, Duke University, Durham, North Carolina

MARK SAGOFF   Institute for Philosophy and Public Policy, University of Maryland, College Park

RICHARD SANDBROOK   International Institute for Environment and Development, London, United Kingdom

E.F. SCHUMACHER   former Economist, Surrey, England (deceased)

KLAUS SCHLÜPMANN

VANDANA SHIVA   Third World Network, New Delhi, India

JASON SHOGREN   Dept. of Economics, Iowa State University, Ames

MALCOLM SLESSER   Centre for Human Ecology, University of Edinburgh, Scotland

GERALD ALONZO SMITH   Dept. of Economics, Mankato State University, Mankato, Minnesota

PETER SÖDERBAUM   Dept. of Economics and Statistics, Swedish University of Agricultural Sciences, Upsala

CHRISTOPHER D. STONE   School of Law, University of Southern California, Los Angeles

JAN TINBERGEN   formerly Erasmus University, Rotterdam, The Netherlands (deceased)

MICHAEL TOMAN   Resources for the Future, Washington, D.C.

JOHN F. TOMER   Manhattan College, Troy, New York

KENNETH N. TOWNSEND   Dept. of Economics, Hampden-Sydney College, Hampden-Sydney, Virginia

F.E. TRAINER   School of Education, University of New South Wales, Kensington, Australia

DANIEL A. UNDERWOOD   Dept. of Social Science, Peninsula College, Port Angeles, Washington

LYNN WHITE, JR.   formerly Dept. of History, University of California, Los Angeles (deceased)

JEFFREY T. YOUNG   Dept. of Economics, St. Lawrence University, Canton, New York

Series Introduction

Neva R. Goodwin

The Nature and Purpose of this Series

This is the first volume in a series. The purpose of the series is to provide a convenient way for people of various interests and backgrounds to familiarize themselves with intellectual developments in areas in which important, everyday human concerns (about, for example, happiness, justice, or the health of the ecosystem) significantly influence, and are influenced by, economic behavior. The first such area, surveyed in this volume, is Ecological Economics; later volumes will survey such topics as The Consumer Society; Definitions and Assessments of Human Welfare; Sustainable Development; Meaningful Work; and Economic Power.

We have identified these topics as issues on the frontiers of economic thought because they share three characteristics: (1) they are subjects which, we believe, have extremely important implications for the nature and the consequences of human economic behavior; (2) these topics have not been treated as central to the discipline of economics as now defined; and (3) they have a strong intrinsic interest for other areas of intellectual endeavor in addition to economics.

These Frontier areas are also the focus of considerable intellectual liveliness. Many individuals, recognizing the centrality of these issues for the world of the late twentieth century, have been thinking and writing about them. Among these:

(1) Some are trained economists; of these, some have retained their identity as professionals within this discipline, but many others have found their concern with the "frontier issues" to be incompatible with the systems of rewards and recognition in the field, especially in the United States.

(2) Some people who think and write about ecological economics, the consumer society, sustainable development, and other frontier issues come to these subjects from other disciplines such as anthropology, sociology, geography, political science, history, and philosophy.

(3) Other Frontier thinkers are hard to place; they cross the usual lines between "intellectual" and "activist," as well as the disciplinary lines between, for example, economics and philosophy, or sociology or ecol-

ogy. As often occurs, some of the needed new theory is being pioneered in practice before it is generalized and abstracted conceptually. Thus there are also writers in what we have identified as Frontier areas who are more readily identified as activists than as academics.

As an economist myself, I first began to think about the six Frontier areas listed above primarily in relation to the discipline of economics. From that perspective it seemed that there would be great value to the creation of a practical and convenient method for economists of all kinds to become familiar with work being done in areas that should be—but are not now—studied within the core of the discipline. As the research into the first Frontier area progressed under the leadership of Rajaram Krishnan, it became increasingly clear that everything about the project is interdisciplinary. We found it necessary to search far beyond the borders of economics for work on any one of the Frontier topics, and to read work by authors from the wide range of disciplines suggested above; we also recognized that the results would be useful to people with quite varied reasons for their interest in areas in which economic concerns overlap issues that are more often thought of as environmental, psychological, ethical, etc.

The method used in this project is a novel one, providing not just new information but a new *genre* of information presentation. It is, perhaps, most similar to the collections of abstracts of articles in a given area that are available for various disciplines; however, the summaries that will comprise the largest part of each volume in this series are very different from abstracts. They are considerably longer, since they are designed not only to list the topics that are covered in each article but also to present, in a readable, abbreviated form, the most important arguments made about those topics. As compared to more complete bibliographical listings, the Frontiers volumes are selective, representing the judgment of well-informed research teams about which are the critical writings in each area.

How do we expect these summaries to be used? Clearly, reading a summary of two or three pages is not the same as reading the original article, which might be anywhere from five to fifty pages long. Some lines of thought will be compressed; others will be omitted. Initially, we wondered whether there might be a danger that the Frontiers summaries would be read *instead* of the articles that they describe. In one sense, that may be true: someone who would not have the time, patience, or research knowledge to read 100 articles in ecological economics might, nevertheless, read through the approximately 100 Frontiers summaries in this area. However, just as radio technology increased the purchase of musical recordings by introducing listeners to new music that they then wanted to hear again, we believe the net result of the Frontiers publications will be an increase in the number of articles read. Where the reader finds something of special value or pertinence, s/he is likely to want to go to the original to grapple with the details and to get the full context. Someone who is interested in one of the Frontiers topics but does not know where to begin can browse through that volume, find the parts of greatest interest, and locate therein the articles that s/he will then search out to read in full.

The primary purpose of each volume in the series will be to provide a good overview of one of the areas we have identified as being on the frontier of the field of economics. As an overview, the intention is to address such questions as: What is included in contemporary understandings of this area of thought? What is the research agenda? Which, to date, are the most important writings in the area?

Regarding the last question, the research team for the Frontiers series takes responsibility for determining "importance" on two grounds. One of these is the ultimately subjective decision of which articles will add to the collection valuable ideas that are not readily found—or that are not so well expressed—elsewhere. The same principles are true of the selection of *which* arguments within a given article are to be summarized—and which will be left out. That is to say, particularly in the case of long articles, some parts will only be mentioned, while more attention will be paid to the sections that help to round out the volume's presentation of the whole Frontier area. Thus, the subjectivity of the judgment used in compiling the volume must again be acknowledged; nothing but individual judgment can be used to determine which are the "critical" ideas. This is noted without apology—indeed, if anything, the reverse; a large part of the value of this project depends upon the fact that critical judgment has been used in selecting and summarizing the articles included herein.

Our second criterion for determining "the most important writings" is somewhat more objective; here "importance" refers to the impact that an article has had upon other thinkers in the area. This is in part inferred by noting which articles are most frequently referenced in the literature. Additionally, near the beginning and the end of the research work for each volume we communicate with a few (perhaps a dozen) outstanding writers and thinkers in the area to request their comments on the project. At the beginning we ask them for bibliographies of works they have found especially useful or illuminating; at the end we request their reaction to our final selection list.

In attempting to provide an overview of each Frontier area, we have found it helpful to break it down into parts. Each part is preceded by an essay that analyses the state of that part of the field—what it has to offer, where it is perceived to be weak, where we feel that additional research is most needed, etc.

The users of the Frontiers volumes are expected to include people from the following groups:

(1) *Researchers coming from the discipline of economics* who are working on—or are curious about—the particular Frontier areas dealt with in each volume. These will include those who think of themselves as in the "mainstream" of neoclassical economic thought, but who are interested in what is going on at what they regard as the margins of the field. It will also include others who have already focused on the areas of our summaries and who may regard them as the proper core of economics. (We hope that the term *Frontiers* is meaningful from both points of view.)

(2) *Researchers in other academic areas.* We are especially aware of connections among the social sciences (sociology, anthropology, geography, political science, history, etc.). This series will provide a source through which such researchers can understand and thereby contribute to the analysis of issues on the margin between economics and their own fields without having to penetrate the barrier of the language and techniques of neoclassical economic presentations.

In addition to social scientists, we expect to find other academic readers such as philosophers (especially philosophers of science), as well as some engineers and natural scientists who have a professional interest in the various areas of intersection with economics that will be surveyed in the Frontiers volumes.

The project is undertaken on the assumption that this segment of our audience will have as much to contribute to the development of a more appropriately contextualized economics as economists have to contribute to their fields.

(3) *Teachers and students at the graduate and undergraduate level* who can use the Frontiers summaries as a basis for interesting reading and classroom discussion on alternate viewpoints.

(4) *Activists* seeking to understand academic arguments in a nontechnical form.

(5) *Foundations, government agencies, and other sources of research support and employment of economists* who can view the volumes as guides for shaping research agendas. Characteristics of the Frontiers areas selected for this project include novelty and contentiousness: the old borders of economics are being stretched because some thinkers, both inside and outside of economics, believe that there are critical subjects not being adequately served by the existing paradigm. The mainstream is bound to resist such redefinitions, and the process of redefinition will inevitably be accompanied by differences among the new thinkers.

The Frontier project aims to hasten the process of sorting out the leading contributors to the new ideas.

The Need for New Approaches to Economic Theory

This section of the Series Introduction will lay out, in more philosophical terms, the reasons why we believe that the areas we have identified as Frontier issues are, themselves, of critical importance at this time; and why we have chosen the method of these volumes for giving wider currency to intellectual developments in these areas.

What matters? That first question of philosophy should also be the first question of economics; for if the study of economics is to be of value to society it must stress the aspects of economic behavior that matter the most.

This series, *Frontier Issues in Economic Thought,* arises out of the conviction that while the focus of economic theory has shifted over time, it has not done so in ways that, as of the 1990s, have brought it abreast of the most important aspects of economic behavior. A number of critical areas which should be at the center of the mainstream of thinking about economics have, instead, been left to the margins. It is arguable that those margins, viewed by the most conservative members of the mainstream as "fringes," are more properly seen as the "frontiers" of economic thought. They include the topics we have selected for this series: ecological economics; the consumer society; definitions and assessments of human welfare; sustainable development; meaningful work; and economic power.

How—and why—has the content of the field of economics diverged from the subjects that are of prime economic importance in evolving modern societies? A full answer to that question, as well as a defense of the premises on which it rests, would require a much longer exposition than is possible here.[1] In suggesting some of what would be included in a fuller argument, I will start with some perceptions of what economics was about in the eighteenth century.

Adam Smith, for the titles of his two great works—*The Theory of Moral Sentiments* and *An Inquiry into the Nature and Causes of the Wealth of Nations*—chose three of the concepts that were of paramount importance in his time—*morality, wealth,* and the *nation*—as an especially appropriate level of analysis for economic thought. In the eventful two centuries since then (with an appreciable part of that eventfulness attributable to Smith's influence) some priorities have shifted. For example:

(1) The role of the nation is different, its singular importance challenged by supra- and sub-national allegiances and powers. Some examples

include multinational corporations, the Bretton Woods institutions, newly energized religious movements, the as yet hardly realized impact of the mega-cities (those with over 10 million inhabitants), and a variety of local movements and ideologies (some, but not all, formalized in NGOs).

(2) Wealth—the power to command resources—has different meanings depending upon the type of need or want for which it is sought. When the most pressing needs are directly related to survival, then acquisition of the necessary resources for survival requires no explanation; survival and the means for survival are so clearly and obviously connected that it hardly seems necessary to make a means/ends distinction. However, when the basic needs have been secured, then another issue arises concerning the acquisition of wealth. Wealth must be regarded as a means—to what end? One word used to indicate the end, or purpose, of wealth is *well-being*.[2] To the extent that progress (or development, or the accumulation of capital, etc.) brings people to a state of affluence where their individual and family survival appears assured, wealth as an end in itself should cease to be the focus of economics. The coexistence of unprecedented affluence with extreme poverty,[3] as well as the impacts upon our environment and the implications thereof for the future, strongly suggest that the focus of economics should shift from wealth per se to the purpose of wealth.

(3) Morality was assumed by Smith as an essential backdrop for all human behavior; this was not less so in economic behavior than in other areas. As the discipline of economics developed, subsequent writers increasingly looked only to *The Wealth of Nations*, forgetting that its author wrote it in the context of *The Theory of Moral Sentiments*, and also downplaying the moral arguments that thread through *The Wealth of Nations*. This is a topic which has not become less salient for economic behavior; however, it has been pushed to the fringes of the field of economics.[4]

It is interesting—and perhaps a little depressing—to see how the evolution of the field of economics has diverged from the evolution of economic issues and realities. Take, for example, Adam Smith's focus on the nation. As taught in colleges and universities, economics is generally viewed as composed of two approximately equal halves: micro- and macroeconomics. The field of macroeconomics, essentially invented by John Maynard Keynes at the end of the depression of the 1930s, accepts Smith's assumption of the nation as an especially appropriate level of analysis for economic thought. Microeconomics, by contrast, focuses on what are regarded as individual economic actors, such as families, firms, and labor unions. There is no developed field of global economics; trade theory, for example, is largely based on standard micro and macro concepts. By now the field of macroeconomics is in considerable disarray, as successive attempts to make tight logical connections between micro and macro have failed. However, economics curricula have not yet been changed to reflect the fact that the old micro–macro division no longer works.

The failure by economists to elevate the concept of *well-being* to an importance equal to that given to *wealth* is related to the loss (from most writing in economics since the time of Alfred Marshall) of an appreciation of the salience of *moral issues* to economic behavior. It may be said that the basis of human morality is human values—our identification of *what matters*. In the mainstream, neoclassical economics paradigm the single value admitted to is efficiency. Efficiency, however, is only a means. When pressed to name the end to which efficiency is a means, neoclassical economists offer the maximization of utility. In practice, most economic writings admit that utility is undefinable (or, at least, unobservable and immeasurable). They therefore use as a proxy goal the maximization of consumption—and thus of production—within feasibility constraints. The growing recognition that the feasibility constraints must include such ecological issues as carrying capacity and sustainability has not succeeded in changing neoclassical economics' orientation to growth in production and consumption. That orientation can only be affected by a much deeper alteration in our appreciation of what constitutes human well-being, with renewed attention to both the individual and the societal goals whose realization promotes well-being.

The Mainstream and the Frontiers

The foregoing description of changes in economics since Adam Smith provides a very cursory look at some of what we believe to be missing from the contemporary mainstream paradigm. Within this synopsis may be seen the germs of the ideas that have been developed into what we are calling Frontier areas.

The definition of "Frontier" areas implies, by contrast, the existence of "core" or "mainstream" areas. Any body of knowledge that has received systematic academic attention develops a mainstream following. A mainstream represents a core of knowledge, theory, methodology, approach, and point of view which is widely accepted. At the same time, it imposes a degree of conformity upon views and methods; indeed, it may so take for granted large parts of its world view (i.e., the bundle composed of knowledge, theory, methodology, approach, and point of view) that it would deny that it possesses them—just as some people deny that they have any kind of accent in their speech: an accent (or an approach, or a point of view) is what *other* people have.

The mainstream determines the boundaries of the discipline within which debate is acceptable—given a methodology, the fundamental questions to be asked, and the areas of investigation; however, it precludes serious debate about the methodology, the fundamental questions, and the areas of investigation. That part of the literature which asks and answers questions on these fundamental issues constitutes the frontier of a discipline. A frontier area whose existence questions the premises of the mainstream and develops different analytical frameworks is likely to be marginalized and ignored by the mainstream until something like a paradigm shift occurs (approximately along the lines suggested by Thomas Kuhn's 1962 book, *The Structure of Scientific Revolutions).*

This conception of what constitutes a "Frontier" area both permits and justifies this project. It permits it because mainstream areas tend to be so well explored, and to have generated such a large literature, that it might not be feasible to survey any comparable mainstream area in the depth supplied in the Frontier volumes. The only comparable efforts in the field of economics—for example, the abstracts published quarterly in the *Journal of Economic Literature*—are far briefer, and are narrowly focused on subjects that fit within the methodological approaches and subject categories currently in (mainstream) fashion. While modern information technology is likely to make it progressively easier to stay current even in areas that lie on the edges of disciplinary divisions, technology cannot substitute for the selective judgment that is essential for this project. Right now, and for at least a few years to come, it will be feasible to gain an overview of the Frontier areas we have identified because, while the expansion of new areas and new kinds of economic thinking is very rapid, this development is of recent origin, and the material to be surveyed in these areas is still of a comprehensible volume.

At the same time, this project is justified by its focus on fast-changing Frontier areas where there is a special need for clarification and systematic comparison and sorting out. The Frontiers volumes will have an exceptional value in this period, when so much is, so to speak, up for grabs. While the very foundations of economics (the psychological assumptions, for example, upon which the whole system of theory is axiomatized) are being questioned and reevaluated, new thinkers cannot turn to the standard body of accepted knowledge as background for their original work. The question, "where shall I look?" then becomes exceptionally poignant; guidance in finding individual answers to that question is needed more now than in times of less questioning and seeking.

Many thoughtful commentators now perceive a need of great scope; in the end, what is required may be nothing less than one or more whole alternative systems of economic theory. Any alternative that is to be adopted must be able to show that it can, under reasonable goal definitions, rival the achievements of the currently dominant paradigm—achievements which represent the efforts of a vast amount of human talent, operating cumulatively over all of this century. To take on the task of erecting a viable challenge to the existing economic paradigm, each thinker needs as much assistance as possible. Even if, in normal times, few expect to find what virtually every researcher would always like to have—a volume of extracts surveying his/her area of interest—such an aid will be of exceptional significance in this transitional era.

Another justification for this project is the growing number of scholars from all disciplines who believe that the future of the social sciences must include a strong move toward interdisciplinary teamwork. On the one hand, they point out, we encounter ever growing scale and complexity among the human problems that the social sciences are designed (in their applied form, and in the theory formulated to underpin their application) to address. On the other hand, expansion of the knowledge which could conceivably be used in addressing these problems invites ever more minute specialization as the only way for a single individual to be master of all the information in a single (ever more narrowly defined) area. Only by integrating the masters of many specialties into teams, and by developing creative new models for interdisciplinary social science teamwork, can we take advantage of all the information needed to deal with problems of growing complexity.

It is worth exploring whether the Frontiers publications may be able to play a useful role in allowing individuals who wish to make connections with disciplines beyond their specialty to take the kind of quick survey that will allow them to decide where and with whom they could most usefully connect. If this project can, indeed, give this kind of assistance, it will also strengthen the argument for working on the technology that might make it possible to continue publications of this sort even in mature fields.

Finally, given that this is a time of exceptional ferment and creativity in the field of economics, there will also be an historical value to the Frontiers publications. They have the potential to be viewed, in the future, as critical records of a pivotal moment in the history of economic thought—one of the interdisciplinary periods when traditional disciplinary boundaries are reevaluated and redrawn.

Conclusion

In concluding this Series Introduction a few explanations and disclaimers are in order.

To make the Frontier summaries as readable as possible, we have tried to minimize direct quotations from the articles being summarized. Where we have used quotations from the original it has been either because the author stated an idea so succinctly and precisely that it seemed any other wording would be much inferior, or else because a particular phrase or expression is so distinctively associated with its author that direct quotation was important to give the flavor of the article. We have tried to be scrupulous about using quotation marks to indicate when a summary includes material quoted directly from the original. We have generally omitted articles that describe specific techniques and articles that are empirical in nature, as they are very difficult to summarize in a manner that would make sense to the general reader.

The pool from which our selections were drawn was not, as we would ideally have liked it to be, a global one, since our resources did not permit us to undertake a multi-language survey. We are aware, however, that this limitation makes the survey less complete than we would have wished. We do not assume that articles omitted because they were not printed in English are necessarily of lesser importance than the ones to which we had ready access.

Even within the universe of articles printed in English, our selection is fairly U.S.-centered. Although, after publication, we will undoubtedly discover additional papers that we never knew existed, and that we wished we had read before going to press, we nevertheless feel that we have made a quite comprehensive survey of the literature in ecological economics that has been current in the United States in recent years and decades. Where we have encountered English-language papers on ecological economics that were written or published outside of the United States we have included them in the pool from which we have drawn our final selections; but we have not made the kind of systematic search outside the United States that we made within this country. Again, we do not claim any better reason for this than limitations of time and resources.

We have especially regretted that the necessity to draw boundaries about what we could survey has caused us to make the somewhat arbitrary decision to summarize articles, but not whole books. In some cases, where it seemed especially salient, we have summarized an individual chapter out of a book, and we have felt free to summarize individual articles from collections published in book form. However, the task of reducing the content of a whole book to a few pages is very different from that of summarizing even a long article; for this Frontiers volume, at least, we decided not to undertake it.

Finally, while considering what we have left out, we should mention the historical classics in the field—works like Ronald Coase's "The Problem of Social Cost" (1960), Garett Hardin's "Tragedy of the Commons" (1968), or Allen Kneese's "Analysis of Environmental Pollution" (1971). In deciding not to allocate research time to reading and summarizing the variety of writings that one would have to consider for this category, we were influenced by our awareness of how much movement there has already been in this Frontier area. The works just mentioned were written when ecological economics was not yet thought of; the principal reference point was neoclassical economics, with its emerging subfield of "environmental economics." The latter, as a neoclassical offshoot, essentially applies the tools and approaches of the mainstream paradigm to issues of environmental importance. It does not include any dramatic shift of world view, such as the ecological economics view of the world's economies as being embedded within the earth's ecologies, rather than vice versa—an assumption that radically reverses the neoclassical view of reality. The "classics" cited above made great contributions in establishing the importance of environmental issues. However, they are no longer on the ecological economics frontier of the discipline of economics.

Mention was made earlier of the element of subjectivity involved in selecting and summarizing papers for this work. It is important to add that the determination by the Frontiers research team of the most important ideas does not necessarily connote agreement with those ideas. In fact, members of the team have strongly disagreed with some of the papers which are nevertheless represented in the present volume because it was felt that they articulate ideas which are important in the present development of ecological economics.

A related point should be made. Ecological economics, like the other Frontier areas, is rapidly evolving. Among the ideas which we believe to be central to the area now, it is almost certain that some will, over time, lose their salience, while others that do not seem so important now will come to command greater attention. It would be surprising if the team of researchers that has been deeply immersed in this topic for nearly three years did not possess opinions as to which ideas deserve to drop out and which should be given more attention.

We have tried to be moderate in our representation of these opinions, steering a middle course between, on the one hand, a positivist view that there is an objective reality to the existence of the area of study called ecological economics; and, on the other, a relativist recognition that such conceptual categories are created in the minds of people, including ourselves.

Positivistically, we have included in this volume ideas and papers with which we do not necessarily agree, but we feel that they are important to a generally held definition of the area. Relativistically, we have tended to give somewhat more emphasis to the ideas that we feel will or should increasingly define this area in the future, and less to those that seem to us due to diminish in influence. This balance is evident in the essays introducing each section as well as in the selection of papers summarized.

Our definition of what constitutes a Frontier in relation to economics is highly dynamic. We expect that the boundaries of the whole discipline will continue to evolve, both because of progress that has been made in the field and because of changes in the real world. We hope that our project may contribute usefully to an evolution of economics wherein some subjects that now constitute the Frontiers of the field will continue to move closer to its core. We perceive considerable tension between the methodology and general approach of the existing core, and the topics which—partly because they are not so amenable to analysis through the neoclassical approach and methods—have been left out of the core. For this reason we anticipate that the field may have to undergo some difficult, even wrenching, changes if it is to adapt as suggested here. It is comforting to find such a possibility anticipated by so eminent an economist as Sir John Hicks:

> Our theories, regarded as tools of analysis, are blinkers. . . . Or it may be politer to say that they are rays of light, which illuminate a part of the target, leaving the rest in darkness. As we use them, we avert our eyes from things which may be relevant, in order that we should see more clearly what we do see. It is entirely proper that we should do this, since otherwise we should see very little. But it is obvious that a theory which is to perform this function satisfactorily must be well chosen; otherwise it will illumine the wrong things. Further, since it is a changing world that we are studying, a theory which illumines the right things at one time may illumine the wrong things at another. This may happen because of changes in the world (the things neglected may have gained in importance relatively to the things considered) or because of changes in ourselves (the things in which we are interested may have changed). There is, there can be, no economic theory which will do for us everything we want all the time.[5]

We are not more optimistic than Hicks that any economic theory—even one that took full account of all of the important issues now lying on its frontiers—could do everything one would want for all time. However, we believe that an economic theory that is to be truly useful and appropriate for the times just ahead will need to take account of the Frontier areas described in this series.

In stressing the importance of these areas we do not regard them as of concern only to economists. We offer this project to our colleagues, to researchers, activists, and the intellectually curious, with mingled conviction and humility. We hope that we are contributing to movements that will not only change some disciplinary boundaries and broaden the real-world usefulness of economics, but will also assist in the development of more fruitful teamwork and interdisciplinary research. However, whatever intellectual structures, or disciplinary boundaries, emerge from this transitional era, we have to anticipate that a time will come when they, too, will no longer be able to keep step with changing circumstances, and will need to be challenged and changed anew.

Notes

1. See Neva R. Goodwin, *Social Economics: An Alternative Theory, Volume 1: Building Anew on Marshall's Principles* (London: Macmillan, and New York: St. Martin's Press, 1991). See also Neva R. Goodwin, Silvio O. Funtowicz, Jerome R. Ravetz, and Bruce Mazlish, *Intellectual Trends into the Future: Neoclassical Social Science and the Possibility of Social Progress* (in preparation).

2. Another word, favored by many economists, is *utility*. In its most general sense (where it means something like "whatever it is people want"), utility is, if anything, less well defined than well-being. When a more concrete definition is needed, utility is often defined as consumption of goods and services. That definition also has its problems (see below).

3. Given that the absolute size of the human population is now about five times greater than it was when Smith wrote, and that approximately one-fifth of all people now living suffer from severe deprivation of the basic requirements of life, it is evident that the absolute number of people for whom "wealth" is a simple survival issue is larger than it was in the eighteenth century. At the same time, however, far more human beings than at any previous time in history are now enjoying sufficient command over resources that they can consider other goals of wealth than simple survival.

4. See Neva R. Goodwin, "Economic Meanings of Trust and Responsibility," in *As If the Future Mattered: Translating Social and Economic Theory into Human Behavior*, ed. Neva R. Goodwin (Ann Arbor: University of Michigan Press, forthcoming).

5. John Hicks, *Wealth and Welfare: Collected Essays on Economic Theory, Vol. 1* (Cambridge, Massachusetts: Harvard University Press, 1981), 232–33.

Preface

How can we define ecological economics? Is it a sub-field of economics, an interdisciplinary area, or a discipline in its own right? As the field has developed, it has shown aspects of all three categorizations. After exploring the expanding literature of ecological economics, the researchers for this volume have leaned toward the third proposition: a new field of study is being defined which is independent of the standard economic paradigm.

This is an ambitious claim, and the reader will have to make his or her own judgment as to how well it is supported here. After surveying hundreds of books and articles, however, the editors of this volume feel that a strong case exists for the emergence of ecological economics as a new field of research and study. Not that the discipline lacks historical roots—but it is only within the past decade that it has emerged from marginality to play a significant role in shaping serious thought about global economic and environmental issues.

The field of "environmental economics," as distinct from ecological economics, already exists in mainstream economics. However, that mainstream approach is felt by many theorists and practitioners to be inadequate to deal with the contemporary crises of environment/human interactions. The "environmental" area within the existing discipline of economics is too constrained by its requirement of market valuation to respond adequately to the complexities of issues such as global warming, species loss, ecosystem degradation, intergenerational equity, and non-human values. Ecological economics, by contrast, starts from a recognition of the biophysical realities underlying the operations of the economic system. Economic issues are then viewed in this context, rather than attempting a monetary price valuation of all aspects of the environment.

The issues which ecological economics brings to the fore are especially important in a long-term perspective and on a planetary scale. Much of human economic activity has been directed toward stretching ecological limits, notably through high-input agriculture and the use of fossil fuels. In some senses, this enterprise has been phenomenally successful, but over the long term and in a broader perspective we find that natural systems react adversely to the ever-increasing pressure to produce for human use. Effects which are subtle at first gradually become overwhelming. In agriculture, such effects include cumulative soil erosion and nutrient loss, water overdraft and pollution, and the emergence of resistant pest species. The inexorable buildup of carbon dioxide in the atmosphere has no immediate effect on economic activity, but eventually it may threaten the climatic stability of the entire planet.

Such issues are by now well known but often fail to register on the monetary scale of standard economic analysis. Attempts to reflect these ecological developments in economic cost terms inevitably fail to capture the full scope of the problems. For some time, however, writers in the ecological economics tradition have warned of just such problems, basing their analysis on such concepts as energy flows and ecological system stability. The steady drumbeat of news on growing global ecological problems signals a need to treat the field of ecological economics much more seriously than it has been treated hitherto by most economists.

The reason why this paradigm shift is particularly important now has to do with the issue of scale, a concept much emphasized by ecological economists. In standard economic analysis, there are no inherent barriers to the scale of the macroeconomy. This vision of unlimited growth is in fundamental conflict with the ecological perspective, which sees scale and carrying capacity limits as central to the analysis of any biophysical process. It is precisely this issue which undergirds almost all of our current environmental problems. The human race has doubled in numbers in less than forty years, and may well double again in the next forty. Economic activity has at least quadrupled over the same period, and according to World Bank forecasts will nearly quadruple again by 2030.[1] Whether we are thinking of the loss of open space in the United States, water limits in India, over-harvesting of fisheries worldwide, or the enormous potential coal use of China in the coming decades, environmental problems are driven by the pressures of growth. Scale issues can be ignored up to a point, as they are in mainstream macroeconomics, but we are now well past that point.

If we accept the case for a more careful consideration of ecological economics, what do we find? This is the question which motivated our research for this volume. The organization of the volume is intended to present the full scope of the field, starting with its historical roots and the definition of the field. We then move to general and specific theoretical concepts, then to energy and resource flow analysis and national income accounting techniques. Applications to North–South/international relations and to social, ethical, and institutional issues round out the volume. Several hundred articles and books were surveyed in the search for those which would best represent the field. Our selection principle has favored those articles which we believe best express a key concept or argument. Rather than reprinting full articles, we have chosen to summarize articles or book chapters. In this way, the reader will get the benefit of the essential content of an article—which would not emerge from a shorter abstract—but a far larger number of authors can be included than would be possible if the full text was reproduced. In every case, the authors have reviewed the summaries to check that their work is adequately and clearly presented. These summaries, however, are in no way meant to substitute for the original articles. We strongly recommend that readers seek out the full texts in their areas of interest.

The overview essays at the head of each part attempt to synthesize the diverse selections to give a sense of the nature of the field. Despite the varied views and theoretical perspectives represented, we feel that a certain *Gestalt* emerges, a sense of a viable field of analysis with its own parameters and techniques. There is certainly some overlap with standard economics as well as with ecological, political, historical, and ethical analysis. But we feel, and have some confidence that the reader will also feel, this emergence of a new and essential discipline.

Such a far-reaching enterprise has necessarily involved the contributions of many people. Rajaram Krishnan, an economist specializing in agricultural and labor issues in development, has coordinated the selection and preparation of summaries, as well as providing a summary essay for Part VI. Jonathan Harris, who has published work on the economics of agriculture, trade, and global institutions, has written most of the overview essays that introduce the parts of the book. Neva R. Goodwin, the originator of the project and author of *Social Economics: An Alternative Theory,* has contributed the Part VII overview. The research team for this volume included Andrew Morrison, Daniel Von Moltke, Daniele Guidi, and Kevin Gallagher. For tireless editing work we are indebted to Carolyn Logan. Associates of the Global Development and Environment Institute including Jeffrey Zabel and Elliott Morss contributed to the shaping of this volume in its early stages. The final responsibility for the selection and content rests with the three editors. We hope that we have done justice to the field of ecological economics, and perhaps helped to define this emerging discipline.

Most of the funding for the research and writing of this volume was provided by the John D. and Catherine T. MacArthur Foundation, as part of a grant to the Program for the Study of Sustainable Change and Development. Tufts University administrative staff have provided essential support throughout. We are very grateful for the active support of these institutions, without which the project would not have been possible.

Note
1. World Bank, *1992 World Development Report: Development and the Environment* (Oxford University Press, 1992), 9.

Note to the Reader

In general, the summaries presented here do not repeat material from the original articles verbatim. In a few instances it has seemed appropriate to include in the summaries direct quotations from the original text ranging from a phrase to a few sentences. Where this has been done, the page reference to the original article is given in square brackets. The complete citation for the article always appears at the beginning of the summary. References to other books or articles appear in endnotes following each summary.

A SURVEY OF
ECOLOGICAL
ECONOMICS

PART I
Historical Perspectives

Overview Essay
by Jonathan M. Harris

The history of economic theory is today a neglected field. If the evolution of economic ideas is studied at all, it is generally viewed as a linear, progressive process leading inevitably to the highest embodiment of economic analysis: today's neoclassical model. The average student of economics will encounter the names of some bygone economists appended to concepts: Smith's invisible hand, Ricardian rent, Keynesian fiscal policy, Marshallian demand curve, Walrasian general equilibrium. But these concepts are merely embedded in what is generally taken to be a complete and consistent theory of economic activity. Missing is any sense of intense controversy, internal conflicts, fundamental divisions, wrong turns, and neglected insights in the history of theory. The major remaining controversy centers on the efforts of "new classical" economists to purge the last vestiges of the Keynesian heresy from the field, against the resistance of aging Keynesians and a few Post-Keynesian radicals. But little attention is given to the history of theory for insights into this or any other modern issue.

The selections in this part offer a contrary perspective. From varying viewpoints, they suggest that crucial issues raised by pre-classical and classical economists have been neglected, leading to fundamental weaknesses in present mainstream theory. New life is thus breathed into old controversies, and apparently minor or outdated views are seen to hold clues to modern dilemmas. Issues such as the productivity of land, population growth, resource and energy limits, and the moral/philosophical basis of economic activity gain a new currency in the context of modern environmental crises. This discussion defines the theoretical background for the emergence of ecological economics as a discipline.

Paul Christensen outlines the major theme of this part: the roots of ecological economics are to be found in the physiocratic and classical schools of economics. Both placed emphasis on the productive power of "land," a concept which is usually taken broadly in economics to encompass all natural resources. Specific attention to the importance of energy flows is also

seen in the works of some pre-classical and classical authors. However, these
concerns were then lost in the further evolution of neoclassical economic
thought. As economics moved toward analytical formalism and mathematical modeling, material and energy flows were subsumed under the
homogenous categories of "capital" and "labor." "Land" survives in formal
models only as a one-dimensional concept which fails to reflect the physical realities of natural resources and energy. The complexities of the real
world are sacrificed on the altar of mathematical simplification.

Christensen suggests that these neglected themes from classical thought
can form the basis of a new "biophysical economics" focusing on energy
and resource use in production, and on the specific and complementary
nature of productive inputs. (*Complementary* here refers to the essential
role of energy and resources in the operations of physical capital, in contrast
to the neoclassical convention of viewing all productive inputs as substitutes.) A convergence is seen between this classically based alternative theoretical approach and some of the twentieth-century non-mainstream
theories such as Sraffa's commodity analysis and Post-Keynesian disequilibrium theory. Christensen thus draws together some of the threads of
opposition to the formal mathematical models of equilibrium which dominate contemporary economics.

Gerald Alonzo Smith offers an overview of a different but equally important dissenting theme in the history of economic thought. Early opponents
of the doctrine of economic growth, such as Sismondi and Ruskin, argued
that true human welfare is not best served by expanding production of
material goods. Hobson and Tawney continued this critique of consumption as the goal of economic activity. None of these thinkers had much
impact on the course of standard economic theory, but their ideas have
gained new relevance in the post–World War II period, as mass consumption has expanded beyond anything they could have foreseen. As we will see
in later parts of this volume, the moral/ethical critique of economic growth
deriving from their work combines with the biophysical critique of ever-
expanding production to shape the world view of ecological economics.

D. H. Judson pursues the issue of convergence between ecological economics and neo-Ricardian value theory. In both, the source of value is identified with productive factors, a theme common to the Physiocrats, Smith,
Ricardo, and Marx. This contrasts with the neoclassical derivation of value
from individual demand or utility. Energy theorists share with neo-Ricardians several important assumptions about the nature of value: they both
proceed from the social rather than the individual level, see value as objective rather than subjective, and are concerned with dynamic processes of
growth and change. Differences arise, however, over the delicate issue of
whether a single ultimate determinant of value can be identified, or should
even be sought. Neo-Ricardians tend to look to commodity inputs as the

basis of value, while ecological economists favor energy content or entropy measures.

Some energy theorists have attempted to formalize value determination in analytical paradigms demonstrating that embodied energy is the source of all value—reminiscent of the Marxian labor theory of value. This initially attractive identification of a basic source of value runs into numerous problems of consistency and application to actual prices. Philip Mirowski's "Energy and Energetics in Economic Theory" notes that this "neo-energetics" school can be criticized for oversimplifying the problem, just as neoclassical theory oversimplifies it in a different way. Objections to identifying energy as a unique source of value include the problem of quality differences in energy, the difficulty of actually measuring net energy use, and the many important properties of materials which are not correlated with energy content. But even if it falls short of offering a complete theory, the focus on energy opens up new and important lines of theoretical and empirical investigation.

Juan Martinez-Alier's book *Ecological Economics: Energy, Environment and Society* offers an extensive discussion of the history of energy flow analysis in economics and related fields. Although much of the work on energy analysis has been done by noneconomists, there has been a fascinating, intermittent dialogue between economists and natural scientists on the role of energy in economic analysis. Agricultural energetics, energy use in industry, and issues of resource use and conservation, among other themes, are prominent in this dialogue, involving economists such as Jevons, Marx, and Walras as well as ecologists and energy theorists such as Podolinsky, Sacher, Popper-Lynkeus, Liebig, Clausius, and Soddy. Martinez-Alier also discusses a possible convergence between Marxism and ecology, proposed by Podolinsky but resisted by Marx, Engels, Lenin, and other orthodox Marxists.

Robert Kaufmann also suggests that Marxist and ecological analysis need each other's insights in order to explain the interplay of social, technological, and environmental factors in shaping economic history. Theories of the exploitation of labor under capitalism can find some common ground with theories of exploitation of resources. Kaufmann presents only a sketchy outline of the complementarity of the two approaches, and a very simple thesis relating energy availability to class conflict, with echoes of familiar Marxist dogmatism. Whether or not this line of thought is considered fruitful, it certainly raises the issue of the relationship between ecological and social/political critiques of economic theory, a topic which is pursued further in Parts VI and VII of this volume.

Cutler Cleveland goes further into the issues associated with the evolution of energy theory and biophysical economics. Tracing the line of descent from the Physiocrats through Joseph Henry, Herbert Spencer, Wilhelm Ostwald, Frederick Soddy, W.F. Cottrell, and M. King Hubbert to today's energy and ecological theorists such as Howard Odum, Robert Costanza, Nicholas Georgescu-Roegen, and Herman Daly, he identifies two central themes. These are the limitations imposed on economic activity by the laws of thermodynamics, and the complementary nature of energy and capital in production. Taken together, these place strict limits on the ability of economic systems to expand based on technological progress and flexibility in production. Standard economics, of course, has been far more influenced by the immense potential of technological progress and market adaptability. This faith in technology has been embodied in a formal neoclassical theory which essentially recognizes no limits to technological progress, substitutability in production, or economic growth. The experience of two centuries of economic growth, and especially the rapid expansion of the past fifty years, might seem to support this more optimistic paradigm. The case for the alternative must then rest on the argument that conditions are changing, in accordance with the physical laws of energy and resource flow, in such a way that the next fifty or one hundred years of economic development will look fundamentally different.

The articles by J.F. Richards and Lynn White, Jr. introduce the historical perspective which is essential to this debate, and which is often lacking in mainstream economics. Richards ties the history of economic development to the massive impacts of human activity on soils, forests, wetlands, arid lands, and grazing lands throughout the world. This offers a systematic view of environmental impacts which appear only as disjoint "externalities" in most standard economic analysis. Lynn White, Jr. discusses the ethical world view which has accompanied the ever-increasing technological appropriation of Nature for human purposes: a predominantly Christian anthropomorphism which justifies resource expropriation and even ecological vandalism in the cause of economic growth.

Robert Goodland's article presents "The Case That the World Has Reached Limits," an application of these themes to the current world economy. Numerous "red flag" indicators show that resource use trends which have accompanied economic growth for centuries are now stressing ecosystems to the point of collapse. Goodland focuses on biomass appropriation, CO_2 emissions, ozone depletion, land degradation, and biodiversity loss; other such indicators could be cited. While there is controversy over the specifics, a good case is presented for the proposition that population and economic growth have now fundamentally altered the relationship between human activity and planetary ecosystems.

If indeed the current ecological crisis necessitates a reevaluation of the "neglected" trends in economic theory emphasizing energy and resource use, there will be major implications for development theory. One of these implications, of course, is a renewed emphasis on population. Paul Harrison provides an overview of the history of the population growth debate, counterposing the Malthusian tradition with pro-natalist theories maintaining that population growth complements and stimulates technological and economic progress. Economic theorists in general have not worried much about population; as world population approaches six billion they clearly must. Issues of carrying capacity, food production, and environmental stress, as well as the more general issue of quality of life, are all dramatically affected by population size and growth rates. This insight must become fundamental to theories of economic development.

A second major implication of an ecological perspective on economic development is the obsolescence of what F.E. Trainer calls the "indiscriminate growth and trickle-down-someday" approach. Trainer argues that it is patently impossible for the growing population of the less developed nations to attain "first world living standards" as they are currently conceived. Yet this is the implicit goal of current development theory: to make the poor richer, while the rich become richer yet. In a world of biophysical limits, development must be redefined in terms of adequacy and self-sufficiency for all rather than ever-increasing affluence for the rich with the rest coming along in their wake. The implication of this redefinition is that material improvement for the poor is linked to a kind of "reverse development"—*reduction* of resource consumption by the rich. (A notable example of this is seen in current proposals for a "trade-off" of CO_2 emissions whereby increased developing nation emissions would be balanced, or exceeded, by developed nation cutbacks.) Clearly this line of thought requires overturning economic assumptions which have predominated since the time of the later classical economists.

Thus the historical background for ecological economics unfolds. Debates in history of theory are seen to have a strong relevance to current environmental crises; yet the answers to current problems cannot be discerned merely by reviewing historical controversies. A new theoretical enterprise is indicated, the development of which is the subject of this volume.

Summary of

Historical Roots for Ecological Economics— Biophysical Versus Allocative Approaches

by Paul P. Christensen

[Published in *Ecological Economics* 1 (February 1989): 17–36. Reprinted with kind permission from Elsevier Science B.V., Amsterdam, The Netherlands.]

Economic theory has become a highly axiomatic and deductive science. While institutionalists have attempted to use results from other social sciences in their analysis, the biophysical foundations of economic activity are still missing. The other social sciences as well as physics, chemistry, biology, and ecology must inform economic analysis. The foundations for a theory that can do this are found in the works of the pre-classical Physiocrats and the classical economists. This essay considers these foundations and traces the genealogy of modern economic theory. It establishes the links between a biophysical theory of the economy and the classical economists.

The Classical Production Approach

The early classical economists saw production as a set of sequential activities. The extraction of materials and food preceded the processing and fabrication of materials. The capital stock was divided into fixed capital—machines and structures—and circulating capital—food, fodder, raw materials, and working finance. A distinction was made in the production process between land and industrial machinery. Earlier the Physiocrats had regarded land as productive and manufacturing activities as unproductive, because it was thought that land created a surplus, whereas machinery only transformed materials. Similar views on the differences between land and machinery were also held by classicists such as Malthus, who argued that only "the machinery of the land" could produce food and raw materials, and Ricardo, who spoke of the "original and indestructible powers of the soil." They recognized the inability of industrial machines to produce without materials and sources of power, and believed that all surplus was due to the productive power of land. However, only the Italian writer Pietro Verri made it clear that productivity is not an inherent property of land, but rather is dependent on material and energy flows through the land.

The importance of power (energy) in the new technologies of the industrial revolution was also recognized by the post-Ricardian classical economists, under the influence of technical writers such as Smeaton, Babbage, and Ure. The industrial prosperity of Britain was seen as a result of the use of coal as a source of fuel. In analyzing the use of coal, some writers emphasized its physical aspects, while others emphasized its commercial aspects.

Influenced by engineering mechanics (via Babbage), Senior[1] emphasized a physical taxonomy of production inputs: labor and skills, natural agents, and capital. Capital was divided into fixed and circulating, the former being tools and machines, the latter the *materials* embodied in the product (production obeyed the law of conservation of matter: a doubling of material output required a doubling of raw material input). Machines were further divided into engines producing power and machines transmitting and applying power. Senior put food and coal (energy resources) with fixed capital since these were not embodied in output. He needed another category for motive powers.

Mill maintains Senior's tripartite classification but includes motive powers (food, coals, and other natural powers) with materials, judging the distinction between materials and fuels to be of no scientific importance. This lack of differentiation between inputs contributed to the absence of an appropriate terminology for understanding physical processes of production. Marshall's[2] choice of a "commercial" rather than scientific terminology for capital appears to follow Mill.

Neoclassical Production Theory

Neoclassical theory shifted from a production approach to the economy and prices to an exchange approach. Eventually this resulted in a model which combined a marginal utility theory of demand and a marginal productivity theory of supply (the latter was only developed in the 1890s). Early theorists first had to grapple with the classical legacy of a materials–energy–machine conception of production. A common feature of all early models was the elimination of the distinction between fixed and circulating capital (and thus the most obvious problem of complementarity between inputs). Jevons[3] took the approach of reducing fixed capital to a version of circulating capital. The latter in turn was reduced to the subsistence of workers. Materials, fuels, and fixed capital as direct inputs in production were thereby eliminated.

Menger[4] and Walras[5] were influential in the further elimination of raw materials from the production theory. Menger supports his theory of prices with a universal assumption of variable proportions. Thus the possibility of substitution of techniques (with their distinct material and machine requirements) was confused with factor substitution along an isoquant. Walras formalized the elimination of raw materials from the production process by vertically aggregating manufacturing and agricultural production. Walras argued that final products are obtained by combining raw materials, land, labor, and capital, but raw materials themselves are obtained by combining land, labor, and capital. Consequently, raw materials and time do not need to be included explicitly along with the other factors, and they are therefore eliminated from the representation of production. Marshall further excludes raw materials, referring to them as incidental expenses. Marshall's neglect may be attributable to a recognition of the incompatibility of their inclusion within the marginal framework of analysis. This incompatibility arises because the marginal framework requires substitutability among inputs, while raw materials are clearly complements to other inputs in the production process, and are therefore not substitutable.

Thus the neglect of raw materials, energy, and complementarity in production facilitated development of marginal productivity theory. However, this theory is not based on a physical analysis of production activity. Resource valuation depends only on individual preferences and initial endowments as determinants of prices, ignoring the importance of environmental and social systems in shaping these processes.

A Biophysical Approach to Production

A biophysical approach, like the classical one, sees production as the starting point of economic theory. From a biophysical perspective the basic factors of production are materials, energy, information flows, and the physical and biological processes which convert, transmit, or apply them. Solar energy is identified as the primary net input. Neoclassical factors of production are seen as hopelessly aggregative and incomplete.

Complementarity of inputs is also a central component of the biophysical approach. All inputs in a production process are seen as complements rather than as substitutable, and machines and other capital equipment must be designed with this in mind. This notion of complementarity is extended across sectors; technologies, organizational structures, and resource and energy needs are seen to co-evolve across sectors and activities. The neoclassical notion of marginally changing one factor while holding all else constant is therefore not viewed as an appropriate form of analysis, nor is partial equilibrium analysis.

There are several other differences between the biophysical and neoclassical approaches. One is the recognition in the former of the fundamental differences between resource extraction and resource processing, as opposed to the neoclassical view of production as a one step process, from primary factors to final products. Another is the claim of the biophysical approach that movement from a largely renewable resource base to the use of large stocks of coal and petroleum implies inherent limits to economic growth—limits that are not recognized by neoclassicists. Biophysicists see a cycle set up whereby resources are used to produce machines, which are used to extract materials, which are used to produce more machines, and so on. Several problems can be expected to arise from this. First of all, resource inputs may become scarce. Second, natural systems may not be able to absorb increasing levels of material and toxic wastes. These inconsistencies between maximizing the use of high-grade nonrenewable sources of energy and environmental limits indicate the need for control mechanisms to keep economic systems in balance with environmental systems.

Classical/Post-Keynesian Production Prices

The biophysical approach to production calls for a reformulation of the theory of interactions within the economy. For example, the effects of primary commodity price shocks on output, productivity, and inflation are not fully explained by conventional economic theory. This deficiency calls for a macro model that incorporates sectoral pricing and a focus on the short run price and quantity dynamics of commodity price shocks.

The early classical economists developed a sectoral model of asymmetric price behavior in which manufacturing prices were determined by cost of production, and agricultural and raw material prices were determined by the forces of supply and demand. More recently, such a dual pricing model—mark-up pricing for manufactures and market prices for natural resources—has been taken up by some post-Keynesian economists. The differences in the nature of price formation in the two categories and the underlying physical conditions that cause them are important determinants of the behavior of broader macroeconomic variables. A materials- and energy-based, cost-plus pricing model can account for these effects, and is consistent with a Keynesian process of quantity adjustment at the macro level.

From the biophysical point of view, neoclassical price theory has significant shortcomings. Neoclassical price theory values resources at marginal costs of extraction (not reproduction) and values environmental effects in terms of disposal costs. While the existence of user costs and external costs is recognized, these tend to be undervalued based on current market prices. Sraffa[6] attempted to address these shortcomings by extending the classical model to incorporate reproduction prices. He did not, however, incorporate the reproduction of materials and sources of energy from natural systems. Such an incorporation into the Sraffian framework would provide a different policy emphasis, focusing on the long-term maintenance of environmental and resource systems rather than on short-term market price adjustment.

Notes

1. N. Senior, *An Outline of the Science of Political Economy* (New York: Kelley, 1965; original publication 1836).

2. A. Marshal, *Principles of Economics* (London: Macmillan; 8th ed. 1920).

3. W.S. Jevons, *The Theory of Political Economy* (London: Macmillan, 1871; reprinted by Penguin, 1970).

4. C. Menger, *Principles of Economics* (Glencoe, Illinois: Free Press, 1950; translation of Grundsätze der Volkswirtschafts-lehre).

5. L. Walras, *Elements of Pure Economics* (London: Allen and Unwin, 1954; tr. W. Jaffe).

6. P. Sraffa, *The Production of Commodities by Means of Commodities: Prelude to a Critique of Economic Theory* (Cambridge University Press, 1960).

Summary of

The Teleological View of Wealth: A Historical Perspective
by Gerald Alonzo Smith

[Published in *Valuing the Earth: Economics, Ecology, Ethics,* ed. Herman E. Daly and Kenneth N. Townsend (Cambridge: Massachusetts and London: The MIT Press, 1993), and in *Economics, Ecology, Ethics: Essays Toward a Steady-State Economy,* ed. Herman E. Daly (New York and San Francisco: W.H. Freeman and Company, 1980), 215–237.]

"The practice of medicine may require the prescription of an addictive stimulant for the sake of good health. The amount of the stimulant is finite and limited by the end. When, however, one takes a stimulant for its own sake, the desire for it becomes infinite since it is no longer limited by a final goal but is an end in itself. The same is true of the output of the economic process which, rather than being used for the sake of achieving the final goal of life, tends to become the final goal itself. . . . We get hooked on economic growth."[215]

Economists have tended to formulate their perceptions of social welfare based upon the nineteenth century philosophies of individualism and utilitarianism. Happiness is equated with the consumption of goods: the more goods available and consumed in society, the higher the level of social well-being. Individuals are considered the best judge of their own happiness, so the individual's choice of economic goods as expressed in the marketplace must be taken as given, and is thus beyond analysis. The key to the greatest happiness for the greatest number is to simply allow people to follow the dictates of their acquisitive, self-interested nature. There have been economists who have questioned this premise. In what follows, the thoughts of four such economists are examined. Each in his own way rejects the conventional wisdom that economic growth is an end in and of itself. They have all viewed the growth of production and consumption as a means rather than an end. They define that end as life in all of its dimensions, especially the higher, immaterial dimensions.

J. C. L. Simonde de Sismondi (1773–1842)

Sismondi was writing during the period of transition from craft production to industrialization, and his views were shaped by the excesses of that time. He was the first economist in modern times to question the notion that growth in economic productivity was an end in itself, tantamount to an enhancement of the public good. He began his analysis by rejecting the notion that the goal of an economy was the maximization of wealth itself. Sismondi turned to the Greeks, most especially Aristotle, for his inspiration. "But at least they [the Greeks] never lost sight of the fact that wealth had no other worth than what it contributed to the national happiness."[1] From this perspective, he disagreed with the conventional economists' standard prescription of expansion of production to ease the massive social misery of the early industrial period.

Sismondi, who coined the term "proletarian," developed his analysis by comparing the disappearing system of craft production, in which a man worked for himself, to the emerging industrial system, in which he works for others. In the former system, an individual who reaped the fruits of his own labor could simply work until the point at which the value of leisure exceeded the value of producing additional goods. For such a person, "it would appear as folly to accumulate still more [wealth], since such a laborer would not be able to increase his consumption in a proportional amount."[2] Moreover, "every craftsman [who] compares the almost imperceptible pleasure that he would receive from a slightly finer suit of clothes with the additional work that such a suit of clothes entails, would not wish to pay this price. Luxury is not possible except when it is paid for by the work of others."[3] Thus, the decision to continually expand production and accumulate wealth is made by those who profit from production, rather than by those who must bear the real cost of production.

Sismondi looked around him and witnessed an expansion of production and technology that was without precedent, but for what purpose? His historical studies had taught him that there was more to a superior civilization than increased material production. He recognized that if this increase in productivity was brought about by an unjust economic system, then it may well do more harm than good.

John Ruskin (1819–1900)

Ruskin's investigations into the life of laborers in England quickly led him to the conclusion that something was very wrong with a system that produced so much quantity of so little quality, and brutalized so many people in the process. He denounced the gospel of greed advocated by the conventional political economy of his time. Of all the humanistic critics of his age, only Ruskin attempted to challenge the economic theorists on their own ground and attempted to distinguish true political economy from the "bastard science" which merely attempts to maximize economic productivity.

Like Sismondi, Ruskin turned to the Greeks for a definition of wealth, which he finds in Xenophon's *Economist*: those economic possessions that aid man in living are true wealth, while those that contribute to the destruction of man's nature are not true wealth—Ruskin labels these "illth." For Ruskin, those possessions that aid man in living are only those that he can use, and in the case of a single being, uses are necessarily limited. Excess in possession, i.e., the accumulation of goods for which man has no use, is ill for that man, and is therefore illth. Thus the accumulation of wealth for its own sake ought not be the final goal for any individual or society.

John A. Hobson (1858–1940)

Hobson considered himself a disciple of Ruskin and, like Ruskin, subjected conventional economic theory to the test of humane assessment. More than Ruskin, Hobson accepted that there was some validity in orthodox economic theory. He felt, however, that the discipline had to be moderated by a social ethic and brought under the umbrella of a broader science: the art or science of human welfare.

Hobson focused first upon the flawed ways in which economists treat consumption. They see consumption as the formal end of an economic process, in which goods are passed from the farmer, manufacturer, and trader into the hands of the consumer, where they disappear in privacy and obscurity. The pattern of demand is taken as a given and is thus nobody's concern. Hobson, however, questioned the extent to which current tastes and appetites are reliable indices of human utility, and further doubted man's capacity to distinguish between the desired and the desirable. One need only "cite the ample evidence of the errors and wastes that are represented in every human standard of consumption."[4] The theory of demand "does not yet accord the disinterested valuations of consumptive processes required by a theory in which consumption is the 'sole end.' For consumption here only enters the economic field as a factor in markets and the determination of prices, not as the means of realizing the purpose of which the whole economic system is directed."[5]

Hobson then attempted to determine what it was that was desirable, or, in other words, what was the ideal "Ultimate End" by which the system could be judged. He identified this ideal as organic welfare, by which he means "good life," including a material component as well as non-material artistic and spiritual factors. The practice of equating current patterns of income and consumption with the desirable or organic welfare in society is not acceptable since the entire system contains large elements of human waste or error. He decried the absence of any study either of the evolution of actual standards of consumption or of desirable standards. The status quo, with its elaborate apparatus of selling and technological innovation, has a built-in bias toward excess production and consumption. When narrow-minded, tunnel-visioned economists blindly accept current consumption as the inevitable and desirable outcome of individual preferences, they describe only a minute portion of the canvas.

Richard H. Tawney (1880–1962)

Tawney, like the others, took the false equation of wealth and consumption with happiness as his starting point. He was troubled by the modern belief that the "principal aim of man, what should be taught to children, . . . what merits approbation and respect, is the attainment of a moderate—or even immoderate—standard of comfort."[6] With such a standard, the goal of society must be to produce and then produce more. Yet the philosophical road which views economic productivity as its own end, the road that has given us the greatest increase in productivity since the fall of the Roman empire, has at the same time produced greater and greater levels of economic discontent. The frenetic rush to produce with no guiding principle other than the accumulation of wealth creates a situation where "part of the goods which are annually produced, and which are called wealth, is strictly speaking, waste."[7] Tawney compared British industrialism with Prussian militarism, both of which have killed the souls of men by allowing a subordinate social system to dominate their societies.

Like Ruskin, Tawney saw the correct path as one in which the purpose of industry "is to supply man with things which are necessary, useful or beautiful, and thus to bring life to body or spirit. In so far as it is governed by this end, it is among the most important of human activities."[8] He greatly emphasized the centrality of religion, art, literature, and learning to human happiness and well-being. These are ends which must not be secondary to production and the accumulation of wealth, for "if they are sought second they are never found at all."[9]

Conclusion

The four economists reviewed in this study have examined the economic system in which they lived and the economic thinking regarding that system, and found both wanting. It is a system in which doing becomes its own justification. We no longer ask "doing what?," or explore "doing what for what?," or analyze "doing what for what and with what?"[232] Man has sought the false remedy of gaining power over things and persons, and thus economic production and power have become their own ends. In pursuing this path, the sickness of society is exacerbated. It is only through returning to a study of man and the appropriate final goal of human association that this sickness can be healed.

Notes

1. J.C.L. Simonde de Sismondi, *Nouveaux principes d'economie politique ou de la richesse dans ses rapports avec la population, Vol. II*, 2nd ed. (Paris, 1827), 140, translation by G.A. Smith; cited by Smith, 218.

2. Sismondi, 75–76; cited by Smith, 219.

3. Sismondi, 79; cited by Smith, 219.

4. John A. Hobson, *Wealth and Life: A Study in Values* (London, 1929), 328; cited by Smith, 225.

5. Hobson, 304–6; cited by Smith, 226.

6. J.M. Winter and D.M. Joslin, ed., *R.H. Tawney's Commonplace Book* (Cambridge, England: Cambridge University Press, 1972), 60–62; cited by Smith, 228.

7. R.H. Tawney, *The Acquisitive Society* (New York, 1920), 37-38; cited by Smith, 230.

8. Tawney, 8; cited by Smith, 230.

9. Winter and Joslin, 60–62; cited by Smith, 228.

Summary of

The Convergence of Neo-Ricardian and Embodied Energy Theories of Value and Price

by D.H. Judson

[Published in *Ecological Economics* 1 (October 1989): 261–281. Reprinted with kind permission from Elsevier Science B.V., Amsterdam, The Netherlands.]

Ecological economics theories have much in common with classical theories. This can be demonstrated by examining both the roots of energy theorists, which can be found in classical economic thought, and the parallels between energy theorists and the neo-Ricardians. Some attempts to integrate the equations of neo-Ricardian and energy theories can therefore be made.

Foundations of a Theory of Value

There are three important dimensions to consider when answering the question "what gives a commodity worth or value?":

(1) The analysis may be at the micro or the macro level. At the root of this dimension is whether the individual or society is made the starting point of economic analysis. Neoclassical economists (the marginal utility perspective) argue that it must be the individual; value is based on individuals exchanging so as to maximize utility. On the other hand, classical economists (with an embodied labor basis for value) argue that society must be the starting point. They see society as reproducing itself over time through the productive activities of its members.

(2) The analysis of value may be subjective (a human projection onto commodities), or objective (value is inherent in a commodity).

(3) The analysis may be static or dynamic. Neo-Ricardian economists argue that marginal utility analysis is essentially static, equating the economic process with a mechanical analog. Such an analysis suggests that the economic process cannot affect the environment of matter and energy in any way. Energy-based analysis argues that the material universe and hence the economic system is subject to irreversible qualitative change, i.e., to a dynamic evolutionary process. This perspective bases itself on the law of entropy.

The Sraffian Challenge to Marx (A Neo-Ricardian Perspective)

In his book *Production of Commodities by Means of Commodities* (1960), Pierro Sraffa argued that:

(1) The exchange value of any particular commodity in relationship to every other commodity is entirely determined by the sociotechnical conditions of production. This was a critique of the neoclassical theory of value which argued that the forces of demand and supply were crucial in determining the value of a commodity. The major implication of this critique is that the value of a commodity is a function of the costs of production of its various commodity inputs, and not of the exchangers' personal preferences.

(2) Given certain technical assumptions, the value of all commodities can be expressed in relation to a standard commodity whose price is equal to unity. This was the neo-Ricardian argument against Marxian theories of value which argued that only labor could create value. Neo-Ricardians do not dispute that labor values can be calculated, but rather object to the Marxian view that labor should be the only input considered.

Energy Theorizing about Value and Price

Early energy theorists concluded that "value in general rests on the transformation of energy."[1] In comparison, modern ecologists have taken several different approaches to measuring value:

(1) Value can be measured as the energy content of a commodity expressed as the amount of energy that can be released from it in combustion or behavior. This view has been criticized since it only recognizes the energy constraints in the system. More specifically, it does not consider the heterogeneous forms of matter (as opposed to energy, which is homogenous), each of which has characteristic properties.

(2) Value can be measured as the energy cost of production of a commodity, i.e., the energy used up in its manufacture. This view has been seen as a useful foundational principle for an ecological critique of economic theory.

(3) Energy content or input can be considered to be one of several important factors that determine the value of a commodity. This is seen as the most fruitful integration of ecological and orthodox economics.

Convergence between the Neo-Ricardian and Embodied Energy Approaches to Economic Valuation

The common threads between neo-Ricardian and energy theorists include:

(1) the use of input–output analysis as a tool;

(2) the reliance on cost of production theories to explain exchange value (neo-Ricardians believe that exchange value can be expressed in terms of any "standard commodity," while energy theorists use energy cost of production as a measure);

(3) the view that economic evolution is an irreversible process; and

(4) the belief that demand schedules are unimportant as a determinant of value.

Critiques of the Embodied Energy Approach to Value

Embodied energy approaches have been criticized for failing to consider the role of matter in creating value. The crux of this argument is that in the production of commodities some materials are fundamentally nonsubstitutable.

Another problem with embodied energy approaches to value is their failure to account for the importance of exchange processes in the realization of value. Sraffa (and thereby neo-Ricardian analysis) ignored the problem of exchange processes and their role in the determination of value by assuming that markets cleared and by arguing that all outputs are reintroduced into the economy as factor inputs. For goods which did not fit the above assumptions (called "nonbasic" or "luxury" goods), Sraffa argued that their value and distribution was determined by some other process. Energy theorists have not dealt with the problem of whether the value of nonessential luxury commodities can be determined by their energy cost of production.

Finally, energy theorists have not yet addressed the relationship between the long-run energy value of a commodity and its short-run price.

The Fundamental Theoretical Problem

While economists from the time of the Physiocrats have recognized the interconnected nature of economic processes, in which one set of outputs become inputs in another process, a fundamental question that arises is whether or not there is a point at which the circle should be broken to establish a first cause of economic value? This question has implications for whether exchange values can be expressed in terms of any standard commodity or a specific input.

The Physiocrats broke the chain, attributing all value to agriculture. The classicists—for example, Smith, Ricardo, and Marx—argued that labor is the source of all value. The neo-Ricardians claimed that no commodity can be singled out. Now energy theorists are arguing that energy is the common factor in all the inputs of production.

Integrating Neo-Ricardian and Embodied Energy Theories of Value—Theoretical Developments and Recommendations for Empirical Testing

There are several points of convergence between neo-Ricardians and embodied energy theorists. For example, both groups argue that value is inherent in objects. These similarities can be shown through the use of a simple mathematical model. Thus, neo-Ricardian theory might be advanced by integration into the embodied energy framework, where prices can be described in terms of energy costs of production and wages can be described by the energy input. However, energy theorists must still deal with the issue of how prices are derived from values expressed in energy terms. Other theoretical issues to be addressed include basic versus nonbasic commodities; the relationship between money, energy, and prices; a theory of capital; the role of technological change; and the heterogeneous quality of energy from different sources. Suggestions for empirical work include attempting to compare energy intensities and dollar values of commodities, cross-national testing of energy theory hypotheses, and studies relating energy and international trade.

Note
1. W. Ostwald, *The Modern Theory of Energetics* (Monist, 1907), 513; cited by Judson, 266.

Summary of

Energy and Energetics in Economic Theory: A Review Essay[1]
by Philip Mirowski

[Published in *Journal of Economic Issues* XXII (September 1988): 811–830. Summarized by special permission of the copyright holder, the Association For Evolutionary Economics.]

A striking and little-noticed aspect of anti-neoclassical thought in the twentieth century is the number of natural scientists who have thought that they were the first to believe that the only "true" economic value is energy. Two groups can be distinguished among the group of scientists under consideration: the *neo-energeticists*, who believe that energy is identical to economic value, and the *neo-simulators*, who regard physics only as a metaphor and as a source of ready-made mathematical models. This article reviews some of the unorthodox economics views of the neo-energeticists, who can be further sub-divided into three categories: (1) those who never ventured beyond a crude theory of energy and value; (2) those who attempt to quantify energy and implement their theory of energy as a value substance; and (3) Nicholas Georgescu-Roegen.

The conviction that there exists a literal identity between the physical concept of energy and the economic concept of value has always had currency in the scientific community. For over a century it has drawn the attention of distinguished scientists and moved from one academic discipline to another. By 1880 the physicist Georg Helm and the physical chemist and Nobel Laureate Wilhelm Ostwald claimed that all of the sciences, including the social sciences, could be united under a small set of principles and concepts. It was believed that energy would form the basis of a unified theory. Others who attempted to advocate the integration of energy theories into the social sciences included the Marxist Sergei Podolinsky, the biologist Patrick Geddes, and the physical chemist Ernest Solvay. Solvay funded the *Institut des Sciences Sociales* to forge a link between the physical and social sciences.

In the 1920s, the research of population biologist Alfred Lotka attempted to lay bare the "biophysical foundations of economics," with energy being the fundamental underlying principle. Frederick Soddy, a physical chemist and Nobel Laureate, was the most consistent advocate of an energy theory of value. Soddy wanted "to obtain a physical conception of wealth that would obey the physical laws of conservation."[2] He had a crude energy theory of value and showed the existence of monetary divergences from those value principles.

The American engineering profession also contributed toward an energy theory of value. Frederick Taylor, the father of "scientific management," set out to discover the relationship between fatigue and the number of foot pounds of exertion in order to identify the parameters of a "full day's work" in energy terms. In the 1930s, Howard Scott told *The New York Times* that a group of engineers were working for more than a decade on a survey of the industrial system of the United States in terms of energy consumption rather than in dollars, because dollars were a "rubber yardstick." More recently, an energy theory of value has been adopted by some anthropologists, ecologists, and sociobiologists. Among anthropologists, Leslie White proposed that all culture should be conceptualized as manifestations of "the amount of energy per capita per year harnessed and put to work."[3] Ecologists who have popularized an energy theory of value include Frederick Cottrell and Howard and Elizabeth Odum.

There has therefore been a nearly continuous espousal of the energy theory of value since the 1880s by groups that did not accept the hegemony of neoclassical economic theory. Two conditions that have contributed to the persistence of this theory are the fact that no single group ever developed the theory with any seriousness, and its movement from one fledgling discipline to the next. Recently a new breed of energeticists have started grappling with some of the analytical objections to earlier energy theories of value. The OPEC oil crisis of 1973 provided a boost to this new group. Energy is now treated as an embodied value similar to the classical labor theory of value, and input–output analysis is employed to facilitate calculations of energy values. There have also been further attempts to synthesize biology, physics, and economics into a single science.

Neoclassical economics first ignored these theories but then took notice of the new breed of neo-energeticists by developing a field of economics called "energy economics." They attempt to elevate energy to the status of land and capital in the production function, and to arrive at a price of energy. Neoclassicists such as Ernest Berndt argue that energy is neither a homogeneous nor a distinct commodity.[4] He takes the neo-energeticists to task for ignoring the Second Law of Thermodynamics: the entropy law. However, the neoclassical solution of putting energy into the production function makes a mockery of physics. Moreover, the neoclassical approach shares many of the weaknesses of neo-energetics, and thus cannot provide a compelling critique of it.

Nicholas Georgescu-Roegen, who ironically is perceived as a neo-energeticist, is the only economist who has provided such a critique. A neoclassical economist in his earlier days, Georgescu-Roegen later turned to a critique of neoclassical mathematical formulations. His book, *The Entropy Law and the Economic Process* (1971), criticized neoclassical production functions for neglecting the dictates of the laws of thermodynamics. However, while he did disassociate himself from an embodied energy theory of value, a number of his passages sounded like endorsements of this theory. As a result, a number of neo-energeticists have quoted him in support of their theory of value. Georgescu-Roegen responded with explicit critiques of the embodied energy theory of value, making four main points:

(1) it is wrong to equate matter and energy, and to believe that energy can be transformed into matter;

(2) the neo-energeticists do not offer a rigorous definition of "net energy";

(3) they ignore the implications of the Second Law of Thermodynamics by overlooking quality differences in energy; and

(4) while in theory the neo-energeticists reduce all of their phenomena to energetic essences, in empirical work they derive their embodied energy coefficients from monetary or pecuniary values.

These criticisms can be modified and laid at the doorstep of neoclassical economics, something Georgescu-Roegen has not done in a thorough manner. His promises of the outlines of a new bioeconomics that will lay out the "proper laws" of the economic sphere have not materialized.

Notes

1. An author's note indicates that this article was prompted by two books: J.C. Dragan and M. Demetrescu, *Entropy and Bioeconomics* (Nagard SrI Editrice, 1986), and W. van Gool and J. Bruggink, eds., *Energy and Time in the Economic and Physical Sciences* (North Holland/Elsevier, 1985).

2. Frederick Soddy, *Wealth, Virtual Wealth and Debt* (Hawthorne: Omni, 1961), 21; cited by Mirowski, 814.

3. Leslie White, "Energy and the Evolution of Culture," *American Anthropologist* 45 (1943); cited by Mirowski, 816.

4. Ernst Berndt, "Aggregate Energy, Efficiency, and Productivity Measurement," in *Annual Review of Energy* 9: 409–26 (1978).

Summary of

Introduction to *Ecological Economics:* *Energy, Environment and Society*

by Juan Martinez-Alier with Klaus Schlüpmann

[Published by Blackwell Books, Oxford, England and Cambridge, Massachussetts, 1987, 1990, 1–19.]

The focus of this volume is the study of energy flow, a unifying principle in ecological analysis, and its application to the economic system. Although the "energetic dogma," which seeks to trace all value to embodied energy, is rejected (following Georgescu-Roegen), the relation between energy flow and economic activity can still provide a fruitful field of study, drawing on an extensive literature dealing with the interaction between human ecological energetics and economics.

This book covers the period between Jevons' *The Coal Question*[1] and the 1940s. The object of the volume is to make a contribution to the ecological critique of economic theory "by resurrecting the arguments of half-forgotten authors."[2] The existence of an historical school of ecological economics is often not acknowledged, even by its current advocates; this book may serve to rectify this omission.

Agricultural Energetics

Until recently, most applied work on the economics of energy has been done by noneconomists. The results of energy analysis often seem to contradict standard economic theory, for example, in the finding that modern agriculture is less efficient than traditional agriculture (i.e., has lower energy return per unit of energy input). The apparent increase in agricultural productivity is actually a result of the low price of oil used for energy-intensive agriculture. If oil has been undervalued, however, then this productivity increase is fictitious. In addition, standard economic theory heavily discounts the value of resource conservation, using an interest rate based on the assumption of future growth, as Frederick Soddy has emphasized. The critiques of this orthodox theory of exhaustible resources are among the topics addressed in this volume.

The concept of energy return to energy input was first developed by Sergei Podolinsky,[2] who combined an ecological approach with Marxist value theory. His views, however, have not been considered in later Marxist theory. Eduard Sacher[3] and Josef Popper-Lynkeus[4] also studied agricultural energetics and the relation of energy use to economic development, prefiguring modern discussions of a shift to renewable resource use. Around 1840, Liebig, a founder of the discipline of agricultural chemistry, predicted the dependence of European agriculture on nonrenewable imported energy sources (guano imports from Peru at that time, and inorganic chemical fertilizers later).[5]

The "Entropy Law" and the Economic Process

Jevons, one of the originators of marginalist economic theory, also brought his knowledge of natural science to bear on the issue of coal use and reserves, though he did not consider intertemporal resource allocation analysis. Walras, whose work is central to modern neoclassical theory, corresponded with Patrick Geddes, who challenged the lack of a physical/energy basis for Walras' theories. Rudolf Clausius[6] criticized humanity's profligate use of irreplaceable fossil fuel. Many other natural scientists, mathematicians, and engineers were concerned with the efficient use of energy in industry, while physiologists considered energy efficiency in plants, animals, and humans. A physicist, Leopold Pfaundler,[7] analyzed the earth's carrying capacity based on solar energy and photosynthesis. However, the relation of the entropy law to the economic process did not become a well-established field of study.

Social Darwinism and Ecology

Species may adapt to the limited availability of energy in two ways: either by becoming very efficient in their use of available energy, or by devising means to capture more extensive sources of energy. Clearly, the human species has excelled in the second approach. However, extending the ecological principle of *interspecific* competition for solar energy flux to *intraspecific* competition among individuals or classes is not a sound approach. Alfred Lotka[8] and others seem to have leaned in the direction of an energy-based social Darwinism; this line of thought is criticized in this volume.

Ecological and Chrematistic Economics

Soddy, the 1921 Nobel Laureate in chemistry, is a prominent figure in the history of ecological economics. From 1903 onward, he urged economists to devote greater effort to the study of energy use. He argued that economists typically mistook real capital for financial capital, and chrematistics (maximization of short-term exchange value) for economics.[9] In Soddy's view, the payment of interest and the maintenance of economic growth depended on the availability of energy and natural resources to fuel real economic activity. Ostwald, a chemist, developed the field of social energetics, arguing that the development of culture depended on an improvement in the efficiency of energy transformation. Max Weber criticized this view, pointing out that in energy terms, hand-weaving of cloth was cheaper than machine-weaving. (The similar issue of energy use in traditional and modern agriculture has already been observed.) However, the cost of machine-weaving depends on the intergenerational valuation of fossil fuels and their externalities. Such a conflict of views pointed the way toward an integration of the social and natural sciences.

"Social Engineering" and the "History of the Future"

Energy and material resources have generally been absent from the discipline of economic history, and the study of ecological history has developed only recently. Faced with the ecological critique, economists have fallen back on a deeply rooted belief in economic growth. However, it is crucial to consider physical limits on potential growth paths. Economics should not *merely* be human ecology, but economics alone cannot explain either the history or the possible futures of economic systems. In addition, the individualistic economic methodology favored by some—for example, Hayek—fails to consider the fact that individuals not yet born cannot express their preferences in today's markets.

A fruitful dialogue between socialism and ecological economics should be possible, drawing out the differences of opinion among socialist thinkers on the question of the "boundless" possibilities of technological advance once capitalist relations of production are overcome. Some socialists have rejected this technological optimism in favor of a greater emphasis on equality and "ecological utopianism." This ideology might be more appropriate for the poor people of the world than either traditional Marxism or the "growth with inequality" offered by market economists.

In summary, the elements of ecological economics have existed for some time, and the field could have been developed long ago. That this did not happen was due in part to disciplinary divisions.

Notes

1. W. Stanley Jevons, *The Coal Question* (London: Macmillan, 1865).

2. Serhii Podolinsky, "Le Socialisme et l'unité des forces fisiques," *Revue Socialiste,* June 1880.

3. Eduard Sacher, *Grundzüge einer Mechanik der Gessellschaft* (Jena: Gustav Fischer, 1881), and *Die Gessellschaftskunde als Naturwissenschaft* (Dresden and Leipzig: Pierson's Velag, 1899).

4. Josef Popper-Lynkeus, *Die allgemeine Nährpflicht als Lösung der sozialen Frage* (Dresden: Reissner, 1912).

5. Justus von Liebig, *Letters on Modern Agriculture,* ed. John Blyth (London: Walton and Maberly, 1859).

6. Rudolf Clausius, *Über die Energievorräthe der Natur und ihre Verwerthung zun Nutzen der Menschheit* (Bonn: Verlag von Max Cohen & Sohn, 1885).

7. L. Pfaundler, "Die Weltwirtschaft im Lichte der Physik," in *Deutsche Revue* 22 (2), April–June, 1902.

8. A.J. Lotka, *Théorie analytique des associations biologiques* (Paris, Hermann, 1934).

9. Frederick Soddy, *Cartesian Economics: the Bearing of Physical Science upon State Stewardship* (London: Hendersons, 1922).

Summary of

The History of the Future

by Juan Martinez-Alier with Klaus Schlüpmann

[Published as Chapter 14 in Juan Martinez-Alier with Klaus Schlüpmann, *Ecological Economics: Energy, Environment and Society* (Oxford, England and Cambridge, Massachusetts: Blackwell Books, 1987, 1990), 206–231.]

Unified Science and Universal History

Economics should include physical aspects of human ecology, as well as the study of cultural, social, and ethical influences on production and consumption. Ecological political economy must be integrative, bridging some of the gaps between the natural and the human sciences; economic propositions should not be made without consideration of the physical, sociological, and psychological factors affecting economic activity. For example, analysis of the market for automobiles must encompass consideration of many issues, including the efficiency of the internal combustion engine, petroleum geology, the social forces leading to urbanization, moral issues such as global inequity and the increase in mortality associated with auto accidents, environmental impacts, the contribution to global warming, and so forth. Several of these issues involve intertemporal and intergenerational issues that are especially hard to fit into a reductionist, chrematistic framework. Otto Neurath realized already in the 1920s (in the context of the debate on the rationality of a socialist economy) that elements of the economy were *incommensurable*. Neurath's proposal for a "unified science" that would attempt to clarify relationships such as these, based on contributions from the individual sciences involved, might also be viewed as a form of "universal history."

One example from agrarian history of using such a unified science approach would be to go beyond economists' assertion of rising productivity in agriculture to investigate the declining energy efficiency and loss of biodiversity of modern agriculture. This analysis would take into account solar radiation and photosynthesis, the cultural and biological history of food, and the ideology of ever-increasing yields through use of chemical fertilizers. An identification of those propositions of economic science that are contradictory or doubtful from an ecological standpoint would emerge from this kind of analysis (a task undertaken by Nicholas Georgescu-Roegen, among others).

The concept of a universal science echoes the work of utopian socialists such as Saint-Simon, and therefore came under attack from Lenin and other orthodox Marxists, as well as from conservative theoreticians such as Hayek and Karl Popper. However, much can be learned from various "utopian" writings. They explore the connection between technological imperatives and social organization, suggesting new and desirable social relations based on moral values of equality and freedom and on feasible productive bases.

Marxism and Ecology

Marxists have no commitment to market-determined prices or interest rates, and Marx wrote of capitalism misusing natural resources. However, Marxists also tend to view ecological protest against capitalism, like the moral and aesthetic protests of Ruskin, Morris, and other utopian socialists, as being of little analytical value. There is no analysis of exhaustible resources and intergenerational allocation in either the Marxist or the Sraffian schemes. Marx did favor Liebig's argument for small-scale, nutrient-recycling agriculture, although he rejected the Malthusian analysis of food supply. Moreover, he did not consider energy flow, and his limited ecological observations have not been integrated into the Marxist view of history.

Engels did consider energy flow and the entropy law, as well as the "squandering" of energy resources, but he considered a specific energy analysis to be of little value. Marx showed his awareness of the importance of physical factors underlying the economic process in his critique of Ricardo, arguing that Ricardo's theory of agricultural rents ignored the further development of agricultural fertilizers. Marx and Engels did not, however, pursue Podolinsky's effort to develop an ecological Marxism, and their followers have moved further away from this approach. Lenin rejected Ernst Mach's "empirio-criticism," despite its potential for integrating the history of science with Marxism, and in so doing created (for Marxists) a cloud of suspicion around social energetics. Bogdanov and Bukharin both considered energy analyses of production; Bukharin foresaw a communist utopia based on abundant energy. However, ecological Marxism never took hold, a fact that had significant adverse effects on the theory and practice of economic planning in the Soviet Union.

Ecological Anthropology

The historical (rather than functional) school of ecological anthropology has much in common with ecological Marxist approaches. Leslie White, a founder of modern ecological anthropology, analyzed human history in terms of the interplay between technological development, the social system, and the cultural-symbolic level. Cold War restrictions, however, prevented the development of an American school of thought dealing with the relations between Marxism and ecology. Nonetheless, Podolinsky's ecological Marxism still provides much of the inspiration for this volume.

Summary of

Biophysical and Marxist Economics: Learning from Each Other
by Robert Kaufman

[Published in *Ecological Modelling* 38 (September 1987): 91–105. Reprinted with kind permission from Elsevier Science B.V., Amsterdam, The Netherlands.]

The attempt by the Ukrainian socialist Sergei Podolinsky to use the laws of thermodynamics to analyze agricultural and industrial energy flows was rejected by Marx and Engels, leading later Marxists to disregard biophysical analyses of production. This paper suggests that both ecological economists and Marxists can benefit from a reconciliation of physical analyses of production with theories of valuation and distribution.

The Marxist labor theory of value accords no inherent value to natural resources. Biophysical or ecological economists, on the other hand, see the capture of low entropy as the fundamental requirement for production, although they do not emphasize theories of value. Many Marxists share with neoclassical economists a vision of unlimited resource abundance without physical constraints on production. Nevertheless, the fundamental requirement for growth in production is net or surplus energy, rather than labor. This is consistent with Marx's analysis of the crucial role of the steam engine and the use of coal in the development of modern capitalism.

Natural Resources and Surplus Value

The Marxist focus on extraction of surplus value from labor needs to be complemented by an understanding of the essential role of the environment in economic production. Both the concentrated nature of natural resources and the capture of low entropy by biological systems are essential for mobilizing surplus. Much more energy must be expended to recover low-grade resources compared to high-grade ones. The environment therefore affects the organization of production. At the same time, the organization of production affects the environment. Capital accumulation makes much more rapid exploitation of natural resources possible. This modification of the Marxist dialectic also creates a contradiction overlooked by Marxists, because by depleting high-quality resources, advanced industrial production undercuts its own productivity. Energy supply conditions also affect class relations. An abundant energy supply in the United States prior to the early 1970s allowed both rising real wages and increasing surplus. Stagnant energy input from the early 1970s to the mid-1980s was associated with declining real wages and increasing class conflict.

Managing Socialist Economies

Marxists have asserted that socialist economies should not degrade their resource base because they are free of the contradictions of capitalism. This is false, as empirical evidence from communist economies amply demonstrates. Both capitalist and socialist economies are constrained by the same physical laws.

Dialectic of Resource Quality

Biophysical economists might benefit from a less reductionist, more dialectical approach to the relationship between technology and resources. New technologies make more effective resource recovery possible, but they simultaneously speed up resource depletion. This depletion in turn drives the development of technology.

Social Forces and Biophysical Economics

A consideration of social forces—central components of Marxist theory—needs to be added to the biophysical analysis of energy flows, as these flows are mediated by social relations. Similarly, economic relations cannot be reduced to physical interactions. For example, the technical availability of more concentrated sources of energy in the twentieth century (e.g., petroleum and nuclear energy) has had a mediating effect on class conflict; the shift to these new energy sources was readily implemented for this reason. This technical strategy has become less effective during the last two decades, as energy returns to investment have declined for petroleum, and nuclear power has proved to have a lower energy return on investment than hydropower. The result has been a reduction in the amount of energy consumed by wage earners, which is consistent with Marxist analysis.

Summary of

Biophysical Economics: Historical Perspective and Current Research Trends

by Cutler J. Cleveland

[Published in *Ecological Modelling* 38 (September 1987): 47–73. Reprinted with kind permission from Elsevier Science B.V., Amsterdam, The Netherlands.]

In the midst of current debates regarding environmental policy, standard economic models have often been criticized for their unsophisticated and unrealistic treatment of the crucial role of natural resources in human economic affairs. Many of these critiques spring from a broad body of research known as biophysical economics. Biophysical economics uses thermodynamic and ecological principles that emphasize the role of natural resources in the economic process. Although the emergence of a palpable environmental and ecological consciousness is a relatively recent phenomenon, the origins of biophysical economics are, in fact, far older. Dating back as far as the Physiocratic economists of the eighteenth century and the formulation of the laws of thermodynamics in the early nineteenth century, it is an area of research that has continued to evolve up to the present.

Two themes characteristic of biophysical economics will be used to trace its development. The first theme is the emphasis on the physical laws governing the energy and matter transformations that form the basis of the production process. Ignoring these constraints has resulted in an inadequate accounting of the qualitative changes in natural resource inputs and the vast quantity of wastes that the natural life support system has had to absorb. The second theme is the physical interdependence between the factors of production. The supply of capital and labor depends upon inputs of low-entropy matter and energy, since neither labor nor capital can physically create natural resources. This approach challenges the "omnipotent technology" hypothesis central to neoclassical analysis, which claims that factor substitution will be an adequate response to resource depletion.

Physiocracy, a French school of thought developed in the 1750s, had as its first premise the principle that natural resources, and especially arable land, were the source of material wealth. The Physiocrats maintained that economic processes could be understood by focusing on a single physical factor: the productivity of agriculture. If human society accurately deduced the proper economic behavior implied by "natural law," social welfare would then be maximized. Although few of the Physiocrats' biophysical principles are evident in subsequent theory, their steadfast belief that nature was the ultimate source of wealth has become a recurring theme throughout biophysical economics.

The physical and ecological basis of economic production intuitively grasped by the Physiocrats was formalized by the discovery of the laws of thermodynamics. Thermodynamics and the study of energy flows became a universal index by which many disparate biological and physical processes could be quantified and compared. Carnot showed that thermodynamic laws are essentially economic formulations of physical relations, as they concern the ability of the economy to use energy to upgrade the organizational state of natural resources into useful goods and services. Some nineteenth century scientists, including the physicist Joseph Henry and the biologist-philosopher Herbert Spencer, emphasized the energy flow basis of social and economic action. The German chemist Ostwald attempted to incorporate thermodynamics into a general theory of economic development, while the Ukrainian socialist Podolinsky tried to reconcile the labor theory of value with a thermodynamic analysis of the economic process. Podolinsky's biophysical analysis led him to conclude that the ultimate limits to growth lay not in the relations of production but in physical and ecological laws.

The early twentieth century was characterized by a growing body of literature devoted to the analysis of the role of natural resources in human affairs, particularly in economic production. Among the most notable contributions were those of Frederick Soddy, a Nobel Laureate in chemistry, who applied the laws of thermodynamics to economic systems and devoted a significant part of his life to a critique of standard economic theory. Like the Physiocrats, Soddy maintained that a comprehensive theory of wealth must have biophysical laws as its first principles since "life derives the whole of its physical energy or power . . . solely from the inanimate world."[1] He particularly emphasized the centrality of solar energy in empowering the life process.

The use of energy as a unifying concept for social, political, and economic analysis reached a zenith with the technocratic movement in the United States and Canada during the 1930s. Members of this movement believed that energy was the critical factor determining economic and social development, and they advocated the idea of measuring vital economic parameters in energy units instead of dollars. They believed that politicians and businessmen could not manage a rapidly advancing industrial society and should therefore be replaced by scientists and engineers who possessed the requisite expertise to manage the economy toward a highly idealized future.

The 1950s was an exceptional period for research on the role of energy and natural resources in social and economic development. The most comprehensive study was made by a sociologist, W. F. Cottrell, whose work focused on what he termed "surplus energy," i.e., the difference between the energy utilized in energy delivery and the amount of energy recovered. He also stressed the role of energy in enhancing labor productivity. Cottrell examined the differences between biophysical and humanist approaches to biological and cultural evolution, and he argued that resource availability and energy use set the general direction for social change.

Like Cottrell and others, M. K. Hubbert, a geophysicist writing at about the same time, was impressed by the correlation between the burst of human civilization and the transition to a fossil fuel economy. He used his vast knowledge of physics, mathematics, and geology to revolutionize the way in which the supply of nonrenewable resources was analyzed, and was the first to predict that the fossil fuel era would be relatively short-lived. Hubbert's petroleum supply models have proven to be remarkably accurate; it is ironic that the only model to correctly predict the peaking of domestic oil production in the United States was from a physicist.

The amount of research devoted to energy–environment–economic interactions increased substantially in the wake of the environmental movement and the petroleum crisis of the 1970s. H. T. Odum developed a systematic methodology using energy flows to analyze the combined system of humans and nature. One of Odum's most important contributions was an analysis of the countercurrent flows of energy and money in the economy. He pointed out that whenever a dollar flow exists, there must be an energy flow in the opposite direction. Moreover, while money circulates in a closed loop, low-entropy energy enters the system and is consumed in economic tasks. Other essential energy flows (e.g., solar, water, wind, etc.), have no associated dollar flow, leading to their misuse. Empirical support for some of Odum's ideas was provided by Costanza, who analyzed the relationship between the "embodied energy" (direct and indirect energy) used to produce a good or service in the U.S. economy and the dollar value attached to that good or service in market transactions. Geologist Earl Cooke provided a comprehensive overview of energy systems and industrial society in his 1976 book, *Man, Energy, Society.*

The Energy Research Group (Hannon, Herendeen, Bullard, et al.) at the University of Illinois greatly enhanced the empirical methodology of biophysical economics with an input–output model of the U.S. economy based on energy flows, from which the direct and indirect energy cost of any good or service could be calculated. Hannon used this information to argue for a strong energy conservation ethic. Like Soddy and the technocrats, he believed that the existing economic system was an inadequate allocator of energy and other natural resources. Robert Ayres developed a materials–energy balance model to describe the inconsistency of the closed, cyclic model of standard economics. He showed that economic production necessarily generates high-entropy wastes—i.e., negative externalities—which are treated in standard economic theory as isolated market failures, but which are in fact an inevitable and pervasive outcome of economic production.

Some of the most insightful developments in biophysical economics during the 1970s are from Nicholas Georgescu-Roegen and Herman Daly. Georgescu-Roegen depicted a unidirectional flow in the economy, from inputs of low-entropy energy and matter, to outputs that included both useful goods and services and valueless high-entropy waste heat and degraded matter. By focusing on the circular flow, standard economic theory loses sight of the sensitivity of economies to changes in the quality of nature's low-entropy stocks of resources and the degrading of basic natural life support processes.

In his 1977 book, *Steady State Economics*, Daly points out the logical inconsistency of the emphasis placed upon growth in the context of the energy and environmental realities that we confront. Like Ayres, Daly criticizes the failure of standard economics to take account of the throughput of low-entropy natural resources, from which all goods and services are ultimately derived. Our preoccupation with monetary flows at the expense of thermodynamic principles misleads us into believing that perpetual economic growth is not only possible but morally desirable as well.

The majority of economists reject biophysical economic models, arguing that they underestimate the ability of technological innovation to offset changes in resource quality [e.g., Barnett and Morse,[2] and Solow[3]]. While the biophysical perspective does acknowledge the importance of human ideas, it also stresses that they must be firmly rooted in the biophysical world; to date, most of our technological innovations have relied upon increased fossil fuel use per worker. Economics can no longer afford to ignore, downplay, or misrepresent the role of natural resources in the economic process.

Notes

1. Frederick Soddy, *Cartesian Economics* (London: Hendersons, 1922), 9; cited by Cleveland, 52.

2. H.J. Barnett and C. Morse, *Scarcity and Growth* (John Hopkins University Press, 1963).

3. R.M. Solow, "Intergenerational Equity and Exhaustible Resources," *Review of Economic Studies*, 1974, pp. 29–45.

Summary of

World Environmental History and Economic Development

by J. F. Richards

[Published in *Sustainable Development of the Biosphere,* eds. W.C. Clark and R.E. Munn (New York and Cambridge, England: Cambridge University Press, 1986), 53–74. Reprinted with the permission of Cambridge University Press. © International Institute for Applied Systems Analysis, 1986.]

Over the past 300 years the earth's biota has undergone massive changes, natural environments have been removed or fundamentally altered, and the world's land and sea animal populations have been sharply reduced in number and range. At the same time, human control over the natural environment has risen to the point that it is virtually an anthropogenic system. Most historians dealing with the vastly complex social, economic, and political transition to modernity have neglected the human species' changing relationship to the environment, treating this relationship as a constant that can be safely ignored rather than as a significant variable. The great task for environmental historians is to record and to analyze the effects of humanity's recent encroachment upon and control of the natural world over the course of the last three to five centuries. Environmental history must proceed from a global perspective because of the integrated global nature of the world's economic and ecological systems.

Improving our understanding of environmental change in the early-modern and modern worlds has a singular urgency. The cumulative effects of human activity upon water, soils, and vegetation throughout the world have drastically accelerated, setting in motion physical processes of change that may be irreversible. In addition, it is important to consider the extent to which the development of the modern economy has relied upon the consumption of nonrenewable natural resources. Analysis of the implications of this exploitation of resources may suggest issues and questions for future human development.

Expansion of World Arable Land

In every region of the world, the expansion of arable land has proceeded at a startling pace. The conversion of "wild" lands to regular cropping has been as vigorous in the lands of the old world as in the new. It was not until the 1920s that research and investments in agricultural productivity shifted from extending cropped areas to intensifying production on existing arable land through improved biological inputs (e.g., fertilizers, high yielding varieties, etc.). The Food and Agriculture Organization of the United Nations estimates that globally there were around 1.5 billion hectares (ha) of land under cultivation in 1980, and much of that land was brought under cultivation relatively recently. Indeed, it has been estimated that 852 million ha—over half of the present total—were brought under cultivation between 1860 and the present. This phenomenon cannot be adequately explained by citing population pressures alone. Instead, it is the transition from peasant agriculture to mass commodity production for the expanding world market that is the primary cause.

One of the immediate consequences of this expansion of cropped land is the profound impact it has had upon soils. Estimates show that water-induced soil erosion has increased to 91 billion tons of soil each year, a rate twice that of 1860, and a five-fold increase compared to the pre-agricultural past. Moreover, it is the pressing need for agricultural land, as well as land to meet other demands of modernity (e.g., urbanization, transportation systems) that has fostered the encroachment of civilization upon forest, wetlands, and drylands.

Deforestation

Depending on scale and definition, there could be more than 100 major forests worldwide that no longer truly exist in recognizable form. Getting an historical measure of this deforestation can be an immensely difficult task, as neglect of the natural environment by traditional historians leaves us with no reliable inventory of the missing forests. We do know that the patterns of deforestation have directly followed patterns of economic development, and there are some areas for which we can produce a picture of the process, including:

(1) *European USSR*: 67 million ha of forest was lost between 1700 and 1917, with deforestation continuing apace after the revolution.

(2) *Coastal Brazil*: In 1500, it was estimated that 500,000 square kilometers of thick forest blanketed the coast, but by 1900 most of this forest had disappeared.

(3) *Burma*: It is estimated that there were 4 million ha of forest in lower Burma in 1850, but by 1914 only several hundred thousand hectares remained.

Completion of a global inventory of this type would be an invaluable first step in better defining the recent forest history of the world, and more precise, better-documented data on the extent and rate of forest depletion would do much to correct our perspectives on the global process.

Land Reclamation: The Drainage of Wetlands

In the last decades of the nineteenth century the pace and scale of land reclamation through drainage of wetlands increased dramatically. Improved technology and increasing demand for agricultural land combined with the growing intervention of the state to foster this trend. One of the largest of these efforts occurred in the United States. It is estimated that 42.6 million ha were under drainage in 1978. Similar efforts in Australia (1.7 million ha), Europe (21 million ha), Africa, Asia, and Latin America testify to the brisk pace at which the world's swamps, bogs, and marshes have been cleared over the past century. Economic pressures suggest that this drive into the wetlands will continue apace into the future.

Land reclamation by drainage has had significant environmental and social effects, including the release of stored carbon into the atmosphere, altered water tables affecting local watersheds, and disappearance of plant and animal species. A preliminary inventory of worldwide land reclamation through wetlands drainage is an essential first step for environmental history. Economic development may make it desirable to encroach even further on the world's wetlands. If so, an historical perspective on the impact of disappearing wetlands will allow for more informed decisions in this area.

Land Reclamation: Irrigation of Arid and Near-Arid Lands

Irrigation is a much more visible and appealing form of land reclamation. Making the deserts bloom draws upon our deepest aesthetic and cultural instincts. The best known and one of the largest social investments in irrigation has been in the American West, with up to 17.7 million ha under irrigation. Globally over 200 million ha of land are irrigated, and that figure is expected to reach 300 million ha by the year 2000. The more than 13,000 large capacity reservoirs in use have a capacity equal to 12% of the entire annual runoff of the world's rivers.

The physical changes wrought by irrigation are substantial. Waterlogging and increased salinity and/or alkalinity are long-recognized problems. Other threats include the destruction of species adapted to minimal soil moisture, coupled with the enlargement of animal and plant populations and diseases previously held in check by water shortages. The magnitude of world irrigation developments over the past two centuries provides strong justification for systematic, intensive historical review.

Grazing Lands, Large Grazing Animals, and Man

Grazing lands throughout the world are of crucial importance to the global economy. Domestic livestock and wild herbivores provide an important source of nourishment and a vital economic resource. Since 1700 there has been a steady reduction in the extent of the world's grazing lands as many of the great grasslands have come under the plow. In spite of a counter-vailing trend, as forest clearing creates new grazing lands, the overall trend has been a net loss of grasslands. Another significant factor has been the intensifying human intervention in and control of world grazing lands, and the concomitant decline in wild animals. This, in turn, is part of a conscious effort to depose the wild herbivores in favor of domesticated animals, which has led to significant problems of overgrazing in many areas.

Conclusion

These enormous changes in human habitat since 1700 have forced new adaptations in culture and institutions upon human society. It does not appear as though these trends will be slowed or reversed in the near future. The great task for environmental historians is to record and analyze the pace and impacts of these transformations. What is needed is a long-term global comparative historical perspective that treats the environment as a significant variable. More and better data are essential both for under-standing the impact of these environmental changes on our past, and for enabling us to understand problems and prospects for the future.

Summary of

The Historical Roots of Our Ecologic Crisis

by Lynn White, Jr.

[Published in *Science* 155 (10 March 1967): 1203–1207. © 1967 by the AAAS.]

All forms of life modify their natural environment as a basic condition of their existence, and man is of course no exception. Indeed, since becoming a numerous species he has vastly altered his environment. The history of ecological change is still so rudimentary that we know little about what has really happened. From the extermination of the monster mammals of the Pleistocene to the reclamation of land from the North Sea in Holland, unknown numbers of species of animals, birds, fish, and plants have died out, with uncertain implications for the quality of human life. The threat today has expanded many orders of magnitude beyond the preindustrial destruction of French forests or the smog problem in London. Our present levels of fossil fuel consumption and overwhelming deposits of sewage and garbage threaten the entire ecosphere. What shall we do? No one knows for sure, and unless we carefully consider the fundamentals, our best measures may provoke ecological backlashes with dire consequences. As a beginning, we ought to try to clarify our thinking by looking at the historical presuppositions that underlie modern technology and science.

The Western Traditions of Technology and Science

It is important to stress that both modern science and technology are distinctly Occidental. It is beyond question that Western technology has inherited crucial knowledge in mathematics, optics, medicine, and navigation from the great civilizations in Asia, and that it continues to absorb elements from all over the world. Yet today, around the globe, all significant science is Western in style and method, whatever the race or language of the scientists. It is also important to emphasize that the leadership of the West in science and technology considerably predates the so-called Scientific and Industrial Revolutions of the seventeenth and eighteenth centuries, respectively. (These terms are outmoded and tend to obscure the true nature of what they seek to describe.)

Between A.D. 800 and 1000, the West had begun to apply water power to industrial processes, and by 1200 it was harnessing wind power as well. From these simple beginnings, the West rapidly expanded its technological skills in the development of power machinery, labor-saving devices, and automation. In basic technological capacity, the Latin West of the latter Middle Ages far outstripped its elaborate, sophisticated, and esthetically magnificent sister cultures, Byzantium and Islam. "In 1444 a great Greek ecclesiastic, Bessarion, . . . [upon visiting Italy was] amazed by the superiority of Western ships, arms, textiles, glass. But above all he [was] astonished by the spectacle of water-wheels sawing timbers and pumping the bellows of blast furnaces. Clearly he had seen nothing of the sort in the Near East."[1204] By the end of the fifteenth century the technological superiority of Europeans was such that they were capable of sailing the globe and conquering, looting, and colonizing the world over.

Modern science is supposed to have begun in 1543 with the publication of the great works of Copernicus and Vesalius. These brilliant works did not, however, appear overnight. The distinctive Western tradition of science begins, in fact, in the late eleventh century, with the translation of Arabic and Greek scientific works into Latin. Within 200 years, Greek and Islamic science was being avidly read and criticized in new universities. Out of this criticism arose new observation and speculation, and a growing distrust of the ancient verities. By the late thirteenth century the West had seized the mantle of scientific leadership from the faltering hands of Islam. Prior to the eleventh century science had scarcely existed in the West, but from the late thirteenth century onward the scientific sector of Occidental culture has increased in a steady crescendo.

The Medieval View of Man and Nature

Since Western science and technology as we know them today acquired their distinctive character during the Middle Ages, we cannot understand their nature or their present impact upon ecology without examining medieval assumptions and developments. Human ecology is deeply conditioned by beliefs about our nature and destiny, beliefs which in turn are profoundly influenced by religion. In its Western form, Christianity is the most anthropocentric religion the world has ever seen. The Judeo–Christian tradition is one in which the whole of nature and the planet itself were created for the distinct purpose of serving man's needs. Man, created in the image of God, is not a part of nature, but is its master. Christianity, in contrast to paganism and the Asian religions, not only creates a pronounced dualism between man and nature, but also insists that it is God's will that man exploit nature for his own purposes.

This view has implications for the everyday conduct of people. In antiquity it was believed that every hill, tree, and animal had a guardian spirit that had to be honored and placated before using the resource. By destroying pagan animism it became possible to exploit nature with absolute indifference to the feelings of these natural objects. Man thus developed a monopoly over the spirits of this world, and the old inhibitions surrounding the exploitation of nature crumbled. Moreover, the Christian dogma of creation and rapture suggests that there is a discreet beginning and end to man's existence on earth. This creates the basis for a linear concept of time and existence, in contrast to the more cyclical perceptions of existence in antiquity. This linear concept is accompanied by an implicit faith in perpetual progress, which was unknown in our Greco-Roman past or in the Orient.

It is significant that all of the great Western scientists—Copernicus, Grosseteste, Bacon, Galileo, and even Newton—cast their scientific inquiries within a matrix of Christian theology. It was not until the late eighteenth century that scientists began to dispense with God in their scientific inquiries.

An Alternative Christian View

The implications of this argument may be unpalatable to many Christians. If modern science and technology are historically an extrapolation of Christian theology, and if this science and technology is judged to be out of control in terms of its ecological impact, then Christianity bears a huge burden of guilt. It is doubtful that the further application of science and technology alone will enable us to evade the disastrous ecological backlash with which we are confronted. Our science and technology have evolved from Christian attitudes about man's relation to nature, and even today, despite all of our progress in the natural sciences, we continue to view ourselves as the center of the cosmos, as beings apart from the natural process. We are superior to nature, contemptuous of it, and entirely willing to use it for our slightest whim. The whole concept of the sacred grove is alien to Christianity and thus to the ethos of the West.

What we do now about ecology depends upon our ideas today about the man–nature relationship. More science and technology will not relieve the ghastly ecological pressures we confront until we find a new religion, or rethink the one we have. Perhaps we should ponder the theology of the greatest radical in Christian history since Christ: St. Francis of Assisi. St. Francis' heresy lay in his belief in the virtue of humility, not merely for the individual, but for mankind at large. He endeavored to dethrone man from his monarchy over creation, to establish a democracy, a brotherhood of all God's creatures, from the smallest ant to man himself. His view of nature and man rested on the idea that all things, animate and inanimate, were created for the glorification of God, and are thus equal in God's eyes. Our present science and technology are still tainted with the orthodox Christian arrogance toward nature. Instead, "we must rethink and refeel our nature and destiny. The profoundly religious, but heretical, sense of the primitive Franciscans for the spiritual autonomy of all parts of nature may point a direction. I propose Francis as a patron saint for ecologists."[1207]

Summary of

The Case That the World Has Reached Limits

by Robert Goodland

[Published in *Population, Technology and Lifestyle:*
The Transition to Sustainability, eds. Robert Goodland,
Herman E. Daly, and Salah El Serafy (Washington, D.C. and Covelo,
California: Island Press, 1992), 3–22. © 1992 The International Bank
for Reconstruction and Development and UNESCO.]

Since the publication of The Brundtland Report, the United Nations, the World Bank, and most nations have advocated sustainability as a goal. However, the world is currently being run in unsustainable ways, so we must explore the implications of creating a sustainable world.

The Global Ecosystem and the Economic Subsystem

One measure of the size of the human economic subsystem relative to the total global ecosystem of which it is a part is the level of throughput of resources from the ecosystem to the economic subsystem. This level can be measured by the product of population times per capita resource consumption. The global ecosystem is the source of all material inputs, as well as the sink for the wastes of the economic subsystem, and it has limited regenerative and assimilative capacities. Since the size of the human economic subsystem relative to the total global system is very large today, the limited capacity of the global system to support the economic subsystem is being stretched. It is important to ensure that the human economy be limited so that the ecosystem can support it. This will require throughput reduction.

Localized Limits to Global Limits

Human economic activity and the resulting pollution have reached all parts of the world. The current constraints on economic activity are due to the sink limits of the global system. The key limit is the sink constraint on absorption of wastes produced by fossil fuel use. There are a number of signs that the limits have been reached. Five of them are discussed below.

(1) *Human Biomass Appropriation:* As calculated by Vitousek et al.,[1] the human economy uses about 40% of the net primary product of terrestrial photosynthesis today. Thus, with one doubling of the world's

population we will be using 80% of the net primary product of terrestrial photosynthesis, and shortly thereafter 100%. This scenario is ecologically impossible and socially undesirable. The time has come to ask when we will be willing to say enough.

(2) *Global Warming:* The second evidence that limits have been exceeded is global warming. Carbon dioxide accumulation is pervasive and it is expensive to cure. Furthermore, cropping patterns will be affected by the resulting climatic changes. Significant changes in temperature have been recorded in the recent past. There is still uncertainty about whether global warming has actually started, but all evidence suggests that it may have. Neither the effects nor the required policy responses are yet clear.

The dominant cause of the accumulation of greenhouse gases is the fossil fuel–based human economy. Other contributors to global warming are pollutants like methane, CFCs, and nitrous oxide. There is no price to polluters for using atmospheric sink capacity, although the real opportunity costs may be very high. The costs of rejecting the greenhouse hypothesis, if it is in fact true, are far greater than the costs of accepting the hypothesis even if it proves false. If nothing is done until irrefutable evidence comes in, the costs of the influx of millions of refugees from low-lying and coastal areas, of damage to ports and coastal cities, and of damage to agriculture will be exorbitant. Action is necessary, if for no other reason than to insure against these possibilities. Prudence should be paramount. As Amory Lovins has suggested, abating global warming may save, not cost, money.

To the extent that energy use reflects economic activity, carbon emissions are an index of the scale of the economy. Decoupling economic growth from energy throughput and increases in CO_2 seems achievable, as the recent experiences of Japan, the United States, and Sweden attest. This can be accomplished by making a transition to renewable forms of energy, including biomass, solar, and hydro.

(3) *Ozone Shield Rupture:* The third evidence that limits have been reached is the rupture of the ozone shield. Two ozone holes have now been detected: one over Antarctica and another over the Arctic. The consequences of these ozone holes include increases in the incidence of cancer and many other diseases, as well as upsetting balances in natural vegetation. Even if CFC emissions cease today, it will take 100 to 150 years for pre-damage levels to return. The global nature of this problem is made evident by the fact that while 85% of the CFCs are released in the Northern Hemisphere, the main hole appeared over Antarctica.

(4) *Land Degradation:* Land degradation—i.e., "decreased productivity such as caused by accelerated soil erosion, salination, and desertification"[13]—is not new, though the scale of degradation has mushroomed. About 35% of the earth's land is now degraded. Soil loss rates range from 10 to 100 tons per hectare per year, seriously affecting the world food economy. In addition, the shortage and subsequent overharvesting of fuel wood also lead to land degradation.

(5) *Decrease in Biodiversity:* The increase in the size of the human economy has resulted in the extinction of species at the fastest rate in recorded history. The tropical forests are being destroyed at a rate of 168,000 square kilometers per year. While estimates of the number and rates of species extinction vary, they are all large. The destruction of the tropical forests increases poverty, and there is little beneficial trade-off with development.

Population

Reducing population growth in developing and developed countries is essential to achieve sustainability. Population control is needed in the developed countries, as they consume a large part of the world's resources and hence overpollute, and help must also be provided to the developing countries for family planning. Moreover, poverty in any country stimulates population growth, so direct poverty alleviation is essential. Developing country populations are increasing at a faster rate than their economies can provide for them. Even if energy consumption remains at its current inadequate levels in these countries, population growth will increase their commercial energy consumption 75% by the year 2025. To provide the resources needed for poverty alleviation in developing countries, developed nations must shift from input growth to qualitative development.

Growth Versus Development

Given the size of the economic subsystem relative to the global system of which it is a part, as well as the strains on the regenerative and assimilative capacities of the global system, opinions differ as to how much the economy needs to continue to grow. While some authors, including Brundtland, call for continued growth, others believe that to achieve sustainability quantitative growth should stop and give way to qualitative development. According to Brundtland, some necessary conditions for sustainability include: production of more with less through conservation, technological improvements, and recycling; reduction of the population explosion; redistribution from overconsumers to the poor; and—a point Brundtland was fuzzy on—the transition from input growth to qualitative development. Poor countries must be spared further hardship during the transition to sustainability. While Brundtland commendably advocates growth for poor countries, with respect to the resource consumption of different groups of human beings, sustainability will require both raising the bottom and lowering the top.

Conclusion

As economies move toward service-oriented growth and away from industrial growth, there is less damage done to the source and sink functions of the globe. The transition to sustainability will be assisted by technologies that are less throughput intensive. However, these changes will be insufficient, as the potential growth of the service sector relative to the production of goods has limits, and many services also have high throughput. In addition, "hi-tech" growth that is less throughput intensive may not be affordable in those places that need the most growth, i.e., developing countries. Part of the solution will be massive technology transfers from industrial to developing countries.

Note

1. Vitousek, Peter M., et al., "Human Appropriation of the Products of Photosynthesis," in *BioScience* 34 (6): 368–73 (1986).

Summary of

One Part Wisdom: The Great Debate
by Paul Harrison

[Published in Paul Harrison, *The Third Revolution: Environment, Population and a Sustainable World* (London and New York: I.B. Tauris & Co. Ltd., 1992 and Penguin Books, 1993), 7–20.]

(This is a summary of the first chapter of Paul Harrison's book in which the author traces the evolution of the debate about the effects of population growth.)

Human population growth has been through five phases since the beginning of the Christian era. The growth rate in the first phase, between A.D. 0 and 800—a period of economic stagnation, political chaos, and mass migration—was 0.03% per year. In the second phase, between 800 and 1700, the growth rate rose to 0.11% as a result of agricultural improvements, mainly in Europe and China. Between 1750 and 1900, the third phase, the growth rate increased to 0.57%. The fourth phase was between 1950 and 1980. This period saw death rates falling in developing countries because of the introduction of preventative and curative medicine and the agricultural revolution. Growth rates peaked in the 1960s at 2.05%. Since 1980 we have been in the fifth phase, with growth rates declining to 1.74%. However, while the growth rate is falling, in absolute numbers the decade of the 1990s will see the highest annual additions to world population. Are these increases in population something we should worry about, or are they beneficial?

The beginnings of the modern debate as to whether population growth is a positive or a negative factor can be traced to the late eighteenth century. In 1761, in his *Various Prospects of Mankind, Nature and Providence*, Robert Wallace argued that an obstacle to a world of equality was that children would be so well taken care of that infant mortality would fall and population would increase. This increase in population would finally lead to an overstocked world, and cruel and unnatural practices would be necessary to reduce the numbers. In *Enquiry Concerning Political Justice* (1793), William Godwin objected to this vision and argued that because three-quarters of the earth was uncultivated, population growth would never be a problem.

In 1798, Thomas Malthus published *Essay on the Principle of Population*, arguing that while population grew in geometrical ratio, food production grew in arithmetical ratio. As a result, population has a tendency to grow faster than food production. Since food is necessary for survival, population growth is equalized with food production by excess populations dying. Malthus argued that in this way natural checks would keep population growth no higher than growth in the food supply. In 1803 Malthus revised his initial essay to argue that population growth could also be limited by the power of self-control.

Malthus' *Essay* was an onslaught against socialism, and socialists reacted to it in strong terms. William Hazlitt called it the "little, low, rankling malice of a parish beadle"[1] disguised as philosophy. Marx accused it of being a "sensational pamphlet." To Marx, overpopulation was caused by the laws of capitalism, not the laws of nature. He argued that population growth produced a "reserve army" of unemployed because of investments in machinery. Friederick Engels argued that "mankind could multiply more rapidly than is compatible with modern bourgeois society."[2]

In America, Henry George argued in *Progress and Poverty* (1879) that the cause of poverty was not overpopulation but unjust laws, warfare, excessive rents, and lack of secure tenancies. To George, population growth was an effect and not a cause of poverty. He also foreshadowed anti-Malthusian theories of the radical right when he argued that higher levels of population lead to greater wealth.

Ester Boserup, one of George's most influential successors, suggested in her 1965 book, *The Conditions of Agricultural Growth*, that population growth determines agricultural change. Boserup argued that the first farmers were shifting cultivators who returned to plots after fifteen to twenty years. As populations increased, they were forced to return to plots more often, resulting in yield declines. Farmers were then forced to improve agricultural techniques in order to maintain food production, and these developments helped food production keep pace with population growth. If population growth had not taken place, primitive agriculture would have persisted and would not have resulted in higher levels of cultural development.

The modern debate on population growth has been similar to the debates of the nineteenth century. Paul Ehrlich, in the role of a modern Malthus, predicted in his 1968 book, *The Population Bomb*, that overpopulation would result in famines and the starvation of hundreds of millions of people. He advocated compulsory population control measures if voluntary efforts failed, and condemned giving aid to health programs in the Third World. In *The Limits to Growth* (1972), Dennis and Donella Meadows and their team predicted, on the basis of computer models, that if present trends continue, a catastrophic collapse of population will occur due to a rise in pollution and a dramatic decline in mineral and land resources. Moreover, they asserted that those who survive will have a dismal, depleted existence. According to the authors of *The Limits to Growth*, the only way to avoid catastrophe is to undertake a comprehensive program of conservation and population stabilization.

The extreme predictions of modern Mathusianism have evoked reactions from the right and the left. From the right, Julian Simon responded with a pro growth position. He argued that throughout recorded history standards of living have risen along with population because higher population leads to bigger markets, the possibility of economies of scale, and more people with more brains to think up technical solutions to problems. All of this results in increasing wealth; resource shortages may occur, but only temporarily. On the left, the response to neo-Malthusian views has suggested that overpopulation is caused by poverty, which results from exploitation, expropriation, inequality, and injustice. This view argues that the poor have large families because children can bring in wages or care for their parents in old age.

It is not easy to see who is right. Ideology plays a role in molding people's views. Free markets are the answer for conservatives, while socialists believe social justice is the solution. Third World nationalists see this concern with population problems as a smoke screen for fears about the increasing strength of countries in the South, or an excuse to meddle in their internal affairs. Religious groups, meanwhile, equate an anti-abortion stance with an anti–family planning position. There is some element of truth on all sides of this debate, and a more synthetic view (see, for example, the rest of *The Third Revolution*) is needed to provide a balanced picture.

Notes

1. Gertrude Himmelfarb, ed., *On Population: Thomas Robert Malthus* (New York: Random House, 1960), *xxvi*; cited by Harrison, 13.

2. Friederick Engels, "Letter to J.B. Schweitzer," *Works* 2 (1965): 391; cited by Harrison, 14.

Summary of

Environmental Significance of Development Theory
by F.E. Trainer

[Published in *Ecological Economics* 2 (December 1990): 277–286. Reprinted with kind permission from Elsevier Science B.V., Amsterdam, The Netherlands.]

While conventional development has been successful in raising growth rates, the primary beneficiaries of growth are those who are already rich. The vast majority of people in the Third World have experienced very little improvement in their real material living standards. However, both conventional and radical (Marxist and dependency) development theories have ignored the voluminous "limits to growth" literature. These schools are premised on the notion that the goal of development is endless economic growth and the achievement for all of the living standards typical of the rich countries. Given present estimates of the world's mineral and energy resources, there is no chance that all of the people in the world can have per capita use rates typical of people in rich countries. At present, the rich countries of the world have $\frac{1}{5}$ of the world's population but consume $\frac{4}{5}$ of the world's annual resource output.

There is increasing recognition that problems of resource depletion, destruction of the environment, deprivation of Third World people, conflicts over resources and markets, and a falling quality of life are all consequences of pursuing a single-minded policy of growth and ignoring the problem of the "limits to growth." Rich countries must, therefore, move toward becoming less affluent, more self-sufficient, conserver societies. In addition, the goal of development must cease to be defined in terms of raising everyone to the "living standards" or the patterns of settlement and industrialization that the rich countries now have, as this will be physically impossible.

Two main reasons why development has done little or nothing for the poorest 40–60% in the Third World are the emphasis on market forces and the inappropriate development that results. The reason that ⅕ of the world's people consume ⅘ of the world's resources is that the global economy is based on the market system. Market forces always deliver scarce and valuable things to the relatively rich, while ignoring the poor. It is these same market forces that ensure that the wrong industries are set up in the Third World, with the result that much of the productive capacity created is inappropriate in view of the needs of most Third World people.

Development, when focused on economic growth or increases in GNP, allocates resources to producing for the relatively rich, especially for those abroad. Development aimed instead at meeting the needs of most people may not yield substantial increases in GNP. Since the 1970s, the inability of growth alone to meet the needs of the poor has led to "growth with equity" and "basic needs" strategies. But these theories still fundamentally rely on growth as a solutions. They mistake the cause of the problem—growth—for the solution. The thrust of development should therefore not be toward increasing GNP, but toward improving the quality of life. A strategy of appropriate development would contribute to better informal security networks, more independent and autonomous village government, and the development of rich and varied forests and "edible landscapes." Development should not only be for the economy, but for the society as a whole.

The "indiscriminate growth and trickle-down someday" approach to development is largely responsible for the damage occurring to the planet's ecosystem. This conventional approach to development advocates importing huge quantities of goods, machinery, and inputs from rich countries. In order to pay for these imports, Third World countries are forced to turn to their natural resources, which are their most readily available export items. In addition to forests being destroyed outright for export purposes, the lack of appropriate development options lead nomads, peasants, and native peoples to exploit remaining forests as well. Forests are cleared for replacement with agricultural activities that have high rates of return, such as export beef production. This destruction leads to less rainfall retention, creeks drying up, soil being washed away, and severe droughts and floods. The expansion of export cropping has resulted in the best lands going toward export crops, driving peasants and nomads toward marginal lands that are prone to overgrazing and erosion. This has resulted in an increase in the number of landless people in rural areas, and large-scale migration to already over-crowded urban areas. Along with the destruction of forests, the use of pes-ticides and fertilizers and the accompanying irrigation changes have led to the loss of a number of plant and animal species and genetic diversity.

Other environmental consequences result from the affinity of the con-ventional development approach for big infrastructure development. For example, the development of dams results in the destruction of forests, dis-placement of native peoples, loss of silt, and the destruction of food chains such as fisheries. These large-scale infrastructure projects take away resources from more appropriate development strategies and add to foreign debt.

The following can be suggested as basic principles for appropriate, eco-logically sustainable Third World development:

(1) *Focus on the concept of appropriateness:* Concentrate on developing the overall quality of life, with a view toward considerations of ecology, resources, and justice, rather than focusing on growth, market forces, and the profit motive.

(2) *Totally abandon Western affluence as a goal of development:* Aim for lower (but still comfortable), stable lifestyles with reasonable levels of nonrenewable resource consumption, rather than an endless increase of material wealth.

(3) *Maximize local economic self-sufficiency:* Aim at self-sufficiency and independence from the global economy via the development of inte-grated, small-scale regional economies.

The above prescriptions, based on self-sufficiency and autarchy, are often dismissed as naive. This is true if the objective of development is heavy industrialization, high levels of GNP, and western lifestyles. However, if the goals of development are seen in an alternative framework in which low lev-els of consumption of resources can achieve satisfactory living standards and a high quality of life, then frugality, self-sufficiency, and stability come into focus.

PART II

Definition, Scope, and Interdisciplinary Issues

Overview Essay

by Jonathan M. Harris

Ecological economics in its modern form is a relatively new field. We have seen that there is a significant background in the history of economic theory for the emergence of ecological economics; but its claim to the status of a discipline in its own right is recent. Mainstream economic theorists would perhaps attempt to subsume it under "environmental economics," a sub-field of neoclassical theory, but the broader logic of analysis already presented in Part I, and developed in greater detail in this part, argues against such a classification. To address the issues of the relationship between the economic system and its resource and environmental base involves more than simply pricing natural resources and environmental services. An attempt must be made to integrate the very different principles governing the operations of the natural world and of the human-made economy.

This effort necessarily requires insights from different disciplines, certainly including the physical sciences, ecology, and economics, but also extending to sociology, political science, psychology, and philosophy. The distinction between positive and normative analysis, so greatly emphasized by economic theorists, breaks down when we attempt to address questions of the large-scale impact of economic activity on the natural world. It is not simply a question of how the equilibrium and feedback mechanisms in economics and ecology interrelate—that is to say, it is not merely a question of economy/ecosystem modeling, important though that effort is. The issues raised include more fundamental questions such as: what is the purpose of economic activity?; what are the goals of economic development?; how important is the preservation of the natural world as compared to the production of economic goods?; how do principles of social and intergenerational equity affect the use of resources and the choice of basic and luxury goods to be produced? Standard economic theory has a limited capacity to respond to such questions, while disciplines other than economics must be supplemented with some form of economic theory to address them. In an era when questions of resource depletion and environmental degradation have come dramatically to the forefront of public debate, the need for a discipline of ecological economics is evident.

The articles summarized in this part address the issues involved in the development of an interdisciplinary approach to the area. They fall roughly into two categories. The first group deals with conceptual and methodological problems of interdisciplinary research. The second focuses on the now widely used, but poorly defined, concept of sustainable development. Properly understood, sustainable development means the replacement of the standard concept of economic growth with a more balanced set of goals taking into account environmental carrying capacity, social and intergenerational equity, and community values, in addition to the production of goods and services. We must draw on all the different disciplines which contribute to ecological economics to get a good sense of what we mean by sustainable development. Once defined, or at least delimited, this concept replaces such abstract constructs as "maximizing utility" for the purposes of economic analysis. The "economic" issues of production, resource use, technology, consumption, income distribution, international trade, etc. can then be addressed in the context of a new perspective on the overall goals of economic activity.

In two of the original articles outlining the need for a field of ecological economics, Robert Costanza, Herman Daly, and David Pearce establish conceptual links between fundamental issues in economic theory and the biophysical logic of ecology. Costanza and Daly provide an overview of the argument, while Pearce goes into more detail on its philosophical underpinnings. Distribution of wealth and income have always been important in economic theory, but this theory has been limited to considerations of human welfare only, and has tended to define welfare in terms of consumption of goods. Treatment of intergenerational distribution has been limited in economics, and heavily dependent on the use of current interest rates to discount future benefits. The importance of natural resource and environmental constraints in distribution has not generally been recognized, but is now inescapable. These two articles grapple with these shortcomings, rejecting the use of interest rates and present-oriented distributional rules in favor of long-term sustainability. Sustainability, it is argued, extends the principle of distributional justice to take into account both non-human species and future generations. Neither article goes very far toward making the concept of sustainability specific, or focusing on whether and how the differing methodologies of economics and ecology can be fruitfully combined. Rather, these two articles can be considered as setting the stage for the more specific methodological and policy issues which follow.

Richard Norgaard's essay, "The Case for Methodological Pluralism," introduces a fundamental proposition of ecological economics—that there is no single formal theory suitable for the analysis of all economic and environmental issues. This contradicts the neoclassical belief that a single theoretical construct based on relatively simple assumptions can be used to analyze all economic activity, as well as environmental issues associated with the economic system. Within economics, critics of the neoclassical market model have argued that it neglects social, historical, and cultural factors and oversimplifies human motivations. When we take into account the complex and multifaceted questions of ecosystems and their interactions with the economy, this shortcoming is even more glaring. While formal theory also plays a part in ecology, the more pragmatic and empirical methodologies common in ecological research provide a contrast to the mathematical formalism of standard economics. Norgaard suggests an approach of drawing insights from varied methodologies without selecting one as superior or rejecting any out of hand. As a general principle, this sounds unexceptionable; but it leaves open the question of how a rigorous body of theory can be developed which is neither solely ecology nor solely economics.

The articles by Jason Shogren and Clifford Nowell, and by Malte Faber and John Proops, go into greater detail regarding different methodologies and the possibility of effective interdisciplinary work. Shogren and Nowell make the point that economic theorizing is generally based on an explicit "objective function," assuming that the goals of economic actors can be expressed simply as utility or profit maximization. This is questionable as a description of economic reality, but becomes even more so when attempts are made to apply market valuations to the environment through "contingent valuation" theory. They suggest that combining the empirical and descriptive efforts of ecologists with more cautious use of formal mathematical models may be productive for both fields. This search for a middle ground is commendable, since much of the debate over the relative merits of theoretical and empirical investigation has so far proved to be more contentious than productive.

Faber and Proops argue more specifically that the physical scientist's understanding of the constraints on energy availability, process irreversibility, and entropy needs to be combined with economic analysis of technical and social responses to these constraints. Disciplinary boundaries in the academic world, however, make such cooperative research difficult to carry out. One of the goals of ecological economics is to legitimize and gain wide support for such research. Perhaps the outlook here can be hopeful, given the obvious importance of such cross-fertilization for discussion of current issues such as global warming, ozone layer depletion, or species loss.

Mary Clark's essay takes us across another interdisciplinary boundary, that between economics and social theory. She focuses on the conflict between competitive individualism and community relationships. She argues that the uncritical acceptance of a competitive individualist model of human motivation ("Gestalt I") has led inevitably to severe conflict between growth-oriented economic activity and the environment, as well as a weakening of community. The effort by economists to convert all values into prices intensifies these conflicts. She proposes a model of a sustainable community as an alternative goal ("Gestalt II"). This implies a reorientation of educational practice away from formal economics and toward developing an understanding of the ecological and psychosocial foundations of sustainability.

If ecological economics represents the synergy of several different disciplines in the theoretical area, industrial ecology can be considered as its practical application. Jesse Ausubel presents some of the main tenets of this emerging field, which spans ecology, economics, and chemical engineering. Industrial ecology replaces a laissez faire approach toward technological change with a conscious process of design aimed at creating industrial structures which are compatible with their environment, emphasizing systematic resource recycling, energy conservation, and reduced outflows of waste. Technological change has always been one of the "black boxes" of economics; industrial ecology attempts to open the box, examining the relationships of information, incentives, and control structures in shaping new technologies. In the past major new technologies have been "forced" by government policy decision—for example, automobile-centered transport and nuclear power generation. The message of industrial ecology is that the process of introduction of new technologies should be better understood, and turned toward the goal of eco-friendly technology and the transition away from fossil fuel and high material-throughput technologies. (The term *throughput*, introduced by Herman Daly, refers to the whole process in which resources enter the economic system as inputs and emerge as outputs and/or wastes. It is discussed further in Part III.)

The six articles dealing with sustainable development attempt in different ways to give focus to the concept. The obvious danger here is the watering-down of the sustainability concept to the point where almost any economic development, including some minimal environmental protection effort, can be described as sustainable. In fact, sustainability is a demanding goal with environmental, social, and economic components. Properly understood, it also implies a fundamental break with the standard theory and practice of economic development, rather than minor modifications of an existing paradigm. Sustainable development is ecological economics in practice, and as such is very different from the economic growth models of standard economic theory. This becomes apparent as we review the contributions of the different authors whose work is summarized here, themselves drawing on the work of others who have grappled with the concept since it was first introduced by the World Commission on Environment and Development's 1987 report *Our Common Future.*

Richard Norgaard's "co-evolutionary" perspective on sustainable development (SD) sees it as grounded in an alternative world view similar to that sketched out by Mary Clark. The interrelationship of environment, technology, social organization, and value systems in shaping development dethrones economics from its position of primacy in shaping development. A local or regional focus for SD is also emphasized, providing a counterpoint to the market economists' emphasis on an increasingly integrated global economy. Sharachchandra Lélé's critical review of SD literature shows that a frequent failure to recognize the broader implications of SD, and an effort to interpret it within the confines of the standard development model, have led to serious policy shortcomings, with examples cited from the areas of international trade, agriculture, and forestry. In each of these three areas, problems of unsustainability have been perpetuated by growth-oriented policies modified only slightly to take environmental considerations into account, and largely ignoring social equity and community sustainability concerns.

Vandana Shiva extends this line of critique, arguing that the ideology of the market system is fundamentally incompatible with sustainability. Development economists take the primacy of human-made capital for granted, seeing the transformation of natural capital (forests, soils, minerals, natural water cycles and ecosystems, etc.) into industrial capital as the essence of development. True sustainability, by contrast, depends on the recognition of the natural systems as primary. Social and economic structures must be adjusted to this reality, rather than the other way round. The clear implication is that a reconceptualization of the whole theory of development is needed, not merely an adjustment of existing theory to internalize environmental factors.

In "The Difficulty in Defining Sustainability," Michael Toman proposes the concept of a "safe minimum standard" as a possible compromise between economists' generally limited concepts of SD and ecologists' more demanding views of ecosystem protection. This approach would establish socially determined limits to the scope of market exploitation of resources, based on environmental cost and irreversibility. Johan Holmberg and Richard Sandbrook suggest a more ambitious policy of "primary environmental care" developed at the community level to meet basic needs, protect environmental resources, and strengthen community. John Dixon and Louise Fallon consider policy implications of SD from the perspective of the World Bank's Environment Department. (It is worth noting that this department has been far more attuned to SD theory than the Bank's growth-oriented loan officers.) These implications include: the importance of equity considerations in development as an alternative to the rising-tide-lifts-all-ships logic of across-the-board growth; resource planning for future generations; population policy; time horizons for planning and project evaluation; evaluation of species extinction and other irreversible ecological damage; and an awareness of the limits of the market mechanism for development policy.

On completing this survey of articles dealing with the field of ecological economics and its policy correlate, sustainable development, the reader may well feel that a better case has been made out for the *need* for such a field than for the proposition that the field is already established. Many of the criticisms of the narrowness of neoclassical economics are trenchant, and the general call for interdisciplinary research seems appropriate to the growing importance of problems involving economic and ecological interrelationships. But we cannot yet point to any large body of successful research or case studies of policy implementation along these lines. Indeed, the development of this area is still rudimentary—but the rudiments may be more significant for future intellectual and policy work than the far more fully developed academic fields which have failed thus far to offer an adequate understanding of, or response to, the global environmental crisis.

With this observation in mind, we move in Part III to a survey of theoretical work in the general area of ecological economics, then in Sections IV, V, and VI to specific areas of analysis and policy evaluation.

Summary of

Toward an Ecological Economics

by Robert Costanza and Herman E. Daly

[Published in *Ecological Modelling* 38 (September 1987): 1–7. Reprinted
with kind permission from Elsevier Science B.V., Amsterdam, The Netherlands.]

(This summary is the introduction to a special issue of Ecological Modelling
devoted to ecological economics.)

Humanity's increasing impact on the earth's environment requires a further synthesis of the disciplines of ecology and economics. The most important theoretical issues that should be encompassed in this synthesis are "(1) sustainability; (2) inter- and intra-species distribution of wealth; (3) discounting and intergenerational justice; and (4) dealing with non-monetized values, imprecision, and uncertainty."[1]

Need for an Ecological Economics

Both the economic and ecological paradigms have fallen short of addressing many of the questions involved with human/natural resource interaction. In economics, "free marketeers" believe that environmental externalities are of little importance and can be adequately addressed by the invisible hand of the free market. Environmental problems are also seen as minor by Marxists, who argue that political education and better planning are simple remedies. In the field of ecology, questions about human cultural behavior are not commonly asked. Ecologists normally concern themselves only with the effects of human action *on* ecosystems, and not with an understanding of human behavior in the context of the ecosystems on which they depend. These combined shortcomings are serious, and extensive changes to each existing paradigm are necessary to alleviate them.

Major Issues, Problems, and Solutions

Economists have a long history of asking questions pertaining to natural resources, but attention in the present century has dwindled. Many problems arise when attention is diverted away from investigating human interdependence with the earth's environment. The following sections outline some of these major problems.

Sustainability: Maintaining Our Life Support System

Economics should remind itself that nature is the economy's "life support system." By ignoring this essential link we could threaten the ability of natural life support systems to maintain themselves and the economies to which they are inexorably linked. David Pearce has investigated the major economic structures of free market, planned, and mixed economies and has concluded that for the most part these structures are unable to guarantee sustainability. In Pearce's view, sustainability is inherently connected with a notion of justice within species, between them, and between current and future generations.

Intra- and Inter-Species Distribution of Wealth

"Wealth is ultimately the capacity to support life and the enjoyment thereof."[3] We generally do not conceptualize the sharing of wealth with other beings or future generations. When we do look at the lives of animals, we see that all members of these populations have more or less the same "standard of living." In addition, they live at roughly the same level of per capita resource use, a level that does not change over time. Neither are animals split into classes that have varying degrees of access to natural resources. In the human case, per capita resource use differs widely for different social classes and is not at all constant over time. To maintain carrying capacity for an animal population, it is necessary to control population while keeping resource consumption constant. In addition, to maintain carrying capacity for the human race, consumption and income distribution need to be controlled in an equitable manner. Modern economics has paid little attention to such contentions.

Modern economics has determined that the human race should receive a continually increasing share of wealth. This assumption ignores the "instrumental value" that other species have in maintaining the earth's economies and life support systems, and it ignores the intrinsic values of other species. In some cases, such as energy analysis, economists have attempted to calculate forms of intrinsic value based on embodied energy, but these examples are not widespread. Ecological economics can act as "a check on human perceptions," and "allow us to study the economies of nature which do not include humans."[4]

Discounting, Intergenerational Justice, and the Time Delay Trap

Intergenerational justice is an important foundation for an ecological economics. Issues in this realm have usually been addressed by discounting. The problem with discounting is that it reflects the value that the present generation places on future generations without the consultation of future generations. It should be recognized that the practice of discounting is just a numerical way to account for the value judgments that "(a) the near future is worth more than the distant future, and (b) beyond some point the worth of the future is negligible."[4]

Discounting may be a symptom of what is known as a social trap. A *social trap* is "any situation in which the short-run, local reinforcements guiding individual behavior are inconsistent with the long-run, global best interest of the individual and society."[4] Sometimes these short-term incentives (money, social acceptance, physical pleasure, etc.) can be misleading. In such cases, too little importance is placed on the future and this "trap" is set. When economists and ecologists assume that individuals are optimizers and then interpret all behavior as optimal, they fall into this trap. Psychology has shown us that humans experience problems in responding to situations that are not immediate. In this context we expect to see situations in which the future is discounted too much, which may not be optimal.

A particular approach to discounting has been to discount future value by the rate of interest. This "provides an extremely tight link between ecological destruction and macroeconomic policy."[5] For an exploited species whose rate of population growth is less than the rate of interest, there is a high probability of extinction. Policy makers rarely consider issues such as the effects of U.S. interest rates on deforestation in the Amazon, yet these effects are significant.

Non-Monetized Values and the Partial Quantification Gap

Not all values can be accounted for in monetary terms with the same level of precision. Values that can be expressed more precisely often dominate because they can fit into the models of the current paradigm more easily. This is an "unfair" advantage to precise numbers, and a compensating weight should be given to values that are more difficult to measure. The beginning of a solution to this problem is to be aware of and deal with the range of imprecision in all decisions by looking at all possible outcomes and to make decisions with those outcomes in mind.

Integration Versus Cross-Fertilization

Some have stated that the disciplines of ecology and economics should fully integrate with one another, while others advocate cross-fertilization whereby each discipline "borrows" necessary traits from the other. Much of the literature in ecological economics discusses how the concepts of ecology must be incorporated within those of economics, but in some cases, such as the use of input–output models, economics has been incorporated into ecology and used to evaluate ecosystems.

Extending the Classical, Neoclassical, and Marxist Analysis

Different economists have chosen a variety of starting points from which to begin an integration or cross-fertilization of the two disciplines. Robert

Goodland and David Pearce are among those who attempt to expand neo-classical theory to incorporate concepts of sustainability and carrying capacity. Paul Christensen has pointed to modern energy analysis as an example of how classical economics can serve as a starting point. Robert Kaufman also refers to modern energy analysis as a starting point, but wonders if Marxist economics is the better point of integration.

Summary of

Foundations of an Ecological Economics
by David Pearce

[Published in *Ecological Modelling* 38 (September 1987): 9–18. Reprinted with kind permission from Elsevier Science B.V., Amsterdam, The Netherlands.]

Ecological economics, with the objective of creating a sustainable society, should employ a Rawlsian concept of distributive justice in an intergenerational context as one of its principal foundations. This concept can apply to non-human species also; however, it is argued that the biophysical requirements of a sustainable society are likely to ensure the preservation of non-human species and habitats. The present forms of economic organization can be examined to test whether they can guarantee sustainability. The conclusion is that none of the existing forms of economic organization can adequately guarantee sustainability, and we should begin to investigate the conditions for an economy that is "ecologically bound."

Justice as Fairness

In 1971, John Rawls outlined a theory of justice concerned with intratemporal fairness. Rawls argued that a set of moral principles pertaining to justice would best be derived under a "veil of ignorance" about the location of individuals in society (whether they are rich or poor). In this context, a principle of justice is "derived from rational life plans, some knowledge of how society functions, and some knowledge of the relationship between life plans and primary goods."[11] From this principle of justice, rules for the organization of society are derived. When these rules are institutionalized, each person will have equal rights to the maximum amount of freedom possible without infringing upon the freedoms of others. When inequalities arise, these inequalities can only be justified if they are potentially advantageous to everyone. This difference principle is the equivalent to the MAX-IMIN principle which implies that each person will opt for the maximum amount of protection possible to avoid the risk of being the poorest person in the society.

Intergenerational Justice

Talbot Page has expanded Rawls' intratemporal theory, which shows how to define justice within a given generation. Page's contribution gives us an intertemporal theory that takes account of issues of justice between generations. In his formulation, one of the tenets added to the Rawlsian "veil of ignorance" is an ignorance of what generation the decision maker will fall in. In this context the MAXIMIN principle will ensure that future life will be possible because no one will want to be put in the last generation. Page has argued that this notion suggests a "permanent livability" criterion which implies that the natural resource base on earth will be kept intact, and that all generations will have equal access to that natural resource base. Page distinguishes natural resources from primary goods. Natural resources are seen as an endowment that helps determine access to primary goods. As time passes, if the natural resource endowment changes between generations, so will the primary goods, and this can only be justified if future generations benefit by this inequality.

Page's extension of Rawls can be criticized on the grounds that in the intratemporal case all the parties are alive, but in the intertemporal case we are asked to make judgments concerning individuals who do not yet exist. In addition, Page's statement that inequality in resource use is unjustified can be countered by the argument that the conversion of resources to capital in the present can be justified by the capital itself being passed on to future generations.

These criticisms are based on standard intertemporal efficiency conditions that can conflict with intergenerational justice. Such conditions state that each generation should maximize the present value of net gains. However, if, for example, the discount rate that is being used is higher than the regeneration rate of a resource, the resource could become extinct and future generations would not have access to it. Thus an intergenerational justice principle is more likely to ensure equality of resource base endowments by generation.

When comparing Page's notion of "permanent livability" to contemporary conservationists' notions of "sustainability," we find that the two are virtually identical. Sustainability is linked to intergenerational justice.

Justice and Non-human Species

It seems difficult to consider non-human species within this intergenerational context because they cannot assemble to debate the rules on which to form a society. However, these beings are sentient, and it can be argued that they have preferences. They are similar to humans in many ways; for example, like humans we know they experience pleasure and pain. Perhaps because of such similarities, an extended theory of justice could see humans as stewards of non-humans, as is widely discussed in environmental ethics literature. Nonetheless, for our purposes we do not need such a concept of justice for non-humans because intergenerational justice implies sustainability, sustainability implies the observation of biophysical constraints, and observation of biophysical constraints implies a general non-elimination of species.

Sustainability and Biophysical Constraints

In order to achieve sustainability, each generation must have equal access to the natural resource base. However, at any depletion rate of nonrenewable resources it is impossible for the resource base to be equal across generations. As a solution, Page argues that the use of a severance or depletion tax, imposed in proportion to the rate at which resources are depleted, will be an incentive for substituting renewable resources for exhaustible resources, as well as increasing the efficiency of use for those resources that are consumed. This analysis is flawed because it "assumes that real resource prices are reasonable indicators of resource scarcity."[14] Two other approaches regulated by the laws of thermodynamics can serve as satisfactory alternatives. First, the amount of renewable resources extracted should never exceed the rate at which the earth replenishes these resources unless substitution with other renewables is possible. Second, wastes should not be emitted at levels that exceed the earth's capacity to absorb them.

Economist Kenneth Boulding reminded us of the First Law of Thermodynamics, which says that matter cannot be created or destroyed. In an economic context this implies that whatever is extracted from the environment will return as waste. Thus the rate of resource extraction is limited by both the absorptive capacity of the earth's environment and the rate of regeneration. The economic implications of the Second Law of Thermodynamics have been outlined by Georgescu-Roegen. This law states the impossibility of total recycling, which is prohibited because of entropy. The phenomenon of entropy, in the context of sustainability, emphasizes the rules pertaining to the absorptive capabilities of the earth's environment, because the extraction of resources in their low-entropy states leads to the emission of high-entropy waste, that is difficult for the environment to recycle. Thus, wastes should be emitted at or below a level that the environment can absorb.

Economic Society and Sustainability

We now need to discuss whether existing economies (free market, mixed, planned) have any mechanisms for achieving and maintaining sustainability. Truly free market and truly planned economies do not really exist in the world, so we will discuss modified market economies and modified planned economies.

Modified market economies tend to deal with environmental problems by regulating pollution and resource depletion through polluter and depletion taxes. In actual fact, many economies regulate pollution but encourage resource depletion. This reflects the conventional lack of understanding of the linkages between resource use and waste disposal. Modified planned economies, in which environmental externalities are supposed to be accounted for in the planning process, assume that the environment is something that can actually be controlled and planned by humans, ignoring strict biophysical constraints.

Neither economic structure has built-in mechanisms for sustainability. For a modified market economy to be sustainable, the public sector would need to operate planning procedures within ecological constraints, and prices would have to somehow incorporate the overall objective of sustainability. For a modified planned economy "it would be necessary for the planner explicitly to acknowledge the biophysical constraints and to secure planning objectives only within those constraints."[17]

Finally, "sustainability as intergenerational fairness" can not be achieved through the conventions of planned, market, or mixed economies. We must strive to define and develop an economy that is "ecologically bounded," with "sustainability as intergenerational fairness" as the foundation for such an endeavor.

Summary of

The Case for Methodological Pluralism
by Richard B. Norgaard

[Published in *Ecological Economics* 1 (February 1989): 37–57. Reprinted
with kind permission from Elsevier Science B.V., Amsterdam, The Netherlands.]

Scholars and practitioners in the developing field of ecological economics are committed to drawing on ideas from both ecology and economics.
The study of ecosystems is traditionally conducted through models of population dynamics, nutrient webs, energetics, foraging and reproduction
strategies, and co-evolution. Economics is studied through the understanding of political economy, markets, institutions, input–output techniques, accounting, and monetary and Keynesian models. Ecology provides
links to other natural sciences, and economics to other social sciences, and
each offers a number of methodological approaches to help in the evolution of ecological economics. However, there are conflicts between the two
fields as well, especially between what each has historically seen as the right
way of asking questions and arriving at answers, and in the methods each
has for predicting consequences. This article argues that there cannot be a
single right way of knowing and predicting, and therefore calls on the field
of ecological economics to adopt methodological diversity and a culturally
adaptive approach.

Essence, Change, and Methodology

Economics and ecology explore systems in a manner sufficiently similar that
there have been important conceptual transfers between them. However,
economists and ecologists have very different world views, which result in
different concepts of how people should relate to their environment. It is
unlikely that the divergence in world views will be resolved by the theoretical similarities that exist.

The dominant model adopted by Western economists is that of the market. Economists have developed highly sophisticated mathematical and
econometric techniques to understand how markets link individuals who
are suppliers of labor, capital, and land with demanders of products and
services. Many economists are convinced that the market model provides
insights into the functioning of markets, economic efficiency, and policy.
Critics argue that, mathematical sophistication notwithstanding, the models are simplistic and can be used to tell any desired story. However, the
market model is not the only economic model that economists use. His-

torical, institutional, and Marxian models are still dominant in a few schools of thought in the West.

It is more difficult to trace the development of methodologies in ecology. This is due in part to the relative newness of the field, as well as to the less clear demarcations between the biological disciplines, all of which have influenced ecology. A distinct methodological literature in ecology has developed only recently.

Logical Positivism and Methodologies in Economics and Ecology

Logical positivism forms the basis of the relationship between science and society in the West and the modern parts of the developing world. This movement toward finding universal truths started in the period of the Enlightenment. The notions of objectivity and universality that dominated nineteenth century inquiry further influence today's thought. Individual disciplines, working separately, are all working toward a consistent set of laws about the nature of all things. Gaps between disciplines, it is argued, can be bridged by interdisciplinary work.

This presumed positive knowledge influences the way the scientific establishment operates and the role of scientific knowledge in policy making. However, in reality, the different types of knowledge, values, and images within different disciplines that inform the development-versus-environment debate have eroded the alliances of the past.

A taxonomy of methodological beliefs will help compare different methodologies in economics and ecology. The taxonomy takes four key assumptions of logical positivism and classifies methodologies according to whether or not they make these same assumptions. This exercise will help bring out the methodological richness of economics and ecology, showing how each discipline approaches problems that do not fit the assumptions of logical positivism.

The four key assumptions of logical positivism that guide the work of most economists and ecologists are:

(1) methods of understanding reality are independent of culture;

(2) reality is independent of methods of understanding;

(3) reality can be understood in terms of universal laws; and

(4) reality can be understood in terms of one set of universal laws.

Logical positivism underlies the methodological approaches of most modern schools of economic thought, including mathematical economists,

Marxists, and institutionalists. An important exception was the German historical school. This school contended that everything social was conditioned by history and differed from place to place, and it argued against the adoption in the social sciences of the positivist, value-free methodology of the physical sciences. Much of the current methodological diversity in economics can be traced to the "Methodenstreit" debates between the German historical school and the positivists. The field of ecology, on the other hand, utilizes a diversity of methodologies, which can be traced to the influence of biology and the long tradition of direct observation in the field.

Methodological diversity within and between economics and ecology can be related to the taxonomy of methodological beliefs in the following ways:

(1) *Methodological dependence on culture:* Marxists, neoclassicists, and institutionalists have sought culture- and value-free explanations. Agroecologists, on the other hand, acknowledge the ways in which culture affects method.

(2) *Dependence of reality on methodology:* Economists and economic thinking have a heavy influence on the shape of the economy. The situation is similar in agroecology.

(3) *Knowledge is universal or useless:* In economics, neoclassicists continue to believe that universal policy recommendations can be drawn, although no universal laws (except that of the downward sloping demand curve) have been found. Institutionalists, on the other hand, argue that knowledge is specific to the situation. Ecologists differ among themselves on the issue, but in general they would like to seek universal laws tempered with pragmatism.

(4) *On the unity of knowledge:* Some economists have argued that the neoclassical model can be applied to explain history, politics, and sociology, but this view is rather recent. Most recognize the limitations of economic theory in realms beyond explaining markets. Institutionalists have always acknowledged the importance of history, politics, and culture as components of economic explanations, rather than as challenges to their theories. Ecologists tend to accept that different theories can explain different phenomena. Some ecologists argue that an eclectic, interpretative methodology is more suitable for use in ecological and evolutionary theorizing than is logical positivism.

The above analysis of economic and ecological methodologies shows that a variety of methodological positions exist that are not rooted in logical positivism.

The Costs of Methodological Poverty

The methodological diversity of ecology has helped it to be more scientific than economics. Both economics and ecology have used theories that have been shown to be logically inconsistent. However, due to a lack of methodological alternatives, economics has failed to address this problem, while the methodological diversity in ecology has helped it respond to the challenge.

In ecology, when "diversity stability theory" was shown to be logically inconsistent there followed an intensive rethinking that led to a better understanding of how different types of diversity related to different definitions of stability. When the logical consistency of neoclassical economics has been questioned, however, the implications of the arguments have been discussed for a while, but then ignored. For example, it has been shown that gains from free international trade depend on a set of conditions that never exist in the real world, yet free trade is advocated. Similarly, Lipsey and Lancaster[1] demonstrated that economic prescriptions must be tailored to specific circumstances except in the rare case where all but one of the assumptions of market theory hold. Yet neoclassicists continue to make universal recommendations based on this theoretical framework, without paying heed to the specifics of a given situation. Ecologists have been able to rethink their position, while economists could not, because ecologists are methodologically more accustomed to thinking that knowledge can be specific.

The Case for Conscious Methodological Pluralism

For a better understanding of the interplay between economies and ecosystems, a methodological stance should be adopted in which both groups are conscious of the advantages and disadvantages of their own methodologies and of those used by others. Tolerance should be shown toward diverse approaches. The reasons for such a "conscious methodological pluralism" are:

(1) Logical positivism is inappropriate but necessary. It is inappropriate because it denies that how we think affects cultural and ecological systems. It is necessary because it is through the lens of logical positivism that most other people perceive things in the modern world. Thus, while using the logical positivist arguments, we must be aware of their problems and attempt to develop more appropriate methodologies.

(2) It is too early to limit methodologies in ecological economics.

(3) Pluralism makes sense. Given the complexity of the interactions concerned, there clearly cannot be one best and all-encompassing perspective for understanding them.

(4) Pluralism prevents brash action. It provides a variety of insights on complex issues, rather than taking only one insight to be *the* answer.

(5) Pluralism can help sustain biological and cultural diversity; i.e., methodological diversity supports real-world diversity.

(6) Methodological pluralism allows more people to participate in the analysis, rather than only the few who are technically endowed to understand a specific methodology.

Note

1. R. Lipsey and K. Lancaster, "The General Theory of One Second Best," in *Review of Economic Studies*, 24(1956): 11–32.

Summary of

Economics and Ecology: A Comparison of Experimental Methodologies and Philosophies

by Jason F. Shogren and Clifford Nowell

[Published in *Ecological Economics* 5 (May 1992): 101–126. Reprinted with kind permission from Elsevier Science B.V., Amsterdam, The Netherlands.]

Views of the proper roles of experiments in environmental economics and ecology have developed quite differently. Until recently, the primary engine of research in ecology has been observation-induced description, while in economics it has been theory-induced propositions. From a philosophical or methodological perspective, the ecologist's focus on description appears pragmatic while the economist's focus on the axiomatic has evolved from logical positivism. Pragmatism implies that methods and choices result from the workability of common sense rather than from formal rules of evidence. This can result in a broad methodological base of competing theories without a hierarchy of theoretical axioms, laws, and "truths." By contrast, the logical positivism of economists rests on two key assumptions: an objective world view and a value-neutral scientist. In such a paradigm, science can only advance if there is an explicit dichotomy between fact and value. This positivism has led economics to a definite hierarchy of theories based on the neoclassical paradigm, and an assumption that this well-defined theoretical structure is inherently correct, thereby eliminating the need for observation.

Theory Versus Experimentation

Ecologists have developed a broad foundation of competing methodologies in which observation and description are the focus, with abstract theoretical work coming second. Armed primarily with the laws of thermodynamics and the evolutionary theory of natural selection, ecology emphasizes observations of the natural environment in both bottle experiments and natural variations. These observations are mediated through organized, formalized models of the structure and functions of a complex system. Clearly this amounts to more than a "stroll through the forest," yet given the extraordinary complexity in ecosystems, ecologists are still far from establishing universal laws.

Some ecologists, such as Lotka, Volterra, and May, have attempted more rigorous modeling. Although the complexity of ecological systems makes the use of mathematical theory difficult, it is not impossible. By developing propositions that identify the key aspects of the natural system, formal theory can reject earlier anecdotal evidence from direct observation. There is thus an antagonism between mainstream, pragmatic, field-oriented ecologists and mathematically inclined theoretical ecologists, leaving the latter largely isolated from the mainstream.

The hold of logical positivism on the sciences has been in decline for decades, but it has left a lasting effect on economics: a methodological paradigm of theory-without-measurement. It is presumed that a well-argued theory, based on explicit, logically consistent assumptions, will lead to specific correct conclusions—what is there in a theory to test? Armed with axiomatic logic and mathematics, economists have often failed to go beyond logic or theory to observational empirical work. However, despite the benefits of formal theory for clarifying hypotheses and providing rigorous definitions of assumptions, there is growing discomfort with theory for theory's sake. This has led to the increased use of experimental methods which, though not totally accepted, are increasingly acknowledged as a low-cost method to isolate and examine abstract theories of individual behavior.

The basic difference between these two fields is the view of the proper place of experimentation. Mainstream ecologists accept experimentation, often at the expense of theory, while mainstream economists do the opposite. There appears to be a need to approach the middle ground in both disciplines.

The Objective Function: Well Defined or Uncertain?

One basic reason for this divergence is that economists and ecologists differ in their assumptions regarding the objective function of a model, which describes the cause–effect or dose–response relationship between inputs and outputs. The ecologist's view is that the objective function is unknown, and the major experimental focus is on trying to describe or define how the function works. A major reason for this approach is that often little is understood about the relationship between the cause and effect—for example, the hotly debated impact of acid deposition on ecosystems. A second reason is that the overall complexity of the ecosystem does not lend itself to axiomatic descriptions.

Economists' perceptions of the objective function are quite different. They generally assume that the objective function is well defined, based on fundamental theoretical axioms of preference or production. They argue that since the market embodies all of the relevant information of the dose–response relationship, specific attempts to observe these relations are not necessary. The key question then is whether or not the basic axioms are satisfied. In the case of utility theory, there is increasing evidence that the answer is no, as both psychologists and economists turn up evidence of systematic deviations of individual choice behavior from the predictions of utility theory. Increasing recognition has been accorded to the argument that economists must step back and further explore the workings of the objective function through direct observation, much like the ecologist.

Experimental Methods in Environmental Economics

Today, experimental research in environmental economics falls into two broad categories: institutional and valuation. Institutional experiments consider the efficacy of alternative mechanisms to reduce the negative impacts of pollution. Valuation experiments examine individual preferences or values for non-market environmental goods. The former have largely remained in the lab, while valuation work has generally been conducted in the field through the use of surveys and bidding games.

The foundation for institutional experiments on environmental issues is found in the public choice literature, and it is based on two notions. First, social policy analysis should evaluate the relative efficiency of alternative institutions in the face of market failure. Second, it is believed that principles of rational choice are central to the behavior of social institutions. Following the general public choice viewpoint, institutional experiments have focused on alternative mechanisms for efficient control of externalities such as pollution. The experiments, which examine the efficiency of market-based incentives relative to traditional command and control regulations, have indicated that the former are more cost effective in achieving identical levels of pollution abatement.

Valuation experiments have utilized the contingent valuation (CV) method. A CV experiment estimates the economic benefit of a public good through the construction of a hypothetical market. By carefully constructing understandable preference-revealing mechanisms, benefits are determined through surveys or interviews that elicit a respondent's implicit price for a good. CV experiments are flexible, relatively inexpensive, and can construct markets where none currently exist.

Although CV use has expanded rapidly, the method has significant drawbacks and many detractors. Most questions center on the hypothetical nature of the "market" being probed in CV, and the minimal formal economic theory presently extant to guide researchers in understanding how individuals form values in CV contexts. In response, both psychologists and economists are now attempting to provide a more rigorous structure to CV. Given concern over CV biases and the value formation process, economists have turned to laboratory experiments to isolate and control the preference revelation mechanisms. The introduction of more controlled settings in which experiments can be replicated under similar conditions should help to increase acceptance of this valuation research.

Lessons from the Desk and the Lab

Economic experiments are designed primarily to test specific economic theories. Though economic theory provides a rich body of material and testable hypotheses, most experiments are based on a few critical behavioral assumptions. Economists need observation-based research to examine these assumptions.

The comparative advantage held by economics over ecology is the long tradition of theoretical modeling. Experimentalists need to recognize that modeling helps theories to mature, encourages consistent use of terms, checks unstated assumptions or boundary conditions, and reduces the derivation of opposite conclusions from the same theory. In addition, ecologists must at times leave their field experiments in complex environments and go back to the lab to evaluate specific hypotheses under controlled conditions.

The field of ecological economics allows both the pragmatist and the positivist to converse over the relative merits of integrating their approaches. Relaxing methodological constraints can lead to higher rewards for both groups.

Summary of

Interdisciplinary Research Between Economists and Physical Scientists: Retrospect and Prospect

by Malte Faber and John L.R. Proops

[Published in KYKLOS 38 (4th Quarter, 1985): 599–616. Reprinted with kind permission of Helbing & Lichtenhahn Verlag AG, Basel and Frankfurt/M.]

Problems of environmental pollution and energy shortage have stimulated interdisciplinary work between economists and physical scientists. This cooperation has resulted in many economists developing an understanding of the physical underpinnings of economies, and many physical scientists realizing that problems of pollution and energy shortage have social and economic aspects. However, this cooperation has led to some mutual incomprehension and hostility between the disciplines as well. Interdisciplinary research and cooperation between economists and physical scientists are urgently needed, although they will be difficult to carry out.

Economists and Physical Science

Economists have a long tradition of employing concepts and methods from the physical sciences. Physical analogies have been used by Proops, Walras, Edgeworth, and Samuelson, among others. Analogies have been drawn to the central concept of thermodynamics—entropy—in measuring industrial concentration, inequalities of income and employment, and geographic concentration. Another analogy used has been that of "gravity models" in regional economics. There is a move to supplant mechanical analogies with "organistic" analogies, because the economy is more like a self-regulating and developing organism than a mechanical system.

The use of analogies has not been the only method of interaction between the two disciplines. Jevons[1] considered the importance of coal to the British economy and its shortage as a constraint upon industrial activity. Georgescu-Roegen[2] has stressed the irreversibility of the productive process and the long-run constraints on economic activity due to finite exhaustible resources. These authors are concerned with the physical limits to social activity; for example, fuel reserves and environmental pollution have interested economists in recent years.

A third and more general relationship between economics and thermodynamics is also being explored. In this case, the question is whether economies can be viewed as similar to dynamic structures, which maintain a constant relationship with their environment via active internal processes.

Physical Scientists and Economics

In the early days of the energy crisis, a view commonly held by physical scientists was that value must derive only from energy, as energy is the only factor of production that is, in principle, nonsubstitutable. However, with many studies showing that labor and capital can, to some extent, substitute for energy, and that energy can be augmented in production by technical progress, physical scientists have come to see that energy is not the only factor in modern economies worthy of study.

Energy, Time, Irreversibility, and Entropy in Economics

All physical processes relevant to the functioning of economies require energy, involve time, and are irreversible, but these concepts have not been given the attention that they deserve in economic theory. Dynamic economic analysis does include the time factor, but it does not deal with the irreversible nature of physical processes. The concept of entropy can incorporate these three aspects simultaneously, and it can be applied to an analysis of resources and the environment. In addition, rather than dealing with time as a mere parameter, the thermodynamic approach forces one to consider real, irreversible time.

Koopmans[3] introduced the postulate of the irreversibility of economic processes: "It is not possible to run some or all activities at positive levels such that the joint effect of the net output is zero for all goods."[1] This postulate essentially suggests that the manufacturing of commodities cannot be reversed in time. This irreversibility follows from the Second Law of Thermodynamics. Economists have also shown that an implication of the Second Law is that you cannot get an output without an input. Georgescu-Roegen has extended this idea to argue that outputs can be obtained only at a greater cost of low entropy. While economists are beginning to accept irreversibility as an axiom, the physical meaning of irreversibility has yet to be fully internalized in the conceptualizations of most economists.

A knowledge of thermodynamics offers many new insights into an understanding of issues in environmental and resource economics. Energy can be divided into useful energy—that contained in foodstuffs and fuels directly used for man's subsistence—and primary energy sources—for example, solar or fossil energy. Primary sources of energy can be transformed by man into useful energy. Until the beginning of the nineteenth century land was used to transform solar energy into useful energy. As populations increased, land became scarcer in Europe. Over the last 150 years, industrial development has required the extraction of fossil fuels and minerals as the principal source of useful energy. Thus land becomes a limiting factor in an even broader sense, i.e., as a surface, as a supplier of resources, and as a receiver of pollutants. Economists have paid attention to the first aspect, but not to the other two. Since the extraction of resources and the disposal of waste increase the entropy or the disorderliness of the system, entropy can be used to connect theories of environment and of resources. The thermodynamic approach is also a way for economics to build a biophysical foundation to understand long-run, macro-level issues, for which the price system does not provide a complete solution.

Physical Constraints, Technical Progress, and Social Change

Economists perceive limitations to economic activity as essentially social in nature. Physical scientists see economies as limited by physical constraints. Both of these viewpoints are valid. Physical constraints generate social responses in the form of technical and social adjustments which move the economy away from the constraint. Thus social transformations, technical change, and physical constraints form a web of recursive interrelationships. Analysis of social and economic activity must integrate technical progress, while physical constraints must be seen as not only influencing human activity in the long run, but also as prominent determinants of social change.

Interdisciplinary Research: Difficulties and Some Tentative Solutions

While the urgency of interdisciplinary work is accepted, psychological and institutional factors impede such cooperation. Some of these factors include:

(1) discouragement from peer groups—either fellow economists or physi-

cal scientists—as work across disciplines is viewed as less "serious" than work within a single discipline;

(2) often harsh criticism of such research, as the criteria used to evaluate new interdisciplinary work is the same as that used to evaluate research in an established field;

(3) difficulty in finding researchers to collaborate with;

(4) differences in the languages and foci of each discipline that make communication difficult;

(5) shortage of journals that publish interdisciplinary research; and

(6) time-consuming learning needed to begin crossover work in a new field.

In the long run it is necessary to establish a wider vision by dissolving established conceptual frameworks. In the meantime, more interdisciplinary conferences, symposia, and seminars must be conducted to bring together interdisciplinary researchers. Training toward interdisciplinary work should be given at the elementary, undergraduate, and graduate levels.

Notes

1. W.S. Jevons, *The Coal Question* (London: Macmillan, 1865).
2. N. Georgescu-Roegen, *The Entropy Law and the Economic Process* (Cambridge, Massachusetts: Harvard University Press, 1971).
3. T.C. Koopmans, "Analysis of Production as an Efficient Combination of Activities," in *Activity Analysis of Production and Allocation*, ed. T.C. Koopmans (New York: J. Wiley, 1951), 48; cited by Faber and Proops, 604.

Summary of

Rethinking Ecological and Economic Education: A Gestalt Shift

by Mary E. Clark

[Published in *Ecological Economics: The Science and Management of Sustainability*, ed. Robert Costanza (New York: Columbia University Press, 1991), 400–413.]

Leaders in many less-developed parts of the world believe that the West has solved all the old economic and social problems, and that if the prescriptions of the West are followed, their problems will also be solved. What they fail to notice is the environmental destruction and social disintegration that Western economic behavior causes. This article discusses two systems of social organization, one based on competitive individualism (Gestalt I) and the other based on the concept of community (Gestalt II). The author concludes that Gestalt II is essential for global sustainability and offers some implications for education in the principles of Gestalt II.

Gestalt I: Linear Progress and Competitive Individualism

By the 1500s, long-standing hierarchical systems in Europe started disintegrating, giving way to a new world view based on new assumptions about human nature and the social order. Contracts between self-centered, competitive individuals with a right to property were viewed as the foundation of societies. Self-interest and competition were seen as ways of maximizing a nation's wealth. Wealth and power were a sign of virtue, and the pursuit of utility and pleasure became the supreme goal of life.

This view of the world has led to problems. Its driving force, material reward, demands constant growth, which results in constant stimulation of throughput. This has run head-on into environmental limits. Other problems that have resulted from this competitive structure are psychological in nature. The pursuit of rank, power, and ability to consume have destroyed meaningful community, creating psychic angst throughout all levels of society. Finally, competitive individualism has led to misconceptions in our understanding of evolutionary and ecological processes. We have mistakenly taken evolution to represent a continuum of "progress" from lower to higher states, with humans at the top. An even more pervasive misconception is that "competition" underlies all of Nature. It must be understood that evolutionary success is not a matter of winning, but one of "fitting in."

Neoclassical Theory and the Problem of Values

Economics as a discipline has ignored or simplified the relations between economic activity, Nature, and the human psyche. Different definitions of value notwithstanding, market prices are the single yardstick of value. One problem with this approach is the conflating of the trivial and the life-giving, and of "costs" and "benefits." Another is how one assigns "prices" to social relations, the environment, and other "goods" that fall outside the market economy. Economists seek to solve this problem by commoditizing everything and attaching a price. Where prices cannot be obtained directly, they invent shadow prices. However, when assigning shadow prices to the loss of a forest, for example, economists tend to estimate transactional prices, not the price of long-term social "income." While less arbitrary measures of value have been suggested for material objects (e.g., embodied energy), no numerical value can be assigned to our affective relations with our surroundings or with each other.

Gestalt II: Dominance of Community/Environment Relations

An alternative gestalt views economic activities and material consumption as a link between Nature and human community. The establishment of viable societies or sustainable ecosystems requires a deep understanding of human nature, its needs, and its proper relationship with Nature as a whole.

Desired Environmental and Social Goals

The achievement of sustainability is the environmental goal, and this can apply to either the global environment or local and regional resources. The former implies a "top down," centralized management style under the direction of existing international power structures. Such a system may be needed in the short run to deal with climate change and other global concerns. However, in the long run effective global management depends on responsible management of local ecosystems, making use of the available knowledge base to answer questions such as "what is local sustainability?" and "who is concerned about maintaining it?"

Fikret Berkes and M. Taghi Farvar[1] point out that the usefulness of the knowledge of local people can far exceed that of scientific "experts." Traditional knowledge and cultural wisdom are usually ignored when a system is managed by such outsiders. The challenge is to integrate scientific and traditional knowledge. However, there is little motivation for outsiders to maintain sustainable local systems, since they can continuously move elsewhere to achieve their aims, as the multinational corporations have done, for example.

Regarding social goals, it is wrong to describe human needs as a "hierarchy" in a Maslowian sense. Such a view takes the isolated individual as the point of reference. Yet the sociology of non-human primates, as well as our own social context, shows that bonding, affection, and social acceptance are primary needs. If the survival of the planet depends on providing people with a sense of community, then the West must abandon competitive individualism and insatiable acquisitiveness and move toward a communally based society with shared social goals.

In the West, the degradation of communally owned resources is seen as inevitable due to the "tragedy of the commons." Berkes (1989) provides a number of examples in which the sustainable use of communally managed resources does occur. It is when social arrangements break down that the resource base may diminish. Thus, if local sustainable development is the aim, then there is a strong argument for strengthening communal property regimes over private property regimes.

Implications for Education

Education must play a significant role if we are to move toward a world view based on Gestalt II. Education is needed in the ecological principles of sustainable systems and in psycho-social factors creating sustainable societies. The following are proposed curricular approaches to global education:

(1) Impart a basic understanding of the principles of energy flow and dissipation; material recycling; services provided by "guilds" of organisms such as nutrient and water retention, pollination, pest-controlling species, etc.; unexpected positive feedback mechanisms;[2] principles of island biogeography; and species survival.

(2) Study the knowledge base of indigenous societies that have successfully managed resource systems for millennia.

(3) Develop an understanding of the complex and reciprocal relations among soil, vegetation, and climate.

(4) Identify and understand the sources of the economic expectations of people in the North, and make an effort to reconcile these expectations with a sustainable level of economic development; this will require a far higher level of popular understanding of how modern industrial economies interface with the natural world.

(5) Assist in the development of sustainability in the South through building a grounding in cultural anthropology, co-evolutionary social theory, and human needs theory.

To bridge from the present to the future we first need to critique current economic theory, redefining "wealth," and clarifying "costs" and "benefits." We then need to weave together new social theory, economic theory, and ecological theory into a comprehensive alternative gestalt that lays the groundwork for development of sustainable local communities globally.

Notes

1. Fikret Berkes and M. Taghi Farvar, "Introduction and Overview," in *Common Property Resources*, ed. Fikret Berkes (London: Belhaven Press, 1989).

2. "Positive feedback" does not mean beneficial, but uncontrolled and destabilizing.

Summary of

Industrial Ecology: Reflections on a Colloquium
by Jesse H. Ausubel

[Published in *Proceedings of the National Academy of Sciences*
89 (February 1992): 879–884.]

Industrial ecology can be defined as "the network of all industrial processes as they may interact with each other and live off each other, not only in the economic sense but also in the sense of direct use of each other's material and energy wastes."[879] This article discusses ten fundamental questions that should shape the field of industrial ecology, spanning the fields of philosophy of nature, history of technology, science, engineering, economics, and management.

(1) Do Sociotechnical Systems Have Long-Range Environmental Goals?

While societies set broad goals such as poverty reduction, universal education, and health care, other sociotechnical systems such as agriculture, transport, energy, and production seem to evolve without a long-range purpose. This evolution results from the interactions among strict rules of choice at the micro level. Economic systems are inherently short-sighted and do not help direct sociotechnical systems toward long-range goals. Industrial ecology can provide direction toward a better environment by aiding in the coordination and creative design of the economy. This field can promote reduction of pollution and throughput, and it can help determine which technologies, products, and enterprises should survive.

(2) How Is the Concept of Industrial Ecology Useful and Timely?

Three fields—ecology, economics, and chemical engineering—lay claim to an understanding of the dynamic flows of energy, resources, and information. Industrial ecology should synthesize the perspectives of all of these fields to incorporate what is valued in economics, to expand the domain of engineering design, and to integrate our understandings of ecology and of the human-made world. The role of industrial ecology is especially important given the scale and rate of growth of the economy and the resulting emissions, pollution, and waste. An understanding of the complex interactions between different systems will help us identify methods to make waste products useful.

(3) What Are Environmental Technologies?

There are still no definite criteria for identifying environmental technologies. At present there are many definitions. Some include technologies that improve the environment relative to present practices, while others focus on technologies that prevent pollution, provide remedies, or conserve resources.

(4) Is There a Systematic Way to Choose among Alternatives for Improving the Ecology of Technologies?

The crux of industrial ecology lies in the search for technologies that reduce throughput in the production process in an efficient manner. This involves both the use of materials with suitable properties at the outset, as well as consideration of the end-of-life recyclability. Industrial ecology needs to explore whether there are systematic ways of transforming present technologies to achieve these desired results, and also whether potential pollution problems can be foreseen when technologies are being developed.

(5) What Are Ways to Measure Performance with Respect to Industrial Ecology?

Performance with respect to industrial ecology can be measured by identifying major transitions expected in the relevant processes, and using these as a base. This is similar to the way in which transitions are used in other fields—for example, the demographic transition identified when fertility rates start to decrease, or the labor force transition signified by a decline in agricultural workers. One transition that can be used as an indicator for industrial ecology is the shift from materialization to dematerialization, i.e., to a decrease over time in the weight of materials or "embedded energy" in industrial products. Another transition could be the shift to decarbonization of the energy system, i.e., a shift from an increasing to a decreasing ratio of carbon to total energy used for economic activity. Industrial ecology should move toward both hastening and analyzing these transitions. Moral and aesthetic criteria should also be included in the evaluation of industrial ecology processes.

(6) What Are the Sources and Rates of Innovation in Environmental Technologies?

Industrial ecology should also explore how environmental innovations come about and how they get diffused. How much can one rely on markets and entrepreneurs? What role should targeting and planning play in the development of environmental innovations?

(7) How Is the Market Economy Performing with Respect to Industrial Ecology?

Environmental concerns have not been well served by the market, primarily because social environmental costs are not easily internalized in market transactions. Industrial ecology should consider five aspects of the interactions between industrial processes and the economy:

(a) *information structures* that transmit information between the economy, the environment and economic agents;

(b) *incentive structures*, i.e., the social and economic rewards and penalties for decisions that are faced by individuals and organizations;

(c) *learning mechanisms* within and between technologies and markets;

(d) *selection processes*, i.e., how consumers and producers can make better choices of products and technologies; and

(e) *control and power structures* that monitor performance and limit the range of acceptable behaviors in the economy.

(8) What Will Be the Effect of the Ecological Modernization of the Developed Nations of the North on the Developing Countries of the South?

The South is an exporter of energy and natural products to the North, so increased environmental efficiency in the North may lead to a widening of the economic gap between the North and South. The effects of the integration of world markets on the environment also need to be analyzed. So far there has only been speculation about what these effects might be, and no real insight has been gained.

(9) How Can Creative Interaction on Environmental Issues Be Fostered among Diverse Social Groups?

Different social groups have different views on a number of issues that have an impact on the environment, including myths of nature, views of resources, scales of activity, aesthetics, notions of fairness, and risk. All of these views must be considered and discussed to build a consensus on the environment.

(10) How Must Research and Education Change?

There is a general feeling that the science and education that brought us to our present state are inadequate to solve our problems. Science and education must move in the direction of a holistic ecological perspective.

Summary of

Sustainable Development: A Co-Evolutionary View

by Richard B. Norgaard

[Published in *Futures* (December 1988): 606–620.
By permission of the publishers, Butterworth-Heinemann Ltd. ©]

The challenges of sustainable development (SD) can be organized around three themes:

(1) Modernization has been unsustainable because it relies upon a use of limited resources, which damages the environment.

(2) Political consensus and bureaucratic mobilization will be more difficult as declining faith in "progress" and growth make the hard choices clearer. Western science is no longer viewed as a panacea, and the decline of the belief in progress has enhanced opportunities for non-Western cultures to define development for themselves.

(3) We are shifting from a mechanical to a co-evolutionary understanding of systems, which helps explain why development has been unsustainable and what we must do to attain sustainability.

The Fall of the Idea of Progress

The idea of progress through the technical mastery of nature has been central to western culture for many centuries. Beginning with the Renaissance, through the demise of feudalism and the rise of capitalism, through the maritime, scientific, and industrial revolutions, a linear image of development has emerged in which each embellishment is tied to knowledge. The spread of knowledge among the populace leads to its application in the development of better technologies for exploiting nature, improved products, easier living, and new institutions for organizing people. This simple image is what Third World peoples saw as they embarked upon the path of development after independence. As economists espoused the wonders of growth, the process was all too often presented as a positive-sum game in which hard choices ultimately could be avoided. The calls for progress and modernization were vague, yet they evolved into a meta-belief system—a great carpet under which old belief systems and new contradictions were swept for centuries.

Widespread belief in technical progress is increasingly in doubt. During the twentieth century we have learned that new technologies not only sequentially deplete resources, but they degrade environments as well. Furthermore, we have become attuned to how our own value systems, to say nothing of those of non-Western peoples, are modified by development, and how these changes in turn affect our choice of social organization and technology. Finally, there is the growing awareness that the products of these technologies do not necessarily enhance human happiness.

The Rise of an Alternative World View

The push for sustainability may be the beacon of another meta-belief system as it becomes the clarion call of a new age. Broadly conceived, the call for SD resonates with the rise of new understandings of environmental systems, technologies, social organization, value systems, and the ways in which all these variables interact. With SD as a meta-belief we enter into a wholly new realm. The changes in our understanding of these factors deserve careful attention, for they indicate how the future will be different.

In this emerging world view, knowledge is intertwined with values, social organization, technologies, and resource systems. People are beginning to recognize that individuals have little identity apart from the organizational or cultural systems of which they are a part. Thus, knowledge and values are a part of the patchwork quilt of cultures around the globe, one in which each patch is complex. No singular understanding is sufficient; rather, multiple understandings are required.

Similarly, our understanding of resource systems and technology is changing. Most ecosystems have been affected by human activity for millennia, and people have always been active agents in the evolution of ecosystems. Understanding ecosystems requires an understanding of how humans have influenced them over time. The notion that technology is neutral with respect to values, organization, the environment, or knowledge is also fading. Technology, by changing how we relate to each other and to nature, has made some values more important and has stifled others.

All of these understandings are giving rise to a co-evolutionary understanding of development. The intertwining of all these variables is more or less symmetrical; no system dominates another, none provides a more obvious starting point for understanding the whole, and each can be understood in the context of the others. This emerging world view is dynamic: not only is each subsystem related to all the others, but each affects the evolution of the others. This co-evolutionary interpretation gives us insights into how development occurred before the use of hydrocarbons, as well as into the nature of unsustainable development, and the challenge of the return to sustainability.

Defining Sustainability

Calls for SD in the latter part of the 1980s are vague, and we need to nail down the concept. Five increasingly comprehensive definitions are proposed, emphasizing the sustainability of interactions between regions and cultures. These are:

(1) Start at the local level and simply ask whether a region's agricultural and industrial practices can continue indefinitely. Will they destroy the local resource base, environment, or people?

(2) Ask whether this locality is dependent upon nonrenewable resources beyond its borders which are not being managed in a sustainable manner.

(3) Ask whether the region is culturally sustainable, and whether it is contributing enough to the knowledge and institutional bases of other regions to balance its dependence upon them.

(4) Question the extent to which the region is contributing to global climatic change.

(5) Inquire as to the cultural stability of all regions in combination. Are they evolving along mutually compatible paths?

Formulating responses to the questions associated with each of these definitions is a major challenge. The transition to SD will be difficult and will require:

(1) A positive sense of interdependence between individuals and cultures, and the evolution of new alliances based on agreement on the appropriate paths to approach these problems rather than upon specific issues or solutions.

(2) A changing political and bureaucratic environment, in which national governments will play a diminished or at least a significantly different role in the global arena.

(3) A new realm for policy processes in which there exists no prior agreement on the key questions, appropriate frameworks, or basic facts—the key will be to produce common understanding among people from different disciplines and culture.

(4) Better information to smooth the process of reaching public decisions—information that must come through contextual/interpretive thinking.

Summary of

Sustainable Development: A Critical Review
by Sharachchandra M. Lélé
[Published in *World Development* 19 (June 1991): 607–621.]

The rhetoric of sustainable development (SD) has become increasingly commonplace in the statements of those making or influencing development policy worldwide. This rhetoric and the SD literature that drives it are, however, afflicted by vagueness, inconsistencies, and oversimplifications. These weaknesses impede the formulation of fresh, consistent, and effective policies, instead permitting the proliferation of programs that only pay lip service to the concept. SD is in danger of becoming just a politically expedient cliché, unless rigor and intellectual clarity replace the current imprecision in the literature.

Mainstream Definition

SD is broadly understood as a form of societal change that unites traditional development objectives with the objective of ecological sustainability. Translating this general definition into specific policies requires the use of a model of the environment–society relationship. The mainstream model in SD thinking may be characterized as follows:

(1) Environmental degradation is severely reducing human well-being in developing countries, and will have global implications in the long run. The principal cause of this degradation is poverty, because the poor have no option but to exploit resources for short-term survival. Moreover, the poor are also often the first to experience the consequences of environmental deterioration and neglect.

(2) Traditional development objectives (meeting basic needs, improving factor productivity, etc.) need not conflict with the objective of ecological sustainability; the latter is necessary for the permanence of the former, while economic development will create the resources and capacities for implementing environmentally sound policies. Moreover, environmentally sound methods are "profitable" in the long run, and often in the short run as well.

(3) For any development program to succeed, even in the short run, it must be based on a participatory process.

Strengths

The SD movement has succeeded in promoting the idea that environmental conservation need not constrain development and that development does not necessarily mean environmental pollution. The literature has highlighted many possibilities for combining the objective of ecological sustainability (less resource use and less pollution) with those of poverty alleviation and community participation, and even with motivations of long-term self-interest. This approach has the potential to unite a broad spectrum of actors and interests.

Weaknesses

There are significant weaknesses in the literature, however, that compromise SD's effectiveness as a paradigm of development. One clear problem is the poor and incomplete characterization of the problems of poverty and degradation. The mainstream conceptualization has emphasized a circular process in which impoverishment and environmental degradation cause and reinforce one another. It has failed to acknowledge that poverty and environmental deterioration may both be the results of overconsumption, particularly in the North, and that all of these phenomena have deeper and complex structural and cultural causes. Consequently, much of the policy discussion focuses on techno-economic solutions: the adoption of "green" technologies, reforming pricing and subsidy policies, etc. Socio-political issues such as land reform or reduction of individual materialist tendencies are either ignored or acknowledged only in passing.

Another difficulty has been the inadequate conceptualization of the objectives of development, sustainability, and participation. The primary goal of development is to ease the crushing burden of poverty in the South. The SD paradigm presents economic growth as the means to reduce poverty and achieve sustainability. Yet the links between growth and either poverty alleviation or achieving environmental sustainability are not at all clear. Indeed, the irony is that SD, a supposed synthesis of previous development thinking, ignores its major lesson, i.e., the need to shift the focus from economic growth to the meeting of "basic needs," the reduction of inequity, and the building of indigenous capacity at the community level. Economic growth may be a product of SD, but the promotion of such growth should not be viewed as an integral part of SD policies.

The concept of sustainability has expanded beyond the management of renewable resource systems to embrace broader themes about the maintenance of essential ecological processes, genetic diversity, and the optimal utilization of nonrenewable resources. The concept does, however, remain disturbingly muddled as it fails to clearly answer the crucial questions: what is to be sustained, how, and for whom? It is vital to understand the conditions under which differing answers to these questions can or cannot be accommodated—i.e., when the well-being of future generations can be safeguarded simultaneously with meeting the needs and aspirations of presently deprived communities and with the protection of non-human species, and when trade-offs will be required. In trying to provide operational principles for achieving ecological sustainability, the literature not only oversimplifies ecosystem dynamics but also loses sight of the complex social conditions that substantially determine ecological outcomes.

Initial attempts to resolve the environment–development dilemma emphasized equity and social justice as fundamental objectives. This emphasis has been quietly dropped in favor of the politically less provocative concept of "local participation." In practice, this is further reduced to "the involvement of nongovernmental organizations." Such "NGO-ization" is, however, hardly tantamount to true local participation. Even significant decentralization of the decision-making process cannot by itself guarantee just and equitable outcomes, as it leaves the distribution of power unchanged. Finally, the relationship between equity, community participation, and environmental sustainability bears greater examination.

Examples

With all this confusion in the terms and concepts in mainstream SD thinking, it is not surprising that many SD policies do not conform to the basic idea of ecologically sound and socially equitable development. Three policy areas exemplify this point.

(1) *International Economic Relations:* An unreconstructed system of monetary and trade relations continues to reproduce patterns of unequal exchange and lopsided flows of resources to the North, undermining the viability of SD in the South. Yet the International Monetary Fund and the SD-friendly World Bank continue to foist draconian structural adjustment programs on developing nations and to promote simplistic free trade policies, measures more likely to exacerbate resource exploitation, inequity, and environmental pollution in the South.

(2) *Sustainable Agriculture:* As one of the key elements of SD, it is ironic that there is such confusion surrounding this concept. The terms *sustainable agriculture, low-input agriculture,* and *organic farming* are often used interchangeably, when in fact they are not the same thing. Moreover, the focus on "agroecology" ignores the social conditions necessary to ensure fair returns to rural factors while meeting urban

food demand. The lack of a clear definition and agenda has resulted in the continued domination of Green Revolution thinking and policies.

(3) *Tropical Forests:* Here a broad spectrum of institutions (Food and Agriculture Organization, United Nations Development Program, International Bank for Reconstruction and Development, World Resources Institute) have identified overpopulation, poverty, and ignorance as the primary culprits in forest degradation. This analysis not only fails to address the ultimate causes of poverty and population growth, but also obscures the more significant causes of tropical deforestation, i.e., state-sponsored "development" schemes and logging policies.

Agenda

In trying to balance the need for rigor and steadfastness to fundamental values and the need for wider political acceptance and support, SD proponents have tilted toward the latter and have adopted vague terminology, simplistic world views, and inconsistent policy mixes. Such an approach, however, is itself unlikely to be "sustainable." Advocates and analysts of SD must:

(1) reject the idea of economic growth as the primary vehicle to achieve SD;

(2) move away from neoclassical economic analysis and toward exploring more relevant empirical questions and approaches;

(3) address the complex causes and consequences of poverty and environmental degradation;

(4) understand the multiple dimensions of sustainability; and

(5) explore what patterns and levels of resource demand and use would be compatible with different forms of ecological and social sustainability.

Summary of

Recovering the Real Meaning of Sustainability
by Vandana Shiva

[Published in *The Environment in Question,* ed. David Cooper and Joy S. Palmer (New York: Routledge, 1992), 187–193.]

The term *sustainable* entered the economic development lexicon in the 1980s when people began to realize that economic growth and continuous increases in per capita income were unsustainable. Instead of living up to its promise to alleviate poverty, economic growth actually undermined ecological stability, thereby destroying people's livelihoods and causing further poverty. Moreover, development strategies have been based on the growth of the market economy, even when large numbers of people operate outside of this network. The emphasis on the market economy has resulted in the destruction of the other economies of nature's processes and of people's survival, but this destruction is seen as nothing more than the "hidden negative externalities" of the development process.

The principles of ecology and survival that maintain and sustain life in society have been neglected as the market and human-made capital have been elevated to the position of the highest organizing principle. However, modern economics and concepts of development are only of recent origin in the history of human interaction with nature. Before the advent of modern economics, humans derived their livelihood directly from nature through self-provisioning mechanisms based primarily on the principle of sustenance. Under this system nature was regarded as a commons. Under the market system, on the other hand, nature is viewed as a resource and is exploited to increase profits and capital accumulation. Processes of nature and society that are outside of the market system are not valued, leading to the destruction of nature and of the material base for people who live outside of the market system. Thus the emphasis on market-related and market-driven activities, undertaken in the name of economic development, has led to underdevelopment and scarcity in the economies of nature and survival.

Sustainable development is being offered as a solution to the ecological crisis that has resulted from economic growth and commercialization. Unfortunately this concept is still embedded in the ideology of the market system, resulting in the loss of the real meaning of sustainability. It is argued that more growth—resulting in greater use of natural resources and higher capital investment—is needed to solve the crisis at hand. The problem with this approach is that it separates the ecological problems from the economic problems. Strategies of economic growth lead to the destruction of nature, exacerbating economic problems. The most widely advocated sustainable development strategy suffers from three flaws:

(1) it assumes the primacy of human-made capital;

(2) it separates production from conservation, making conservation dependent on capital; and

(3) it assumes the substitutability of nature and capital.

To understand the real meaning of sustainability we must realize that nature's economy is primary and the money economy depends on it. The growth of markets and the resulting destruction of nature are at the root of the sustainability crisis. To have truly sustainable development, production and conservation should not be viewed separately, and ecological principles must be incorporated into the production and development processes. Furthermore, the notion that human-made capital and nature are substitutable must be abandoned. While it is true that human-made capital is created from natural resources and life, the reverse cannot take place.

In conclusion, the word *sustainable* can have two meanings. The real meaning refers to nature's and people's sustainability, where nature supports life. The second meaning is the sustainability of the market and the production process, but this path cannot be followed forever as it destroys nature, which is the primary source of support and sustenance.

Summary of

The Difficulty in Defining Sustainability
by Michael A. Toman
[Published in *Resources* No. 106 (Winter 1992): 3–6.]

The terms *sustainability* and *sustainable development* mean different things to different people. In general, sustainability involves some notion of respect for the interests of our descendants. Ecologists have taken this to include preservation of the status and functions of entire ecological systems. Economists have stressed the maintenance and improvement of overall human living standards.

There is also disagreement about the prospects for achieving sustainability. Some scholars argue that in the past humankind, through resource substitution and technological progress, has avoided the specter of Malthusian scarcity. Yet others believe that the human pressure on natural systems has already passed sustainable levels. They argue that it is likely that the world's population will at least double before it stabilizes, and they cannot conceive of ecological systems tolerating the consequences of the economic growth that will be needed to support a decent living standard for this increased population. It is difficult to determine where the truth lies and to identify the appropriate strategies. Progress is hampered by disagreements about basic concepts and terms of reference.

Key Conceptual Issues

There are differences of opinion between economists and resource planners on the one hand, and ecologists and environmentalists on the other, with respect to at least two salient elements of the sustanability concepts: inter-generational fairness, and what is to be sustained.

In economics, the standard approach for dealing with issues of intergen-erational trade-offs is to discount the costs and benefits of future genera-tions, as well as future receipts and burdens of the present generation. Dis-counting is justified on the grounds that present benefits are preferred to future benefits, and future costs to present costs, and that, from the point of view of current decision makers, current receipts are preferred to future receipts as they can be invested to increase capital and future income. Crit-ics of discounting object to its excessively wide application. Ethical objec-tions are raised when present generations exercise influence over future generations. The capital growth argument is criticized on the grounds that in many cases the environmental resources at stake are inherently limited in supply. Critics also object to the preferences of an "average" member of the present generation guiding resource use when such usage may threaten the future well-being of the entire species. "Deep ecologists" object to human values being at the center of the debate, arguing that other elements of the ecological system have an equal moral right to be sustained.

If one accepts that the present generation has collective responsibility to future generations, then the question is: what kind of social capital should be transferred to future generations? Many economists view the natural endowment, physical capital, and human knowledge and abilities as rela-tively fungible. Thus degradation of the environment and ecosystem are not seen as intrinsically unacceptable. The question is whether and what sort of compensatory investments can be undertaken. Such investments include human knowledge, technique, and social organization. Many ecol-ogists and some economists, however, view such a position as untenable. They point out that physical laws limit the possibility of substituting other things for ecological resources. In addition, healthy ecosystems are seen as offering resilience against unexpected changes, and degradation may be irreversible.

Another area of disagreement on this issue is the appropriate level of geo-graphical scale in considering resource substitutability. On the one hand, the larger the geographical scale the greater the opportunities for resource trade-offs. On the other, the smaller the scale the more attention can be paid to unique attributes of ecosystems. This disagreement is especially clear in considering the scale of human impact relative to global carrying capacity. Ecologists believe this to be a serious problem and an immutable constraint. Economists generally believe that substitution and technology will arise from within the system to deal with problems of global carrying capacity.

Safe Minimum Standards

The concept of a safe minimum standard can be applied to concerns about intergenerational fairness, resource constraints, and human impact. The safe minimum standard posits a socially determined, albeit "fuzzy," dividing line between moral imperatives to preserve and enhance natural resource systems and the free play of resource trade-offs. Suppose that the damages to natural systems can be characterized by the size of their cost and degree of irreversibility. The size of costs can be measured in terms of opportunity costs (by economists) or as a physical measure of ecosystem performance (by ecologists). The effects of irreversibility, which reflect uncertainty, cannot be so easily monetized from an environmentalist perspective. The two are therefore treated separately. Following a safe minimum standard, society would rule out actions that could result in natural impacts beyond a certain threshold of cost and irreversibility. Central to the safe minimum standards approach are the role of public decision making and the formation of societal values. The safe minimum standard will be defined differently by ecologists and economists, depending on judgments about moral imperatives and the value of discounting, but the concept may provide a useful frame of reference for discussion.

Research Needs

There is great scope for interdisciplinary work to address some key issues related to sustainability, including defining objectives, identifying constraints, and resolving the relevant disagreements. Economists could make greater use of ecological information and the implications of physical resource limits in an analysis of resource values. Social scientists can contribute to an understanding of how future generations might value different attributes of natural environments. Ecologists should provide ecological information in a manner that can be used in economic valuation. They should also take into consideration the role of economic incentives in ecological impact analyses.

Summary of
Sustainable Development: What Is to Be Done?
by Johan Holmberg and Richard Sandbrook

[Published in *Making Development Sustainable*, ed. Johan Holmberg (Washington, D.C. and Covelo, California: Island Press, 1992), 19–38. © International Institute for Environment and Development, 1992.]

(This is a summary of the introductory chapter of the book.)

The Concept of Sustainable Development

The World Commission on Environment and Development (the Brundtland Commission) brought the concept of sustainable development to geopolitical significance. Today the term *sustainable development* is a catch phrase meaning different things to different people. To some it is a truism, to others a contradiction in terms. Sustainable development is often identified with sustainable growth. Questions about the trade-offs and links between economic development, economic welfare, and the environment remain unanswered.

As the Brundtland Commission and others have defined it, the primary implication of sustainable development is that future generations should inherit an undiminished stock of "quality of life" assets. This is, however, a political concept, and this capital stock can be measured or interpreted in three ways:

(1) as comprising human-made and environmental assets;

(2) as comprising only environmental assets; or

(3) as comprising human-made, environmental, and "human capital" assets.

The notion of intergenerational equity lies at the core of the concept of sustainable development. While there is no solid definition to go by, development that does not meet the criteria of intergenerational equity must be bad development. Barbier[1] has attempted to reconcile different views in a working definition of sustainable development. He identified three systems that are basic to any development process: biological, economic, and social. Society applies sub-goals and targets to be achieved within each of these systems. The objective of sustainable development will be to maximize goal achievement simultaneously across these three systems, through an adaptive process of trade-offs. An unsustainable process would seek to maximize goals for each of the systems separately, without regard for the trade-offs. The choices and trade-offs made in a sustainable development strategy will depend on priorities, time, and scale (local, regional, national, or global).

Four Dilemmas

There are four dilemmas in defining sustainable development and its goals. First, Goodland et al.[2] convincingly argue that economic growth cannot be the unquestioned objective of economic policy. Growth implies more: more throughput, more inputs, and more waste. Human activity has resulted in problems of global warming, rupture of the ozone shield, and the highest rate of extinction of biological species ever recorded in history. The role of conventionally defined growth, in this view, should increasingly be limited to poverty alleviation in developing countries. The rich nations of the world cannot go on increasing their output and must instead concentrate on increasing efficiency in resource use. However, such a conclusion is contrary to the prevailing economic and business ethic.

Second, sustainable development is defined differently from conventional economic development. The change in emphasis from quantitative to qualitative dimensions leads to problems in measurement. Therefore, a new set of indicators and methodologies is needed. Further complications in measuring and comparing success arise when different trade-offs are made at different locations and times.

A third dilemma relates to how trade-offs will be made. As argued earlier, a sustainable development program will call for making trade-offs between different systems. While some broad principles may be agreed upon, such trade-offs are very difficult to make, and the tools needed to make these decisions are poorly developed. Cost–benefit analysis, which attempts to ascribe values to different systems, is controversial. Another dilemma is how to make trade-offs between protecting biological diversity and meeting human needs. Those in favor of development for people are pitted against those in favor of conservation. While both groups support the notion of sustainable development, they disagree on the means and methods of bringing it about. Is it necessary to cop-out by defining sustainable development as a broad guiding principle rather than a methodology in a complex, unequal world?

The fourth dilemma involves the relationship between sustainable development and democratic government. Central to the concept of sustainable development is the notion that future generations should not be made worse off because of today's needs. However, democratic governments cater to the needs and aspirations of people today, which leads them to borrow from the future. Similarly, cross-boundary issues that make for a sustainable world order rarely gain attention from politicians. Politicians alone cannot be blamed for such a situation, as they often reflect prevailing public opinion. The limited time horizon of elected governments is not conducive to a broader perspective on intergenerational or international issues.

It is for these reasons that patterns of sustainable development must be built from the bottom up. When progress at the local level is constrained due to factors beyond local control, public pressure will grow to make changes at the national, and eventually at the international, level.

Primary Environmental Care

Primary environmental care (PEC) is a process for progress toward sustainability at the "grass roots." It combines attempts to raise the productivity and welfare of the poor with concern for protecting the environment. Its three sets of goals, which must be considered together, include: (1) economic (meeting basic needs); (2) environmental (protecting and optimizing utilization of the environment); and (3) social (empowering groups and communities). The success of PEC depends on the involvement of local groups and communities in the organization and decision-making aspects of their communities. In addition, natural and financial resources, political support, and open access to information are required for success. PEC concentrates on empowerment and on building the knowledge of local people and institutions.

Notes

1. Edward B. Barbier, "The Concept of Sustainable Economic Development," in *Environmental Conservation* 14(2), 101–10 (1987).

2. Robert Goodland, Herman Daly, Salah El Serafy, and Bernard von Droste, *Environmentally Sustainable Economic Development: Building on Brundtland* (UNESCO, 1991).

Summary of

The Concept of Sustainability:
Origins, Extensions, and Usefulness for Policy
by John A. Dixon and Louise A. Fallon

[Published in *Society and Natural Resources* 2 (1989): 73–84.
Taylor and Francis, 1989, used with permission.]

The concept of sustainable development (SD) has gradually been accepted as a key organizing concept by a broad spectrum of development and environmental organizations. Indeed it is a mediating term that has bridged the span which often separates these two groups. The difficulty is that the term is so broadly defined and is used so extensively in the rhetoric of often disparate institutions that its real meaning is little understood, and there is an inadequate basis on which to evaluate the aims and outcomes of various projects carried out in the name of SD.

Definitions

The definition of SD has evolved through three stages over the years:

(1) Sustainability originated as a purely biological concept for a single resource, and thus was usually used within the context of a special class of renewable resources such as forests and fisheries. The goal was to establish some biologically determined maximum sustainable yield so as to reap today's bounty while preserving tomorrow's resources.

(2) Sustainability developed into a physical concept for a group of resources or an ecosystem. This level of understanding evolved out of the growing awareness that the first concept paid inadequate attention to the ways different resource bases interact with one another systemically. Thus what appears sustainable for a given resource may prove to be unsustainable for an entire system; so rather than focusing upon a single resource, there is explicit attention to the variety of outputs from an entire system. Of course, not all parts of an ecosystem can be managed in harmony; some resources may be enhanced, while others may be maintained at pre-use levels, and yet others may undergo some degradation. Moreover, social and individual needs must influence the evaluation of these trade-offs in any resource management policy.

(3) It is from this last point that the final understanding of sustainability, that is SD itself, has evolved. The focus shifts from specific physical stocks of given resources and systems to policies that enhance our ability to meet the needs of today without compromising our ability to meet the (larger) needs and challenges of tomorrow. This is a seductively simple concept, and there is little debate as to its basic desirability.

But SD for whom? As Richard Norgaard pointed out, "Environmentalists want environmental systems sustained. Consumers want consumption sustained. Workers want jobs sustained," etc.[1] A lively debate has developed, with people often talking at cross-purposes over what to sustain, how to go about it, how to define sustainability, and how to measure progress toward this ill-defined goal. The fundamental problem is that the term *sustainability*, which was originally developed in a biological/physical context, is now applied in a much broader economic/social context.

Some environmentalists and physical scientists argue that maintenance of physical stocks is the correct path to sustainability. From a socioeconomic perspective, however, because of population growth, especially in developing countries, maintenance of physical stocks will lead to declines in per capita availability of goods—this may occur to some extent even with reductions of physical stocks. It is clear, then, that improved productivity and efficiency are a necessary component of sustainability. However, it is very difficult to say *ex ante* what will be a sustainable economic activity, and far easier to say *ex post* what was not.

A number of authors are grappling with this dilemma. One definition equates sustainability with "ideal income," i.e., the greatest amount that can be consumed today without diminishing productive possibilities tomorrow. This perspective rejects the idea of purely physical measures of sustainability, with a recognition that what constitutes a productive asset may change over time; for example, the substitution of rain forests for equally sustainable rubber plantations in Malaysia. In addition, SD does not require that any particular activity continue indefinitely. Indeed, it will generally involve structural changes and the replacement of old activities with new ones. Additional questions center on how best to handle nonrenewable resources, and on the need to invest income from their depletion in renewable activities for the future. Some suggest that "growth" ought to refer to the quantitative expansion of the economy, and development to its qualitative enhancement. Thus SD need not mean sustainable growth.

All of these issues raise interesting and at times intractable questions which a rigorous assessment of SD must answer:

(1) How should equity, both inter- and intragenerational, be handled with respect to resource management decisions? Overfishing and excessive harvesting of forest products are examples of overemphasis upon the present—a problem that may be brought on by either poverty or greed. The implication is that resource issues cannot be discussed without regard for development issues.

(2) What do we leave to future generations to ensure that they are not worse off? Should we leave the same physical stock of resources, the same resource base per capita, or the potential for being at least as well off as the present generation? Each of these criteria will lead to different patterns of resource use, some of which may not be sustainable in the physical sense.

(3) Will there be enough to go around? Rising population implies increasing resource use merely to maintain current levels of consumption. The implication is that resource issues cannot be divorced from population issues.

(4) How far into the future do we worry about? The shorter our time horizon, the less likely that any pattern of resource use will truly be sustainable over long periods of time.

(5) Are there some patterns of resource use that should not be accepted regardless of their impacts on the resource base? For example, should the negative effects of species extinction always outweigh the social welfare gains of a given activity?

(6) To what extent can market forces intervene in the development process vis-à-vis resource use? Many factors can inhibit the proper functioning of markets, including imperfect information, greed, and uncertainty about the future, all of which tend to lead to unsustainable patterns of development. Nevertheless, market forces can be harnessed and corrected through appropriate macroeconomic policy instruments such as taxes and subsidies.

Clearly a great deal of work needs to be done to define parameters and goals in attempting to answer these questions in a more substantive manner than is currently possible. Nevertheless, the broader thinking engendered by the sustainability discussions has produced positive results, including:

(1) a greater awareness of the necessity of considering the long run in resource management decisions;

(2) enhanced attention to intergenerational concerns and transnational impacts;

(3) greater awareness that reliance solely upon the market may not be compatible with SD; and

(4) a better chance that bad development projects can be avoided.

Note

1. Richard Norgaard, "Sustainable Development: A Co-Evolutionary View," *Futures* (December 1988): 606–20 (see summary in this Part); cited by Dixon and Fallon, 7.

PART III

Theoretical Frameworks and Techniques

Overview Essay

by Jonathan M. Harris

Any theoretical offering in the domain of economics will inevitably be measured against the dominant, neoclassical theory. To its proponents, neoclassical economics represents the accumulated insights of two centuries of economic theory. Further, it presents itself as a complete, axiomatic theory, building its edifice of theorems on specific, testable assumptions. Does ecological economics seek to overturn this edifice and offer a different systematic theory to explain all economic activity? As we have seen, writers in the ecological economics area have raised many criticisms of the narrowness of neoclassical economics, and of its divorce from biophysical principles. But is there a single, sweeping alternative to put in its place? The answer is probably no. Yet the outline of what Daniel Underwood and Paul King call an alternative "metaeconomics" does appear, and significant efforts to advance specific analysis based on this new metaeconomics have been made. Part III summarizes what the editors of this volume consider to be some of the most important contributions to the task of building new theory. As will become apparent, these efforts do not necessarily reject all of the tools and approaches of the neoclassical school but at the least modify them significantly, and in some cases offer completely different analytical approaches.

The new theoretical contributions of ecological economics are clustered around certain key concepts. In each case the task attempted by the authors summarized here is to establish specific theoretical content for each concept. After considering some major concepts as developed in the specific articles summarized here, we will return to the issue of whether something like a complete alternative economics emerges from these efforts.

Sustainability

This much-used term has two components. One is *economic sustainability*—the ability of an economic system to continue operating at some level of output. The other is *ecosystem sustainability*—referring not to an absolutely unchanged ecosystem equilibrium but to what C.S. Holling refers to as ecosystem resilience (see the selection by Mick Common and Charles Perrings). Resilience refers to the bounce-back capacity which allows ecosystems to recover from short-term damage or disruption. True sustainability must include both components. Often only the first is considered, giving a *weak sustainability* concept which is generally compatible with the neoclassical framework. In this formulation, depletion of natural resources and degradation of ecosystem functions is acceptable provided that sufficient human-made capital is accumulated to substitute for these resources and functions. A good example would be depletion of soil fertility through erosion, with attendant substitution of mechanization, irrigation, and fertilizer to give equal or higher yields.

Strong sustainability, by contrast, gives priority to ecosystem resilience, and does not accept human-made capital accumulation as an adequate substitute for *natural capital* depletion. Common and Perrings construct a model which allows rigorous comparison of the two concepts, concluding that the stability conditions for the two types of sustainability differ widely. This is an extremely important result, giving theoretical rigor to the perception that an efficient neoclassical economic growth path is not environment-friendly. Edward Barbier offers a different formal model, starting with a neoclassical production function, but also embodying something similar to the entropy principle. He reaches similar conclusions: the benefits of "efficient" economic growth may be outweighed by increasing environmental degradation.

Scale

Herman Daly has been largely responsible for introducing this central concept to debates on economic growth, and his contribution is reflected in several selections here. He points out that neoclassical economics admits no scale limits—economies in mathematical theory can grow forever—but that the *closed system* of the physical world necessarily imposes some limits on the *open system* of the economy. The real question then is, how close are we to the limits? The question was raised by Kenneth Boulding in his famous "Spaceship Earth" article summarized here. Daly places us somewhere between the "frontier" economy, too small to affect its environment significantly, and the "spaceman" economy, which must manage its entire environment. He posits a "bull-in-the-china-shop" economy, large enough to do significant damage to ecosystem resilience. In this situation, the efficiency criterion advanced by neoclassical economists will not suffice—specific attention must be given to limits to growth, both of population and of per capita consumption. Daly proposes a *steady-state economy* which, rather than maximizing consumption, would minimize *throughput*—the use of resources and generation of wastes.

Thus to the goal of economic efficiency must be added the goals of *sustainable scale* and *equitable distribution*. The theoretical implication of this is that while neoclassical methodology might be very useful in defining economic efficiency and prescribing policies for its achievement, it is wholly inadequate to address issues of scale and distribution, which depend respectively on ecological realities and social, political, and ethical principles. Theories of macroeconomic equilibrium, employment, and income distribution which ignore these factors are therefore highly misleading. This implies a new structure for macroeconomic theory—though neither Daly nor the other authors in this part offer more than a very general indication of what this theory would look like.

In addition to its obvious importance for developing economies, this perspective has a special implication for the formerly communist economies. They clearly suffer from a cancerous growth of high-polluting industry. Will their present transition be simply to a more efficient kind of growth or to a truly sustainable system? Kenneth Townsend discusses this question, offering some prescriptions (transferable pollution permits) which are perfectly acceptable to neoclassical theorists, but also advocating an application of Daly's steady-state goal to Eastern economies. He fails, however, to offer many useful specifics (e.g., energy sector efficiency, agricultural reform) as to how this might be achieved.

A practical application of the scale concept is seen in the case study of Haiti by George Foy and Herman Daly. Some of the severe environmental problems of Haiti are attributed to the resource misallocation issues familiar to standard economic theorists as cases of "market failure." But population pressure and resulting deforestation and soil erosion are seen as an independent cause of environmental degradation. Perhaps a standard economic rejoinder might be that correcting the "market failures" would allow for an expanded population carrying capacity. But it is surely unarguable that so long as resource misallocation problems exist, population pressure will make the results significantly worse, as is dramatically obvious in Haiti.

Entropy

As Underwood and King point out, the "metaeconomics of the steady state" is based on the laws of thermodynamics, as opposed to the formalized mathematical assumptions of the neoclassical model. The First Law, that of conservation of matter and energy, is reflected in the emphasis on limits in ecological economic theory. The planetary stock of resources is fixed; leaving aside exotic schemes of mining other planets, we have a limited resource base to work with. The Second Law, that of increasing entropy, governs our use of the one truly "free" resource, solar energy, and of all existing resource stocks. This law implies that any economic activity, as indeed any life process, inevitably degrades energy and material resources to a more disordered, less usable form. It is not simply a question of energy supply, as some neoclassical economists have suggested. Even more significant is the issue of ecosystem capacity to absorb the high-entropy wastes which are the unavoidable result of economic activity. Herman Daly, in "On Economics as a Life Science," suggests that in economics, as in biology, the critical issue is the ability of the system to adapt to limited sources of low entropy, utilizing the solar flux efficiently and avoiding a buildup of waste products which would render the environment incapable of supporting further life.

Nicholas Georgescu-Roegen, who first proposed the concept of analyzing the economic process in terms of the entropy law (in *The Entropy Law and the Economic Problem*) emphasizes that this perspective does not imply an energy theory of value. Writers in the "energetic" tradition have attempted to measure value in terms of embodied energy. Georgescu-Roegen finds this approach wrong-headed, and strongly differentiates his own view from neo-energetics. But he does see the entropy theory as a fundamental challenge to mainstream economists. Economic growth, he argues, has been dependent on a "mineral bonanza" which is unrepeatable. Mechanistic theories of economic growth which ignore thermodynamic limits are therefore unreliable. This criticism applies to essentially all of neoclassical growth theory.

The introduction of the entropy concept to economic theory raises a question which is well posed by Burness et al. in the article "Thermodynamic and Economic Concepts as Related to Resource-Use Policies." That is, is there a specific role for entropy analysis as distinct from ordinary market price rationing? Is it not true that scarcity of low-entropy resources will be reflected in a high market price? And if so, what does entropy analysis have to add to standard market analysis? Herman Daly's reply to this crucial question is to the effect that we should not seek a new energy theory of value but rather use the awareness of Second Law constraints to formulate policies for long-term sustainability. These policies (such as taxes on energy and virgin resources) would then work through the market price mechanism, internalizing into market decision making a social awareness of ecological limits. Burness et al. feel that this is simply the imposition of an ethical decision, not a modification in theory.

How can we evaluate this debate? One comment might be that Daly may underrate the specific importance of energy and resource analysis. Short of seeking a comprehensive energy theory of value, we may analyze the evolution of many agricultural and industrial systems specifically in terms of energy and resource use (extensive examples of such analysis are offered in Part IV). The heavy dependence of our economy on fossil fuels is a central issue which leaps out of such an analysis, as opposed to its relative obscurity in a standard economic analysis in which energy is but one factor in costs of production. The cumulative impact of pollutants is also evident from physically based analysis of economic activity but will only affect market prices *after* a conscious decision by policy makers, based on non-market factors, to impose quantitative limitations or taxes. (Daly, of course, is well aware of this, and refers, for example, to the importance of expanding input–output analysis to include ecological stocks and flows in "On Economics as a Life Science," but he does not stress it in his reply to Burness et al.)

Another relevant point is that the question of intergenerational patterns of resource use is not solely an ethical issue. It raises the next important area of theoretical difference between neoclassical and ecological economics—the treatment of time.

Time

The essential issue here is the role of the discount rate in balancing present and future values—seemingly a technical issue, but one of sweeping implications. The best work in this area has been done by Richard Norgaard and Richard Howarth, in the chapter summarized here, "Economics, Ethics, and the Environment," and other articles. They suggest that the use of a discount rate—any discount rate—to balance present and future values is fundamentally flawed. This, of course, represents a basic theoretical difference with neoclassical economics. Discounting based on prevailing commercial interest rates (say a real interest rate of 6%) heavily downgrades the interests of future generations. Costs and benefits 25 years in the future will be discounted by a factor of four, and 50 years in the future by a factor of 18. This means essentially that the interests of future generations in avoiding environmental degradation will be disregarded. Nor are we discussing the distant future—these time periods are within the lifetimes of children already born. Norgaard and Howarth show that if we take a different starting point, assuming that future generations have equal rights over resource allocation, a quite different pattern of discounting and inter-period resource allocation would emerge. In effect, using a current discount rate assigns all rights over resources to the present generation.

This point is of extraordinary importance, for it means that hidden in the apparently "neutral" principle of inter-period efficiency is a normative judgment that gives absolute primacy to short-term, present-generation interests over future interests in the resource and environmental area. The only justification for this would be the assumption that future citizens are fully compensated for resource loss and environmental degradation by the accumulation of human-made capital. But since most of this capital itself has a lifetime of only 20 to 50 years, and since the substitutability of human-made and natural capital is in serious question, this clearly shortchanges the future.

The alternative approach suggested by Norgaard and Howarth separates the normative definition of goals from the positive determination of efficient means. We must first determine our principle of long-term resource allocation and environmental preservation (in accordance, they propose, with the sustainability criterion discussed earlier). Then we can proceed to issues of valuation and discounting to achieve these ends. Interestingly, this perspective reverses the burden of normative judgment in the Burness/Daly debate. Rather than seeing the "steady-state" advocates as imposing their own ethical criterion on resource allocation, we see that the current economic allocation imposes a present-oriented normative value in the guise of a neutral market efficiency.

Complexity, Uncertainty, and Irreversibility

Another important tenet of ecological economics is advanced by Peter Söderbaum in "Neoclassical and Institutional Approaches to Development and the Environment." He argues that the inherent complexity of ecosystems is at odds with the reductionist nature of both modern industrial production and neoclassical economic theory. A similar theme is developed compellingly by Norgaard in "Economics as Mechanics and the Demise of Biological Diversity." The rapid replacement of traditional, ecologically integrated agricultural production techniques with uniform, high-input agriculture and commercial production is devastating to the maintenance of biodiversity. The spread of a global trading economy means that local production decisions must be responsive to a global supply and demand balance determined without regard to the nature and capabilities of local ecosystems. Rapid shifts in crop profitability and export demand impose impossible burdens on local ecosystem stability, destroying ecosystem resilience. Thus the spread of free trade, seen from one perspective as clearly beneficial, appears now as a relentless destructive force steadily reducing global biodiversity. Norgaard does not proceed to any theory of ecologically sustainable trade, but his analysis clearly indicates the need for such a theory (this issue will be pursued further in Part VI.)

Allied to the issue of complexity is that of uncertainty. While some environmental impacts are clearly definable in relation to such factors as levels of production and generation of pollutants, in many cases a high degree of uncertainty is involved with the "big" environmental issues such as global warming, biodiversity loss, ozone destruction, and cumulative ocean pollution. The range of "cost" estimates associated with these problems may be immense, and considerably complicated by the discounting issues discussed above. The *precautionary principle* suggested by Charles Perrings ("Reserved Rationality and the Precautionary Principle") implies that when worst-case possibilities involve massive and irreversible damage, standard expected-value cost/benefit methodology is unacceptable. The principle of erring on the side of precaution implies a high premium on preserving the resilience of ecosystems. As we have already seen, this will generally cut against the "efficient market" solution which ignores or downgrades ecosystem sustainability issues.

John Krutilla's "Conservation Reconsidered" approaches similar issues using the more standard theoretical concept of *option value*. He suggests that it is usually impossible for the market to capture the public benefits of preserving unspoiled environments. The ecosystem services provided by these environments, whether practical (water purification), aesthetic/spiritual (enjoyment of nature), or purely ecological (biodiversity) cannot be replicated once destroyed. This argues for a conservation principle which must override market considerations to guarantee the unquantifiable "option value" of ecosystem resilience.

Values and Motives

A theme which runs through all the topics discussed so far is the social and ethical dimension of decision making. In the neoclassical model all actors, whether consumers or producers, are motivated by pure self-interest. Moral considerations, altruistic motives, or public-spiritedness are excluded by assumption. Thus if we agree with any of the ecological imperatives discussed above, we would somehow have to impose them from without on an otherwise self-regulating market. Both John Tomer in "The Human Firm in the Natural Environment" and Peter Söderbaum propose the contrary view: the moral/altruistic motives of protecting the environment may in fact be internalized in the decision making of individuals and firms. Many institutions and social forces affect the behavior of economic actors, and among these is a growing consciousness of the importance of the environment. Thus "socially responsible" firms will seek to modify their own practices to minimize environmental impact; "green" consumers will give preference to sustainably produced goods, and nongovernmental interest groups may effectively influence public policy toward environmental protection.

The significance of this point is that it breaks down the disciplinary barriers between economics, sociology, political science, and philosophy. Neoclassical economists may perhaps try to preserve the purity of their mathematical models by arguing that these considerations simply create new "objective functions" for firms and consumers. But this really begs the question, since the elegance of the original model derives from the simplicity of the profit or utility-maximizing goal. Once a tangled web of social, ethical, and ecological considerations enter the picture, it will no longer be possible for economists to defend the frontier of their discipline against the incursions of other social and physical scientists and even of philosophers. (Perhaps Adam Smith, author of "The Theory of Moral Sentiments," would agree with today's ecological economists that they should not try.)

In summary, three elements of new economic theory emerge from these selections:

(1) *Meta-theoretical Framework:* The interlocking concepts discussed above clearly form an alternative perspective or world view which contrasts with the neoclassical model. The ramifications of this new perspective are extensive, with major theoretical and policy implications.

(2) *Formal Models:* Both Barbier and Common/Perrings construct formal mathematical models which resemble standard neoclassical models but include ecologically derived principles which significantly affect their results. Variations on this technique can be used in many kinds of economic/ecological modeling, some further examples of which will be seen in the Parts IV and V.

(3) *Alternative Theories and Techniques for Specific Fields of Study:* The Norgaard/Howarth critique of discounting implies a completely different approach to cost/benefit analysis and project evaluation. Tomer and Söderbaum suggest new approaches to the theory of the firm and public choice theory. Norgaard's analysis of trade reverses the standard

conception of the benefits of free trade, with profound implications for trade and development policy. Daly suggests (but does not fully develop) a new macroeconomics including limits on growth, bringing to the fore issues of employment and distribution which have hitherto been "solved" by the assumption of continuous growth. Townsend suggests a different goal than that currently being pursued for the post-communist economic transition—a transition to ecological sustainability as well as market efficiency. Though not developed in detail, the issue raised is of critical importance for this area of analysis and policy.

Two additional specific areas of analysis appropriate to the ecological economics perspective will be added in Parts IV and V: energy/resource flow analysis (deriving from entropy theory) and modified national income accounts. The alternative approaches to trade, development, and social/ethical/institutional analysis which have been suggested here are also more fully developed in Parts VI and VII.

Summary of

On the Ideological Foundations of Environmental Policy

by Daniel A. Underwood and Paul G. King

[Published in *Ecological Economics* 1 (December 1989): 315–334.
Reprinted with kind permission from Elsevier B.V., Amsterdam, The Netherlands.]

Arguments in the philosophy of science have suggested that ideological preconceptions underlie all analysis, including economic analysis. The ideological basis of economic analysis is called "metaeconomics." As long as different groups of economists have different ideological (metaeconomic) foundations, an objective resolution of debated issues cannot take place. This article examines the differences in the metaeconomic first principles and the resulting analytic and policy conclusions of two schools in environmental economic analysis: neoclassical economics and the steady-state approach.

Metaeconomics of Neoclassical A-Environmentalism

The ideological basis of neoclassical economics can be traced to Adam Smith's notion that individuals working in their self-interest will promote the welfare of the whole of society. This Smithian view, along with the use of logic, mathematics, and utilitarian Benthamite views, was applied to the concepts of value and distribution. This process of methodological development culminated in Pareto working out the marginal conditions needed for a market system to maximize social welfare.

The belief that individual action would result in maximizing social welfare (albeit under a set of restrictive conditions) was questioned by Pigou, who argued that, due to the nature of property relations, self-interested individuals may behave in ways that are antagonistic to total social welfare. In particular, Pigou claimed that there may be externalities to individual action that, if ignored, would violate Pareto's optimality conditions. This challenge to the neoclassical framework was countered by Coase, who argued that negatively affected individuals would alter the actions of externality producers through a set of side payments. Alternatively, if there were too many individuals to make side payments possible, then the imposition of fines or taxes could correct the actions of individuals and bring the system back to a Pareto efficient point.

Another challenge to the neoclassical position was raised by American conservationists in the early twentieth century who argued that natural resources were being extracted and used rapidly, posing problems for future generations. In response, Hotelling claimed that welfare will be maximized if nonrenewable natural resource extraction is guided by the discount rate and a corresponding growth in resource value over time. If the net value of the resource grows at the discount rate, then future generations will be compensated for a smaller stock of natural resources by a larger stock of productive capital. Once again, the thrust of the argument was that the market, through the price system, could regulate the rate of extraction.

The position of the neoclassical school, therefore, is that there is no absolute scarcity. Scarcity is relative, and the price system will send signals that will lead to appropriate substitutions.

Metaeconomics of the Steady State

Influenced by the work of Nicholas Georgescu-Roegen, Kenneth Boulding, and Herman Daly, the steady-state school questions the notion that the market can dictate a path of sustainable growth. This school adopts the laws of thermodynamics as a metaeconomic first principle. Thus, while steady-state theorists agree with neoclassicists that relative price movements generated by market transactions can result in Pareto optimal resource allocations in the short run, and that welfare can be improved by internalizing externalities, they argue that the problem of assimilation of pollutants by the environment can be solved only by a ceiling on throughputs. They contend that this is because there are biospheric limits to economic activity. The thrust of the steady-state position is that the problem of scarcity is not one of relative scarcity but one of absolute scarcity. Absolute scarcity exists both in terms of resource availability and assimilative capacity.

Contemporary A-Environmentalism

Contemporary a-environmentalism is essentially an application of the neoclassical framework to environmental issues. It argues that the problems of pollution and energy can be solved by substituting for environmental resources in production, while the market will take care of intertemporal problems. Using the past as a guide, it suggests that capital and technology will take care of environmental problems in the future.

There has been a recognition by some economists of the laws of thermodynamics and their implications for substitution. For example, Solow and others see the laws of thermodynamics and conservation as ultimate constraints on economic activity. However, many address the problem primarily as a question of providing adequate energy sources, an approach that separates the problems of the environment from energy issues, although these two issues are actually closely related. In fact, technological energy "fixes" ignore the environmental impacts of increased energy use. Therefore, given that there are no exceptions to the laws of thermodynamics, one of the metaeconomic first principles should be that there is an upper bound to the application of technological innovation.

Is Reconciliation Possible?

The difference in the evolution of economic thought between the neoclassicists and the steady statists rests partly on their notions of value. To the neoclassicist the value of a commodity is its price. Thus environmental resources are valued by the amount people are willing and able to pay to maintain them. Given relative price movements and the changes in value they bring about, neoclassicists do not see any limits to growth. Steady statists, on the other hand, take the limits to growth based on thermodynamic considerations as their starting point. As a result, steady statists' concept of value is grounded in "sustainability" and a moral imperative not to degrade the environment. This transcends the "rational egoism" of the neoclassicists. This difference in viewpoints may not be easily resolved.

Summary of

Towards an Ecological Economics of Sustainability
by Mick Common and Charles Perrings

[Published in *Ecological Economics* 6 (July 1992): 7–34. Reprinted with kind permission from Elsevier B.V., Amsterdam, The Netherlands.]

The discussion of sustainability in environmental economics continues to be plagued by considerable disagreement and obscurity as to both the conceptual and the operational content of the term. These disagreements arise due to different disciplinary perspectives, the axiomatic foundations of the models that are used to explore the concept, and interpretations of sustainability at the policy level. The discussion is further plagued by ill-defined philosophical and ethical differences over issues of both intra- and intergenerational equity. This article seeks to clarify matters through the development of a mathematical model of resource allocation that embraces both economic and ecological concepts of sustainability, drawing on models and insights from both fields. Specifically, the Solow/Hartwick approach from economics and the Holling approach from ecology have been selected.

Economics: Solow-Sustainability

Consumption is the starting point for treating sustainability within the utilitarian framework of the neoclassical model. Consumption refers to that portion of the total goods and services produced that is currently utilized to satisfy a set of wants, all within the constraints imposed by a given set of resource endowments. Wants are determined exogenously, and their satisfaction is used as a measure of system performance. The endowment set is an exogenous heritage of resources, along with the property rights that map these resources into the consumer's constraint set. Property rights are assumed to be external to the productive system as well.

The implications of this definition of consumption for sustainability can be found by relating it to income. The Hicks/Lindahl concept of sustainable net income is defined as the maximum amount that can be spent on consumption during a given period without reducing either the expected capital value of prospective receipts in future periods or the real consumption expenditure in future periods. Income so defined presupposes the deduction of expenditures to make good the depreciation and degradation of the productive asset base such that society is as well off at the end of the period as it was at the beginning. Thus a suitably defined capital stock must be maintained which ensures that the constraint set does not tighten over time.

A theory of sustainable resource utilization based on this definition must establish how a constant real consumption expenditure can be maintained with an exhaustible resource base. Solow, adopting the egalitarian arguments of Rawls, proposed a "Rawlsian" maximin approach to the intertemporal distribution of consumption. Solow, Hartwick, and others produced a simple result known as the Hartwick rule: "Consumption may be held constant in the face of exhaustible resources only if the rents deriving from the intertemporally efficient use of those resources are reinvested in reproducible capital."[10] In other words, the returns from exhaustible assets must be invested in nonexhaustible assets.

The investment rule that this implies rests on an assumption that, although capital inputs are heterogeneous, there exists sufficient substitutability between reproducible and exhaustible stocks within the relevant production functions. Therefore, the rule itself is, in fact, more a condition for intertemporal efficiency than it is for sustainability per se. The well-behaved production functions used by Solow and Hartwick have had to be modified to admit the nonsubstitutability of certain types of natural and produced capital. Thus, in some models upper bounds on the waste absorptive capacity of the environment have been set, along with lower bounds on the level of stocks that can support sustainable development.

Whatever the variations, the notion that some suitably defined capital stock should be kept constant is a crucial component of this definition of sustainability, and it is generally agreed that the only meaningful measure of these stocks is a measure of value. Moreover, for this measure to produce optimal allocations it must not be based on market prices but on shadow prices that reflect the true social value over time. Thus, in order for resources to be allocated according to the rule, there must either exist a complete set of competitive markets from today until infinity, or all economic agents must contract in today's markets on the basis of rational expectations for the future. If one of these conditions cannot be met, then there is no assurance of reaching an efficient, intertemporal, competitive equilibrium.

Ecology: Holling-Sustainability

The difficulty with the above from an ecological perspective is that it ignores the fact that the human economy is an integral part of a closed evolutionary system. The assumptions are often blind to the physical principles informing a materially closed, thermodynamic system, and to the feedback effects of dynamically interactive human and environmental productive systems. To address these shortcomings, Holling's work on resilience and stability of ecosystems is the starting point. He distinguishes two levels of stability: (1) stability per se, i.e., the propensity of populations in an ecosystem to return to an equilibrium condition following a perturbation; and (2) resilience, i.e., the propensity of a system to retain its organizational structure following a perturbation. The distinction between the two implies a difference in the focus of analysis within an ecosystem; there can be either a micro focus on a population of organisms within the system, or a macro focus on the larger community of organisms. Individual populations can only be Holling-stable if the ecosystem is Holling-resilient, though Holling-resilience does not necessarily imply Holling-stability.

Ecosystems that are open with respect to energy flows have a tendency to self-organize within the constraints imposed by an evolutionary and fluctuating environment. Any point at which the self-organizing forces of the system balance the disorganizing forces of the environment may be said to be an optimum operating point of that system. There may therefore be multiple equilibrium points for an individual population that could be considered Holling-stable. The Holling-resilience of the system as a whole may then be measured by its ability to "accommodate the stress imposed by its environment through selection of a different operating point along the same thermodynamic path without undergoing some catastrophic change in organizational structure."[18] The important feature of resilience then is the capacity it implies to adapt to the stresses imposed on a system through its interdependence with other systems.

Holling characterizes endeavors to manage ecosystems as "weak experiments testing a general hypothesis of stability/resilience."[1] This is exemplified by historical attempts to stabilize ecosystems in the Holling-stable sense, which have often been successful in the short term but have led to qualitative changes in the larger system, generally with adverse consequences for the resilience of that wider system. Most often this is due to decreasing diversity of communities within the system due to the economic focus upon a single community. A narrower range of communities reduces the level of interaction and the complexity of the system, characteristics that are argued to be necessary to maintain its resilience.

The Ecological Economics of Sustainability

The fundamental difference between the Solow and Holling models is in the way each perceives the interrelationships between the economy and the ecology. In the Solow model, the economic system does not affect the physical system in which it is imbedded. By assuming that the economy receives free gifts from the environment (as a source of natural goods and a receptor of pollution and wastes) the Solow model does not consider the important dynamic implications of resource use. On the other hand, the Holling model privileges the system over its component parts. The Solow model considers just the economic system, whereas the Holling model takes a macroscopic systems view.

The model presented here takes a systems approach and considers the biophysical and economic system simultaneously. It considers a problem of resource allocation over time given a social welfare function and a constraint. The biophysical system is the constraint on economic activity, and this constraint changes with exploitation of resources and imposition of wastes into the ecosystem by the economic system. Social welfare depends on both the income derived and the state of the resource base that the present generation bequeaths to future generations; i.e., social welfare depends on the welfare of both present and future generations.

The most striking conclusion of the model described above is that the concepts of Solow-sustainability and Holling-sustainability are disjoint. This implies that there may be no close relationship between economic efficiency and ecological sustainability. In fact, historical evidence suggests that economies that have managed the resource base in an ecologically sustainable manner have not performed well by intertemporal economic efficiency criteria. This is not to suggest that economically efficient systems cannot be ecologically sustainable, though for this to be so would require some improbable conditions. An ecological economics approach requires that resources be allocated in such a fashion that they threaten neither the system as a whole nor the key components of the system. For the system to be sustainable it must serve consumption and production objectives that are themselves sustainable. If existing preferences and technologies, as perpetuated and sanctified in the concept of consumer sovereignty, are not sustainable, then the system as a whole will be unstable. The appropriate policy instruments to address these concerns are varied and complex, and are not discussed here. What is important is that ecological economics privileges the needs of the system over those of individuals.

Note

1. C.S. Holling, "The Resilience of Terrestrial Ecosystems: Local Surprise and Global Change," in *Sustainable Development of the Biosphere*, eds. W.C. Clark and R.E. Munn (Cambridge: Cambridge University Press, 1986); cited by Common and Perrings, 18.

Summary of

Alternative Approaches to Economic–Environmental Interactions

by Edward B. Barbier

[Published in *Ecological Economics* 2 (April 1990): 7–26. Reprinted with kind permission from Elsevier B.V., Amsterdam, The Netherlands.]

A central question asked by environmental and resource economists is, "what useful economic functions does the environment provide and how are these functions affected by the process of economic–environmental interaction?"[8] A conventional approach and an alternative approach are outlined here. A model of economic–environmental interaction is constructed based on the alternative approach to show how such a method is suitable for analyzing emerging problems of environmental degradation.

Conventional Approaches

Following Hotelling,[1] the conventional approach defines natural resources as those environmental resources that provide economically valuable productive services. This view sees the natural environment solely as a supplier of raw material and energy inputs to the economic process. When a natural resource becomes scarce, its price will rise relative to that of other goods. Therefore, it is the expected threat of future scarcity from overexploitation and depletion that makes it worthwhile to hold on to certain material and energy-yielding natural resources. This leads one to ask, "what is the ideal rate of depletion?" For nonrenewables it may be optimal to deplete the resource if future technologies and the availability of perfect substitutes make the resource nonessential for future production. For renewables, exhaustion may be optimal if the resource is growing at a slow rate, harvesting costs are low, and its value appreciates more slowly than the market rate of interest. This approach is based on the optimistic expectation that markets will automatically determine the optimal rate of exploitation.

Alternative Approaches

An alternative approach recognizes three important functions performed by the environment and by scarce environmental resources:

(1) providing useful material and energy inputs for the economic process;
(2) assimilating waste by-products generated by the economic process; and
(3) providing utility—i.e., yielding services or ecological functions that are essential for supporting the economic system and human welfare, including recreational, health, cultural, scientific, educational, and aesthetic services, as well as the maintenance of essential climatic and ecological cycles.

As the environment is used by the human economy, the quality of the environment itself may deteriorate, and this is seen as an economic problem. This view may lead to different criteria for the economic exploitation of environmental resources, as it considers the total economic value provided by all functions of an environmental asset. The absolute effects of ecosystem degradation must be considered, rather than only the relative scarcity effects of the conventional approach.

A Model of Economic–Environmental Interaction

The model presented here builds on a number of studies that emphasize the environmental costs of economic activity. It addresses a situation in which economic–environmental interaction leads not only to increasing relative scarcity of utility-yielding environmental services, but also to the possibility of widespread ecological disruption and disturbances.

In the model, a social welfare function is defined based on consumption and on a stock variable that represents environmental quality. It is assumed that over time the capital stock in the economy increases by the difference between output and the sum of three other factors: consumption, resources used for environmental improvement, and capital depreciation. In addition, environmental quality declines over time due to extraction of resources and generation of wastes. It is assumed that the improvements in the environment can never be greater than the deterioration; environmental quality is likely to decline in each period. The existence of a maximum tolerable level of environmental degradation is also assumed, beyond which the economic–environmental system is destabilized.

The planning problem suggested by the model is how best to allocate economic and environmental resources over time, given declining environmental quality and the threat of a future ecological constraint. The model yields:

(1) the optimal trade-off between increased consumption and provision of services to improve the environment; and

(2) the rule governing the optimal rate of capital accumulation, and thus the optimal rate of growth in the economy.

The model is different from the conventional approach in suggesting that at some point the benefits of capital accumulation and growth (in the form of expanding output) may be outstripped by the costs of such growth in the form of environmental degradation. Determination of the optimal allocation of economic and environmental resources clearly depends upon the relative preferences of individuals, the development of technology, and the resilience and regenerative capacity of the ecosystem.

Wider Implications: Technology, Tastes, and Time

Conventional approaches indicate that technological innovation, substitution, and improvements in resource management can help overcome increasing relative scarcity. The model presented here suggests that, with the proper use of technology and environmental management, the rate of environmental degradation can be slowed down appreciably by reducing the inflow of material and energy from the environment and the outflow of waste. Some of the resource saving approaches that can be applied to economic activity include:

(1) factor substitution, e.g., of labor power for energy;

(2) reusing scrap and waste materials;

(3) increasing efficiency of resource conversion and utilization to obtain the maximum amount of end-use energy and material for production of final goods and services from primary inflows of resources;

(4) improving organizational techniques;

(5) changing composition of outputs, e.g., from non-durables to durables, or from resource using goods to services; and

(6) changing product quality and/or design.

The technology needed to achieve these innovations may already exist. However, such technologies may not be adopted unless new conservation-oriented, macroeconomic policy goals are accepted. In addition to technological improvements, better techniques of resource management, appropriate planning of tourist facilities and conservation areas, and training and dissemination of conservation skills will help as well. When applied to agricultural systems, these techniques may also result in the added advantage of increases in production.

However, resource-saving environmental management techniques may not be implemented for a number of reasons. For example, many environmental resources exist outside the gamut of market commodities, so automatic market signals are inappropriate for determining allocation. Moreover, even if external environmental costs of depletion are calculated, there is still no way of accounting for the decay of the ecological process itself, especially since we do not have a clear understanding of the effects of pollutants and resource depletion on ecological systems. In addition, given the First and Second Laws of Thermodynamics, there are limits to how much environmental degradation can be reduced. Finally, there is no way of determining the trade-offs between future consumption and environmental quality, as we do not know the tastes and preferences of future generations.

Note

1. Harold Hotelling, "The Economics of Exhaustible Resources," in *Journal of Political Economy* 39(2), 137–75 (1931).

Summary of

Introduction to the Steady-State Economy
by Herman E. Daly

[Published in *Valuing the Earth: Economics, Ecology, Ethics,* eds. Herman E. Daly
and Kenneth N. Townsend (Cambridge, Massachusetts and London: The
MIT Press, 1993), and in *Economics, Ecology, Ethics: Essays Toward
a Steady-State Economy,* ed. Herman E. Daly (New York and
San Francisco: W.H. Freeman and Company, 1980), 1–31.]

Paradigms in Political Economy

A *paradigm*, according to Thomas Kuhn, is an entire pattern of thought. Discontinuous revolutionary changes in these patterns of thought that occasionally occur are called *paradigm shifts*. When such shifts occur they involve a *gestalt*, an element of faith, personal commitment, and values. Because it changes the entire intellectual framework among scientists within a discipline, a new paradigm must initially rely on its own criteria for justification, because the relevant questions and answers may be absent from the previous paradigm. Proponents of different paradigms may not even agree on the fundamental problems and solutions.

The field of economics can point to several periods of paradigm shift. During the mercantilist period, wealth was seen as based on precious metals that were converted into armies and thus national power. This wealth was obtained by mining, international trade, and conquest. A good balance of trade required low prices, so it was necessary to keep wages low. Later, the Physiocrats shifted the primary focus to agriculture and land as the basis of the economy. The classical economists brought about another shift, as they saw labor as the primary source of wealth and were concerned with how the product of labor was distributed among the social classes that cooperated to produce it. The classical economists thought that "over the long run, population growth and diminishing returns would unavoidably channel the entire economic surplus into rent, thus reducing profit to zero and terminating economic growth."[3] Marx's approach was quite similar to that of the classical economists, but he focused more on the relationship between the owners of the means of production and the non-owners. Marx saw this class distinction as the central economic factor and believed that it would lead to revolution.

Neoclassical economists shifted the paradigm back to the concept of individual competition. Their central focus was on maximizing the amount of wants satisfaction from scarce resources, given a certain wealth and income distribution. The means for this maximization was pure competition. John Maynard Keynes, writing during the economic problems of the 1930s, emphasized unused resources. While classical and neoclassical economists had seen unemployment as an aberration, Keynes recognized it as the general rule. In the present day Keynesian–neoclassical synthesis, economics has become focused on full employment and optimal microeconomic allocation of resources as measured by GNP. Growth in GNP is seen as necessary to maintain full employment. The issue of distribution has receded into the background; the goal of the economy is to make the total pie bigger so that everyone can get more without changing the relative size of the parts. Continuous growth in stocks and income is central to this paradigm, which assumes that aggregate wants are infinite and should be served by making aggregate production infinite.

Ends, Means, and Economics

Political economics has tried to avoid social conflicts by abolishing the idea of scarcity by "promising more things for more people, with less for no one, for ever and ever."[7] Robert Solow has said that "the world can, in effect, get along without natural resources."[1] Barnett and Morse have added to this by stating that there are certain scarcities in nature, but not a general scarcity of resources altogether. These statements have, however, ignored the law of entropy, which tells us that nature does in fact present us with a general scarcity. Nicholas Georgescu-Roegen has pointed out that "any use of natural resources for the satisfaction of nonvital needs means a smaller quantity of life in the future."[2]

Standard economic textbooks have defined economics as the study of the allocation of scarce means among competing ends. We may begin with a reconsideration of these ends and means as the starting point of a paradigm shift in economics toward a steady-state economy.

Humanity's ultimate economic concern is to use ultimate means in the service of ultimate ends. The ultimate end is that which is intrinsically good, while the ultimate means is all of the "useful stuff" in the world, i.e., low-entropy matter-energy. All intermediate categories are ends with respect to lower categories, and means with respect to higher categories. The intermediate ends that can serve as means to the ultimate end include health, education, etc., while intermediate means are the physical stocks, "which can be viewed as ends directly served by the use of ultimate means (the entropic flow of matter-energy, the *throughput*)."[9] The discipline of political economy corresponds to the progression from intermediate means to intermediate ends, while ethics and religion are concerned with achieving ultimate ends. Thus far economics has not dealt sufficiently with either ultimate means or ultimate ends.

Economic growth implies the creation of "ever more intermediate means (stocks) for the purpose of satisfying ever more intermediate ends."[10] The unlimited availability of ultimate means to satisfy the ever-growing demand for intermediate means is never questioned because it is believed that technology can continuously substitute new resources for old ones. It is likewise believed that intermediate means are only scarce because the human capacity to transform ultimate means to intermediate means has not yet reached its full potential. Orthodox economists also view people's intermediate ends as increasing continuously, unconstrained by ultimate ends. From this perspective, then, economic growth is justified and expected to go on forever.

However, economics needs to consider intermediate ends and means in the context of ultimate ends and means. The finiteness of the ultimate means must limit the *possibility* of growth, while competition among ends will limit the *desirability* of growth, and these factors together provide an *economic* limit to growth. A new economics should ask how to use ultimate means to best serve the ultimate end, while viewing the ultimate means in the context of the entropy law and ecology, and the ultimate ends with a "concern for future generations and subhuman life and inequities in current wealth distribution."[11]

The Steady-State Economy

To put our discussion of a steady-state economy in the proper context, it is necessary to consider the quantitative and qualitative differences between rich and poor countries. The ratio of gross national product (GNP) to total population is the measure used most often to distinguish between rich and poor.

Quantitatively, the rate of growth in population is much higher in poorer countries than in rich ones, and the fertility in poor nations is roughly twice that of the rich. Fertility rate is the most consistent index for dividing rich from poor countries. Qualitatively, the incremental population in poor countries tends to be among hungry illiterates. Moreover, each incremental person contributes negligibly to production, but also makes only minimal demands on world resources. In rich countries the incremental population consists mostly of well-fed members of the middle class; each incremental person contributes substantially to GNP and at the same time puts a more severe strain on world resources.

Quantitatively, GNP has grown 4–5% per year in both rich and poor countries, but because poor countries have more population, their per capita growth is much slower. The incremental GNP of rich and poor countries finds qualitative significance in two economic laws: (1) the law of diminishing marginal utility; and (2) the law of increasing marginal cost. The first law states that people act to satisfy their most pressing needs first, and units of income spent afterward satisfy less pressing needs. The second refers to the actions of producers, who use the best quality and combinations of factors of production first and only substitute with lesser ones when they run out of the best. When applied to GNP, the first law suggests that the marginal benefits of increasing output are decreasing, while the second indicates that the marginal costs are increasing.

These laws imply that at some point an extra unit of GNP will cost more than it is worth. This may already be the case in richer countries such as the United States, where growth now means more electric toothbrushes and other luxury items. In poorer countries, however, growth still means more food, clothing, shelter, etc. Thus economic growth should still be advocated in poor countries, but not in the rich ones. Population growth should, however, be discouraged for both.

The Nature and Necessity of the Stationary State

The concept of a stationary (steady) state can be traced to the great classical economist John Stuart Mill, who said that "at the end of what they term the progressive state lies the stationary state, that all progress in wealth is but a postponement of this, and that each step in advance is an approach to it."[3] A steady state means a constant stock of physical wealth (capital) and a constant population. Low throughput rates are also necessary. This means lowering both production and consumption for stocks of wealth, and lowering both the birth rate and the death rate for population stocks. High throughput rates are impracticable because they take more production inputs from the earth and deposit more harmful wastes to it. To maintain low throughput rates it is necessary to focus on both the size and the durability of stocks. Durability of stocks raises not only the question of how long something will last, but also how well it can be recycled (keeping in mind that the entropy law prohibits 100% recycling).

The classical economists expected depletion limits to make the steady state necessary, but in fact the pollution limits seem to be more important. Limits on the pollution side have so far received little attention, however, because while depletion costs are private, pollution costs are social. Air and water are assumed to be free to all and, as Garrett Hardin has pointed out, they are therefore exploited. Of all of the paradigms discussed above, only the Physiocrats emphasized human dependence on the earth. Economics should return to that basic notion.

Economic and Social Implications of the Steady State

The economic and social implications of a steady state are fundamentally different from the neoclassical model, and thus require revolutionary change. "The physical flows of production and consumption must be *minimized, not maximized* subject to some desirable population and standard of living."[21] In addition, the central concept should be the stock of wealth, which must be kept constant, rather than the flow of income and consumption. If production flows are kept low, then the focus of economics will be on the distribution of the stock of wealth, rather than on the distribution of the flows of income.

An interesting analogy can be drawn from the concept of ecological succession to illustrate this point. Young ecosystems have a high production efficiency, while mature ones have a high maintenance efficiency. For a given stock, young ecosystems maximize production flow, while mature ones minimize it. Similarly, if physical stocks are held constant, then in economics "growth must be in nonphysical goods: service and leisure."[22] The price of material-intensive goods and activities should increase relative to that for time-intensive ones. The benefits of technological progress should therefore be in the form of increased leisure as opposed to increased production of goods. Bertrand Russell was a proponent of this approach and expressed it through the hypothetical example of pins. If it takes a certain number of workers eight hours a day to manufacture enough pins for the entire world, and someone then invents a method for making twice as many pins in the same time, then in today's world we would go on working the same amount of time and produce too many pins. In a steady state, however, the world would continue to produce the same amount of pins, but in half the time.

Economic growth continues to be justified on the grounds that it is necessary to maintain full employment to facilitate the "income-through-jobs-ethic of distribution," and because it "takes the edge off of distributional conflicts."[23] If everyone's income is increasing, then there is less tendency to fight over relative shares. However, if we maintain constant physical stocks and utilize technology to create leisure, then "full employment and income-through-jobs are no longer workable mechanisms for distribution."[24] We should therefore try to identify and create institutions that will be able to facilitate keeping stocks of wealth and people constant, while infringing as little as possible on individual freedom.

An Emerging Political Economy of Finite Wants and Nongrowth

The requirement for economic growth has also been linked to the assumption of infinite wants. This is manifest in the definition of GNP, where growth is the "satisfaction of ever more trivial wants while simultaneously creating ever more powerful externalities which destroy ever more important environmental amenities."[25–26] Keynes stated, however, that wants should be separated into two classes: absolute needs and needs that make us feel superior to other humans. Keynes thought that the latter category of wants may be insatiable, but with respect to absolute needs, "a point may soon be reached, much sooner perhaps than we are all of us aware of, when those needs are satisfied in the sense that we prefer to devote our further energies to noneconomic purposes."[4] A steady-state economy focuses on the satisfaction of these absolute needs. Regarding those needs reflecting a desire for superiority over our fellows, we should ask, as the prophet Isaiah did, "Is there not a lie in my right hand?"(Isaiah 44: 14–20)

Notes

1. Robert Solow, "The Economics of Resources or the Resources of Economics," *American Economic Review* (May 1974), 11, cited by Daly, 7.

2. Nicholas Georgescu-Roegen, *The Entropy Law and the Economic Process* (Cambridge, Massachusetts: Harvard University Press, 1971), 21; cited by Daly, 7.

3. J.S. Mill, *Principles of Political Economy, Vol. II* (London: John W. Parker, 1857), 320–21; cited by Daly, 14.

4. J.M. Keynes, "Economic Possibilities for Our Grandchildren," in *Essays in Persuasion* (New York: Norton, 1963); cited by Daly, 27.

Summary of

Allocation, Distribution, and Scale: Towards an Economics That Is Efficient, Just, and Sustainable

by Herman E. Daly

[Published in *Ecological Economics* 6 (December 1992): 185–193. Reprinted with kind permission from Elsevier B.V., Amsterdam, The Netherlands.]

The three basic goals of an economic system must be efficient allocation, equitable distribution, and sustainable scale. The first two have a long history in economic theory, and specific independent policy instruments have been developed for their realization. However, scale has not been formally recognized in economic theory, and no corresponding policy instrument has been developed. In practice, however, where real problems must be acknowledged and addressed, scale has implicitly been recognized as a separate and distinct area of concern. This has occurred especially in the practice of issuing tradeable permits for resource depletion and pollution rights.

The basic definitions of the three goals and their policy mechanisms are as follows:

(1) *Allocation:* This entails the channeling of society's scarce resources to their alternative productive uses. An allocation is considered efficient when resource distribution satisfies material needs in conformity with individual preferences, as weighted by the ability to pay. The policy instrument that produces this outcome is the price mechanism of competitive markets.

(2) *Distribution:* This is the division of final goods and services. A good distribution is one that is considered just or fair, i.e., one in which the degree of inequality is confined within an acceptable range. The policy instruments used to achieve this goal are transfers, such as taxes and welfare payments.

(3) *Scale:* Scale is the "physical volume of the throughput, the flow of matter-energy from the environment as low-entropy raw materials, and back to the environment as high-entropy wastes . . . It is measured in absolute physical units, but its significance is relative to the natural capacities of the ecosystem to regenerate the inputs and absorb the waste outputs on a sustainable basis."[186] Though scale is usually measured in monetary terms (e.g., per capita resource use), throughput might better be measured in terms of embodied energy, and the economy viewed as an open subsystem of the larger, but finite, closed, nongrowing ecosystem. Thus the scale of an economy becomes significant relative to the fixed size of the ecosystem, and it can be considered sustainable if it is not eroding the carrying capacity of the ecosystem. Sustainability is an important characteristic of the optimal scale. We may very generally define the optimal scale as that sustainable scale at which the combined services of both human-made and natural capital are as great as possible.

Standard economic theory has neglected the importance of scale in two opposite ways. First, it has assumed that environmental resources and sinks are infinite relative to the scale of the economy. Second, it has assumed that nature is just one more sector in the economy and that allocative decisions merely move natural resources between alternative uses. Consequently, scale is not seen as a constraint, and policies continue to encourage growth, producing demands on the ecosystem that are increasingly serious and unsustainable. Thus there is a need for a separate policy instrument to control scale.

The usual way of dealing with scale is to subsume it under allocation; i.e., get the prices right and you are assured of an efficient allocation of resources. If productive facilities tend toward larger scales, it is assumed that this merely reflects efficient individual evaluations that the marginal benefits of scale exceed the marginal costs to the environment. Of course, these individual determinations may be biased by externalities, but the "right prices" ought to have internalized those external costs.

In practice, nature is excluded from the world of commodities whose value, or opportunity costs, are measured by market prices. As a result, marginal ecosystem services sacrificed for increased production are not adequately balanced against the marginal social benefit of larger population or greater per capita resource use. Traditionally it has been assumed that by imputing "shadow prices" for these hidden costs a reasonable assessment of opportunity costs can be made. This, however, requires heroic assumptions about our capacity to quantify the costs to the ecosystem; "discontinuities, thresholds and complex webs of interdependence make a mockery of the idea that we can nicely balance smoothly increasing ecosystem costs with the diminishing marginal utility of production at the macro level."[190]

The plain truth is that among the three parameters, allocation is the only one that *can* be satisfactorily resolved through the price mechanism. "Distribution and scale involve relationships with the poor, the future, and other species that are fundamentally social in nature rather than individual."[190] Prices that may reveal the opportunity cost of reallocation are irrelevant to measures of the opportunity costs of redistribution or of changes in scale. These are parameters that are subject to ethical judgments and are not reducible to a simple willingness to pay criterion. Pretending that these social choices exist on the same moral plane as the choice between chewing gum and shoelaces "seems to be dominant in economics today and is a part of the retrograde modern reduction of all ethical choice to the level of personal tastes weighted by income."[191]

Economists today correctly keep distribution and allocation quite separate, and the same must be done for scale issues as well. We may use "the life-saving metaphor of the Plimsoll line on a boat. In loading a boat we also have the problems of allocation and scale—allocating or balancing the load is one problem (a microeconomic problem), and not overloading even a well-balanced boat is another problem (a macroeconomic problem). . . Economists who are obsessed with allocation to the exclusion of scale really deserve the environmentalists' criticism that they are busy rearranging deck chairs on the *Titanic*."[191–92]

Some economists (Norgaard and Howarth) have recently endeavored to subsume scale under distribution by focusing on future generations. A sustainable scale is determined by an intergenerational distribution of the resource base that is fair to those in the future. Thus, through intertemporal discounting we may efficiently provide for the future. Apart from the numerous difficulties with assessing a "discount rate" for the future that will truly produce a just intergenerational distribution, the question of optimal scale is complex and goes beyond merely being able to pass on a sustainable system to the future. For example, the scale of human activities can become too large for the present, resulting in the destruction of nonessential species and habitats, and yet through rigorous and costly management this oversized economy may be sustainably passed to the future. "For this reason scale cannot be totally subsumed under distribution, although it must be admitted that scale issues do overlap with one part of distribution, the intergenerational part, to a considerable degree."[193]

The best policy is to treat the three goals independently. One example of such a policy is the use of tradeable pollution permits. In practice, this policy would require the following steps:

(1) Creation of a limited number of rights to pollute in which the total level of pollution is limited to the absorption capacity of the airshed and watershed and is thus sustainable. Far from ignoring scale, this policy requires us to deal with this issue at the outset.

(2) Distribution of these rights to different people—i.e., to citizens or firms directly, or perhaps to a public body that can auction or sell them to individuals.

(3) Reallocation of the permits among individuals through markets in the interest of efficiency after the scale and distributional issue is settled by the first two steps. This separation of allocation and scale requires the number of permits to be fixed, but the price must be allowed to vary. In this system, environmental costs will be borne by those firms responsible for the generation of pollution that will be willing to purchase the permits if it is profitable and efficient to do so. Those firms unwilling to pay to buy the permit will have to develop sustainable methods of production.

In this example, both scale and distribution are determined by a social decision, not prices. These scarce rights, subject to socially determined limits, are then allocated efficiently through trading. "If operationality (the congruence of abstract concepts with policy instruments) is a criterion for judging theories, then the theoretical separation of scale and allocation advocated here is superior to the neoclassical approach of lumping them together, because the latter requires nonoperational assumptions to save appearances of methodological individualism, while the former is already being accepted in the practical policy of tradeable permits."[193]

Summary of

The Economic Growth Debate: What Some Economists Have Learned but Many Have Not
by Herman E. Daly

[Published in *Journal of Environmental Economics and Management* 14 (December 1987): 323–336.]

It is important to differentiate between the terms *growth* and *development*. *Growth* is a "quantitative increase in the scale of the physical dimensions of the economy; i.e., the rate of flow of matter and energy through the economy (from environment as raw material and back to the environment as waste), and the stock of human bodies and artifacts."[323] *Development* is the "qualitative improvement in the structure, design, and composition of physical stocks and flows, that result from greater knowledge, both of technique *and of purpose.*"[323] An economy can experience development without growth; just as the ecosystem has developed but not actually grown, so can an economy.

On a finite earth there are biophysical and ethicosocial limits to the growth of aggregate output, but there may not be any limits to development. Neoclassical economics assumes, however, that it is biophysically possible and socioethically desirable for aggregate output to grow. This article discusses the biophysical and socioethical limits to growth and the associated welfare losses when these limits are reached.

Biophysical Limits

The economy is a subsystem of a larger, finite ecosystem in which low-entropy raw materials are extracted and high-entropy waste is absorbed. The growth of the subsystem is limited by the size of the overall ecosystem, by the amount of low-entropy raw materials available, by the ability of the larger system to absorb high-entropy waste, and by "the intricate ecological connections which are more easily disrupted as the scale of the economic subsystem grows relative to the total ecosystem."[324] These biophysical limits are interrelated. The finite nature of the larger subsystem would not be an issue if everything could be recycled; however, entropy makes complete recycling impossible. If sinks for high-entropy waste and sources of low-entropy raw materials were infinite, then there would not be an entropy problem; however, "the fact that both are finite, plus the entropy law, means that the ordered structures of the economic subsystem are maintained at the expense of creating a more than offsetting amount of disorder in the rest of the system."[324]

Time and space must also be counted as finite and limited. Tasks or processes (e.g., production, consumption, resource regeneration, and recycling) that can be completed in one time frame may be impossible in another. Linder has shown that the relative price of time in terms of goods has increased because the productivity of labor time has also increased. We then assume that the marginal return on nonwork time should equal the higher productivity of work time, but the congestion of time that results may cause a total welfare decline even as economic welfare increases.

In former peasant economies, the primary source of low entropy was the sun, but modern economies rely on terrestrial ecosystems. However, dependence on energy supplied through terrestrial ecosystems "interferes with the life support services rendered to the economy by other species and by natural biogeochemical cycles"[324–325] and should therefore be counted as a cost to growth. This reliance on terrestrial ecosystems has resulted in both the "drawdown" of mineral stocks and the "takeover"' of the habitats of other species, as suggested by W. Catton. In fact, present growth is based on drawdown.

The laws of thermodynamics are central to the concept of biophysical limits on economic growth. The First Law of Thermodynamics, which states that matter can not be created or destroyed, has been respected in modern economics, as production functions are required to respect this materials balance constraint. However, the Second Law (the entropy law) is not widely understood. "The rearrangement of matter is the central physical fact about the economic process,"[326] and the capacity to rearrange this matter has been termed low entropy, which is easier to rearrange than high entropy. The Second Law of Thermodynamics shows that low entropy is transformed to high entropy during economic rearrangement. Economists have applied their notions of the circular flow of money to flows of matter and energy, but this is incorrect, as the Second Law indicates that the flow of matter/energy is linear. Low entropy is extracted, used, and goes back to the environment as high-entropy pollution.

It is becoming evident that we are approaching these biophysical limits. The Global 2000 report to the President of the United States stated that by the end of the next century we will be approaching a population of 30 billion people, which is estimated to be close to the maximum carrying capacity of the earth. In addition, the per capita production of forests, fisheries, etc. has peaked and even begun to decline. Finally, as a result of the takeover of the habitats of other species, the total number of species is predicted to decrease 20% by the year 2000.

Ethicosocial Limits

Independent of whether or not biophysical limits have been reached, there are four socioethical reasons why growth may not be desirable. They are presented in the following subsections.

Limits to Drawdown

We have a moral obligation to future generations that should limit present growth. Future generations will not have access to the minerals and biological gene pools that are used up by present generations. The basic needs of the present should always come first, but luxuries of the present generation should not. Future generations cannot act in present markets, so our present economic actions should show a moral concern for the future.

Talbot Page has outlined individualistic and collective expressions of these moral concerns for the future. Individualistic concern for the future has been expressed by the discount rate, in which present individuals consider the welfare of future generations. Collective concern is manifest in an empathy for future generations similar to the Rawlsian concept of a "veil of ignorance." In this approach, fairness is achieved because the generation making a choice does not know where in the temporal sequence it lies. The collective concern approach protects future generations more effectively than the individualistic approach (using the discount rate) because the latter is still only limited by the preferences of the present generation.

It has been difficult for humans to include future generations within our moral horizon because we tend to lose the concept of "ours" after great grandchildren. Beyond this, future people are seen as a social product rather than an individual one, and responsibility for them must be effected through collective action. In the end, "present claims should dominate future claims only up to some level of resource use that is sufficient for a good life for a population that is sustainable at that level."[329]

Limits to Takeover

Economic growth requires more space for more stocks of more people and artifacts, and for more sources of raw materials and more sinks to absorb waste. However, it is evident that other species have instrumental value to our economy, and these species need space. On a finite planet the needs for space present an instrumental limit to the amount of takeover. Another limit to takeover comes from the intrinsic value of these other species, regarded as sentient beings whose own "utility" should be taken into account. These claims of intrinsic worth should represent a limit of some kind, although this limit is difficult to calculate. The limits to drawdown are also relevant here because takeover of habitat and extinction are irreversible acts—i.e., a drawdown—and thus represent a cost to future generations.

Limits from the Self-Canceling Effects of Aggregate Growth

Aggregate economic growth may not always mean an increase in social welfare. The Easterlin Paradox questions the supposition that there is a positive correlation between income and happiness: "a larger percentage of rich people rated themselves as 'very happy' than did poor people—just as everyone would expect. But for different countries with very different income levels the differences in reported happiness are small."[331] In view of this, there are four cases that illustrate the self-canceling effects of aggregate growth. First, happiness is a function of relative income, but everyone's relative income cannot increase; aggregate growth therefore has a self-canceling effect. Second, happiness is often a response to a temporary adjustment to a higher income; unhappiness may then be the reverse. Third, as we become goods-rich, we also become time-poor because of the increasing productivity of labor time, so we are less able to afford time-intensive activities. Finally, it has been shown that as growth increases, satisfaction from work decreases. "The implication of these self-canceling effects is that growth is less important for human welfare than we have heretofore thought."[333]

Depletion of Moral Capital as a Limit to Growth

Adam Smith argued that in addition to the restraining hand of competition, individuals in pursuit of their own self-interest would not harm the community because of restraints on behavior derived from shared morals, religion, custom, and education. However, this is contrary to or forgotten in the modern concept of growth. The idea that a type of economic action should not be carried out because of moral constraints is considered "subversive." Theists E.J. Mishan and C.S. Lewis pointed out that our pursuit of the advancement of science has left these moral considerations out of the supply side, to the extent that "scientific materialism and cultural relativism actively undercut belief in a transcendental basis for ethical value, which undercuts moral consensus, which undercuts the minimum moral restraint on self-interest presupposed by Adam Smith and most of his followers."[334] In addition, as Mishan has pointed out, common morality has become fragmented, so it is difficult to argue in favor of underlying morals, and they are therefore scrapped. On the demand side, "the glorification of self-interest and the pursuit of 'infinite wants' leads to a weakening of moral distinctions between luxury and necessity."[335] Moreover, moral constraints on demand are inconvenient in an economy based on growth, so the growth economy leads to the erosion of the very values upon which it is based.

Summary of

The Economics of the Coming Spaceship Earth

by Kenneth E. Boulding

[Published in *Environmental Quality in a Growing Economy,* ed. Henry Jarrett
(Baltimore: published for Resources for the Future, Inc. by The Johns Hopkins Press,
1966), 3–14, © Resources for the Future; reprinted in *Valuing the Earth: Economics,
Ecology, Ethics,* eds. Herman E. Daly and Kenneth N. Townsend (Cambridge,
Massachusetts and London: The MIT Press, 1993.)]

Throughout the ages, man's image of his environment has always been tempered by the existence of an inexhaustible frontier somewhere beyond the known world, an illimitable plane in which respite could be found once one's immediate surroundings deteriorated socially or environmentally. More recently, man has had to become accustomed to the notion of a finite earth and a closed sphere of human activity. However, it was not until World War II and the air age that the global nature of our lives really entered the popular imagination, and in the intervening period we have not entirely come to terms with this transition from the illimitable plane to the closed sphere. Economists in particular have failed to come to grips with the ultimate consequences of this transition.

Humankind is, in fact, quite unfamiliar with closed systems. Almost by definition, an entirely closed system would be unknowable unless we are participants in it. Overwhelmingly it is open systems, structures maintained in the midst of a throughput from inputs to outputs, with which we are familiar. Indeed, human life itself is an open system. We must receive inputs of air, water, and food and give off outputs of effluvia and excrement. Human societies have likewise been open, drawing upon inputs from the earth, the atmosphere, and the waters, and depositing wastes into the same. If there is an infinite capacity to draw upon these inputs and dispose of the outputs in perpetuity, then such an open system can survive indefinitely.

The world economy or "econosphere" is still an open system with respect to three important classes of inputs: matter, energy, and information. For example, materials pass from the non-economic into the economic sphere as they are utilized to produce goods, then pass back into the non-economic arena as they lose their usefulness and are discarded. With respect to the energy system, the econosphere utilizes inputs of available energy in the form of water power, fossil fuels, sunlight, etc. Water and solar power can be viewed as a kind of energy income, while fossil fuels represent a capital stock of stored-up sunshine. Relatively few activities can be based on the available energy income, and so in the advanced societies energy use has been heavily supplemented by the use of fossil fuels, i.e., by dipping into the capital stock. By so doing, we have been able to maintain a vastly larger energy input into the system. However, this supplementary input is, by its very nature, exhaustible. Finally, from the human perspective, information is the most important of the three systems; it is only through knowledge that matter acquires significance and enters the econosphere. Technology is knowledge that has been accumulated and embodied in capital, and this accumulation is the key to human development of all kinds.

Loosely formulated, the concept of entropy can be applied to these systems. In the material system, there are entropic processes that take concentrated materials and diffuse them over the earth's oceans and through the atmosphere. There are also anti-entropic processes, whereby diffuse matter is gathered and concentrated. Since there is no law of increasing material entropy, it is possible to go on concentrating material elements given sufficient energy inputs.

In the energy system, however, there is no escape from the grim Second Law of Thermodynamics. If there were no energy inputs into the earth, developmental processes would be impossible. Moreover, the energy inputs that we extract from the earth are strictly limited. Even the most optimistic estimates suggest that, at current levels of usage, readily available supplies of fossil fuel will be exhausted within several centuries. This rate of use will accelerate with population growth and as other nations begin to approach the levels of energy consumption seen in the United States. Nuclear technologies have not fundamentally changed this picture, as the supplies of fissionable materials remain limited. If fusion should become technically feasible, then the picture would be significantly altered and our time horizon would extend to the point that we would essentially have an open system. Failing this, however, the time when man will be forced once more to rely entirely upon the current energy from the sun is not too far distant.

The closed earth of the future requires economic principles that are entirely different from the open "cowboy" economy of the past, principles best embodied in the imagery of a "spaceman" economy, in which the earth has become a spaceship. In the spaceship we are profoundly aware of both the limited resources available and the limited reservoirs for waste disposal. We must develop a cyclical ecological system that is capable of continuous reproduction of material, in which success is not quantitatively measured in terms of throughput and consumption, but rather is a measure of the nature, extent, quality, and complexity of the total capital stock. "In the spaceman economy, what we are primarily concerned with is stock maintenance, and any technological change which results in the maintenance of a given total stock with a lessened throughput (that is, less production and consumption) is clearly a gain."[259]

This notion that production and consumption are, in fact, bad things is a difficult one for economists who have been obsessed with income-flow concepts to the virtual exclusion of capital-stock concepts. There are indeed tricky and unsolved problems in this issue of whether human welfare is best captured in stock or flow measurements. Is it, for example, eating that is most important, or being well fed? The stock concept is actually the more fundamental one. If it is true that we eat primarily to maintain a condition of being well fed, then the less we can eat to maintain that condition, the better off we shall be. Of course, we can not exclude the possibility that there is also a value in the eating (or producing) in and of itself.

Perhaps we ought not concern ourselves with these questions. The space-man economy might well be a long way off. We could spend, pollute, and extract, go on increasing GNP, and leave these future problems to the future. When problems arise in the future, with respect to scarcity of resources or pollutable reservoirs, the needs of the then present will determine the solutions of the then present. This approach, which leaves to posterity the onus for resolving these issues, can be a difficult one to refute. After all, what can one say to the man who says "what has posterity ever done for me?"

Conservationists must fall back upon vague ethical arguments and principles that rely upon an identification with a larger community, one that extends not only back in time but also into the future. With this in mind, it is important to stress that the welfare of the individual depends in large part upon the extent to which he can identify himself with others in a community, both spatially and over time. Once that identification is secure, then posterity does have a voice in the present. Moreover, it must be stressed that the shadow of the future falls heavily upon us today. This fact is most evident with respect to pollution. Thus it is not only for posterity's sake that we must change our approach.

All of these problems are large scale and may not seem immediate, but our success in dealing with the big problems is not unrelated to our ability to confront the more immediate, less difficult ones. One can only hope that the succession of smaller, immediate crises will, in mobilizing support for solutions to those problems, lead to an appreciation of, and perhaps solutions to, the larger, more intractable problems.

Summary of

Steady-State Economies and the Command Economy

by Kenneth N. Townsend

[Published in *Valuing the Earth: Economics, Ecology, Ethics,* eds. Herman E. Daly and Kenneth N. Townsend (Cambridge, Massachusetts and London: The MIT Press, 1993), 275–296.]

One of the legacies of the centrally planned economies throughout Eastern Europe, the former USSR, and China is the advanced state of environmental deterioration. Lopsided investment in heavy industrialization with little regard for the environment has produced rising morbidity and mortality rates throughout the East. The deceptively green landscape is "contaminated with heavy metals, radioactive fallout, and incredibly high levels of deposits of the oxides of sulfur and nitrogen from the smokestacks of industry. In many command economies water is so polluted that it is often unfit even for industrial cooling applications, and air is so foul that school children must periodically be removed from their homes to more hospitable climes to cleanse their lungs of airborne contaminants. Destruction of the environment points to a critical failure of communism."[276]

Environmental Protection in a Command Economy

The historical emphasis on growth in modern society has led to attempts by humans to control the natural environment so as to yield a higher continuous output than is provided in a state of nature. The Russian mineralogist Vladimir Vernadsky's monumental work, *The Biosphere* (1926), was a recognition that the growth in the scale of human activity would have dangerous consequences for the biosphere and would run up against limits imposed by the finite availability of low-entropy materials and energy. He believed that people must collectively organize and transform the biosphere into a rationally managed system to meet not only their material needs but their aesthetic and spiritual needs as well; this system he called the *noosphere*. This idea is similar to that found in Marxist thought where, once property has been socialized, man "for the first time becomes the real, conscious lord of Nature, because he has now become master of his own social organization."[1]

It is these thoughts that form the foundation of Eastern environmental philosophy. While in the West an ideal environment is pictured as a pristine natural environment, in the East it is seen as rational, ordered structures imposed on the character of nature by human effort. In spite of Vernadsky's prominence during the formative years in the development of the command economy in the East, the type of development pursued in these economies seems to have been little affected by his insight that human growth and activity must be organized on a scale that is compatible with constraints imposed by the biosphere. Thus large-scale projects that fundamentally alter the environment to better suit human needs have been pursued with striking disregard for environmental limits. Attempts to reverse the flow of rivers or drain the Aral Sea for irrigation stand as catastrophic examples of this "rational approach."

In theory, environmental degradation should not have occurred under communism. Marxist–Leninist doctrine held that such problems arise only within a capitalist organization of the means of production. Problems of market failure—for example, when an individual bears only a fraction of an environmental cost of his or her activity by disposing of harmful wastes in the "commons"—should be rendered moot once all property is commonly held and production is managed by the state, since the state will have to bear these external costs as well.

The state's role as the bearer and enforcer of all social cost remained a theoretical one. In reality, overwhelming emphasis in the planning process was placed upon growth. The state "did not wish to slow itself down with anything as mundane as environmental cost, especially when natural resources are in Marxist theory supposed to be free."[281] This perception of costless resources was buttressed by the vastness of the endowment and the sheer size of the environment available as a waste dump in such places as the USSR and China. Thus, the levels of industrial growth achieved in both countries significantly raised the material standard of living, but at a tremendous environmental cost.

In the 1970s, scholars such as Soviet economist V. Alekseev recognized, as Vernadsky had fifty years earlier, that there were limits to growth that even socialism could not overcome. Nevertheless the system of central planning failed to produce policies that substantially reduce the damage being inflicted upon the biosphere. The five-year plans invariably emphasized heavy industrialization, in which large-scale plant design coupled with energy inefficiency produced intense pollution of the immediate environment. Modern enterprises in the Eastern Bloc and China exhibit some of the highest levels of energy use and pollution per unit of GNP in the world. A survey of environmental conditions in the former and present command economies reveals a pattern of advanced ecological deterioration that is a testimony to the irresponsible attempts to dominate nature under communism.

Achieving a Steady State in Eastern Economies

"Marx, Engels, Lenin, and Mao all shared the honorable vision of improving the human condition in advocating a communistic economy. Unlike Vernadsky, however, they shared a preanalytic vision of the world in which the human economy would not likely exhaust the spontaneous gifts of nature."[290] In large measure, the capitalist societies share this preanalytic vision of infinite sources and sinks. Relatively more efficient capitalist economies have been able to get away with this faulty vision for longer, while command economies, with their production and pollution inefficiencies, have collapsed.

One danger is that the East will think that a market system will solve its problems and permit permanent growth on an ever-expanding scale. Instead, policies that will result in the creation of steady-state economies must be advocated. This will involve limiting the throughput of resources used in production to levels commensurate with both sustainability and achievement of reasonable living standards. This is best achieved by allowing maximum individual choice through microvariability in resource allocations made within a "mutually coerced, mutually agreed upon" set of total limits on production and pollution. For example, marketable resource use permits or pollution permits could be used, as opposed to more cumbersome command and control procedures. Limiting births through a system of marketable permits may reduce environmental stresses as well.

Unlimited economic growth is not possible in a biosphere with limited capacity both to yield material and energy resources and to absorb economic wastes. Whatever regulations are ultimately used, it is important to recognize the need to reconsider the efficacy of growth for its own sake. Attempts should instead be made to develop the economy by improving the efficiency with which existing levels of stocks of physical capital yield utility for consumers. "Sooner or later, . . . the economies of the world must achieve a rational, ordered noosphere in which the hallmark of the economy is development, not growth."[293]

Note

1. Frederick Engels, *Socialism, Utopian and Scientific*, ed. John E. Elliot (Santa Monica, California: Goodyear, 1981), 479-80; cited by Townsend, 277.

Summary of

Allocation, Distribution, and Scale as Determinants of Environmental Degradation: Case Studies of Haiti, El Salvador, and Costa Rica

by George Foy and Herman E. Daly

[Published in World Bank Environment Department Working Paper No. 19, 1989, and reprinted in *Environmental Economics*, eds. Anil Markandya and Julie Richardson (London: Earthscan Publications Ltd., 1992), 294–315.]

(Editor's note: The original article classifies and evaluates environmental problems in three Latin American countries: Haiti, El Salvador, and Costa Rica. This summary only includes Haiti because of the similarity in both methodology and content of the three examples.)

Three related, but conceptually distinct causes of environmental problems are considered here in evaluating the environmental problems of Haiti: allocation, distribution, and scale.

Concepts and Theory

The satisfaction of all human wants is ultimately derived from the environment, either directly or indirectly. Economic development has historically been characterized by a shift from direct to indirect use of the environment. Environmental problems are defined as any degradation in the assimilative and regenerative capacities of the environment. This degradation may occur due to reasons of allocation, distribution, or scale.

Allocation refers to the flow of resources among alternative uses. Allocations are said to be optimal or efficient when prices of resources reflect their marginal opportunity costs. Misallocations of resources may occur due to government actions or market failures. Problems of misallocation are solved by encouraging policies that breed competition rather than rent seeking, and by developing institutions that define property rights in public goods settings.

Distribution refers to the division of output among individuals or families. Distributions may be categorized as just or unjust in an ethical sense, and as skewed or even in a statistical sense. Maldistribution of resources in an economy limits people's options and their participation in the political process, which may result in environmental problems.

Scale, which is a macro-level concept, refers to the total flow of resources through the economic subsystem, beginning with depletion of resources and ending with pollution. Scale depends on the population and the per capita resource use in an economy. The most important aspect of scale for an economy is whether it is sustainable or not. Sustainability depends on both the physical scale of the economy and the physical capacities of the environment.

It is important to clarify the distinction between allocation and scale: allocation decisions are micro in nature, and scale issues are macro. The primary reason for allocative efficiency is to maximize the present value of wealth of an economy, while the primary reason for scale criteria is to ensure the sustainability of the economy within environmental limits. Allocative decisions depend on prices, whereas scale decisions depend on ecological criteria. Efficient allocation of resources does not ensure optimal scale of the economy.

Case Study I: Haiti

The case study is divided into five subsections:

(1) key environmental problems;

(2) scale of resource use as a cause of environmental problems;

(3) allocative causes of environmental problems;

(4) distributional causes of environmental problems; and

(5) recommendations.

Key Environmental Problems

Haiti's foremost environmental problems are deforestation and soil erosion. Only 7–9% of forest cover remained in 1979 in a country that was once completely covered by forests. While only 29% of the land is considered suitable for cultivation, 49% is actually cultivated. The depletion of forests has led to soil erosion, and deforestation and soil erosion together have resulted in declining agricultural productivity, increasing urban flooding, rural-to-urban migration, and loss of wood, a primary source of energy.

Scale of Resource Use as a Cause of Environmental Problems

Population increases are the primary cause of pressure on the land in Haiti and are therefore responsible for soil erosion, especially because the fallow period when secondary vegetation and soils can regenerate has been drastically shortened. Haiti attempted to ameliorate its population pressures by encouraging emigration in the late 1970s, but recent policy changes in receiving countries have reduced the level of emigration. Per capita resource use is not high in Haiti, and it does not contribute substantially to the increasing scale of the economy. Population control is a prerequisite for Haiti to develop sustainably.

Allocative Causes of Environmental Problems

There are a number of reasons for misallocation of resources in the Haitian economy, including:

(1) There is inadequate expertise and personnel in both forestry and soil and water conservation.

(2) The government has imposed taxes on coffee exports and import restrictions on staple foods, resulting in a move away from coffee production to the production of staple foods. The local currency has also been artificially overvalued, thus discouraging export crops. Perennial coffee trees hold soil better than staple food crops, so soil erosion is an uncounted environmental cost of these government policies.

(3) There is no mechanism for arranging mutually beneficial trades between those who cause soil erosion (uphill farmers) and those who suffer from soil erosion (lowland farmers and urban dwellers).

(4) Lack of access to institutional credit markets for the majority of people makes investing in increased agricultural productivity difficult. Widespread tenant farming also reduces the incentives for making long-term improvements in land, such as reforestation and soil conservation.

(5) There is only a nominal tax on the collection of wood for energy needs in those areas where forests still exist. The low private costs of harvesting wood therefore provide a disincentive for forestry management and establishing plantations. Haitian energy policy is generally not designed to consider environmental impacts and trade-offs.

Distributional Causes of Environmental Problems

Widespread corruption has resulted in patronage and transfer of public resources to a privileged minority at below-market prices. Corruption and abuse of power have led to a fear of state confiscation of lands from farmers—a major disincentive to invest in agricultural or environmental improvements. The inequitable distribution of land also means that vast numbers of people depend on marginal lands, which causes soil erosion. However, the pressure on land is due more to the scale of the economy than to maldistribution.

Recommendations

Population control must be the centerpiece of any Haitian resource policy. If it is not, anything Haiti does will only delay disaster. In addition, a massive analysis of land use and degradation should be undertaken and used as a basis to recommend suitable land management policies in the context of economic and social policy. Watershed reforestation and hydroelectric planning should also be integrated into a coordinated strategy. Given the political realities, bilateral and multilateral aid agencies should include non-governmental organizations in order to promote sustainable development and poverty alleviation policies.

Summary of

On Economics as a Life Science
by Herman E. Daly

[Published in *Journal of Political Economy* 76 (May/June 1968): 392–406, and in *Valuing the Earth: Economics, Ecology, Ethics*, eds. Herman E. Daly and Kenneth N. Townsend (Cambridge, Massachusetts and London: The MIT Press, 1993).]

This article brings out the analogies between economics and biology. The similarity between economics and biology stems from the fact that the life process is the ultimate subject matter of both disciplines. The views of the total life process presented here derive from the steady-state and evolutionary aspects of the two processes. The article then considers the human economy from an ecological perspective.

The Steady-State Analogy

The within-skin (biologic) life processes of metabolism can be compared to the outside-skin (economic) life processes of production and consumption. The metabolic process consists of anabolism and catabolism. *Anabolism*, the process by which useful matter and energy is converted into living tissues, is similar to production in the economic system. *Catabolism*, which converts living tissue into degraded matter and energy, is similar to consumption in the economic process. The primary purpose of the metabolic process is the maintenance of life, while that of the economic process is the maintenance and enjoyment of life. In both processes, the only material output produced is waste. Edwin Schrodinger[1] described life as a system in steady-state thermodynamic disequilibrium, in which high-entropy outputs are exchanged for low-entropy inputs. A corollary to this is that no organism can live in a medium of its own waste products. Schrodinger's description and its corollary are a perfect physical description of the economic process as well.

The economic and metabolic processes fit together because metabolism is part of the economic subprocess of consumption. Many economic products are inputs into the metabolic process, and some outputs of the metabolic process, such as manure fertilizer and carbon dioxide, can be consumed in the economic process. The physical basis of the metabolic and economic processes undergoes continuous replacement in short periods of time. This replacement constitutes the steady-state aspect of both processes. Capital is essentially matter that is capable of trapping energy and using it for human purposes. Biological organs are endosomatic capital, and the environment, in the form of air, soil, and water, constitutes physical exosomatic capital.

The Evolutionary Analogy

Replacement of the physical basis of metabolic and economic processes is equivalent to short-term depreciation and investment. The physical basis also undergoes qualitative and organizational change over long periods of time. These long-term changes are the equivalent of technological change and represent the evolutionary processes in metabolism and the economy. When the rate of anabolism is greater than the rate of catabolism, growth occurs, and then merges into development by giving rise to qualitative changes as well. In biological evolution, genes transmit knowledge, while gene mutations modify knowledge to adapt to the environment. In economic evolution, economic surplus propels growth, while culture transmits knowledge and generates new ideas that assist adaptation and development. While economic surplus leads to secondary economic activity that is far away from direct contact with nature, the biophysical foundations of economics are always present in the background.

The Human Economy in Ecological Perspective

Ecologists abstract from the human economy and study only natural interdependencies, while economists abstract from nature and study only interdependencies between commodities and man. As the biologist Marston Bates has suggested, ecologists pretend that man does not exist, and economists pretend that nature does not exist. However, the human economy is having serious effects on the ecology. Rather than dismissing these effects as externalities, the study of economic commodities should be integrated into study of the larger economy of nature.

A useful framework for understanding the interactions between the economy and ecology is the Leontief input–output framework. In its simplest representation, the total economy can be divided into human and non-human sectors as shown below.

From	To	
	Human	Non-human
Human	(2)	(1)
Non-human	(3)	(4)

Cell (2) represents the domain of traditional economics. All items exchanged here are economic commodities with positive prices. Cell (4) is the domain of traditional ecology, while cells (1) and (3) represent flows from the economy into the ecology and vice versa. Cells (1), (3), and (4) may be called ecological commodities that capture the biophysical foundations of economics; free goods (zero price) and economic "bads" (negative price) are included in these cells. The non-human sectors include animals, plants, bacteria, the atmosphere, the hydrosphere, the lithosphere, and the sun. The standard Leontief input–output matrix is restricted to the activities in cell (2). This extension into the non-human sectors captures the entry of low-entropy energy and matter into the economic system and the outflow of high-entropy waste into the ecological system. In principle, the suggested extension should pose no problems, but practical problems do exist. The inputs and outputs in cells (1), (3), and (4) have not been measured, and doing so will require the cooperation of many disciplines.

Note
1. Erwin Schrodinger, *What is Life?* (New York: Macmillan, 1945).

Summary of

The Entropy Law and the Economic Process in Retrospect
by Nicholas Georgescu-Roegen

[Published in *Eastern Economic Journal* 12 (January–March 1986): 3–25.]

Twenty years after putting forward the idea that the economic process is entropic in all its material fibers, it is now time, in this article, to comment on and clarify some of the issues that have arisen from this idea.

The Entropy Law and Its Extension to Matter

In an isolated system, the total amount of energy is constant, but it irrevocably degrades from the available to the unavailable state. Available and unavailable energy are anthropomorphic concepts relating to whether humans can use the energy for their own purposes. *Entropy* is the ratio of unavailable energy to the absolute temperature of the isolated system. The entropy law says that the amount of unavailable energy will increase in a system over time. Some economists have argued that the entropy law is irrelevant to the workings of the economic system because it is an open system. However, while it is true that net entropy can increase or decrease in an open system, entropic degradation does occur in all systems, so the entropy law is relevant to economic systems.

Matter, like energy, exists in both available and unavailable states, and over time it also degrades from the former to the latter. An important implication of this is that complete recycling would require limitless amounts of energy and time. Materials that are deemed vital will inevitably become scarcer and scarcer over time. The idea of a steady-state economy, put forward by Herman Daly as a solution to the ecological crisis, does not recognize this, and it is therefore logically weak.

The Fallacy of the Energy Theory of Economic Value

A living organism requires low-entropy energy to support its activities. Since low-entropy energy can only be used once, its scarcity increases over time. The entropy law is therefore at the root of economic scarcity. However, it would be wrong to treat the entire economic process simply as a process of degrading low entropy. A number of writers have drawn close parallels between thermodynamics and the economic process, leading to the energetics approach that equates economic value with net energy. David Huettner rejected this method, although he does claim to have established that economic value is *proportional* to energy content. Huettner's proof, however, is based on a production function that includes only flows, not funds—a formulation clearly not in keeping with economic reality. Robert Costanza attempted an empirical formulation of the "economic value equals energy content" proposition, but his analysis suffers from the same problem as Huettner's: it only includes flows, not funds. Costanza's equation also produces the curious result that the costs of the elements that he does not include equal zero in all sectors. At best, Costanza's analysis reveals that energy is an important stochastic element of cost. The entropic nature of the economic process does not, however, mean that economic value can be determined by energy content.

Lessons for Economics from Thermodynamics

Mainstream economists argue that economic growth is primary and that economic scarcity can be overcome through technological improvements. They view economics as a mechanical process, not a thermodynamic one, and believe that the market will resolve any problems that may arise with respect to the availability of natural resources. While these economists concede that at times markets do not function efficiently, they argue that the imposition of taxes and subsidies can rectify any problems. They point to the continuous improvements in living standards around the world as an argument in favor of a strategy of economic growth.

It must be remembered, however, that the tremendous growth of the past has been fueled by a mineral bonanza that supported technological advances. For these advances to continue, a steady supply of environmental low entropy is needed. In the future, the unavailability of low-entropy energy will be a major constraint on available technologies. For some time now, many have believed that cheap and renewable solar energy will solve the current energy crisis. However, the problem with solar energy is that tapping it requires a disproportionate amount of matter; at this point, using solar energy still depends a great deal on other primary resources. Nuclear energy is another possible future energy source, but here the biggest problem concerns safety issues. Given these problems with solar and nuclear energy, the only reasonable solutions to the energy crisis are to economize in the use of fossil fuels, or to rely on less energy intensive technologies. Any successful program to economize on energy will require international cooperation.

Summary of

Thermodynamic and Economic Concepts as Related to Resource-Use Policies

by Stuart Burness, Ronald Cummings, Glenn Morris, and Inja Paik
[Published in *Land Economics* 56 (February 1980): 1–9.]

In the face of heightened concern over the gathering ecological crisis, issues relating to the optimal use of exhaustible resources can be readily analyzed within the dominant economic paradigm. As various resource bases are depleted, their scarcity value will be reflected in higher prices. Higher prices will in turn reduce demand, encourage conservation, and promote a more prudent allocation of these resources among competing sectors of the economy, as well as intertemporally. The market-based policy implications of this analysis have been a source of frustration for physical scientists for two reasons. First, they feel that market-based solutions result in a wasteful use of resources; second, markets ignore the fundamental laws of thermodynamics—laws that should have some relevance for public policy on the use of exhaustible resources. The First Law of Thermodynamics states that energy is never destroyed, it only changes form. The Second Law implies that the whole of economic life is entropic, feeding on low-entropy matter and generating high-entropy wastes.

A few economists have begun to question the effectiveness of market-based analysis in dealing with resource issues, and to examine the possibility that market solutions do indeed ignore physical laws. The need for clarifying these points is not merely academic. Many people have argued that these physical laws have a direct relevance to resource policy. This article explores the interface between thermodynamic and economic concepts and suggests questions that warrant consideration if a compelling case is to be made that resource policies can be improved via the introduction of thermodynamic laws.

A Heuristic Sketch of Thermodynamic Laws

The First Law of Thermodynamics concerns the conservation of energy and is intuitively relatively easy to grasp. An energy conversion process involves capturing the internal energy stored in a given resource, which is the sum of the kinetic and potential energy contained in its molecules. After the coal is burned, little energy remains in the ashes. The change in the internal or stored energy between the two states is released in the form of work or heat, viewed as a flow of an equal amount of energy. There are many different methods for producing this flow of energy, each depending on the type of system used, which is in turn a function of the type of capital utilized.

The Second Law of Thermodynamics deals with the entropy of a resource, i.e., it concerns the quality of the energy resource, rather than its quantity. Entropy essentially refers to the state of disorderliness or diffusion of energy. A lump of coal has a low entropy value before it is burned, i.e., the energy is orderly and readily available. After the coal is burned, the level of entropy rises; the energy it once contained is now diffuse and unavailable.

The introduction of the Second Law to an analysis of a system has important implications. Entropy limits the ability to extract work from resources and imposes an upper bound on the amount of work that can be performed in our thermodynamic system. As we deplete low-entropy resources, the amount of work that can be derived per unit of resource use declines, which means that we must consume ever greater quantities of increasingly high-entropy resources. In addition, given a particular technology or capital stock, different energy resources will give rise to different entropy changes. System design should, therefore, seek to capture the maximum amount of available work for a given entropic change. This criteria suggests that our current technology is thermodynamically inefficient, as we use a two-step process in which energy produces heat, which in turn is used to perform work, rather than converting energy resources directly to work.

Thermodynamics, Economics, and Resource Policy

Is this analysis of the depletion of stocks of low-entropy resources anything more than the restatement of the economist's formulation of resource scarcity? To answer this we must first consider whether the implications of the Second Law are reflected in markets. If markets are reasonably competitive, this will indeed be so. The market price of goods should rationally reflect the opportunity cost of producing them. Therefore, widespread availability of low-entropy resources should result in relatively low costs, while higher costs and hence higher prices will occur as the level of entropy of resources (or the "scarcity of work") increases. This process will engender capital innovation to extract more work for less energy and less entropic change. Of course, market imperfections and government policies may distort prices, but these problems are well known in economic theory. Policies that take these distortions into account will therefore enable a pattern of resource allocation to emerge that will better reflect relative resource scarcities, thus channeling lower entropy resources into higher value uses.

It is this notion of value that may lie at the heart of the interface between thermodynamic and economic concepts in terms of their relevance to the public debate on resource-use policies. The key question, then, is what determines value? Nicholas Georgescu-Roegen argues for an entropy theory of value. The suggestion is that low entropy has a value that is not reflected in markets, but should be; this implies that proper energy policy is one that conserves energy quality (low entropy). In standard models, on the other hand, consumer preferences for low costs prevail, and the value of energy, as well as of all other inputs, is derived solely from the capacity to serve this goal. This promotes the use of technologies requiring high-quality resources.

It is true that real problems exist with respect to resource scarcity and intergenerational equity as they relate to energy resources, which both government and the markets of the standard model often deal with imperfectly. The case has yet to be made, however, that the introduction of thermodynamic concepts will fundamentally alter the policy-making process. Suggesting that we are wasting energy resources implies nothing more than that energy prices are low, a problem that can be dealt with through deregulation or taxes. Even if we could overcome the many intractable problems associated with actually measuring entropy or energy stocks in resources, it is difficult to determine how it would change economic outcomes, unless there is a fundamental transformation in our system of values whereby energy itself becomes a factor in our sense of well-being. In other words, thermodynamic efficiency in and of itself means little if it is not efficient from the standpoint of societal values as well. Few would deny that artificially low energy prices in the United States have resulted in thermodynamic inefficiency. However, it is not clear that thermodynamic considerations are inappropriately reflected in market prices, nor is it clear that these considerations could be used to enrich public policy.

This article does not reject a potentially useful role for thermodynamic concepts in the making of public policy. Rather, the argument is that the gap in resource-use policies based on economic analyses, which is attributable to the absence of an explicit consideration of thermodynamic laws, has not been made clear. Further interchange between economists who do see the relevance of thermodynamics to economics and those who do not may help to develop a compelling case, if indeed one exists. In order to further this dialogue, the following inquiries are made:

(1) Is the relevant system of values to be one wherein individual preferences determine values? If not, what is the alternative?

(2) Can one define in precise ways those dimensions of the First and Second Laws that are not reflected in markets? If so, by what rationale should they be included?

(3) If we can argue for an energy value that is distinct from market value, what are the manifestations or signals from this value? How is the energy "price" to be determined and used in the process of resource allocation and policy formulation?

(4) Acknowledging market imperfections, equity issues, and market distortions related to government policies, what is the mechanism by which recognition of thermodynamic laws is to contribute to the resolution of these problems? Economic responses to these problems would lead to adjustments in the price mechanisms through taxes, subsidies, deregulation, etc. What is the energy counterpart to these market-related mechanisms?

Summary of

Thermodynamic and Economic Concepts as Related to Resource-Use Policies: Comment and Reply
by Herman E. Daly (Comment) and Stuart Burness
and Ronald Cummings (Reply)
[Published in *Land Economics* 62 (August 1986): 319–324.]

Comment

Before specifically addressing the questions posed by the authors of this article, it is important to correct a misperception held by many neoclassical economists and repeated by Burness et al.: the entropy law does not imply an energy theory of value. Careful reading of a number of economists who do incorporate thermodynamic laws into their economic thinking will reveal that this notion has been explicitly rejected by them. Burness et al. specifically argue that Georgescu-Roegen advocates an energy theory of value, but this is incorrect. If they have misread Georgescu-Roegen, they have misunderstood the issue they are addressing.

As to the specific questions raised by the authors, the following replies are offered (each question is first restated, followed by the response):

(1) Is the relevant system of values to be one wherein individual preferences determine values? If not, what is the alternative?

There is no serious proposal to substitute market values by calculated, non-market coefficients based on work or energy or entropy. Rather, the entropy law imposes a previously neglected constraint on the physical scale of the economy relative to the ecosystem. The market fails to consider this constraint because Pareto optimality of allocation is independent of the ecological sustainability of the throughput. It is worthwhile to take account of this constraint only if we collectively value sustainability which, like justice, is not expressible at the level of individual choices in a competitive market. In order for sustainability and the entropy-driven constraint on physical scale to be reflected in market prices, there must be a collectively imposed constraint on the aggregate flow (throughput) of matter and energy between the ecosystem and the economy. The criteria for setting this constraint must be sustainability. Once established, the markets at the micro level will generate a new set of prices reflecting the social value of sustainability; when the biophysical constraint is explicitly acknowledged, the environment will no longer be treated as a free good.

The constraints imposed by the laws of thermodynamics are twofold. The First Law tells us that matter and energy are extracted from the environment, flow through the economy, and are then returned to the ecosystem. Resources are never consumed, in the sense that what is taken is quantitatively identical to what is ultimately returned. The Second Law tells us that whereas the quantity of the throughput is constant, the quality is not. Raw material is low-entropy matter-energy, while waste is high-entropy matter-energy. Furthermore, both sources and sinks are finite in a finite environment, and sinks cannot be recycled into sources within human time scales. Finitude would not be so troublesome were it not for entropy, for then matter and energy could be recycled ever faster. Nor would the entropy law be a bother were it not for finitude, as there would be no need for recycling at all. However, both finitude and entropy are very real, so it is an unavoidable fact that the scale of our economy cannot expand indefinitely. The market is sensitive to scale at a micro level, but not to the scale of the entire system relative to the ecosystem. It is thus very relevant to economics to measure the qualitative difference between the raw materials and waste products of our economic system; entropy is that measure.

(2) Can one define in precise ways those dimensions of the First and Second Laws which are not reflected in markets? If so, by what rationale should they be included?

What is not reflected in the market is the value of the optimal sustainable physical scale of the economy relative to the ecosystem. There is no distinction made in the market between a scale of throughout that is ecologically sustainable and one that is not. Market prices can only reflect this value after markets are subject to collectively instituted macro constraints. These constraints, determined by ethical and ecological criteria, should be price-determining rather than price-determined. After they are established, the proper allocation of resources among competing sectors can be price-determined. The entropy law helps us to delineate the nature and the necessity of this sustainability constraint on scale and growth, and hence its relevance to policy formulation.

(3) If we can argue for an energy value that is distinct from market value, what are the manifestations or signals from this value? How is the energy "price" determined and used in the process of resource allocation and policy formulation?

This issue is covered in the responses to questions one and two.

(4) Acknowledging market imperfections, equity issues, and market distortions related to government policies, what is the mechanism by which recognition of thermodynamic laws is to contribute to the resolution of these problems? Economic responses to these problems would lead to adjustments in the price mechanisms through taxes, subsidies, deregulation, etc. What is the energy counterpart to these market-related mechanisms?

As indicated earlier, there is no energy counterpart to market-related mechanisms. The policy measures that have been discussed in this context have, in fact, involved standard market mechanisms such as depletion quota auctions, energy tax-cum-rebate schemes, and others. However, the issue at hand is whether the entropy law is relevant to economics, not what is the best policy for dealing with entropic constraints. It has been argued here that physical law is directly relevant to economic analysis.

There has been a common misperception that entropy and sustainability are merely ethical issues, and that the whole issue boils down to a claim that society's values are wrong. It must be made clear that entropy is a physical law, and entropic constraints are objective facts, the ramifications of which are immediately evident. How one reacts to these objective facts does reflect a value judgment. One may reject sustainability as a desirable policy goal, but that will not abolish the entropy law; the objective constraint will still exist. If we accept sustainability as a goal, then the market alone will not reflect this value-laden choice. A sustainable economic system is a public good and can only be achieved through macro policy choices.

Reply

We have no quarrel with the logic of Professor Daly's argument per se. If society could agree on any ethical constraint, then the process described by Professor Daly may in fact take place. He has satisfied our concerns regarding the role of individual preferences, but he has done little in terms of rationalizing the interface between thermodynamics and economics. Professor Daly's formulations of "sustainability" are extraordinarily vague and ill-defined. He says little beyond the well-worn suggestion that markets and economists ignore the finitude of the environment. In fact, we do not know the dimensions of finitude in terms of our resource base, nor do we know the nature of future technologies that may eventually include extraterrestrial components. Unless Professor Daly can lend some substance to his notion of sustainability, the appeal to collective action may appear vacuous.

Pedagogically, sustainability requires only that all processes operate at their steady-state, renewable level, which might require a return to a regulated caveman culture. It is doubtful that such a system could develop in an environment in which individual preferences prevail, but in any case, future generations are unable to participate in this decision process. Thus, if competitively determined market prices lead to a pattern of resource use that some regard as wrong, or unfair, it is not as a result of market failure to recognize the Second Law of Thermodynamics; rather, it arises from an asymmetrical distribution of property rights between generations. Likewise, the neglect of an aggregate constraint on the physical scale of the economy with respect to the ecosystem does not arise as a consequence of ignorance of the principle of increasing entropy. Rather, it reflects the usual problems associated with common property resources.

In the end, Professor Daly's argument does reduce to the claim that society's values are in some sense wrong. His concern is with the imposition of constraints on economic behavior and resource use so as to force a steady-state solution that satisfies his perceptions of an ethically just pattern of resource use. The argument is about ethical issues, not about the allocative efficiency of markets.

Summary of

Economics, Ethics, and the Environment
by Richard B. Norgaard and Richard B. Howarth

[Published in *The Energy-Environment Connection*, ed. Jack M. Hollander (Washington, D.C. and Covelo, California: Island Press, 1992), 347–363. © Island Press, 1992.]

This article argues that questions of economic efficiency should be based on moral decisions about the rights of future generations and that it is fallacious to determine the morality of decisions using a criteria of economic efficiency. Among the many complex, long-term, global environmental issues, global climate change is one that is relatively amenable to conventional economic analysis. However, it is easier for economists to quantify the costs of mitigating climate change through the reduction and absorption of greenhouse gases than to quantify the benefits. Economists are beginning to grapple with these issues and are staking out their positions in public. Based on standard economic assumptions about technological progress and natural resources, economists have generally argued that:

(1) in the long run the costs of most mitigation measures are greater than the benefits;

(2) until present uncertainties are reduced no action should be taken; and

(3) the present generation should not bear the burden of mitigating climate change since, irrespective of what climate changes are occurring today, future people will be materially better off.

There is a flaw in the way economists have framed the questions regarding the mitigation of climate change. At a time when people are concerned that future generations will not be as well off as the present generation, the question that economists are asking is whether mitigation is a good investment decision. This approach implicitly assumes that current generations have the right to exploit the atmosphere and that doing so will not leave future generations worse off. While economists are questioning how this generation might most efficiently exploit the environment, the political discourse is questioning whose environment it ought to be. The critical question is what kind of a world we want to leave to our children and how best to do it, rather than whether mitigation of climate change is a good investment for us.

The important point to be made regarding questions of efficiency and equity is that what constitutes an efficient outcome will vary depending on how the rights to resources are distributed. Present economic cost–benefit analysis takes the existing distribution of rights to resources as given, but other distributions are possible and potentially valid. However, while economic reasoning may incorporate different distributions of rights for the sake of analysis, it cannot determine which distribution of rights should prevail. The moral question as to whether future generations should have rights to a climate approximately like the climate of today must be determined through the political process. Once this is done, then it is appropriate to use economic reasoning to decide how to allocate resources efficiently.

The current efficiency-based approach of economists also conflicts with the concept of sustainability because of the narrow definition of efficiency that economists use. However, when environmental goods and services not traded in the market are included in the analysis, there is less of a conflict between the efficient and the sustainable. In spite of this, a fundamental contradiction exists: all techniques to measure benefits are developed in the context of current generations, whereas sustainability is concerned with the future. Thus sustainability is also an issue of intergenerational equity. Again, this tension between the present and future generations must first be resolved in the political arena, and the questions regarding global climate change correctly framed, before empirical research on the question is pursued. A broad consensus appears to exist in political discourse that sustainability is a minimum criteria for intergenerational equity.

Acknowledging that sustainability involves both equity and efficiency does not necessarily define the rights of future generations or the responsibilities of the present generation. However, it does clarify some of the issues regarding the efficient allocation of resources, non-market valuation, and contradictions of discounting the future.

The Allocation of Resources

Based on a seminal paper by Hotelling,[1] an extensive literature has developed on the optimal depletion of stock resources. Hotelling argued that in a perfectly competitive world producers would extract resources up to the point at which the returns from holding units of the resource for future extraction equaled the returns from extracting the resource and investing the net revenue earned in the capital markets. While economists have looked into the equity implications of this analysis, they have not developed models which show that different intergenerational distribution of assets will result in different efficient solutions, and that the equity implications of different efficient allocations can be significant. Instead, economists have implicitly assumed that technological progress will make resources available to future generations. Questions of intertemporal resource use have been addressed only from the framework of efficiency, as if the present generation had all the rights to resources, and research has focused only on how efficiency can be improved within these narrow limits. If questions of equity and the rights of future generations are not incorporated, then although efficiency of resource allocation may improve, we may still only be moving from one unsustainable point to another.

The Discount Rate Controversy

On the one hand, low discount rates aid sustainable development, since the lower the discount rate is the more concern it shows for future generations. On the other hand, low interest rates lead to higher investments, including investments in capital necessary for mineral extraction and the transformation of environmental systems, leading environmentalists opposed to water development projects and other major investments to argue against subsidizing discount rates. The issue of using lower discount rates to protect future generations becomes moot if instead we think in terms of the intergenerational distribution of rights to resources and environmental services. The interest rate would not be seen as the instrumental variable, as it is really just another price. The emphasis should instead be on what rights are passed between generations. Transferring rights to future generations will itself affect the interest rate. Bringing equity back into neoclassical analysis resolves the contradiction between efficiency and the concern for the future.

Environmental Valuation

The value of environmental services is a function of how environmental and other rights are distributed across generations. Lowering the rights of the present generation to the environment will result in a higher marginal value of environmental services. Economists have argued that environments are misused and degraded because the costs of using environmental services are not fully reflected in markets, and that by introducing the valuation of non-market goods and services—i.e., internalizing externalities—a more efficient use of environmental services will result. However, internalizing externalities will not always ensure that the economy will move closer to sustainability; present methods of environmental evaluation will not be effective in protecting the welfare of future generations. Therefore, given the moral issues at stake, the ethical questions should be answered first before valuations are made. In other words, issues of sustainable development must be tackled first as issues of equity, and then as issues of efficiency.

Note

1. Harold Hotelling, "The Economics of Exhaustible Resources," in *Journal of Political Economy* 39(2), 132–175 (1931).

Summary of

Neoclassical and Institutional Approaches to Development and the Environment

by Peter Söderbaum

[Published in *Ecological Economics* 5 (May 1992): 127–144. Reprinted with kind permission from Elsevier Science B.V., Amsterdam, The Netherlands.]

Differences between neoclassical and institutional economists cannot be described in terms of black and white. Rather, we must address their divergent approaches, i.e., the reductionist-mechanistic tendencies of neoclassical economists, and the holistic-evolutionary tendencies of the institutionalists. Neoclassical economists tend to believe in very clear boundaries between economics and other disciplines, and between the various fields of economics. For example, environmental economists are expected to take care of environmental problems and policies, while other economists can continue in their detached fields of study. In addition, an example of neo-classical reductionism is the rendering of all practical economic analysis in monetary terms. Mainstream neoclassical economics was not developed to deal with environmental problems. It therefore seems reasonable to consider alternatives to the neoclassical paradigm when facing a new category of problems.

Holistic and Evolutionary Economics

Institutional economics emphasizes a holistic or inclusionist approach to economic policy making. The different disciplines are seen as overlapping, rather than as distinct and separated by clearly delineated boundaries, and scholars are expected to try to achieve a balance between specialized knowledge and knowledge at a holistic, interdisciplinary level. Thinking in environmental terms should then permeate all sub-fields of economics and all policy areas. In addition, institutional economists have a preference for evolutionary thinking, i.e., an interest in how technology, institutions, habits, values, and the economy at large evolve through time. Institutionalists also prefer models that are open ended or only partially closed.

Institutional economics focuses both on actors—their world view, habits, etc.—and on institutional arrangements, i.e., the organizations, rules of the game, power relationships, entitlements, and other types of control over resources. Whereas neoclassicists take institutions (and technology) for granted, institutionalists treat them as crucial variables and are ready to question current institutional arrangements. For example, they see all commodity prices on national and international markets as being contingent upon the prevalent institutional structure; depending upon the value perspective, these may or may not be regarded as reasonable. The market, then, is just one relevant institution among many, a part of the structure of rules governing social and economic outcomes, which happens to be a useful decentralizing mechanism. Institutionalists do not, however, evince the enthusiasm shown by neoclassicists for the market as a problem solver.

A Strategy of Disaggregation

The history of natural resource and other environmental deterioration indicates that something is wrong with the objectives, decision-making methodologies, and accounting practices that mainstream economists have developed and upon which society has relied. Reliance upon standard economic policy instruments does not seem to be enough in view of the many failures that have occurred and the difficulties ahead. Attempts to modify measures of GNP by adding components that are judged valuable and subtracting others that are judged environmentally harmful may improve things somewhat, but it will not eliminate the dogma of thinking in terms of money values. This dogma must instead be replaced by a strategy of disaggregation, whereby monetary and non-monetary impacts are kept separate.

In addition, a distinction must be made with respect to resources and pollutants between flows over periods of time and positions at a point in time. For example, the reduction of mercury effluence into a lake may decline (an improvement in pollution flow), but stocks of mercury in fish may continue to increase (a deterioration in position). None of this can adequately be aggregated in monetary terms and thus cannot be fruitfully used (e.g., in cost–benefit analysis) to inform the decision-making process. Impacts of different kinds, impacts relating to different interests, and dynamic impacts over time should all be disaggregated and considered separately.

Sustainability as Ecological Ethics

Neoclassical economics tends to support and legitimize a view of progress that is limited to the traditional indicators of growth: balance of payments, inflation, etc. Sustainable development has evolved as an alternative concept of progress. One problem with this term is that each scholar can choose a definition for it that fits into his or her pre-established world view. We need instead to be able to determine whether a specific development trend will lead to degradation or improvement in the state of the environment. The following set of principles is formulated to guide decision making concerning energy, transportation, forest projects, etc.:

(1) Alternatives that involve irreversible environmental degradation within the region should be avoided.

(2) Alternatives that involve irreversible environmental degradation in other regions or globally should be avoided.

(3) A philosophy of cautiousness should prevail in situations of uncertainty with regard to environmental impacts.

(4) When possible, environmentally positive or neutral alternatives should be chosen. If no such ready alternative exists, then a search should be initiated to find new alternatives in terms of different technology, new rules, reconsideration of lifestyles, etc.

These imperatives are deliberately limited to environmental impacts and therefore do not represent a complete ideological standpoint. Formulating environmental ethics represents an effort to extend the ideological options available for politicians and other citizens. Specific activities may be scrutinized with respect to the above ethics, and traditional GNP-based measures of success may be questioned on the grounds of environmental degradation. Economic growth strategies and expansion of international trade, commonly accepted by most political leaders, may also be questioned on the grounds that they underrate community sustainability and diversity. Public choice theory, based on the assumption of group self-interest, can also be challenged by a view of political actors with complex motives, including moral considerations. This in turn may lead to a more optimistic view of the possibilities for sustainable development.

Summary of

Economics as Mechanics and the Demise
of Biological Diversity
by Richard B. Norgaard

[Published in *Ecological Modelling* 38 (September 1987): 107–121. Reprinted with kind permission from Elsevier Science B.V., Amsterdam, The Netherlands.]

Macro explanations of the loss of biodiversity have emphasized how higher population levels have forced the transformation of relatively undisturbed areas, and how industrial pollutants and energy intensive agriculture have put new and relatively uniform selective pressures on species. This article explores how a third macro phenomenon—social organization based on specialization and exchange—has contributed to the demise of biological diversity.

Development and Diversity Before the Global
Exchange Economy

People have coexisted with other species for some three million years. While there is evidence that humans have caused species extinction in the past, earlier rates of extinction were far lower than current or projected rates. The world before the rise of the global exchange economy can be viewed as a mosaic of co-evolving social and ecological systems. Within each area of the mosaic, human selective pressure operated upon other species according to how well their characteristics fit the evolving values, knowledge, social organization, and technologies of the local peoples. At the same time, each of these components of the social system was also evolving under the selective pressure of how well it fit into the evolving ecosystem and the other social components. These mosaics were not entirely self-contained; elements spilled over into other systems where they may have thrived, adapted, or died out. But to some extent they all influenced the further co-evolution of system characteristics in their new areas, resetting the dynamics of the system. This co-evolutionary vision of our past combines the evolution of belief systems with biological systems and suggests how each has contributed to the diversity of the other.

Remnants of co-evolutionary agricultural developments remain today, providing clues to the past. In a wide array of traditional agroecosystems we find traditional farmers deliberately intermixing crop, noncrop and sometimes animal species over different places at different times. This is a system that has co-evolved in the societies of traditional peoples over centuries or millennia, and was designed to ensure a dependable food supply. This dependability relied upon the ecological stability achieved through high species diversity within each system. On the basis of Western experience, natural historians have portrayed man's influence on natural systems as destructive; however, we are now beginning to learn how traditional peoples contributed to the growth and maintenance of genetic diversity.

Global Exchange Economy

Recent development has been distinctly different from the co-evolving mosaic of the past. The mechanistic grid of universal truths developed by Western science and the global adoption of Western technologies has boldly overlaid and destroyed most of the mosaic. The environment has not been immune to this global unifying process. Environments are merging through common land management practices, while biological diversity is declining from the common cropping, fertilization, and pest control practices of modern agriculture. Much of this has come about as a consequence of the pressures of global markets.

The global exchange economy evolved over several centuries and began to characterize the global order during the past century. While exchange was going on well before economists began to theorize about it, their models have affected policies and helped rationalize the global exchange economy. Development policies are heavily influenced by institutions like the World Bank, where in 1986 there were 692 designated economists on staff, and one biologist. Thus, how economists conceptualize social systems affects the maintenance of existing features and the design of new components of the global order.

The concepts of comparative advantage, specialization, and the gains from trade are central to the Western economic model. This framing of social order has affected diversity in two ways. First, the encouragement of development through trade has fostered specialization and a reduction in the diversity of crop and supporting species in every region. The implementation of free trade policies has encouraged Third World farmers to respond to international agricultural markets, supported by development efforts in road and port construction. Those who continue to practice subsistence agriculture are simply moved out by larger commercial or centrally planned agricultural ventures. The global exchange economy further transforms local agroecosystems because it forces farmers to produce as much as possible at low cost in order to remain competitive. Thus high-yield seed stocks, fertilizers, and pesticides are widely adopted, further reducing the remaining regional diversity.

A second cause of species extinction is that the global exchange economy induces temporal variation for which species have not evolved coping mechanisms. In market economies, individuals rapidly respond to exogenous factors (changing prices, tastes, institutions, technology, weather, etc.) that redefine which people, land, or tools have a comparative advantage. This flexibility in factor allocation is viewed as a crucial component of the dynamic efficiency that makes market economies so attractive. Thus if poor rice crops in Brazil induce a sharp rise in the price of rice, other global regions will substitute rice production for their current crop in a rational market response. This increased variability at the individual level actually contributes to the decline of diversity in the ecosystem.

Expanding on this further, we can see that the economic model is designed with the explicit assumption that land can move between uses much like people and tools. Land, however, is more complex than a tractor, and economists have given little thought to the environmental services that help give the land its value. The problem, put simply, is that environmental services cannot freely shift from the support of rice to the support of cotton, and then to the support of suburban lawns, to alfalfa, and back to rice, with the same ease with which a farmer may adapt to these different systems. There would not be a problem if the species that supply the environmental services appropriate to particular crops could co-evolve to fill their supporting niches as rapidly as the global economy leads farmers to shift crops; but this is not the case.

The difference between how economic and ecological models are presumed to respond to change stems from different degrees of mechanical and evolutionary thinking in the two disciplines. The economy is modeled as if it had predefined atomistic parts that will mechanically adjust through market signals or planning to optimize the systemic performance. However, believing that species and their interrelations co-evolve in response to the particular conditions of the place and time, ecologists are more hesitant to generalize than economists. These differences help explain why the use of the neoclassical paradigm has contributed to species extinction.

People and the economic decisions they make are an integral part of the ecological system. The diversity of the ecological system is intimately linked to the diversity of the economic system. Local biological and social systems and the culture of agriculture are destroyed when international markets dictate that corn should be planted one year, wheat the next, and soybeans the year following that. Species conservation, as well as the continued co-evolution of cultural knowledge, local technologies, and unique forms of social organization, all need more spatial diversity and temporal stability than the global exchange economy permits. Our economic model is well specified but barren, positing only exchange relations. The result is a failure to acknowledge the evolutionary basis of ecological systems, while fostering a policy-making process that is wiping out species at the most rapid rate since the hypothesized meeting with the asteroid that raised the dust that terminated the dinosaurs.

Summary of

Reserved Rationality and the Precautionary Principle: Technological Change, Time, and Uncertainty in Environmental Decision Making

by Charles Perrings

[Published in *Ecological Economics: The Science and Management of Sustainability*, ed. Robert Constanza (New York: Columbia University Press, 1991), 153–166.]

Many of the most serious potential environmental problems are those for which the effects of certain processes are highly uncertain with respect to both their spread and duration. As the uncertainty increases, so does the difficulty of evaluating the associated environmental damage or the marginal social costs. Moreover, the wider the spread and the longer the duration of these problems, the narrower is the scope for a market solution involving the allocation of property rights. Intractable problems of this sort have led to strong support for the "precautionary principle," which involves the commitment of resources today in such a way as to safeguard against distant and potentially catastrophic outcomes in the future. This article's main concern is the identification of the conditions in which the precautionary principle is appropriate, and the way in which the principle modifies the decision-making process. It is argued that it leads to a sequential approach in which the decision maker reserves judgment about the uncertain outcomes of each activity, assuming the worst-case outcome until evidence is provided to the contrary.

Discounting, Valuation, and Treatment of Future Generations

The strongest argument in favor of the precautionary principle is the fact that environmental effects which are both distant in time and have a low probability of occurring receive very little weight in the decision-making process. There are two main reasons for this: (1) the rate of discount; and (2) the valuation of resources under the current structure of property rights. Both raise ethical questions with respect to the right of present generations to put at risk not only the marginal economic benefits but the very survival of future generations.

The social discount rate is a measure of the rate at which it is considered socially desirable to substitute consumption in the present for consumption in the future. This is an issue because it involves ethical judgments concerning intergenerational equity. If discount rates are positive, a development strategy that is unsustainable may seem optimal today. If the discount rate is set at zero, on the other hand, then a development strategy will only be considered optimal if it yields a constant stream of income in all periods. The discount rate implies a judgment about the responsibility of the present to the future for distant but catastrophic impacts. Positive discount rates screen out even major future costs from present decision making.

Historically, mainstream economics has been strongly critical of the ethical judgments inherent in positive discount rates. More recently, however, the sovereignty of the current generation of consumers has been invoked to support the propriety of discounting and to deny any role to the state in safeguarding future generations. The rationale for discounting in this work lies in the notion that future generations are compensated through the growth of capital. Much of this work, however, relies on models that exclude the natural capital base from consideration, so that capital expenditures today appear to yield only growth benefits for the future. This is a highly misleading proxy for the growth potential of the entire system, which relies as much on natural capital as on produced capital.

The authority for ignoring the future costs of present activities stems from the structure of property rights. Under the existing system, environmental resources are not allocated on the basis of their full intertemporal opportunity cost. Rather, property rights tend to be such that resource users are confronted only by the direct costs of resource use, and can ignore the uncompensated costs that are imposed on the future, as well as those externalities that are imposed on the present. The issue of intergenerational compensation becomes more difficult when these uncompensated costs are discontinuous and uncertain. Thus, there is no way to estimate costs to the future directly, and there is no means to assign property rights to unborn generations. The net result is that future costs are only taken into consideration insofar as the present generation chooses to take an ethical responsibility for them. The precautionary principle merely confronts this reality.

Decision Making under Incomplete Information and under the Precautionary Principle

Decision making under risk occurs when there is a well-defined set of possible outcomes. When it is not clear that an outcome will belong to the set of outcomes, or what the probability of that set is, then we have decision making under uncertainty. It is a characteristic of decision making under uncertainty that new information is acquired over time. Uncertainty typically occurs when there is no historical precedent for the activity or its impacts from which to gather data. As time passes and the historical record is enhanced, information will accumulate, thus pushing forward the boundary between the known and the unknown. Hence, the decision-making process will evolve sequentially in response to the changing information available to the decision maker. Decision makers will reserve judgment about uncertain outcomes (and act accordingly) until they are sure of their ground.

The class of problems for which the precautionary principle is advocated as an alternative to conventional decision-making models is that for which the level of uncertainty and the potential costs of current activities are both high. Global warming is one such example. Application of the precautionary principle in such cases involves a highly normative judgment about the responsibility of the present to the future—a judgment that can not be captured in existing models of rational decision making. The precautionary approach nevertheless accepts that every decision problem has elements of the standard problem. Uncertainty is treated as a *residual*—a property of the unobserved part of the system. The approach assigns a worst-case value to the uncertain outcome of current activities. The optimal policy is then the one that minimizes the maximum environmental costs over variation in the unobserved part of the history of the system.

The link between the worst-case scenario approach embodied in minimax and the precautionary principle seems quite obvious. The problem, however, is to define the worst case under conditions of incomplete information. It is not possible to select the worst case out of a known range of possibilities since that range remains unknown. Nor can we simply select the worst possible imaginable consequences, for it is always possible to envision apocalyptic scenarios. Such a construction would necessarily paralyze all activity. Since the worst-case scenario must be believable enough to capture policy makers' attention in order to be operational, something else is needed.

Shackle's concept of the "focus loss" of a decision is a good starting point. A set of possible future states is projected in connection to any given action. An opinion is formed as to the degree of disbelief in the occurrence of each state—a measure of the potential surprise they would experience if this state actually came about. These outcomes are then ordered according to an attractiveness function that would register the power of each outcome to command the attention of the policy maker. Thus, low probability yet believable outcomes that would involve high costs will command attention (such as a Chernobyl type event), while catastrophic but barely believable outcomes of vanishingly small probability will be ignored. The central point here is that the "focus loss" of a decision is adopted as the point of reference in a decision process of "reserved rationality." Decision makers confronted by uncertainty will reserve their position on some outcomes, and pending receipt of additional data they will adopt policies that will minimize the worst believable case.

Under the precautionary principle, decision makers who are ignorant as to the magnitude of potential losses will proceed cautiously to safeguard against the possibility of unexpectedly severe future costs. This seems prudent in those cases where certain policies have the potential for destroying crucial life support systems. Under such conditions of uncertainty, it would also be prudent to allow some margin for error, precisely because the impacts are unknown. This approach provides a method for determining the future costs of potentially catastrophic outcomes, and thus a yardstick against which to measure the net benefits of committing preventative expenditures today. As new information accrues, the sequential decision-making process envisioned here will allow for adjustments in policy over time.

It is worth stating that a normative ethical set of judgments is necessarily embedded in these procedures, as the decision maker must attach relative weights to various outcomes and to the populations that may be affected. In particular, the issue of responsibility to the future is involved, for even if the possibility of future devastation seems quite remote, it may well be as unacceptable to pursue the causative activities as if that outcome was assured.

Summary of

Conservation Reconsidered
by John V. Krutilla

[Published in *American Economic Review* 57
(September 1967): 777–786.]

From the time of Pigou until recently, the primary issue for economists with respect to the conservation of natural resources has been the optimal intertemporal utilization of these resources. However, the rates of consumption of natural resources during both world wars began to indicate that the resource base would ultimately be depleted. Nevertheless, the view that modern industrial economies can gain a large measure of independence from natural resources due to technological advances has more recently been gaining popularity. The core of this argument is that technological progress compensates for the depletion of higher quality natural resource stocks. There have, however, been warnings that the level of pollution and the deterioration of the physical landscape are increasing.

The traditional focus of conservation economics on reserving natural resource stocks for future generations has been outmoded by technological advances. This concern has therefore been replaced more recently by a focus on how to preserve natural environments for future generations. Traditional conservation economics does not, however, address this issue. In fact, use of Pigou's social time preference to determine the optimal rate of resource use may hasten the conversion of natural environments into low-yield capital investments. This article therefore discusses how decisions should be made with respect to choices involving actions that will have irreversible adverse effects on natural phenomena. It should be the task of a new economics of conservation to confront the "problem of providing for the present and future the amenities associated with unspoiled natural environments."[778]

At present unspoiled environments are not sufficiently valued. When deciding on the utilization of unspoiled environments, a private resource owner typically looks at all of the alternate uses of the resource and considers the prospective discounted net income of each use. It is possible that such an analysis would find that the option with the highest net income is also an option that is detrimental to the preservation of the unspoiled environment. The private resource user may then choose this option despite its detrimental effects, although from a social perspective this choice may not be the most efficient.

The efficiency of market allocations is uncertain for several reasons. First of all, unspoiled environments have no substitutes, while natural resource commodities often do. Thus, the private resource owner can not actually appropriate through gate receipts the total social value of the resource when it is used in a manner that preserves the unspoiled environment. The present value of the owner's expected net income values is therefore not a valid measure for evaluating the efficiency of resource allocation. It is also impossible to determine the efficiency of market allocations when many individuals are dependent on the preservation and availability of an unspoiled natural environment for their real income. In this case, the maximum willingness to pay could be less than the minimum amount that would be necessary to compensate these individuals if they were to be deprived of the natural phenomena in question, so it is not possible to determine whether or not the market allocation is efficient.

Option demand is another basis for questioning the efficiency of market allocations. This demand can be characterized as "a willingness to pay for retaining an option to use an area or facility that would be difficult or impossible to replace and for which no close substitute is available."[780] Option demand may exist even if there are no current plans to utilize the area or facility. If an option value exists but there is no way for the private resource owner to actually appropriate this value, then the resulting resource allocations may not be efficient.

Option values for unspoiled environments may exist for a number of reasons. For example, scientific research is often dependent upon an unspoiled environment to preserve the objects of study, and these environments are also important to maintain genetic diversity (e.g., in agriculture) and to serve as a source of new medicinal drugs (in fact, "approximately half of the new drugs currently being developed are obtained from botanical specimens"[780]). In other cases, the option value may have only a "sentimental basis." Many Americans rallied to preserve the national historic relic "Old Ironsides"; although many of them will never visit the site, they still derive satisfaction from knowing that it exists. Membership in the World Wildlife Fund is similar: individuals contribute to preserve endangered species in parts of the world that they will probably never see. Option value can therefore be relevant both among people active in the market for a particular "object of demand," and for those who place a value on the mere existence of this object.

In practice there are several examples of what a market for these "options" might look like, but they are very imperfect. For example, a small natural area or historical site may be purchased by the Nature Conservancy, an American nongovernmental organization. However, the investor often has little knowledge of the special characteristics of the ecosystem in question. In addition, "the serendipity value may not be appropriable by those paying to preserve the options."[781] Most importantly, the greatest unspoiled environments are large scale and not merely of local interest, so all of the problems associated with markets for public goods are encountered in these cases.

The formation and growth of demand for unspoiled environments is also relevant. Of particular interest is the "learning-by-doing" approach outlined by Davidson, Adams, and Seneca, which "suggests an interaction between present and future demand functions, which will result in a public good externality, as present demand enters into the utility function of future users."[1] That is, as present populations begin to learn to use these unspoiled environments in situations requiring less advanced skills (e.g., car camping), then in the future the "greater will be the induced demand for wild, primitive, and wilderness-related opportunities for indulging self interest."[782] Thus, the utility gained from the existence of unspoiled environments may continue to rise, although the supply of these environments can not be increased. At the moment little is known about these relations, and it is an area needing further research.

In expanding our concept of conservation, we must look further at the potential of technology. While technological advance may help compensate for the depletion of specific resources, the same cannot be said for natural phenomena. Neither extinct species nor the grand wonders can be replicated, and even if they could, the replicas would probably be of little worth compared to the originals. Technological advance may allow ever-increasing production from a given resource base, but "the supply of natural phenomena is virtually inelastic"[783]; we can only preserve these phenomena, as they can not be reproduced. Consumption-saving behavior is therefore motivated by both the desire to leave one's heirs an estate and by the utility that is obtained from consumption. Maintaining the option to enjoy these scenic wonders will depend on their provision as public goods. Given the increasing demand for unspoiled environments and the irreversibility of past losses, it is already clear that the level of well-being in the future will not be as high as it could have been if the conversion of natural environments had been stopped earlier.

At present very little is known about the possible magnitude of the option demand. We need to determine the type and minimum scale of reserves of land-based and aquatic environments needed to avoid grossly adverse consequences for human welfare. On land this could mean setting aside approximately 10 million acres for North America, which is not likely to affect the supply or cost of material inputs to the manufacturing or agricultural sectors. We also need to develop learning-by-doing markets in areas suited to specialized recreation where the preservation of biodiversity is crucial. This policy will help maintain biodiversity for scientific research and educational purposes and will provide the widest choices for future consumers of outdoor recreation.

Note

1. P. Davidson, F.G. Adams, and J.J. Seneca, "The Social Value of Water Recreation Facilities Resulting from an Improvement in Water Quality: The Delaware Estuary," in *Water Research*, eds. A.V. Kneese and S.C. Smith, (Baltimore, 1966), 186; cited by Krutilla, 76.

Summary of

The Human Firm in the Natural Environment: A Socio-Economic Analysis of Its Behavior
by John F. Tomer

[Published in *Ecological Economics* 6 (October 1992): 119–138. Reprinted with kind permission from Elsevier Science B.V., Amsterdam, The Netherlands.]

Firms are developing new managerial approaches to deal with the growing public alarm over environmental degradation, as well as the regulatory, consumer, and technological challenges that result from this degradation. The neoclassical model of the firm that underlies the environmental thinking of most economists cannot adequately explain firm behavior. This article develops a socioeconomic model of the "human firm" that incorporates managerial, social, environmental, and ethical realities not found in the neoclassical model. The article focuses on the pollution aspects of environmental problems that are by-products of the production and consumption of firms' goods and services.

The Neoclassical Model of Firm Behavior

The neoclassical model of the firm assumes that the firm is perfectly knowledgeable about alternative courses of action and that it maximizes profits. The profit-maximizing assumption means that firm behavior depends on economic incentives, which derive from the product and resource markets in which the firm participates, and from regulators who attempt to modify the firm's behavior. The latter do this because firms may act in a manner that creates negative externalities. Firm behavior with respect to the natural environment is, therefore, seen simply as reactions to market and regulatory incentives, unrelated to the character or quality of particular firms, or to society's influence.

Managerial Approaches to the Environment and Changing Realities

Traditionally, problems of pollution have been dealt with by disposing of pollutants with an "out-of-sight, out-of-mind" perspective. This has resulted in attempts to conform to environmental standards merely by adding equipment to existing production processes at the lowest possible costs. Traditional managerial thought has been opportunistic and oriented to the short term in its decision making.

However, new realities confront management today, including:

(1) the alarm of the public at the level of environmental degradation, and increasing support for environmental protection efforts;

(2) the ability of the environmental movement to create coalitions that seek technically and politically feasible solutions to various environmental issues;

(3) the government's requirement that companies meet increasingly stringent environmental standards;

(4) the preference shown by consumers and consumer groups toward environmentally friendly products; and

(5) the development of new technologies that avoid pollution.

These new realities have given rise to new managerial approaches. Environmental management is now recognized as a separate field by both businesses and universities. Environmental goals are being integrated into the overall strategies of companies in an attempt to harmonize environmental and economic goals. Companies are realizing that "pollution prevention pays." Operations are becoming cleaner and cheaper. While not all companies have made the shift, the new environmental realities have resulted in managerial approaches that are long term, rational, nonopportunistic, and responsible.

A Socioeconomic Model of the Human Firm's Environmental Behavior

The new behavior of firms described above indicates a failing of the neoclassical model. The environmental behavior of firms is not simply a response to market or regulatory incentives, but could be consciously chosen behavior that goes beyond the interests of firm owners. Such behavior cannot be accounted for by the neoclassical model. A model of the firm is needed that incorporates managerial, social, environmental, ethical, and economic considerations, and that has clear alternative policy implications.

As in the neoclassical model, firms in the socioeconomic model are affected by market and regulatory incentives, as well as by the existence of market failures that offer economic incentives to pollute the commons. However, the socioeconomic model incorporates five additional factors that determine the firm's ability to improve the environment, taking into account the macro and micro social influences and regulatory effects that encourage or discourage the firm from undertaking environmental activities. These factors are as follows:

(1) *Environmental Opportunities:* These are known or knowable developments that the firm can utilize to reduce environmental impacts. The opportunities to improve the environment may be either in the manufacturing process or in providing consumers with environment-friendly products.

(2) *Internal Organizational Capabilities:* There are six internal organizational capabilities that determine how a firm responds to the opportunities and incentives confronting it:
   (a) The ability of the firm to incorporate environmental considerations into other aspects of the company's operations.
   (b) The ability of firms to make rational decisions: The socioeconomic model assumes that firms are boundedly rational. Firms can improve the rationality of their environmental decision making by investing in organizational capital.
   (c) The ability of the firm to be socially responsible: The social
   · responsibility of a firm depends on its ethical standards and its willingness to make short-term sacrifices for long-term gain. The level of social responsibility of firms can range from firms that are

opportunistic and oriented toward the short term to highly patient
and ethical firms that act in ways that transcend their self-interest.

(d) The ability of firms to envision and carry out change: This capability is called *entrepreneurship*.

(e) The capacity of the firm for organizational learning.

(f) The firm's level of environmental concern and awareness.

(3) *Macro Social Forces:* Community and societal influences that reflect public concerns, societal goals and demands, and society's support for environmental improvements can all influence firm behavior.

(4) *Extra-Firm Institutions and Infrastructures:* These are micro forces that influence a firm's environmental behavior, including educational institutions, trade associations, consultants, the firm's suppliers (including its suppliers of pollution control technology), lawyers and lobbyists, and standard industry and managerial practices.

(5) *Other Regulatory Influences:* Some regulatory administrative operations may have undesirable effects on firms' environmental behavior due to unintended social and economic consequences of the regulatory operations.

Thus, in the socioeconomic model of the firm, a firm's behavior is determined by its internal organizational capabilities and the external social and regulatory influences upon it. Pollution is a product not only of market failures but also of insufficiently developed firms and a lack of appropriate social and regulatory support.

Implications for Government Policy

The main implications of the socioeconomic model for government policy are that it should:

(1) encourage the development of firms' internal organizational capabilities;

(2) provide firms with knowledge of environmental opportunities or opportunities to learn about them;

(3) identify and reduce the undesirable micro social influences emanating from extra-firm institutions and infrastructures, and strengthen the desirable influences; and

(4) identify and reduce the undesirable, unintended influences from regulators' administrative operations.

PART IV

Energy and Resource Flow Analysis

Overview Essay

by Jonathan M. Harris

The structure of ecological economic theory, as we have outlined it above, clearly implies a more central role for the analysis of energy and biophysical resource use than does standard economics. The articles in this part go into greater depth concerning the implications of this perspective for analysis and policy. Some of the discussion here is still on a theoretical level, but there are also significant efforts to develop specific techniques appropriate to this new perspective. These offer insights into economic theory, data analysis, and policy formulation which are significantly different from those derived from the neoclassical model. We can also note here that as ecological economists attempt to come to grips with the real-world implications of their theory, differences of opinion and of interpretation within the field become more pronounced.

The fountainhead of energy and resource flow analysis is found in the work of Nicholas Georgescu-Roegen. As we have already seen, there is considerable controversy over the value and implications of his theories. The most detailed exposition of his thought is in his 1971 book *The Entropy Law and the Economic Problem*, but his short article on "The Entropy Law and the Economic Problem" is more accessible to most readers. Here is set forth the basic view of the economic system as an "open" subset of a larger biophysical system, with matter and energy crossing the boundary into the economic system in a low-entropy state and returning in a high-entropy state. This unidirectional flow differs fundamentally from anything in standard economic theory, which sees the economy as a closed system balanced by internal market equilibrium. From this basic analysis Georgescu-Roegen draws some lessons of sweeping importance. One is that the production process necessarily results in an *entropy deficit*, a draw-down of "wealth" in terms of available energy and resources. Another is the fundamental distinction between the *stock* of terrestrial resources, analogous to capital, and the *flow* of solar energy, analogous to income. The difference between living on income and living on capital is clear, but prior to Georgescu-Roegen's work it had rarely been applied to energy and resource economics.

Georgescu-Roegen uses the inexorable logic of entropy to define the limits of economic activity. No industrial system can continue indefinitely drawing down terrestrial stocks of low entropy. (Note that this argument is not framed simply in terms of quantities of available resource reserves but takes in the logic of rising costs and increasing environmental damages as production proceeds.) Also, there are strict limits to what can be achieved through technological progress or resource recycling. Technological optimism must be subordinated to the entropy law; what Georgescu-Roegen calls "entropy bootlegging" is as impossible as perpetual motion. Even a steady-state, nongrowing economy will progressively degrade its terrestrial resource base. Hence the unique importance of solar energy—it is the only truly "free" good, but a difficult one to utilize well due to its diffuse nature.

What are some of the practical implications of the entropy analysis? We must remember that Georgescu-Roegen's original work was published prior to the wave of awareness generated by environmental problems that have drawn wide public attention in the last twenty years. His work can certainly be regarded as prescient in providing a theoretical framework to explain concerns about both resource adequacy and global environmental pollution. But how can it be applied to economic analysis? Some economists have argued in response that while the entropy limits posited by Georgescu-Roegen must undoubtedly apply to economic activity in the long term, their practical impact is so far off as to be irrelevant to current economic analysis. In this view, the entropy law provides a nice metaphor for an over-consuming, over-polluting society, but nothing more. Policy issues of resource management and pollution control will not be subject to binding entropy constraints for centuries, according to many leading economists (see, for example, Robert Solow's 1974 article on "The Economics of Resources or the Resources of Economists"[1]).

The energy and resource flow analyses in this part are predominantly oriented toward proving this critique wrong by developing practical applications of analyses of energy and resource flows. (Only the article by Young endorses the neoclassical skepticism about the relevance of entropy theory.) Some respond directly to the issue of relevance to economic theory. Tran Huu Dung sees entropy as compatible with mainstream economics, and distinguishes between the entropy implications of consumption, production, and "pure" utility. Pure utility refers to satisfaction derived from the natural world without intervention in it, and it is neutral in entropy terms. Consumption necessarily increases entropy. Production is more complex: it decreases entropy in some parts of the system while increasing it in the larger environment. This gives a new twist to "technological optimism." The true potential of technology is seen to lie in its ability to achieve utility while minimizing increases in entropy. This has a clear parallel with the standard economic conception of maximizing utility while minimizing costs, but also a crucial difference. The difference is that the entropy implications of a particular production process will probably not be reflected in market prices, nor will consumers be encouraged to favor "pure" utility over consumption through market processes (quite the contrary if advertising is taken into account).

Jeffrey Young, by contrast, defends the mainstream economists' treatment of the entropy law as irrelevant to economic analysis. The essence of his critique is the proposition that technological progress can overcome any growth limitations imposed by entropic degradation. This is linked to an assertion that the entropy concept is meaningless as applied to matter, since improved technology can render previously unusable materials useful. Counter-arguments by Townsend and Daly reemphasize the point that technological progress is always subject to the entropy law, which as a matter of scientific definition applies to both matter and energy. Daly also points out that improved information may constrain rather than expand our choices in use of matter and energy, when we discover unsuspected environmental damage from existing technologies such as CFCs. This is a point of far-reaching importance: the environmentally destructive nature of the "unforeseen consequences" attendant on technological progress often seem to be associated with efforts to "bootleg entropy." For example, the spread of energy-intensive agriculture has brought in its wake a multitude of negative environmental impacts not associated with traditional agriculture. One interpretation of this would be that traditional agriculture, like natural ecosystems, was well-organized for the capture of the solar low-entropy flux; intensive agriculture expands apparent carrying capacity at the expense of polluting the environment with high-entropy waste products. In any event, one inference is that the specific examination of production processes in entropy terms will be intellectually fruitful.

R. Stephen Berry's article moves toward a practical application of entropy analysis with an examination of the thermodynamic efficiency of automobile production. He identifies enormous inefficiency in production techniques viewed not from a least-cost point of view but in terms of energy requirements. Significant energy savings are also possible from recycling or improving product durability, but these are dwarfed by the potential of highly energy-efficient production techniques. Oddly, this thermodynamic inefficiency is probably "efficient" from the point of view of standard economic theory—energy prices are too low relative to capital and labor to justify private investment in an energy-efficient plant or social investment in the appropriate training and infrastructure for a high energy-efficiency economy.

The contrast between economic and thermodynamic efficiency is further developed in the article by Robert Ayres and Indira Nair. They criticize the standard economic concept of a production function with unlimited substitutability between labor/capital and matter/energy. Technology which operates specifically to increase thermodynamic efficiencies can lower matter/energy requirements, subject to entropy law limits, but will not eliminate the problem of economic dependence on high-quality fossil fuel resources. This suggests that analysis of fossil fuel use, reserves, and efficiencies has a specific importance which is not adequately reflected by changes in market price. Such analyses have been attempted by, among others, Robert Costanza, Cutler Cleveland, and Howard and Elizabeth Odum.

What is meant by the "energy cost" of production? The question is trickier than it might appear. One approach is simply to measure the money costs of directly purchased energy (e.g., coal burned in the production of steel). But this leaves out many indirect energy inputs (e.g., energy used to make machinery for the steel mill). It also omits solar energy. We can also consider labor inputs to be indirect energy inputs, at least in part, since the provision of labor requires food energy, energy for housing and transportation, etc. An early review of these issues by P.F. Chapman sets out these problems, and some of the methods appropriate for resolving them, with some specific industrial applications. It is notable, however, than no single entirely consistent technique is identified. Chapman warns that energy studies are subject to misinterpretation if their assumptions and methods are not made clear. These potential ambiguities in energy analysis can become the source of considerable controversy, as the selections in this part demonstrate.

In "Energy and Money" Howard and Elizabeth Odum identify virtually all economic activities as energy flows, balanced by money flows in the economic system. In effect they pose an "energy theory of value" analogous to Marx's labor theory of value. They do not come to grips, however, with the many economic theory difficulties created by such a sweeping simplification. Marx and his followers spent much time grappling with the "transformation problem" of labor value and market prices, but the Odums simply overlook any such problems arising from an energy theory of value. They maintain, for example, that inflation arises when money supply growth exceeds available energy supply—an apparently apt description of the energy price-driven inflation of the 1970s, but not very useful analytically in explaining varying rates of inflation during other periods in economic history.

Costanza's 1980 paper, "Embodied Energy and Economic Valuation," also grapples with the problem of energy valuation. Input–output techniques allow economic inputs to be reduced to primary factors—the question is which primary factors to select. Costanza starts with the conventional categories of capital, labor, natural resources, and government services, then moves by stages to include solar energy, to convert labor and government services to their embodied energy equivalents, and then to combine these two steps to produce an economic system where energy is in effect the only ultimate input. His main conclusion from a statistical analysis of this model is that embodied energy values are closely related to dollar values of output. Unfortunately this result is vulnerable to the criticism raised by Georgescu-Roegen in "The Entropy Law and the Economic Process in Retrospect" (summarized in Part III above). Once all inputs are reduced to energy, the assertion of a constant relationship between energy and output value becomes a tautology. Energy intensity can only vary across sectors if there is some other primary factor contributing to cost of production. By eliminating *all* other primary factors, Costanza may have gone a bridge too far. It might have been better, for example, to base the analysis on the primary factors of solar energy, fossil fuel and nuclear energy, materials, and labor. This would allow investigation of economic shifts over time from dependence on labor and solar energy to fossil fuel/nuclear reliance, and perhaps provide insight into the possibility of an information-intensive future economy based on skilled labor and efficient capture of solar energy. By contrast, what Georgescu-Roegen refers to as the "energetic dogma" is ultimately barren of analytical value.

The article by Cleveland, Costanza et al. on "Energy and the U.S. Economy" focuses on some more practical conclusions. The authors demonstrate a strong link between fossil fuel inputs and economic output using a conventional GNP measure. Growth in labor productivity over time is seen not as a disembodied technological advance but as resulting specifically from increased use of energy in combination with labor. Both of these are important empirical results (though subject to challenge—see, for example, work by Moomaw and Tullis on differing national energy development paths[2]). Their comments on inflation are similar to those of the Odums and subject to the same criticism. Perhaps the most important finding of this article is that the energy costs of obtaining energy itself are steadily rising for all fossil fuel sources. This is a more sensitive gauge of the limits of the fossil fuel age than simple estimates of existing reserves.

Cleveland extends this approach in his 1990 article "Natural Resource Scarcity and Economic Growth Revisited" to examine energy use in all major natural resource sectors of the U.S. economy. Energy costs per unit of physical output are found to be rising in many sectors, giving an important new perspective on the analysis of resource scarcity. Net costs of resource extraction may be falling due to lower labor and capital costs, and still-cheap fossil fuels. But this standard economic measure of costs masks the increasing dependence on energy inputs—and, as noted above, the energy cost of extracting fossil fuels is itself rising. Without significant future increases in energy efficiency or shifts to solar energy, this indicates a predictable future economic crisis, one which is not likely to be reflected in standard economic analyses until it is well under way. The article by John Peet supports this point, using the concept of net energy to measure resource quality and predicting much higher long-term costs of energy resource development as more easily available, higher-return sources are exhausted.

Bruce Hannon suggests that in this context of energy limits, we face a choice between continuing our energy-intensive economic strategies or shifting our ethos and incentive systems toward a "conserver society." In such a society, labor and capital would be substituted for energy use. In addition to the environmental advantages, this approach would promote full employment of labor. A tax on energy is the obvious policy tool to promote this economic transition. Such a tax need not be an *additional* burden on taxpayers, but rather should partly replace present taxes on labor and capital. To those who complain that such a tax would distort free market pricing, one might suggest that the present tax system is an equal distortion, but one which is not so benign in terms of its effects on employment and the environment.

A different perspective on the "conserver society" is offered in articles by Robert Ayres and Faye Duchin. Ayres interprets physical flows in the economy in thermodynamic terms: a massive one-way flow of energy and materials being converted to wastes. The emerging concept of industrial ecology suggests a goal of improving process efficiency and reuse of wastes, just as natural ecosystems have evolved for efficient use of low entropy. Ayres points out that the economic incentives of market price often work against this goal, rewarding throwaway products and reliance on virgin materials. He discusses a possible future economy using a solar/hydrogen energy base, and eliminating dissipative uses of heavy metals and other long-lived pollutants. His article is rich in specific examples of the physical and chemical characteristics of industrial processes. It is clear from the discussion that an unguided market economy lacks appropriate incentives to promote the transition to a thermodynamically efficient industrial ecology.

Faye Duchin offers a specific analytic framework for evaluation of material and energy flows and waste reduction. Her adaptation of dynamic input–output analysis to the industrial ecology perspective crosses the disciplinary boundaries of economics, engineering, and the physical sciences.

Its physical focus distinguishes this approach from standard economic optimization techniques based on price signals. Dynamic input–output analysis is particularly appropriate in meeting the challenge posed by Ayres of massive industrial adaptation rather than incremental change. Duchin has also applied this analytical approach to specific areas of industrial ecology, including biomass waste recycling and global strategies for reduction of atmospheric pollutants.[3]

A more specific approach to industrial ecology is presented by T.E. Graedel et al. Three subsystems of the industrial process are identified: materials production, product manufacture, and consumer product cycle. Each can include both recycling and waste disposal. An overall systems analysis is needed to identify possibilities for more effective materials reuse, reduction, or recycling. The institutional requirements for linking these separate phases of the industrial process may be lacking, with materials producers, manufacturers, and consumers responding to market price incentives only. Modification of these market incentives through, for example, a tax on virgin materials, is one policy tool available for industrial ecology. In other cases more specific regulations aimed at emissions reduction, institutions for collecting and recycling wastes, toxic materials manifest systems, and so on are essential. None of these policy tools are new in themselves, but their comprehensive application to the materials/manufacturing/consumption cycle is the special domain of industrial ecology.

Thus the field of energy and resource flow analysis has developed considerably beyond the broad world view of economic activity and entropy set forth by Georgescu-Roegen in 1971. Specific techniques and methodologies have emerged, not without controversy, and have been successfully applied to practical problems. Much remains to be done in this area. If the general trends indicated by Cutler Cleveland's work are confirmed by further studies, the importance of this area of investigation will grow. Industrial ecology studies, whether of regional or global scope, will clearly be in greater demand as nations struggle to integrate environment and development issues. The techniques of standard economics are not irrelevant to the investigation of these areas, but a strong case has emerged that they are not sufficient, and may be misleading without a stronger focus on the physical basis of economic systems.

Notes

1. Robert M. Solow, "The Economics of Resources or the Resources of Economics," *American Economic Review* (May 1974).

2. William R. Moomaw and D. Mark Tullis, "Charting Development Paths: A

Multicountry Comparison of Carbon Dioxide Emissions," *Industrial Ecology and Global Change*, eds. Robert Socolow, C. Andrews, F. Berkhout, and V. Thomas (Cambridge, England: Cambridge University Press, 1994).

3. Faye Duchin, "The Conversion of Biological Materials and Wastes to Useful Products," *Structural Change and Economic Dynamics*, 1 (December 1990); and Faye Duchin, "Prospects for Environmentally Sound Economic Development in the North, in the South, and in North-South Economic Relations: the Role for Action-Oriented Analysis," *Journal of Clean Technology and Environmental Science*, 1(3–4), 225–38 (1991).

Summary of

The Entropy Law and the Economic Problem

by Nicholas Georgescu-Roegen

[Published in *University of Alabama Distinguished Lecture Series*, No. 1, 1971, and in *Valuing the Earth: Economics, Ecology, Ethics*, eds. Herman E. Daly and Kenneth N. Townsend (Cambridge, Massachusetts and London: The MIT Press, 1993).]

The influence of a mechanistic approach on the founders of neoclassical economics can still be seen today in, for example, the representation of the economic process as a pendulum movement between production and consumption within a completely closed system. The mutual influences that the economic process and the material environment have on each other are not recognized by standard economics. Marxian economists also represent the economic process as a completely circular and self-sustaining system, and they do not recognize the interrelations between the economic process and nature. However, the history of mankind unequivocally shows that nature plays an important role in the economic process. This article considers the consequences of this role and seeks to show that some of them are of utmost importance in understanding the linkages between nature and the evolution of man's economy.

Given the First Law of Thermodynamics—that matter and energy can neither be created nor destroyed—it is worth asking what the economic process actually does. When viewed from the purely physical perspective, the economic process continuously absorbs and throws out matter-energy. This is a partial process, circumscribed by a boundary across which matter and energy are exchanged with the rest of the material universe. Valuable natural resources enter the economic process, and valueless waste is thrown out. In thermodynamic terms, the economic process converts matter-energy from a state of low entropy to a state of high entropy.

What is entropy? The 1948 edition of *Webster's Collegiate Dictionary* defines entropy as "a measure of the unavailable energy in a thermodynamic system." Energy exists in two forms: available or free energy, and unavailable or bound energy. Man has almost complete command over free energy, but cannot use bound energy. For example, the chemical energy in a piece of coal is free energy, whereas the heat energy contained in the water of the seas is bound energy. Free energy implies the existence of ordered structure, while bound energy is energy dissipated in disorder. The Second Law of Thermodynamics, the entropy law, states that the amount of bound energy of a closed system continuously increases. Once a system has reached thermodynamic equilibrium (i.e., when all energy is bound), the only way to lower its entropy is to bring in free energy from outside the system. However, the decrease in entropy of the closed system can be obtained only at the cost of higher entropy elsewhere. When man converts copper ore (relatively higher in entropy) to copper metal (relatively lower in entropy) there is a more than compensating increase in the entropy of the surroundings. The lesson from thermodynamics is that, in entropic terms, the cost of any biological or economic enterprise is always greater than the product.

Why does the economic process go on? The purpose of the economic process is the enjoyment of life, but both the enjoyment of life and continued economic progress depend on the availability of environmental low entropy. Every object of economic value has a highly ordered structure. In fact, a number of historically important events have begun as searches for environmental low entropy. Thus, it is apparent that the economic process is not an isolated, circular affair but a unidirectional, irrevocable evolution, tapping low entropy and inevitably producing high entropy, because it is anchored in a material base subject to definite constraints.

The Industrial Revolution saw economists beginning to ignore the natural environment when representing the economic process. The powers of science were exaggerated, and it was argued that there were no real obstacles to progress; constraints imposed by the material environment were not recognized. In fact, serious thought was given to the notion that it was possible to unbind bound energy. As a result, scientists and economists failed to realize that "better and bigger" products could not be made without "better and bigger" waste as a by-product. Even now some suggest that problems of pollution can be dealt with either by producing no waste, or by recycling wastes. While recycling can take place, the entropic cost of recycling is much greater than its entropic benefits.

Although the globe may be surrounded by free energy, either the costs of tapping it are too high to be worthwhile, or the technology does not exist. For example, the immense thermonuclear energy of the sun cannot be directly tapped as no material container exists that can resist the massive temperatures of the reactions. Two sources of free energy are accessible to man. The first, the energy from mined sources, is a stock, while the second, solar radiation intercepted by the earth, is a flow. There are three important differences between these two sources:

(1) man has almost complete control over energy from terrestrial stocks, but has no control over the flow of solar radiation;

(2) terrestrial sources provide low-entropy energy to manufacture our most important implements, whereas solar radiation, which is the

source of chlorophyll photosynthesis, is the primary source of all life; and

(3) the existing energy in terrestrial stocks is a small fraction of that contained in the sun.

In light of these differences, the population problem assumes a new dimension. There are differences of opinion about the effects of population growth and the world's ability to support increases in the short run, but no one has asked how long any given total population can be maintained over the long run. It is this second question that brings to light the true complexity of the population problem, and which shows that even the concept of an optimum population level is an inept fiction.

The mechanization of agriculture is unanimously advocated as the solution to meeting the world's food demands. What does this mean in entropic terms? Mechanization has meant replacing draft animals with tractors, i.e., shifting from solar (via chlorophyll photosynthesis) to terrestrial sources of low entropy inputs. Thus, viewed in entropic terms, the mechanization of agriculture is anti-economical in the long run. To secure our biological existence we increasingly depend on the scarcer of the two sources of low entropy.

Moreover, the problem of depletion of terrestrial stocks of low entropy is not limited to the mechanization of agriculture. Given the disproportion between the amount of energy available from the sun compared to that in the earth, the industrial phase of man's evolution will cease long before the sun stops shining. The higher the degree of economic development, the sooner the end will come.

What does all this imply? Present economic development and production are using limited supplies of available low entropy at the cost of future generations. Even if we realize the entropic problem, we may not be willing to give up our present luxuries. It seems mankind is doomed to have a short life.

Summary of

Selections from "Energy and Economic Myths"

by Nicholas Georgescu-Roegen

[Published in *Southern Economic Journal* 41 (January 1975) and in *Valuing the Earth: Economics, Ecology, Ethics,* eds. Herman E. Daly and Kenneth N. Townsend (Cambridge, Massachusetts and London: The MIT Press, 1993).]

(In this summary, a discussion of bioeconomics has been omitted, as it is very similar to the issues raised in "The Entropy Law and the Economic Problem," also summarized in this part.)

A number of strands of economic thought can be identified, but when seen from the perspective of the laws of physics, many of them are myths. These "myths" can be classified into three broad categories, each of which is discussed below.

Entropy Bootlegging

There is a notion that sources of usable energy are infinite because of man's inherent ability to defeat the entropy law. However, given that there can only be a finite amount of low entropy in a finite space, which continuously and irrevocably dwindles, we must recognize the finiteness of accessible resources. Even scientific authorities have voiced the hope that energy can eventually be made a free good. For example, some suggest that sea water could be decomposed into oxygen and hydrogen, the combustion of which will yield great amounts of energy. However, this is an impossibility because the entropy of water is higher than that of oxygen and hydrogen after decomposition. Others hope that nuclear energy will produce more energy than is consumed—another false hope. These proposals do not recognize that any activity must consume a greater amount of low entropy than is contained in the product; this is the deficit principle of the entropy law.

Economic Myths

Standard economists argue that, since the definition of resources changes over time, there cannot be an absolute limit on natural resources. It is true that estimates of available natural resources have often proved to be lower than the actual amounts; there may, for example, be more metal in the earth's crust than we know of at present. However, the issues of accessibility and disposability of those unknown reserves must not be ignored. More importantly, irrespective of how resources are defined, the total amount available must be finite. No taxonomic switch can change that.

Standard (neoclassical) and Marxist economists also argue that we will always be able to find substitutes for resources and to increase the productivity of any kind of energy or material. The basis of this assertion is that it has been done in the past and will therefore be possible in the future. However, the same kind of linear thinking would lead to the conclusion that no healthy young person will ever die. Extending the same logic, it is argued that only a few resources are incapable of eventually yielding extractive products at constant or declining costs, and that technology improves exponentially. While it is true that technological advances induce other advances, there may be an upper limit on the level of technological progress related to resource extraction.

Finally, there is what may be called the fallacy of endless substitution, which has both a theoretical and an empirical dimension. Theoretically, according to this argument nature imposes particular scarcities, not an inescapable general scarcity. Substitution for resources that run out is nonproblematic as there are very few resources that defy economic replacement. Substitution will take place because of changes in relative prices; for example, it will take place first within the spectrum of consumer goods, with decreasing purchase of resource-intensive goods, and increasing purchase of other things. Similarly, in production, as natural resources become scarce other factors of production will take their place. There are two problems with these arguments. First, substitution within a finite stock of accessible low entropy cannot go on indefinitely. Second, with respect to substituting other factors for natural resources, we must recognize that there are no material factors other than natural resources. To think otherwise is erroneous.

On the empirical front, Solow[1] has shown that for a number of different minerals, consumption per unit of GNP fell in the United States between 1950 and 1970. However, this in no way shows that technological improvements led to a greater economy of resources. GNP may increase more than any input of minerals even if technology remains the same, or even deteriorates. More importantly, we do know that between 1947 and 1967 the per capita consumption of basic materials increased. What is relevant is not only the impact of technological progress on the consumption of resources per unit of GNP, but also the increase in the overall rate of resource depletion.

Another piece of empirical work to support the substitution thesis is the work of Barnett and Morse.[2] They showed that between 1870 and 1957 the ratios of labor and capital costs to net output decreased in agriculture and mining, and argued that these numbers show that technological progress will render accessible resources that were previously thought to be un-usable. However, while their numbers are indisputable, their interpretation is flawed. Economic history shows that great strides in technological pro-gress have been touched off by discoveries of how to use new kinds of ac-cessible resources. These technological innovations must be followed by a great mineralogical expansion to increase known reserves, which leads to a fall in energy prices. It is this cheaper energy that is substituted for capital and labor in the production process. Rising output and falling capital and labor costs can lead, then, to the results shown by Barnett and Morse, but this does not change the fact that the amount of energy being used has in-creased.

The Steady State: A Tropical Mirage

Some writers who have wanted to show that continuous growth will lead to all kinds of disasters have concluded that the solution is to achieve a steady-state or stationary-state economy. Their error is in not recognizing that a positively growing, a no growth, and a declining growth economy all converge toward annihilation in a finite environment. The essential point is that the total accessible resources that exist in the crust of the earth are bound to run out at some point if we assume, for example, that each indi-vidual will use up a positive amount of resources each year of his or her life. The only way in which a stationary state can go on forever is if accessible resources in the crust of the earth are inexhaustible.

There are other problems with the vision of a steady state. Apparently a stationary state is equated with an open thermodynamic steady state, which maintains its entropic structure through material exchange with its envi-ronment. But for such a state to exist, special conditions need to be met that make its perpetual existence close to an impossibility. Another problem with the concept is that while, on the one hand, throughput in such a state would be constant, on the other hand, the society would be forced to change its technology and mode of life to adapt to decreases in resource ac-cessibility. This would call for the right innovations at the right time, and if this does not happen, as it inevitably will not, the state will collapse.

It is also argued that in a steady state there is more time for pollution to be reduced by natural processes and for technology to adapt to reductions in accessible resources. But the route to efficient and clean technologies may be through a system of trial and errors. Also it is argued that in a sta-tionary state people will have more time for intellectual activities. History contradicts this point. There have been instances of quasi-stationary soci-eties where the arts and sciences were practically stagnant. Finally, there is no way of determining, even in principle, what the optimum levels of population and capital must be at which the steady state will come to rest. However, the enormous disproportionality between the flow of solar energy and the much more limited stock of terrestrial free energy suggests a bioeconomic program emphasizing such factors as solar energy, organic agriculture, population limitation, product durability, moderate consumption, and international equity.

Notes

1. Robert M. Solow, "Is the End of the World at Hand?" *Challenge* (March–April 1973), 39–50.
2. Harold J. Barnett and Chandler Morse, *Scarcity and Growth* (Baltimore: John Hopkins Press, 1963).

Summary of

Consumption, Production, and Technological Progress: A Unified Entropic Approach
by Tran Huu Dung

[Published in *Ecological Economics* 6 (December 1992): 195–210. Reprinted with kind permission from Elsevier Science B.V., Amsterdam, The Netherlands.]

The Second Law of Thermodynamics has been recognized and incorporated into economic analysis by only a small number of economists, primarily in the fields of resource and environmental economics. Even here the law has done little more than reinforce the sense that there is a limit to boundless economic growth. Beyond this, the impact upon mainstream economic thinking has been negligible, a testimony to the durability of the neoclassical model and its world of infinite substitutability between relatively scarce and relatively abundant resources.

However, even this limited emphasis on the enveloping implications of the Second Law has ignored other equally important entropic properties of economic processes. The Second Law can be taken beyond dictums regarding the inevitability of the end of the world and viewed instead as the delineator of contours within which myriad economic activities can yet take place for a considerable time. It is proposed that an entropy-based characterization of three constituent economic phenomena—consumption, production, and technological progress—can provide an additional dimension in which the economist's traditional building blocks can be further distinguished and analyzed. The incorporation of the Second Law into economics is therefore not incompatible with the existing economic paradigm; it is not a replacement of the mainstream approach, but a complement to it.

The basic premises for this approach are as follows:

(1) entropy is an objective physical magnitude;

(2) many entropies can be ascribed to a system depending on the parameters selected and the level of description, but it is possible to speak of an absolute value of entropy; and

(3) the apparent arbitrariness of an entropy can be explained by distinguishing between "randomness" and "disorder."

Consumption and the Second Law of Thermodynamics

In its simplest version, the Second Law of Thermodynamics asserts that, as time passes, closed systems function in a manner that produces a state of increased entropy or randomness. A closed system is one in which there is no gain or loss of energy from the surroundings. The economic ramifications of this are evident in the observation that human biological life depends upon the consumption of low-entropy inputs and the consequent generation of high-entropy outputs, or waste. Human economic life is the same. Some economists have seized upon this notion to argue that it is economic life itself that creates the tendency to move toward increasingly disordered, high-entropy states, but this is not quite correct. It is actually the consumptive process that purely manifests this property, while the entropic ramifications of both production and technological progress are less clear in this regard.

The relation between the usefulness of materials and their entropy level is an important one. If all things in the universe were to be ranked by their entropy levels, those that are most useful would clearly be grouped at the lower end of the scale. This idea becomes more precise and testable if we recognize that not only will the entropy output from any consumptive process be high relative to the entropy levels of the inputs, but in addition, it will be well above that of the consumed system had it not been consumed at all.

It is also important to recognize that, even without human intervention, the entropy of a system will increase continuously due to the "natural evolution path" of the system. This concept offers a new way to approach the measurement of consumption. To begin with, increasing entropy above its natural state is not a necessary condition for the creation of utility. Utility can be derived from transformations occurring along the natural evolution path (e.g., watching leaves fall from a tree); this is "pure use." Alternatively, utility may be derived from transformations affected by intentional human intervention; this is "active" or "non-pure use." Human intervention will normally cause greater increases in entropy than transformations that occur along the natural evolution path. Consumption can then be associated with active or non-pure use and is the difference between the entropy level that results after human intervention and that which would have resulted from the natural evolutionary path. If there is no difference, then we have pure use and no consumption, but if there is a difference, then we have consumption, and the magnitude of the difference can be thought of as the degree of consumption.

Production Versus Consumption

In many conceptualizations, production and consumption are viewed as sharing a number of properties; in particular, both involve the utilization of inputs and the generation of outputs. If this is so, then it might be assumed that production shares with consumption the entropic characteristics discussed above. From a physical point of view, however, production differs from consumption in that it is "an *intentional* act which causes a certain physical system to be more orderly, less random *from a certain point of view*."[204] That is, organizing a productive process requires the rearranging of a set of inputs to conform to a preconceived set of relationships. This notion must be qualified by observing that the Second Law renders it impossible to rearrange a total system so that the new state is completely orderly; thus it is only from "a certain point of view" that orderliness is enhanced. The Second Law dictates that the system must simultaneously become more random from other points of view, producing a net increase in total disorderliness.

Thus, in economic production, the entropy level will necessarily increase above that which would exist due to the natural evolution path, but for given subsystems within the system we can locate areas of decreasing entropy. This suggests a way to measure the eco-thermodynamic efficiency of the process. An activity that minimizes the output of high-entropy wastes and enhances the degree of orderliness, as suggested above, would imply a greater systemic efficiency.

Usability and Technological Progress

Mainstream economists remain optimistic in the face of the Second Law by suggesting that continuing technological progress will indefinitely postpone the limits to growth. The entropic framework can be used to put this argument in a more constructive perspective. Levels of knowledge and technology determine the usability and reusability of a physical state. As knowledge accumulates, an increasing number of systems previously thought to be unusable are found to contain usable orderly patterns; or a state may become more orderly in response to improved knowledge and the resulting technology. However, it must still be stressed that the natural evolution path produces increasing entropy, implying that the Second Law dictates the eventual triumph of the natural evolution path over technological ingenuity.

Conclusion

Both production and consumption can be characterized by their distinctive thermodynamic properties. Consumption generates an increase in disorder, whereas production may result in an increase in orderliness in some parts of the system. The increase or decrease in the local degree of orderliness can be measured in terms of entropy. Following this unified approach, economic processes can produce three outcomes:

(1) consumption, if the post-use state is more disorderly than the natural state;

(2) pure use, if the post-use state is the same as the natural state; and

(3) production, if the post-use state is on the whole more disorderly, but contains subsets that are more orderly.

This approach is not only consistent with the Second Law but it gives the law a more constructive role. Specifically, it provides a common ground for discussion upon which those afflicted with unbridled optimism and those suffering from doomsday gloom can meet, and thus it enhances the possibility that solutions can be found.

Summary of

Is the Entropy Law Relevant to the Economics of Natural Resource Scarcity?

by Jeffrey T. Young

[Published in *Journal of Environmental Economics and Management* 21 (September 1991): 169–179.]

Mainstream economists have ignored the entropy law in their models of production and economic growth, in spite of the of the strong resemblance that entropy has to the laws of diminishing returns and the concept of scarcity. This article argues that mainstream economists are right in ignoring the entropy law, as it does not add anything new to what is already considered in models of long-run economic growth with respect to the availability of environmental resources.

Conservation and Entropy Laws in Economic Discourse

Ayres and Kneese[1] introduced the law of conservation of matter into economic discourse. They argued that technological external diseconomies are inherent in the process of production and consumption. The implication was that matter was not destroyed during consumption, and hence exhaustion must be an economic as opposed to a physical phenomenon. While the importance of the conservation law has been established in economic analysis, this is not the case with the entropy law. This seems strange, because if matter and energy are neither created in production nor destroyed in consumption, then they must have dissipated, suggesting that the entropy law must be intimately connected with the depletion of natural resources and the buildup of pollutants in the environment.

The energy and environmental crisis of the 1970s resulted in a vast literature on the economics of natural resource scarcity. Only a few economists, including Georgescu-Roegen and Daly, made the entropy law an important part of their analysis. Both see entropy as the basis by which nature imposes a general or absolute scarcity. Daly therefore advocates a steady-state economy. Georgescu-Roegen disagrees with Daly on the efficacy of the steady-state, but he is still critical of economic growth.

For the most part, however, economists have ignored the entropy law. In his 1978 book *Resources, Environment and Economics*, Ayres pointed out that the mainstream theories on exhaustible resources have not taken into account the environmental costs of entropic buildup as natural resources are extracted. Typical neoclassical formulations have argued that a constant per capita output with an exhaustible natural resource is possible under certain condition that are generally based on Cobb–Douglas production functions. These claims of the typical neoclassical formulation do not hold up if the amount of natural resources falls below a certain level; irrespective of the elasticity of substitution between capital and resources, capital must have more than a vanishingly small flow of material resources in order to produce material output. However, while this point seems to lend validity to the Georgescu-Roegen/Daly/Ayres arguments, it actually follows from the conservation laws, not the entropy law. Moreover, this problem with the typical neoclassical formulation is easily dealt with by introducing a constraint in the production function which states that the level of resources should have a lower bound. Such a reformulation may decrease optimism about the sustainability of economic growth, but it still does not clarify the role of entropy in the economics of long-run resource scarcity. In fact, there is some evidence that economists view the entropy law as a glorified law of diminishing returns. However, the difference between the law of diminishing returns and the entropy law is that while the former assumes a certain order of use of natural resources from a given stock, the latter assumes no such ordering.

A Model Incorporating Conservation and Entropy Laws

It will be useful to consider a simple model of the economic process that attempts to incorporate the conservation laws and the entropy law. The inputs in the production process are capital, labor, and two generalized but nonhomogeneous natural resources: matter and energy. The conservation laws and the entropy laws impose the following constraints on the system:

(1) All production, including that of labor and capital, requires matter and energy.

(2) All materials and energy must be accounted for both before and after production has taken place.

(3) Stocks of matter and energy are constant over time, though at any point in time these stocks are partly *in situ*, partly dissipated from previous extraction, and partly embodied in durable goods. The entropy law requires the "orderliness" of these stocks to decrease over time, provided that the system is closed.

It is assumed that the economy is an isolated system, with no flow of matter or energy between the system and the rest of the universe. It is also assumed that capital and labor are produced inputs, i.e., matter and energy are used up in the creation of capital and labor.

This model represents a general equilibrium system that focuses on reproduction, in which outputs are simultaneously inputs. There are four production functions (for capital, labor, refined energy, and refined matter), and capital, labor, refined energy, and refined matter are inputs in each of these as well. Following from the assumptions of the model, relationships are derived between original and current stocks of matter and energy, reflecting the conservation laws. Similarly, relationships are derived showing the difference between the total stocks and the available stocks of matter and energy based on entropic dissipation. As production takes place, each unit of matter and energy used decreases in quality because of the entropy law. This increase in entropy will result in the absolute general scarcity that Daly and Georgescu-Roegen discuss.

However, introducing technological change raises an interesting question: can there be a technological change that is fundamentally anti-entropic, i.e., one that increases order? This can happen if the technological change creates economic resources out of previously non-economic material. Low-entropy matter and energy are anthropomorphic concepts associated with what is useful and are therefore defined by current technology. Visualize a system with two resources "a" and "b." At the outset, let a be a useful resource and suppose that there is no known use for b. As a is used there will be an increase in the level of entropy of the system, i.e., order decreases. However, if through a technological change b becomes a resource, it is possible that entropy (the level of disorderliness or unavailability) will decrease. This is because the system is open with respect to knowledge, which increases exogenously.

The notion of entropy can be applied to energy, since available energy can be measured independently of the state of technology needed to convert the energy into useful work. This is not the case with matter, as its availability depends on the state of technology. However, the absence of a technology that can use dissipated matter does not mean it is unavailable matter. Since there is no measure of the entropy of matter in a closed system, there is no way of defining the materials entropy of a system. Moreover, even if the materials entropy of a system could be defined, there is no way of knowing whether it is increasing or decreasing over time. Another problem in applying the concept of entropy to matter is that there is no neutral aggregation principle that can be applied across different types of material resources. For example, in recycling, when one kind of matter is dissipated while another is collected and made more available, it is difficult to say whether the entropy of the entire system is decreasing or increasing.

Conclusion

The entropy law is not relevant to the economics of long-run resource scarcity. With respect to energy resources, the system is open, so while limits on the flow of solar energy may impose a long-run energy constraint, this is hardly relevant to current resource allocation issues. With respect to matter, the entropic analogy is only relevant if system boundaries are drawn in very peculiar ways, since it is difficult, if not impossible, to define available matter in a technically progressive world with many material resources.

Provided that the materials/energy balance is satisfied, consideration of the entropy law adds little to traditional models.

Note
1. R. Ayres and A. Kneese, "Production, Consumption and Externalities," in *American Economic Review* 59, 282–97 (1969).

Summary of

Is the Entropy Law Relevant to the Economics of Natural Resource Scarcity?: Comment
by Kenneth N. Townsend

[Published in *Journal of Environmental Economics and Management* 23 (July 1992): 96–100.]

(This summary comments on the article by Jeffrey T. Young, "Is the Entropy Law Relevant to the Economics of Natural Resource Scarcity?" also summarized in this part.)

The scientific basis of Young's claim that natural resource economics can be divided into conservation-law orientations and entropy-law orientations, and that the entropy law pertains to energy but not to matter, are questionable. Young argues that the production of nonrecyclable resources in economic production and consumption is a consequence of the conservation principle, and further, that the thermodynamic critique of economic modeling stems from the same principle. He is wrong, because the conservation law only ensures that no economic process can destroy energy or materials. The production of pollution, in the form of disorganized, nonrecyclable waste, is distinctly a Second Law proposition. The economic analysis of the phenomenon of pollution is thus grounded in both the First and Second Laws of Thermodynamics, which jointly describe the characteristics of the changing states of physical systems.

Young further claims that " 'the entropy law as a physical principle applies only in a closed system and then only to energy.' "[97, cited from Young, 167] This claim is wrong on two counts. First, entropy is a concept that applies to both matter and energy. The standard definition of entropic change is the quantity of heat received or lost by a body divided by the temperature, and this applies to all spontaneous changes with respect to energy and matter equally. Young is also wrong in suggesting that the entropy law applies only in closed systems. It is true that it may be possible to reduce the entropy of an open system. However, when changes in all systems—

including the sun—are taken into account, the overall entropy level will increase.

Another more minor problem arises from Young's closed-system model, in which the decision to leave materials that have no known uses *in situ* implies that no discharge or dissipation has occurred. While it may be true that in an economic sense no waste has occurred, as a consequence of the entropy law resources *in situ* will also become increasingly disordered over time. However, although Young's model is technically incorrect, this process is slow enough to make the model heuristically useful.

Young's views on technology are interesting and merit reflection. He wonders if technological change may spontaneously order a system, producing useful materials from waste. The question that Young poses is whether a system will become more ordered if technological change can find an economic use for heretofore useless material, or if a new technology can help recycle some material. However, it must be recognized that even intellectual discovery operates in accordance with the principle of thermodynamics. Technology changes the rate of entropic change but will not reverse the direction of the change. Improved knowledge may increase the efficiency with which we use matter/energy to produce services, but it does not increase the physical availability of matter/energy.

What then is the significance of the entropy law for the economic process? The tendency of the environment to depreciate over time in its functions as both a source and a sink must be understood. While economic growth provides people with services, it reduces the potential for generation of services from stocks for future generations. Thermodynamics provides us with an awareness of a biophysical constraint to economics, rather than with a new economics.

Summary of

Is the Entropy Law Relevant to the Economics of Natural Resource Scarcity?—Yes, of Course It Is!

by Herman E. Daly

[Published in *Journal of Environmental Economics and Management* 23 (July 1992): 91–95.]

(This summary comments on the article by Jeffrey T. Young, "Is the Entropy Law Relevant to the Economics of Natural Resource Scarcity?" summarized in this part.)

The first part of the article is fine except for Young's statement that " 'the entropy law is being recommended to us as the basis of a new energy and/or entropy theory of value.' "[91, cited from Young, 170] This statement has been taken from Burness, et al. (1980) and, as a comment in the same journal points out, is incorrect.[1] It must be noted that Young's model of the "entropy view" neither requires nor implies an energy or entropy theory of value, making the introduction of this error difficult to understand.

Young's main criticism is that entropy is "'an anthropomorphic concept intimately associated with what is useful and, therefore, defined by current technology.'"[91, cited from Young, 177] However, to suggest that entropy is an anthropomorphic concept in no way implies that it is defined by current technology. In addition, Young argues that a material interpretation is critical to the relevance of entropy to economics. While he applies his criticism only to entropy as material dispersion, the same argument should extend to energy as well. However, this extension would imply that the entropy law is false in its classical formulation for energy, and while Young does not try to make this claim, he also does not explain why his arguments do not apply to energy. The lack of a common denominator for different forms of matter does create a problem, but even so, physicists routinely apply entropy to matter, just as they do to energy. Such an application of entropy to matter is more than a mere analogy.

Young's argument that a system may become less entropic (more ordered) thanks to a new technology is strange in several ways. New knowledge will change any system, and we must redescribe the system taking into account the new information. While the new description may record a higher level of low-entropy materials than before, it does not mean that the economic process is not entropic. It simply means that the description of the initial stock of low-entropy materials was incomplete in the light of the new knowledge. In a given year, a greater increase in the inventory of low-entropy materials than the increase in entropy due to resource extraction would not mean that the entropic direction of economic activity has been reversed. New knowledge may expand available matter (and energy) faster than economic activity will convert it into unavailable matter (and energy), but new knowledge may also reveal new limits and reduce available matter-energy (e.g., the discovery of the greenhouse effect lowers the effective availability of fossil fuels, and the discovery of ozone layer depletion places new limits on our ability to use CFCs).

There is a nonsequitur in Young's fundamental argument. Young asks, "Is b available matter when there are no known uses for it? If so, then how can we know that dissipated a is unavailable? The absence of a technology for using dissipated a would not mean it is unavailable matter. The point is that available matter is dependent on the existence of appropriate technologies. It is not a purely physical concept."[92–93, cited from Young, 178] The problem with Young's argument is that he is equating dissipated a and concentrated b, by calling them both "unavailable matter." The reasons for their unavailability are very different: a is unavailable because it is physically dispersed, while b is unavailable because of a lack of knowledge of how to use it. When a technology makes a previously useless material into a useful resource, the technology for using the resource is economic. However, even if a technology to gather and use dispersed material is found, it is not likely that it will be economic, because enormous amounts of energy, time, and labor are required to recycle dispersed material. Moreover, recycling energy is always uneconomic. Even neoclassical economists emphasize substitution rather than recycling because it is easier to find new resources than to recycle old ones.

Young is wrong when he states that "'the model of entropic decay is not relevant for modeling open systems.'"[94, cited from Young, 178] Economies, like organisms, are open systems, resisting entropic decay by importing low-entropy matter-energy from the environment and exporting high-entropy matter-energy. The environment is both the source for low-entropy matter-energy and the sink for high-entropy matter-energy. Absolute scarcity results as the sources become depleted and the sink fills and becomes polluted. The entropy law suggests that the sink cannot serve as a source. Even the notion that the sun is an infinite source of solar energy is wrong, since the level of available solar energy is limited by its flow rate of arrival.

While thermodynamics should not be the basis of a theory of value or relative scarcity, it does help to understand issues of absolute scarcity and the optimal sustainable scale of the economic subsystem as a part of the overall ecosystem.

Note:

1. See summaries in Part III of Stuart Burness, Ronald Cummings, Glenn Morris, and Inja Paik, "Thermodynamic and Economic Concepts as Related to Resource Use Policies," the comment on this article by Herman Daly, and the reply by Burness and Cummings.

Summary of

Recycling, Thermodynamics, and Environmental Thrift

by R. Stephen Berry

[Published in *Bulletin of the Atomic Scientists* 28 (May 1972): 8–15. From the
Bulletin of the Atomic Scientists. © 1972 by the Educational Foundation for Nuclear
Science, 6042 South Kimbark, Chicago, IL 60637, USA.
A one year subscription to the Bulletin is $30.]

As environmental considerations become more important in policy decisions and planning, a compelling need has emerged for reliable and robust indices of environmental use. This is particularly true when choosing between alternative policies, which requires the identification of variables that can be quantified, that are general enough to allow comparison between quite different sorts of processes, that provide key measures or indices, and that yield true measures of the amount of use of the environment. Toward this end, the quantities derived from thermodynamics are the most obvious and natural, and they meet all of these criteria.

Thermodynamic potential is a fundamental measure of a system's capacity to perform work. The science of thermodynamics enables us to determine the minimum expenditure of thermodynamic potential to achieve a given physical change. Since every process requires the consumption of some thermodynamic potential, we are able to compare different processes and select that which is the most thermodynamically efficient. The change in thermodynamic potential associated with a process will measure all of the energy exchanged as well as the effects upon the degree of disorder or dilution, i.e., the entropy of the system.

The two essential forms of stored potential are energy and order. There are multiple forms of energy storage, including hydroelectric facilities, fossil fuels, solar energy, and nuclear technologies. Order is used when, for example, we obtain materials from concentrated ore bodies rather than by finding them distributed evenly over the planet's surface. Some forms of stored potential are readily accessible, while others require considerable effort and energy expenditure before they can be used. Measuring the total stored potential can be quite difficult and involves a considerable amount of guesswork. However, it is possible to measure accurately the change in potential associated with different processes, so that the thriftiest process can be identified and adopted.

This approach is different in practice from the money-based "least cost" method of optimizing production, so it is important to stress the differences between economic and thermodynamic analysis. Economic analysis is based upon perceptions of present value and scarcity as expressed in the marketplace, where the supply and demand framework is modeled on an instantaneous evaluation of the popular perception of shortages. However, "one cannot take seriously using a short-term market analysis to decide, say, in the year 2171, whether all the remaining fossil fuel should be reserved for the chemical industry."[9] But if economists were to determine their estimates of shortage by undertaking increasingly long-term analyses, even with discounting, their estimates would come closer and closer to those made by thermodynamicists. In a sufficiently long time frame, it becomes evident that the most important scarcity is of thermodynamic potential; thus thermodynamic analysis becomes essential.

System Defined

Our system is one in which the manufacture of goods consumes materials and other resources from the environment. To calculate the real thermodynamic cost of a manufactured object, we evaluate the amount of thermodynamic potential that was extracted from the environment to produce the good and then subtract the amount of thermodynamic potential that remains stored in the object. In the unrealizable, idealized thermodynamic limit, the thermodynamic potential that resides in an object is identical to the potential extracted from the environment, the net change in potential is zero, and the process has merely transformed one form of potential into another. However, this naive ideal can never be reality; the net costs are always greater than zero, and there is always a loss of potential both in producing the good and in discarding it. This net loss from production is a true loss as it can not be recovered.

Thermodynamic Estimates

As an example of this thermodynamics-based approach, the thermodynamics associated with the manufacture of automobiles can be examined. Specifically, we can consider the amount of thermodynamic potential consumed in mining and manufacturing from "new" raw materials, the amount consumed in recycling processes, and the minimum requirements for an ideally efficient process. The criterion used is one of "thermodynamic thrift," i.e., the idea that it is desirable to minimize the consumption of thermodynamic potential in achieving any particular goal. There are three policies to consider in this regard: (1) maximizing recycling, (2) extending the useful life of goods, and (3) developing more thermodynamically efficient processes for producing the goods in the first instance.

Each step of the manufacturing process involves the transformation of matter from one state to another, via transformation processes that include mining and smelting, manufacturing, normal use, recycling, junking, and natural degradation. Through numerous, complex calculations, actual figures for loss of thermodynamic potential have been calculated in units of total kilowatt hours (kwh) per automobile. An estimate of 5000–6525 kwh per automobile emerges. The estimate of the *ideal* thermodynamic potential requirement for producing an automobile, on the other hand, is only about 30 kwh.

The enormous magnitude of the gap between actual and ideal thermodynamic potential costs is striking. From this it is evident that our current manufacturing and mining processes "are reflections of the historically developed means of production and transport, rather than of the thermodynamic requirements for creating the ordered structure of an operable machine."[12] The staggering inefficiency manifest in these figures clearly implies the existence of possibilities for vast savings in thermodynamic potential. Even modest improvements in productive processes could generate savings of thousands of kilowatt hours per vehicle.

The potential savings from the alternative policy approaches of recycling or extending product life are smaller but significant. Recycling might save between zero and a little over 1000 kwh per vehicle at best. A limitation of these savings from recycling is the need of new car manufacture for some new materials, mostly to maintain the strength of the vehicles, so the savings figures should be halved. Furthermore, even these savings may not be realizable with current recycling technologies. This assessment could change, however, with improved recycling technologies or an increase in the energy costs of mining and smelting.

The savings associated with an extension of the useful life of a product—for example, through enhanced precision in the manufacturing process itself, or improved maintenance procedures—are somewhat harder to quantify. It is certain, however, that the increased costs of more durable manufacture would be somewhat less than the costs associated with the manufacture of a new product. Doubling or tripling the useful life of an automobile could reduce the overall manufacturing costs by perhaps 1000 kwh, and when the reduced mining and smelting needs are factored in, the net savings increase to 2750–4500 kwh per vehicle.

These figures provide a compelling picture of the differences between these three choices: given current technologies, recycling provides small savings at best when compared to those associated with extending product life, which are in turn small compared with the possible savings from new technologies. However, while it is clear which policy would maximize thermodynamic thrift, the relative ease of adopting one policy over another must also be considered. A policy to encourage maximum recycling would require a relatively small perturbation of existing processes. The extension of useful product life, however, would be more difficult, as it requires a change in both manufacturing techniques and consumer attitudes. The basic technologies to implement the ideal system probably do not yet exist, and the costs of developing and especially of implementing them will be very large indeed. However, the potential savings from their development are so vast that the costs will be insignificant in comparison. For example, it is estimated that saving 1000 kwh per vehicle would equal the output of 8 to 10 large power generation facilities.

It is clear from the example of automobile manufacturing that a policy of thermodynamic thrift ought to be pursued as a national goal. A three-stage course seems desirable: to encourage recycling, to develop extended life machines, and to pursue the longer term goal of developing technologies that would operate with efficiencies closer to the ideal limits. However, the policy implications of this last and most crucial goal are at odds with much current federal policy. We should include in the training of scientists and engineers a specific orientation to conducting this type of research. We should also direct public funds and effort into the development of these technologies since, like military and space technologies, the requisite scale of development is too vast for the private sector.

Summary of

Thermodynamics and Economics
by Robert U. Ayres and Indira Nair
[Published in *Physics Today* 37 (November 1984): 62–71.]

Because the manufacture of goods and services incorporates matter and energy, the physical sciences are clearly relevant to economics. In particular, the laws of thermodynamics can be expected to impose constraints on economic processes just as they do on physical processes. The Second Law of Thermodynamics—the law of increasing entropy—constrains economic processes to those that increase the entropy of the universe. This fact has significant, even world-shaking, implications for economic theory, especially as it is applied to resource, environmental, and technology policy.

Economics

Many economists regard their field as the science of the allocation of scarce resources. The economists' definition of scarcity is important: a resource is considered scarce if it cannot be acquired or used without exchanging another scarce resource for it, i.e., if the available quantity of the resource is insufficient to satisfy all demand for it at a price of zero. As a consequence, it will command a money price in the marketplace that reflects both its value and scarcity. In addition, some resources may command no market price but still be considered scarce, as their use by one person deprives other potential users of their benefits. However, such situations are difficult for economists to handle because of the absence of a market price.

The term *resources* as used in economics is a slippery one. It refers variously to land, labor, capital, materials, energy, or all of these simultaneously under the nonspecific rubric of "factors of production." If the resource in question is not "scarce" as defined above, it will not be considered at all. Since scarce resources command a market price, economists can express all inputs and outputs of a productive process in monetary terms, allowing a straightforward aggregation of these fundamentally different quantities.

Much of economic theory is built upon the simple but powerful notion that economic agents seek to maximize their utility through the buying and selling of economic goods in a free and competitive market. Thus, under a specific set of assumptions, it can be shown that a unique price exists in all markets that will simultaneously maximize the utility of both producer and consumer. Much depends on this simple contention; for example, in the nineteenth century Walras provided mathematical proof that a general equilibrium exists under these assumptions. However, many economists fail to recognize either the nineteenth century roots of this philosophy or that this simplistic form of utilitarianism conspicuously fails to account for much observable phenomena. While this original model has been made more sophisticated with respect to technology and growth in the twentieth century, despite all the embellishments the economy continues to be viewed and modeled as a closed system with a circular flow of money and goods.

However, this view is fundamentally flawed, as the closed system model departs from physical reality in important ways that are apparent once the underlying physical mass and energy flows are considered. All goods, capital and consumer, embody both materials and energy, as do most services. The standard circular flow model has a source of goods (production) and a sink for goods (consumption). However, real materials are not actually consumed, they are returned to the environment as wastes. Thus the economic system cannot be closed if one includes the extraction and disposal of materials, since a closed system in thermodynamic equilibrium is necessarily passive and inert, without flows of matter or energy. The flows of matter and energy through a system also preclude the existence of an economic equilibrium, except in the special case of zero growth.

It is clearly more realistic to regard the economy as an open system through which materials and energy continuously flow. Once this is recognized, the laws of thermodynamics assert themselves and have significant implications for economic theory. The first of these, derived from the First

Law of Thermodynamics, is that the output flow of matter and energy into wastes must be matched by the input flow, i.e., that which was extracted from the earth. The second implication of physical laws, derived from the Second Law of Thermodynamics, is that the available energy contained in the output is less than that contained in the original inputs. In other words, materials tend to be entropically degraded during each stage of the production process, so there is a global increase in entropy as economic production proceeds.

Efficiency

The concept of thermodynamic efficiency was first developed in connection with steam engines: an engine was more efficient if it could pump more water while using the same quantity of coal. This is considered first-law efficiency and is concerned with the quantity of work generated from a given volume of heat input. A process that is more efficient requires (or wastes) less heat and thus uses less energy to accomplish a particular task. Second-law efficiency is measured by taking the ratio of available energy contained in the output to that contained in the input. A process that is second-law efficient generates outputs with available energy levels that are not substantially less than those of the inputs. Thus a simple heating system may be considered first-law efficient if only 30% of the heat goes up the chimney to heat a space, but it may be second-law inefficient in that a large volume of low-entropy matter is used to warm a room to a few degrees above the natural environment, while producing a large volume of high-entropy waste in the process.

However, in economics, efficiency tends to be conceptualized qualitatively rather than quantitatively, and derives from a competitive free market. In this free market, rational maximizing economic agents will generate a Pareto optimal equilibrium if no possible reallocation could be effected that would make one person better off without making another worse off. This implies that the output has been maximized for the economy given well-defined preferences and the available inputs (resources). However, in reality this is a remote abstraction—one that denies any relationship between economic and thermodynamic efficiency.

Production Functions

The divergence between these two concepts becomes clearer when production processes are considered. Economics uses production functions to describe mathematically the relationships between various inputs and the volume of outputs. These functions, subject to a strict set of assumptions, presumably reveal the substitutability between various factors of production, and also measure the maximum potential output given a particular technology set. As one resource becomes more costly, perhaps reflecting greater economic scarcity, it may be replaced by other factors of production at precise, measurable rates derived from the production functions. This approach may be valid when measuring small substitutions at or near the current market equilibrium, but it is clearly problematic when used—as it often is—to draw conclusions about more remote situations involving the entire system over longer time horizons.

This flaw is particularly evident when it comes to resource economics. In spite of the physical impossibility of indefinitely substituting labor and capital for matter and energy, economists have continued to insist on using production functions for this purpose, thereby basing policy analysis on the flawed supposition that constant levels of output can be maintained through input substitution. For example, much of the economic analysis done during the energy crisis was inconsistent with the known laws of physics, making it a kind of reinvention of the perpetual motion machine.

Negentropy

For some time a connection has been seen between entropy and information: the greater the knowledge about the microscopic state of a thermodynamic system, the lower is the entropy of the system. Knowledge or information (orderliness) tend to increase the available energy in a given quantity of matter and are thus the negative of entropy, or negentropy. A production process may therefore result in decreasing entropy locally even as global entropy is increasing due to the generation of waste material and heat. As nonrenewable resources are used up, it is necessary for technical knowledge and capital to accumulate at a sufficient pace to provide a steady increase in negentropy to offset the rise in entropy. For example, in this fashion it is possible, through knowledge, to substitute types of matter (e.g., plastic for aluminum) within the production process. However, these observations do not remove the central limit imposed by the Second Law; no amount of knowledge will enable us to substitute labor and capital for all matter and energy.

Resource Depletion

While the technologies of resource exploration and extraction have become more sophisticated over the past several centuries, it is equally clear that the highest quality and most readily available of those resources have already been discovered. What remains is less pure and less accessible, and will consume more available work or energy to retrieve it. At present, a large proportion of the world's energy comes from fossil fuels, a resource that is necessarily finite. The economic system as a whole may be considered a stable, dissipative system that functions far from a thermodynamic equilibrium, and it cannot be sustained in its present form.

It is possible to avoid a resource-depletion catastrophe, but only through an enormous, conscious effort to do so. The inevitable alternative is a bleak future. Massive R&D efforts can increase the negentropy embodied in knowledge—the orderliness of our system—to increase the available matter and work and to increase the thermodynamic efficiencies of processes to offset the catastrophic rise in entropy associated with our present system. But higher energy prices or other decentralized market forces will not automatically induce these investments, and there is a significant danger that we may not react in time; the necessary investments will become increasingly expensive and the available energy increasingly scarce as we delay. We may find ourselves on a downward escalator from which a democratic, free-enterprise society could find it impossible to disembark.

Summary of

Energy Costs: A Review of Methods

by P.F. Chapman

[Published in *Energy Policy* 2 (June 1974): 91–103.
By permission of the publishers, © Butterworth-Heinemann Ltd.]

The inadequate description of real input costs and the assumption of substitutability inherent in financial analysis of production systems can lead to false conclusions and poor decision making. As an alternative, a number of investigators have turned their attention to the energy costs of production. There are many methods used to evaluate the energy cost of a product, often yielding substantially different results. The purpose of this review is to explain these variations in results, which are often due to the different aims of the investigations.

The Nature of the Problem

There are three problems in evaluating the energy cost of a product. The first is in choosing a subsystem for which all the inputs and outputs are known. For example, there are three simple subsystems for production of a loaf of bread: the bakery, the bakery plus the baker's shop, and the entire production system (e.g., including all farming and transport systems, etc.). The energy costs increase as the size of the subsystem increases, but it is not possible to include all production processes in the world. The subsystem must therefore be restricted in such a way that those inputs that are left out make an acceptably small difference in the total energy cost. The second problem is in deciding what types of energy must be included and how they should be added together. Solar energy is usually not included in energy cost calculations, and energy that is consumed in the production and delivery of fossil fuel may or may not be included. Energy inputs in the form of calorific value of food are also usually ignored. A third type of problem arises in dividing up energy costs when more than one product is produced. These problems do not have a single correct solution, but appropriate conventions for obtaining satisfactory results are needed.

Aims of Energy Studies

The aims of energy studies can be classified in four categories:

(1) Deducing the energy efficiency of processes and making recommendations for conserving energy: Such studies are often carried out by individual industries using data that is not widely available.

(2) Analyzing energy consumption on a large scale so as to forecast or reduce future energy demand: This is the most popular type of study, and it is usually carried out using published national statistics.

(3) Analyzing the energy consumption associated with basic technologies (e.g., for food production, mineral extraction) in order to gauge the consequences of technological trends or energy shortages: These studies are often carried out in areas where conventional economics and "conservationists" disagree, and the conclusions are generally based on published data and presented in terms of national and global averages.

(4) Understanding the thermodynamics of an industrial system.

Methods

There are three methods used to calculate the energy costs of products:

(1) *Statistical Analysis*: This method takes data on the supply of energy to various industries and on industrial output to estimate the energy cost per unit of output. For example, the *Digest of Energy Statistics* shows that the energy supplied to the iron and steel industries in the United

Kingdom in 1968 was 6871×10^6 therms, and the *Iron and Steel Industry Annual Statistics* gives the output of crude steel as 25.86×10^6 tons. This yields a value for energy cost per unit of steel produced of 265.7 therms/ton. This result does not take into account the energy costs involved in generating the electricity and coke used in steel production, the energy sales by the iron and steel industry, and the energy costs of other inputs in the production process. However, these shortcomings can be overcome by using other available statistics. While this method gives a broad estimate of energy costs in an industry, it cannot distinguish between different products within the same industry.

(2) *Input–Output Table Analysis:* An input–output table is a square matrix that includes all inputs and commodities necessary to make other commodities and relates the currency values of the various inputs needed to produce a unit currency of output. One problem with the input –output table is that all firms in an industry are lumped together. In addition, the data is in financial rather than physical terms, so price fluctuations may lead to errors.

(3) *Process Analysis:* The three stages involved in process analysis are:

(a) identifying the network of processes that lead to a final product;

(b) identifying the inputs involved in each process; and

(c) assigning an energy value to each input.

The two problems associated with this method are choosing an appropriate subsystem and assigning energy values. The problem of assigning energy values arises because in some cases an output is also an input in its own production process (e.g., machines that are made of steel are used to produce steel). Therefore, to calculate the energy cost of producing steel, this same energy cost is needed as an input in the calculations. This problem can be solved by making an initial estimation of the cost and then using a set of simultaneous equations to further refine this estimate.

Results

Several examples of different energy value calculations indicate the care that must be taken in interpreting results:

(1) *Copper Smelting:* This example of a detailed process analysis shows how the choice of subsystem influences the results. In copper smelting, an electric furnace has a 61% thermal efficiency and fuel-heated furnaces a thermal efficiency of 27%. The industry therefore finds that the electric furnace provides a substantial energy savings. However, if the subsystem is enlarged to include electricity supply and the produc-

tion of electric furnaces, the opposite results emerge. Thus the copper smelting industry is improving thermal efficiency within its limited subsystem but decreasing efficiency within the larger national subsystem.

(2) *Supply of Electricity:* This example shows how the aims of a study can alter the results. According to the *Digest of Energy Statistics*, the primary inputs in the United Kingdom are coal, oil, gas, nuclear electricity, and hydro-electricity, all of which are converted into coal equivalents. Using this convention, the energy cost of one kilowatt-hour of electricity (kWhe) consumed is 3.91 kilowatt-hours of thermal energy (kWhth). However, if the inputs are instead taken to be either the output of nuclear and hydrostations and/or fossil fuels, different energy costs result. Similarly, differences in how the indirect energy consumption of power stations is accounted for will further affect results.

(3) *Oil Refining:* This is an example of an industry where there is more than one output, so the question arises as to how inputs should be partitioned between different outputs. Crude oil is refined into fuels and chemical feedstock in oil refineries, and the chemical feedstock is then processed into organic chemicals. Different conventions can be adopted, including assigning all of the calorific value to the fuels, or dividing it between fuels and chemical feedstock.

Conclusions

Energy analysis is valuable because it can show ways of conserving energy and highlight particular problems. But the results of energy studies must be carefully interpreted with regard to the subsystems being analyzed and the methods used to measure energy inputs. Neglect of these factors could lead to misleading conclusions.

Summary of

Energy and Money

by Howard and Elizabeth Odum

[Published in Howard and Elizabeth Odum, *Energy Basis for Man and Nature* (New York: McGraw-Hill, 1976), 49–59. Summarized with permission of McGraw-Hill, Inc.]

To understand the economic system as a whole, it is important to understand the relationship between money, which flows in circles within the system, and energy, which flows through it. The effects of energy flows and the circulation of money on both economic growth and on inflation will be considered.

The Money Cycle

In economic process, flows of money and of energy are closely intertwined. For example, in the production process on a farm, high-grade potential energy flows in and low-grade dispersed heat flows out. Money flows in from the townspeople to pay for farm produce and then flows back to the town when farmers buy machinery and fertilizer. Some of the energy that flows into the system is used to support the work involving these transactions with money. The money paid to the farmer by the townspeople pays only for the work of the farmer but not for that of the rain, soil, wind, etc. To capture the contribution of nature, energy rather than money must be the measure of value.

The circulation of money is dependent on the inflow of energy; money will not circulate unless materials and energy are flowing as well. In turn, money facilitates the flow of material and the receipt and processing of energy, and money must therefore be seen as affecting energy flows as well.

In the United States in 1973 there were approximately 25,000 calories[1] used for every dollar in circulation. This means that if a person earned and spent $10,000 in 1973, some 250,000,000 calories were used to support that person. Since only 1,000,000 of these calories were needed to support the individual as represented by the food energy requirements, the difference represents work done by farm machines, power plants, industry, and nature.

Increases or decreases in the level of money supply are thought to influence the level of production in the economy. However, this is true only if the "externals" to the economy—i.e., sources of energy from outside of the money circle—are constant. When the availability of energy changes, the economy changes in ways not correctable by manipulations of the money supply.

Inflation

The buying power of money is the amount of real goods and services that it can buy. If the amount a dollar can buy diminishes, this is called inflation. Inflation can be caused by increasing the amount of money circulating without increasing the amount of energy flowing and doing work, for example, when more money is printed. It can also occur when the money supply is constant but less work is done, for example, because energy becomes scarce. As long as there is unused fuel energy to be tapped, increasing the money supply can increase the flow of energy through the system, causing growth as well as some inflation.

During wartime, even when the money supply is not increased inflation occurs, because energy is diverted away from normal production into military activities. This reduces the energy available per dollar in the main economy, causing inflation.

Depression and Recession

The depression of 1929 was caused by a shortage of circulating money, a shortage of institutions to process money, and a lack of spending. At that time, the government undertook massive efforts to increase the circulation of money and the flow of energy. Energy was abundant, so stimulating the flow of money increased the inflow of energy. The recession of the 1970s, however, was caused by a shortage of energy. Increasing the money supply did not help in this case, as there was no increase in the inflow of energy. Thus, if the economy is in a period of low growth, increasing the money supply will increase the amount of work in the economy only if there are untapped fuel reserves available. If not, increasing the money supply will only increase inflation.

Note

1. To compare energies of different kinds, it is necessary to express them each in units of one kind of energy required. In this paragraph the numbers are in kilocalories of coal energy required. A new word, "eMergy," spelled with an "M," was coined for energies of several kinds expressed as one kind. Thus these numbers are in units of coal eMergy.

Summary of

Embodied Energy and Economic Valuation
by Robert Costanza

[Published in .*Science* 210 (12 December 1980): 1219–1224. © 1980 by the AAAS]

It has long been recognized that available energy governs and limits the structure of human economies. While mainstream economists have not paid much attention to energy analysis, which is primarily concerned with the flow of energy, almost everyone has recognized the importance of energy to the functioning of economic systems. The nature, details, and conclusions of the energy connection are important to several aspects of national policy. This article extends earlier input–output analyses of energy–economy linkages by incorporating the energy costs of labor and government services and solar energy inputs.

An important part of energy analysis is the determination of the total or embodied energy—i.e., direct plus indirect energy—required for the production of economic or environmental goods and services. For example, the embodied energy in an automobile is the energy consumed in the manufacturing plant (direct energy), plus the energy consumed to produce the glass, steel, labor, capital, etc. (indirect energy). A key problem in determining the amount of embodied energy is the choice of methodology used to calculate indirect energy requirements, since different methodologies will yield different results. Input–output analysis, adapted by Hannon[1] and Herendeen and Bullard,[2] is well suited to calculating indirect effects, although controversy still exists concerning the relevant system boundaries for these calculations.

System Boundaries

The choice of system boundaries is important because it distinguishes net inputs from internal transactions. Net inputs are independent and exogenously determined, whereas internal transactions are endogenous and interdependent. Net inputs are what economists call primary factors, and are referred to as "value added" in national income accounts. In essence, the input–output technique distributes a net input vector through a matrix of internal interactions to balance against a net output vector. In recent embodied energy calculations, net input vectors include labor, government services, capital services, energy, and other natural resources. The dollar sum of the net inputs is the gross national product (GNP). The share of energy (from fossil fuels, nuclear fuels, and solar) in GNP is small in dollar units, leading to the conclusion that energy is a minor input in economic production. This conclusion is based on the assumption that the different components of net input are mutually independent. This article argues that the different components are not mutually independent, and it contends that capital, labor, natural resources, and government services have indirect energy costs. A method of using input–output data to calculate embodied energies that takes the interdependencies into account is proposed.

Primary Factors

From a physical perspective, solar energy is the principal net input. Practically everything on earth can be considered a direct or indirect product of past or present solar energy, including all other "primary" factors. In an input–output framework, the interdependence of primary factors can be taken into account by expanding the boundaries so that the net input to the model coincides with the net input to the real system. In practice this can be done by considering households and governments as endogenous sectors. The system boundaries are then defined in such a manner that only current solar energy and the energy embodied in fuels and other natural resources enter as a net input.

Input–Output-Based Energy Accounting

The input–output technique for calculating embodied energy involves defining a set of energy balance equations, with one equation for each sector. The resulting set of simultaneous linear equations can be solved to yield an energy intensity coefficient vector that represents the energy required directly and indirectly to produce a unit of commodity flow. When the transaction matrix is expanded to include the household and government sectors, GNP as currently defined is no longer the net input or output of the model. The new net input is made up of capital consumption allowances and payments to land and resources, and the new net output is gross capital formation, net inventory change, and net exports. Even with these changes there are some problems with the input–output calculations adopted in this article. Specifically, some categories that fall into consumption (like education) should be accounted for under capital formation. Also, while capital stocks are accounted for implicitly when gross capital formation is included, the picture is somewhat distorted because by convention gross capital formation is credited to the industries producing the capital, not to those using it. However, while only approximations were used, solar energy inputs were added to the vector of direct external energy inputs after correcting for the lower thermodynamic usefulness of direct sunlight as compared to fossil fuels.

Results of Modifications to System Boundaries

Embodied energy intensities were calculated for each of four alternatives:

(A) using conventional economic input–output categories;

(B) including solar energy inputs;

(C) including labor and government as endogenous sectors; and

(D) including the modifications of alternatives B and C taken together.

The variance of the energy intensities was greatly reduced under alternatives C and D as compared to alternatives A and B. A lower variance implies a more constant relationship from sector to sector between direct-plus-indirect energy consumption and dollar value of output.

Regressions were run for the four alternatives, with the direct-plus-indirect energy intensity as the independent variable, and the total dollar value as the dependent variable. Since the primary energy sectors were outliers, regressions were also run excluding them. When labor and governments are included as endogenous sectors, there is a significant relationship between embodied energy and dollar output. The more indirect energy costs are taken into account, the more constant is the ratio of embodied energy to dollar output from one sector to the next. The only exceptions to this rule are the primary input sectors, where the energy intensities are high. This may be because the energy embodied in their outputs is much greater than the direct and indirect energy costs involved in their production.

Ratios of Energy to GNP

There have been suggestions that economic growth can be pursued while reducing energy consumption by shifting from high energy intensity sectors to low energy intensity sectors. These suggestions are based on calculations of sector-to-sector differences in embodied energy intensities using conventional system boundaries. This study shows that decoupling energy and economic activity by shifting production between sectors is not a possibility. Given that total energy efficiency is fairly constant across sectors, any reductions in direct energy consumption will be offset by increases in indirect energy consumption through the increased use of labor, land, or capital.

Double Counting

Slesser[3] has argued that including labor costs in embodied energy calculations involves double counting. This criticism is valid when using the conventional system boundaries. With modified system boundaries, the support of labor is an internal transaction and is not included in net output. The problem of double counting is therefore eliminated.

Embodied Energy Theory of Value

Neoclassical economists have rejected various proposals for an energy theory of value on the grounds that energy is only one of a number of primary inputs to the production process. The results presented in this article indicate that if there are interdependencies among the currently defined primary factors, then embodied energy values show a very good empirical relation to market-determined dollar values. It can be asked whether the same thing that has been done with energy cannot be done with any of the other currently defined primary factors, resulting in capital, labor, or government service theories of value. While on paper this could be done, we must look to physical reality to distinguish net inputs from internal transactions: no one would seriously suggest that labor creates sunlight. If the system boundaries are properly defined, an embodied energy theory of value makes theoretical sense.

Conclusion

The results presented in this article indicate that given appropriate system boundaries, market values and embodied energy values are proportional for all but the primary energy sectors. Embodied energy values may therefore be used to determine "market values" where markets do not exist, and these "market values" can be used for "internalizing" externalities. The most important implication of the results for policy is that there cannot be unlimited economic growth with reduced energy consumption. This only appears to be true when looking at small sectors of the economy in isolation. When the whole system is analyzed, it is clear that, when output is constant, energy costs can only be transferred between sectors, not eliminated entirely.

Notes

1. B. Hannon, *Journal of Theoretical Biology* 41, 575 (1973).

2. R.A. Herendeen and C.W. Bullard, *Energy Cost of Goods and Services, 1963 and 1967* (Document 140, Center for Advanced Computation, University of Illinois, Champaign-Urbana, 1974).

3. M. Slesser, *Science* 196, 259 (1977).

Summary of

Energy and the U.S. Economy: A Biophysical Perspective

by Cutler J. Cleveland, Robert Costanza, Charles A.S. Hall, and Robert Kaufman

[Published in *Science* 225 (31 August 1984): 890–897. © 1984 by the AAAS]

Between the mid-1940s and the early 1970s, the U.S. economy showed generally good performance. Since 1973, however, performance indicators such as labor productivity, inflation, and growth rates have been relatively disappointing, and mainstream economic models can not entirely explain this shift and its underlying causes. A theoretical perspective that recognizes the importance of natural resources, especially fuel energy, may help; some economic problems can be understood more clearly by explicitly accounting for the physical constraints imposed on economic production.

In this perspective, the focus is on the production process, i.e., the economic process that upgrades the organizational state of matter into lower entropy goods and services. This process involves a unidirectional, one-time throughput of low-entropy fuel that is eventually lost as waste heat. Production is a work process, and like any work process it will depend on the availability of free energy. The quality of natural resources is also important to this process, because lower quality resources will always require more work to upgrade them into final goods and services.

Based on this biophysical perspective, four hypotheses are presented and discussed below.

Energy and Economic Production

Hypothesis 1: A strong link between fuel use and economic output exists and will continue to exist.

Rather than viewing the economy as a closed system, it must be seen as an open system embedded within a larger global system that depends on solar energy. The global system produces environmental services, foodstuffs, and fossil and atomic fuels, all of which are derived from solar and radiation energies in conjunction with other important resources. Fossil and other fuels are used by the human economy to empower labor and to produce capital. Fuel, capital, and labor are then used to upgrade natural resources to produce goods and services. Production is a process using energy to add order to matter. Since fuels differ in the amount of economic work they can do per unit heat equivalent, both quantity and quality of fuel play a role in determining levels of economic production. An important quality of fuels is the amount of energy required to locate, extract, and refine the fuel to a socially useful state. This can be measured by a fuel's Energy Return on Investment (EROI), which is the ratio of the gross fuel extracted to the economic energy required directly and indirectly to deliver the fuel in a useful form.

Standard economic theory views fuel and energy as just one set of inputs that is fully substitutable with other inputs, but this is incorrect. Free energy upgrades and organizes all other inputs, and it is a complement in the production process that cannot be created by combining the other factors of production. The specific amount of energy needed to produce goods and services is called the *embodied energy*.

If one considers the last one hundred years of the U.S. experience, fuel use and economic output are highly correlated. An important measure of fuel efficiency is the ratio of energy use to the gross national product, E/GNP. The E/GNP ratio has fallen by about 42% since 1929. We find that the improvement in energy efficiency is due principally to three factors: (1) shifts to higher quality fuels such as petroleum and primary electricity; (2) shifts in energy use between households and other sectors; and (3) higher fuel prices. Energy quality is by far the dominant factor.

Labor Productivity and Technical Change

Hypothesis 2: A large component of increased labor productivity over the past 70 years has resulted from increasing the ability of human labor to do physical work by empowering workers with increasing quantities of fuel, both directly and as embodied in industrial capital equipment and technology.

Economic models generally present technological advances as means to increasing labor and capital productivity. These effects of technological change are measured as a residual after accounting for all tangible factors; energy and natural resources are not considered tangible factors, thus leaving a large residual. From an energy perspective, however, the increases in labor productivity are actually driven by increased fuel use per worker-hour. In the pre-1973 period, when fuel prices were falling relative to the price of labor (the wage rate), labor productivity was rising as fuel was substituted for labor due to the change in relative prices. In the post-1973 period, as the price of fuel rose relative to wage rates, the data indicates declining labor productivity.

Energy and Inflation

Hypothesis 3: The rising real physical cost of obtaining energy and other resources from the environment is one important factor that causes inflation.

High inflation rates can be explained by the linkages between fuel use and money supply. If the money supply is increased, stimulating demand beyond levels that can be satisfied by existing fuel supplies, then prices will rise. This implies that when the costs of obtaining fuel are high, fiscal and monetary policies may not be successful in stimulating economic growth.

Energy Costs and Technological Change

Hypothesis 4: The energy costs of locating, extracting, and refining fuel and other resources from the environment have increased and will continue to increase despite technical improvements in the extractive sector.

It has been argued that technological innovations for mining low-quality ores can address the problems associated with the depletion of high-quality mineral deposits. Evidence of this is seen in the constant or declining amount of inputs used per unit output in the extractive sector during this century.

From a physical perspective, however, such a sanguine view of the depletion and scarcity of important natural resources is unwarranted. The extraction of lower quality ores requires the use of more energy-intensive capital and labor inputs. Over the last few decades, there has been an increase in the direct fuel input per unit of output of fuels and minerals. The present rising energy costs of fuel extraction do not bode well for future exploitation of nonrenewable resources.

The EROIs for natural gas, petroleum and coal have fallen dramatically over time in the continental United States. In Louisiana, the EROI for natural gas declined from 100:1 in 1970 to 12:1 in 1981, and a similar decline was observed in the petroleum industry. Nationally, the EROI for coal has fallen from 80:1 in the 1960s to 30:1 in 1977. Another indicator of the increasing cost of fuel extraction is the rise in the real dollar value of the mining sector share of real GNP, from 3–4% over most of this century to about 10% by 1982. Continued economic growth depends on our ability to develop sources of energy with more favorable EROIs.

Conclusion

Declining EROIs for fuels and increasing energy costs for nonfuel resources will have a negative impact on economic growth, productivity, inflation, and technological change. To maintain current levels of economic growth and productivity we will need to either develop alternative fuel technologies with EROI ratios comparable to those of petroleum today, or the efficiency of fuel use to produce economic output must increase.[1]

Note

1. Author's note: The empirical analyses in this article have been enriched and updated. An additional decade of information substantiates the basic conclusions of the article. The interested reader is referred to Robert K. Kaufmann, "A Biophysical Analysis of the Energy/GDP Ratio," *Ecological Economics* 6 (July 1992): 35–56; and Robert K. Kaufmann, "The Relation Between Marginal Product and Price: An Analysis of Energy Markets," *Energy Economics* 16 (1994): 145–48.

Summary of

Natural Resource Scarcity and Economic Growth Revisited: Economic and Biophysical Perspectives

by Cutler J. Cleveland

[Published in *Ecological Economics: The Science and Management of Sustainability*, ed. Robert Costanza (New York: Columbia University Press, 1991), 289–317.]

Many people believe that human ingenuity and technological change will mitigate scarcity problems, but biophysical analysts generally argue that basic physical and ecological laws must constrain (not determine) economic choices. A biophysical model of natural resource scarcity has been developed and is applied here to an empirical analysis of scarcity trends in the U.S. mining, forestry, fishing, and agriculture sectors. The theoretical model and empirical results are compared to their counterparts in neoclassical economics.

The Neoclassical Model of Natural Resource Scarcity

The nineteenth century classical economists Ricardo and Malthus argued that nature was the primary constraint to economic expansion. According to Malthus, the fixed supply of arable land would be limiting, while Ricardo thought the constraint would be declining land quality as production expanded.

Following Hotelling's (1931) theory of optimal depletion and the empirical analysis of resource depletion by Barnett and Morse (1963), the neoclassical school rejected the classical view that nature was a constraint to economic expansion. The Barnett and Morse study found that there was no increasing scarcity between 1870 and 1957 in the United States in the agriculture, mining, and fishing sectors, despite massive physical depletions of the highest grade resources during this period. Increasing scarcity was only found for forest resources. The neoclassical model argues that the solution to increasing scarcity lies in the market mechanism. That is, as a resource becomes scarce its price will increase, and this will lead to a number of endogenous changes, including increased explorations for new deposits, recycling, substitution of alternative resources, increased efficiency and, most importantly, technological innovations.

A Biophysical Critique of the Neoclassical Model

The neoclassical model of scarcity assumes that labor, capital, and land (and sometimes energy) are primary, independent factors of production. A biophysical perspective, on the other hand, distinguishes between "primary factors" of production and "intermediate inputs." A primary factor of production cannot be produced inside the economic system. Low-entropy energy-matter is therefore the only primary factor of production. Intermediate inputs are produced or recycled by some combination of primary factors and other intermediate inputs. Capital, labor, and technology are considered intermediate inputs, as they are produced from low-entropy energy-matter.

According to Daly and Cobb,[1] the neoclassical model frequently ignores land as an input in the production process. Land is seen as property, rather than for its unique role as a provider of natural resources and environmental services. When perceived as property, land is no different from capital and labor, making the importance of nature disappear from the neoclassical model.

The neoclassical model also ignores the massive amounts of energy used to harvest resources. From a biophysical perspective, an important relationship exists between energy costs and the quality of resources, since energy is required to upgrade the organization of resources. Moreover, the declining labor costs of resource extraction documented in the Barnett and Morse study were not due to "self-generating" technological change, as the study suggests, but rather resulted from the substitution of higher quality surplus fossil fuel energy for labor in the resource transformation process. The extraction of a fossil fuel results in a net energy surplus, i.e., the quantity of energy available in the fuel, less the energy costs of extracting it. The quantity of goods and services that can be produced in an economy is then limited by the absolute amount of surplus energy available and the efficiency with which it is used. The period that Barnett and Morse studied included two complete transformations in which high-quality fuels displaced the use of lower quality fuels: first coal replaced wood, and then oil and natural gas replaced coal. It was these substitutions of higher quality fuels that reduced the labor-capital costs of extracting fuels.

Resource Scarcity from a Biophysical Perspective

The two fundamental points underlying the biophysical model of the production process are:

(1) High-quality resource deposits require less work to locate, upgrade, and refine than low-quality resources. In addition, in the process of the transformation of resources, some high-quality economically useful energy is degraded into lower quality economically useless energy. The laws of thermodynamics dictate that, for any given material and given amount of increase in order, there is a minimum amount of energy required; in the real world, even more energy must be used than the minimum energy requirements. Technological change cannot change the minimum energy requirements in the transformation process, but it can help move toward the minimum requirements.

(2) The technological change in industrial countries has a physical basis. Historically, mechanical energy from humans, draft animals, and inanimate energy converters powered by fossil fuels and electricity were the main sources of energy in the extractive sectors. During the last century, however, fossil fuels have become dominant, replacing humans and draft animals. Most importantly, increasing amounts of energy subsidize the efforts of labor, boosting labor productivity.

Humans usually use natural resources in order of decreasing quality. The relationship between energy costs and resource quality can be obtained by constructing the biophysical resource conversion function, which describes the amount of direct (E_d) and indirect (E_i) energy used to upgrade a unit of resources with heterogeneous, lower quality physical and locational attributes (R_u) into a unit of a "standard resource" with homogeneous physical and locational attributes (R).

The Energy Cost of Extractive Output

This section tests the hypothesis that the energy costs of natural resources have increased over time in the United States due to changes in the relative strength of depletion and technical innovations. The hypothesis is tested by calculating the direct and indirect fuel used to produce a unit of resource in the mining, agriculture, forest products, and fisheries industries, where Q is the total output of the industry, and $Q/(E_d + E_i)$ is the output per unit of energy input in the industry.

Mining

Empirical Results: In the metal mining industry, $Q/(E_d + E_i)$ increased from 1919 through the mid-1950s and then decreased by a factor of two by the 1980s. The nonmetal mining sector shows varying trends for different types of output, but the general trend in the sector was substantially decreasing energy costs per unit of output. In the fossil fuel sector, output per unit of energy input is measured by the energy return on investment (EROI). The EROI for the fossil fuel sector rises in the first half of the century and then declines in the 1960s and 1970s. The EROI for petroleum peaked in the early 1970s and then declined by a factor of two in the 1980s. Coal production showed a similar decline, beginning a decade earlier than petroleum.

Discussion: In the metal mining industry, resource depletion is the main cause of the increasing energy costs. The declining quality of ores and the increased mine depth, which results in increases in the amount of waste rock mined per ton of ore, contributed to the increasing costs. While the nonmetal mining sector also saw increases in the amount of waste rock mined per ton of ore, energy costs still decreased because of improvements in recovery techniques. Increases in the energy costs in the coal industry were a result of depletion, with anthracite showing greater levels of depletion than bituminous coal. Energy costs in the oil and gas industry have increased because depletion has outstripped the gains from technical innovation.

Agriculture

Empirical Results: Measuring the output of the agricultural sector in physical terms is not straightforward. Three different measures can be used: gross domestic product originating on farms, the USDA farm output index, and the total calories produced in principal crops. For all three measures, the energy cost of producing a unit of output increased between 1910 and 1973, and it decreased between 1974 and 1988.

Discussion: While energy costs in agriculture increased between 1910 and 1970, prices to consumers generally declined over that period. This apparent paradox arises because savings from innovation and improvements in labor productivity offset the increases in direct and indirect energy use. The fall in energy costs per unit of output between 1974 and 1988 was a consequence of the energy price shocks of the early 1970s, which caused major reductions in farm energy use.

Forest Products

Empirical Results: In the forest product sector, output per unit of energy used declined between 1950 and 1973, and it then increased by 40% between 1974 and 1986.

Discussion: The forest product sector has been similar to the agriculture sector. Between 1950 and 1973, increased mechanization and energy use increased total output and labor productivity but decreased $Q/(E_d + E_i)$. The energy price increases of the 1970s then increased the energy efficiency of the sector. These interpretations of the forest sector must be qualified by noting that wood waste fuel use—the main energy source in this sector— can only be estimated, and the uncertainty associated with these estimates may be substantial.

Fisheries

Empirical Results: National data on energy use in fisheries is not collected, so the trends presented here are based on the energy use and output of the New Bedford, Massachusetts fleet, which has the largest catch by value and the sixth largest by poundage in the country. Between 1968 and 1988, there have been sharp increases in the energy costs per unit of output. At present, 35 BTU of fuel are used to harvest 1 BTU of edible fish protein.

Discussion: The rising energy costs are a result of increases in the total number of vessels in the fleet, in the average horsepower per vessel, and in the time required to travel to and from the point of harvesting due to the depletion of fish stocks. On the output side, there have been sharp declines in output due to decreased fishing effort and competition from foreign fleets.

Conclusion

Economic models showing declining dollar costs of resource extraction mask significant increases in energy costs per unit of output in several sectors. Of these, the increase in the energy costs of obtaining fossil fuels have the most serious long-run implications, since these fuels are essential for the extraction of all other resources. In addition, declines in the quality of non-fuel resources will cause positive feedback effects, accelerating the depletion of fossil fuels and the accompanying increase in their own energy costs.[2]

Notes

1. Herman E. Daly and John B. Cobb, *For the Common Good: Redirecting the Economy Toward Community, the Environment, and a Sustainable Future* (Boston: Beacon Press, 1989 and 1994).

2. Author's note: The empirical analyses in this article have been enriched and updated. An additional decade of information substantiates the basic conclusions of the article. The interested reader is referred to: Cutler J. Cleveland, "Energy Quality and Energy Surplus in the Extraction of Fossil Fuels in the U.S.," *Ecological Economics* 6 (October 1992): 139–62; Cutler J. Cleveland, "An Exploration of Alternative Measures of Natural Resource Scarcity: The Case of Petroleum Resources in

the U.S.," *Ecological Economics* 7 (April 1993): 123–57; and Cutler J. Cleveland and David I. Stern, "The Scarcity of Forest Products Revisited: An Empirical Comparison of Alternative Indicators," *Canadian Journal of Forest Research* 23 (1993): 1537–549.

Summary of

The Biophysical Systems World View
by John Peet

[Published in John Peet, *Energy and the Ecological Economics of Sustainability* (Washington, D.C. and Covelo, California: Island Press, 1992), 83–95.
© John Peet, 1992.]

The biophysical systems perspective sees the economy in terms of the physical activities that take place in it, while the political–economic perspective focuses on the social aspects of the activities of society. From the biophysical point of view, the continuing transformation of available and unavailable energy resources in accordance with the Second Law of Thermodynamics is the fundamental fact of life in the functioning of all economies; there is no known economic process that does not begin by using some sort of raw material and eventually generating waste. The interaction between energy and matter is the basis for life itself, including human life and culture. The inclusion of energy in a world view based on a physical systems perspective can therefore help to clarify the relationship between a social system and its environment. Energy analysis may also help us see where the biophysical and political–economic viewpoints differ, and it may indicate areas in which conventional assumptions need deeper examination.

Energy Analysis

Matter normally enters an economic system as raw materials from the environment. The flow of useful matter into and through an economic system can be characterized in terms of the available energy expended in carrying out the transformation processes in which the matter is involved. Thus, energy can be used as a numeraire or unit of account, enabling a wide variety of goods to be accounted for in terms of the quantity of the energy used in the process of transforming them into marketable products. From the biophysical systems perspective, it is the amount (the physical cost) of energy embodied in a product that is important, not its market price. Therefore, only physical processes of production are considered, and not the social valuation of the product in the marketplace.

The branch of physical science that follows economic production and consumption through their energy consequences is known as energy analysis. It involves the determination of the amount of primary energy that is dissipated in producing a good or service and delivering it to market. There are two common techniques for accomplishing this: process analysis and input–output analysis. Process analysis systematically determines the energy requirements for each stage of a productive process, and by summing the energy added at each stage, it provides the total energy requirement of the product. Input–output analysis is a modification of a standard economic tool. It requires a detailed survey of the economy with an explicit accounting of the direct and indirect energy requirements for producing goods and services. "Thus, all of the energy inputs to the processes that precede the output of a given good or service in the economy are evaluated, right back to the coal mine, oil well, power station, or gas field."[87] As a rule, input–output analysis is appropriate when examining events that affect an entire economy, whereas process analysis may be more appropriate for the study of a specific process.

Net Energy and Physical Accessibility

Energy transformation systems normally begin with a coal mine or an oil or gas well from which the resources are physically extracted, followed by facilities that generate power and produce fuels. Thus, in this approach the energy transformation sector is treated exogenously, not simply as another part of the productive sector of the economy. An important characteristic of this sector is that it absorbs capital as well as operating and maintenance inputs from the economy, which themselves absorb energy. It is when the flow of useful energy to the economy exceeds these input energy flows that there is a supply of net energy to the economy.

The net energy criterion is a means of indicating the physical accessibility of an energy resource; it is a measure of the effort required to extract and deliver a resource expressed in energy terms. The evolution of the industrialized economies over the past century has witnessed a progression to cheaper and increasingly accessible energy sources, but only after the development of the technologies necessary to extract these new resources. Not surprisingly, societies have exploited the resources that were most accessible first.

There is increasing evidence, however, that energy is becoming more difficult to obtain and process into readily usable forms. This implies that escalating resource inputs (and higher pollution levels) will be required to maintain the same net energy supply into the economy. Improvements in technology will not resolve this dilemma. The Second Law of Thermodynamics states that there is an absolute minimum energy requirement for any process—for example, lifting a ton of coal to the surface or pumping a liter of water—that is absolutely unalterable by technology. Thus, in time, the energy transformation industry will have to grow and absorb a steadily increasing quantity of economic activity just to maintain the system at its current level.

Neither should much faith be placed in new energy technologies. For example, much of the optimism surrounding "breeder" type nuclear reactors, a process that allegedly produces more fuel than it consumes, has proved to be illusory. These reactors were merely converting nonfuel uranium (U-238) into fuel grade plutonium (Pu-239) for use in conventional (fission) nuclear power plants, not creating new fuel out of nothing. Nuclear fusion (rather than fission) is seen as the ultimate unlimited energy source, which is supposed to duplicate the reactions that occur in the sun at millions of degrees, transforming hydrogen into unlimited amounts of energy. However, so far these efforts have succeeded only in absorbing vast sums of money and energy, producing no tangible results.

Technology, then, will not provide any relief, and the consequences of this are clear: "When resources are relatively inaccessible, the primary resource flow will be greater than it was for the earlier, high-accessibility case. Thus, the rate of depletion of primary resources will also increase for a given (constant) flow of net energy to the economy. Pollution and other externalities will also be greater due to the increased rejection of unavailable energy."[90] As primary resources become less accessible, it is possible to predict very rapid rises in energy input for very modest increases in nonenergy output. Under conditions of rapid energy-intensive capital investment, it is possible for energy supply programs to be net consumers of energy.

Aims of the Biophysical Systems World View

The implications of the foregoing analysis are that:
(1) the long-term economic costs of energy resource development are likely to be much higher than currently believed; and
(2) costs are likely to increase at an accelerating rate over time.

Energy analysis provides strong indications that there are limits to economic growth, and that current predictions of future energy prospects seriously underestimate the current value of energy resources and encourage wasteful use. If these insights were incorporated into economic analysis, sustainable alternatives would be viewed in a more favorable light.

Summary of

Energy, Labor, and the Conserver Society

by Bruce Hannon

[Published in *Technology Review* (March/April 1977): 47–53.
Reprinted with permission from Technology Review, © 1977.]

There are two paths that America can adopt with respect to future energy use. On the one hand, we can optimistically increase our per capita energy use, relying on new technologies, energy price controls, and statesmanship to postpone shortages. On the other hand, we can be more realistic and become more of a conserver society that recognizes the limited availability of low-cost energy. A conserver society would need to forecast energy shortages and consider the technological, social, and economic problems that would be associated with substituting renewable capital and labor for labor when shortages of nonrenewables arise.

The Relationship of Energy, Wages, and Employment

The use of the three basic inputs in the production process—capital, labor, and energy—are determined by a combination of market forces and regulations in the form of price controls, taxes, and subsidies. The ratio of the prices of any two inputs represents the ratio of their marginal productivities; the lower the relative marginal productivity of a commodity, the more widely it is consumed. Between 1935 and 1970, as industrial workers' wages rose faster than the price of industrial electricity, electricity was substituted for labor. Unemployment did not increase during this time period because of an increase in total economic activity that created as many jobs as were lost due to the substitution of electricity for labor. However, steady employment could have been insured during this period even with zero economic growth if the price of energy had been raised relative to the wage rate. This is apparent between 1970 and 1975, when the real wage rate, and hence the ratio of wages to the price of electricity, fell; although the level of economic activity dropped, the level of employment still rose as labor was substituted for energy during this period due to the relative price changes. A reduction in energy use may, however, mean less material wealth, so "the principal problem of the conserver society becomes one of providing and maintaining an equitable distribution of reduced energy and material flows"[47]

Since 1950, labor and capital have not been substituted for one another, but electricity has been substituted for capital. Evidence of this is seen in the increase in centralized production facilities that conserve labor and capital but are energy intensive.

The Constraints of Energy

A conserver society will increase the use of labor and capital and reduce energy use. The efficient use of energy should be guided by two important physical rules: the Second Law of Thermodynamics, and the concept of net energy. The Second Law suggests that a given quantity of energy has a higher quality (in terms of its ability to do mechanical work) at higher temperatures than at a lower ones. The concept of net energy suggests that it is more economic to transmit high-quality energy than low-quality energy. These two physical laws should constrain the planners of a conserver society, requiring them to match the quantity and quality exchanges of energy. To achieve maximum efficiency, energy exchanges should be organized in a cascading manner, so that the output of one process becomes the input of another. Raising the relative price of energy will result in more intensive use of energy and the development of energy-conserving communities.

As a first step the conserver society must work toward reducing total energy use. Care must be taken to ensure that changes resulting in reduced energy use at one point do not result in compensating increases at another. Such increases might occur, for example, if reducing energy use results in income increases that then increase energy demand when they are spent. The main issue facing conserver society planners is therefore to identify "specific changes in the present economy (that) will reduce energy demand and increase employment, under conditions of income equilibrium."[48] One way that this issue has been approached is by comparing high-energy-using decisions with low-energy-using alternatives while incorporating re-spending effects, to determine the energy and employment changes caused by substitutions. Based on these calculations the job potential per unit of energy saved for each conservation project can be determined by dividing the net change in employment demand by the net change in energy demand.

Relating Energy and Jobs

Aggregate behavior of the U.S. economy in 1974 indicates that 930,000 new jobs were created for every quadrillion Btu reduction in energy use. Given that present U.S. energy use is about 80 quadrillion Btu, it would therefore be possible to reduce unemployment by up to 4 million people (i.e., full employment) by reducing energy use approximately 5–10%. In some cases jobs are lost when energy is expended. For example, in the short run about 75,000 jobs are lost for every new quad of primary energy that is transformed into electricity. This is because increasing energy purchases require a corresponding reduction in costs, which must be brought about by reducing the demand for labor. More jobs are lost due to reduced labor demand than are created by the increased electricity generation.

Strategies for Conservers

Energy conservation policy must be approached on a case-by-case basis. For this purpose, a series of calculations outlined in this article could be used to establish priorities. Examples of ways to increase employment and reduce energy use include shifting from personal autos to buses, trains, and bicycles, or from bulk materials trucking to retail transport. However, not all shifts toward lower energy use will generate employment.

Another option is to promote lower energy use through a tax on energy at the point of production based on the energy content. This will result in increasing prices for goods and services, with greater price increases resulting for the more energy-intensive commodities. Consumers would then shift from energy-intensive commodities to relatively labor-intensive ones. This tax would result in lower energy consumption at home and in industry, but the increased revenues generated for the government would create their own energy demands when they were spent. The government could use this additional income to reduce the personal income tax on individuals, or to subsidize energy conserving capital investments in the economy. Another way to promote energy efficiency is through rationing, which focuses on the finiteness of the energy supply, and which is a more precise method of controlling energy flows in the economy than taxation

It is only through government intervention, not individual voluntary action, that a culture of conservation can be developed. It is possible to achieve declining energy use without compromising the issues of equity and full employment.

Summary of

Industrial Metabolism

by Robert U. Ayres

[Published in *Technology and Environment,* eds. Jesse H. Ausubel and Hedy E.
Sladovitch (Washington, D.C.: National Academy Press, 1989): 23–49. Adapted with
permission from *Technology and Environment.* © 1989 by the National Academy of
Sciences. Courtesy of the National Academy Press, Washington, D.C.]

The biosphere and the industrial economy are both systems that transform materials. While the biosphere is a nearly perfect system for recycling
materials, industrial systems need to be modified to increase their efficiency
in production and recycling. Like the early stages of biological evolution,
modern industrial processes are discrete, irreversible linear sequences that
are energized by fuels which are not regenerated within the system. Modern biological processes, on the other hand, are regenerative. Industrial metabolism—i.e., the energy- and value-yielding processes of economic development—can gain from the lessons learned from the biosphere. This article
discusses the environmental significance of industrial processes, as well as issues related to waste emission.

Each year more than ten tons of "active" mass is extracted per person in
the United States. In principle, 75% of this is nonrenewable and 25% renewable. However, only about 6% of this extracted mass becomes embodied in durable goods, while the remaining 94% is ultimately converted into
waste material that includes highly toxic, carcinogenic, and mutagenic materials. Most of the extracted material is transformed into waste rather
quickly and is degraded, dissipated, and lost in the course of a single normal use. The environmental impacts of this unused waste are harmful and
can be linked to the greenhouse effect, the ozone hole, acid rain, smog, etc.
The total production of waste exceeds the tonnage of crops, timber, fuels,
and minerals recorded by economic statistics. Also a number of services
provided by the environment are derived from common property resources
like air, the oceans, the biosphere, and the sun. Many of these factors are
underpriced in the marketplace, resulting in their overuse. While the industrial system may be in equilibrium in terms of market relationships, this
is not so in thermodynamic terms. Waste materials may disappear from the
market, but not from the physical world. "The economic system is stable
somewhat in the way a bicycle and its rider are stable: if forward motion
stops, the system will collapse. Forward motion in the economic system is
technological progress."[32]

Industrial metabolism can, however, play a role in the recycling of materials and waste products. In fact, there are many examples in the chemical

industry in which the existence of waste and by-products has led to important innovations. For example, the Leblanc process used in the production of sodium bicarbonate now makes use of sodium sulfate, which was previously an unwanted by-product of the production of ammonium chloride. Also, a systematic search by German chemists to utilize by-products resulted in the use of coal-tar, leading to the development of the modern organic chemical industry. Until recently, natural gas, a by-product of petroleum production, was "flared," but it is now used in the production of synthetic rubber.

Technological innovation that will result in economic benefits should be explored as a means to reduce the amount of waste generated. We should seek innovations that can:

(1) *Shorten and/or reduce the process chains in a production process:* This will result in overall gains in efficiency and reductions in costs. The savings in materials and energy inputs and/or capital requirements will in most cases justify a new process that saves one link in the chain between raw materials and finished materials or final goods. The use of first-tier intermediaries or primary feedstocks can enhance the overall efficiency of production systems. Since complex molecules can be developed from biological organisms with few intermediates, biotechnology offers the prospect of long-term productivity gains at lower costs.

(2) *Make better use of by-products and wastes generated in the production process:* When a process can be justified economically based on the market for its primary product alone, then selling by-products as well can be highly profitable. In addition, firms are now sometimes forced to clean up their wastes retroactively, but increasing the recycling of by-products and wastes could prevent such problems in the future.

Economic evolution may be directed by a variety of either long-term or short-term goals. It may be, however, that there is a long-run evolutionary imperative that favors dematerialization of the economy. This could be accomplished through the development of industrial metabolism technologies that reduce the extraction of virgin materials, reduce wastes and dissipative uses of toxic materials, and increase multiple use and recycling of materials. Short-term economic incentives, on the other hand, are often inconsistent with this hypothesized long-term imperative. For example, market forces promote product differentiation and specialization, both of which increase the costs of repairs and recycling. Repair, reuse, and recycling occur in poor countries to such an extent that wastes or "junk" are practically nonexistent, while in advanced countries goods that are difficult or impossible to repair accumulate as wastes. In addition, as products become more reliable and their warranties lengthen, they are increasingly designed in such a manner that disassembly is discouraged and often can only be done by the manufacturer. Incentive structures necessary to encourage the long-term goals proposed here must therefore ultimately arise out of social and political responses to perceived environmental problems.

Materials-balance principles can be used to analyze economic and technical data together, yielding more reliable estimates of waste residual outputs than those found by direct measurement. Technological evolution that is oriented toward long-term goals can also be used as a basis for forecasting the future of industrial processes. For example, it seems likely that the industrial system of the future will use hydrogen as a bulk energy carrier, recycle wastes with high efficiency, and eliminate the release of biologically active toxins into the environment.

Summary of

Industrial Input–Output Analysis: Implications for Industrial Ecology
by Faye Duchin

[Published in *Proceedings of the National Academy of Sciences* 89 (February 1992): 851–855.]

Industrial ecology (IE) is an emerging field that deals with conserving and recycling energy and other materials in the production process. IE faces two challenges. First, practical methods must be identified for reducing and recycling wastes in a wide range of situations. While some changes may be profitable in the short run and therefore adopted voluntarily, these may not be the most important ones from a system-wide or long-term perspective. Second, IE should provide a framework both for evaluating the long-term advantages and disadvantages of different patterns of industrial change and for identifying the short-term bottlenecks that may be associated with these changes. These studies will assist in both public discussions and private calculations. This article discusses how structural economics and an input–output model can assist in the development of the IE framework.

Structural Economics

Structural economics attempts to provide a detailed, disaggregated description of an entire economy in terms of its concrete and observable constituent parts and the interrelationships between them. The constituent parts include natural objects, technologies, and social institutions. The analysis is carried out using both mathematical input–output models and qualitative analysis for those issues that are difficult to formalize. The qualitative aspects of the analysis help in the formulation of questions and the evaluation of results. Of particular interest to the structural economist are the dynamics of long-term structural changes under different assumptions, rather than analysis of static or equilibrium states. Unlike mainstream economic models that are used to arrive at unique solutions to optimization problems, structural economics models are used to arrive at a set of possible solutions. In addition, Structural Economics considers changes in input structure in terms of both process changes that may originate outside of the system and substitutions of sets of inputs rather than of individual inputs. The input–output model is central to the formalism of structural economics models.

Input–Output Models

The input–output model[1] is based on the interdependence of the productive sectors of an economy, where every sector's output is an input to every other sector and to itself. The input–output framework relates output, prices, deliveries to final users, and factor costs per unit of output in matrix form through a set of equations. There is no attempt to discover an optimal strategy because issues may not be purely economic. Rather, the effects on all sectors of the economy of a range of technically feasible scenarios can be examined, as well as the implications of different policies.

The simple static input–output model has been extended to consider dynamic issues. This dynamic input–output model can be used to describe and analyze changes in the economy over historical time. The simple model has also been extended to include an optimization framework used to identify the least-cost technological options faced by different sectors. This optimization framework can distinguish between those cases where the application of formal optimization is appropriate and those where it is misleading. A third extension is the development of a model of the world economy that incorporates international resource flows and can be used to investigate strategies for environmentally sound economic development.

Implications for Industrial Ecology

A program to reduce the input of raw materials and to recycle wastes often gives rise to questions about the *costs* and *benefits* of undertaking the program and the policies that will lead to the *optimal* level of recycling. While these questions are relevant and need to be raised, the first question that should be asked is, *how* can this source reduction and recycling be achieved? This question of *how* has been largely ignored by economists because of their conviction that, given the right incentives, firms will always seek to minimize costs, and thus will know *how* to do things. This may be true in situations where the changes in the economic environment have been small. However, when significant changes are called for, analysis of alternative techniques is necessary to explore the possible paths. Undertaking this task of analyzing the outcomes resulting from different techniques requires cooperation among economists, engineers, and natural scientists. Once plausible and acceptable scenarios are identified, further analysis can reveal the extent of incentives, disincentives, and regulations that might be needed to encourage their adoption.

Note

1. The article includes an example showing input–output computations that has been omitted in this summary.

Summary of

Implementing Industrial Ecology

by T.E. Graedel, B.R. Allenby, and P.B. Linhart

[Published in *IEEE Technology and Society Magazine*
12 (Spring 1993): 18–26 © 1993 IEEE.]

Industrial ecology (IE) can be defined as a concept wherein "economic systems are viewed not in isolation from their surrounding systems but in concert with them. As applied to industrial operations, it requires a systems view in which one seeks to optimize the total materials cycle from virgin material, to finished material, to component, to product, to waste product, and to ultimate disposal. Factors to be optimized include resources, energy, and capital."[18] This article discusses some issues related to the industrial ecology of manufacturing processes.

Systems Description

R.A. Frosch and N. Gallopoulos[1] have argued that industrial systems should attempt to mimic the biological ecosystem. Biological ecosystems are a complex network of processes in which everything produced is used by some organism for its own metabolism; the wastes of one organism are food for another. During the earliest periods of life on earth, material cycles were actually linear systems in which organisms had unlimited resources and produced wastes without recycling. As resources became limited, flows into and out of the ecosystem (resources and wastes) became limited while recycling increased, i.e., the flow of materials became semicyclic. While this type of materials flow is more efficient than the linear system, it is still not sustainable over long periods of time. To achieve sustainability, ecosystems have evolved to become almost completely cyclical; resources and wastes are undefined, as residues from one component of the system are resources for another. The only exception to complete cyclicity in the biological ecosystem is that energy in the form of solar radiation enters as an outside resource.

During a period of global plenty, the industrial revolution, coupled with increases in the human population and agricultural production, led initially to the development of industrial processes similar to the linear systems described above. However, the effects of both resource constraints and limited waste disposal sites are beginning to set in. There is increasing pressure to change the patterns of material flows in industrial systems from linear to semicyclic. Industrial ecology is intended to promote this transformation in an efficient manner. The domain of IE consists of four central nodes: the materials extractor or grower, the materials processor or manufacture, the consumer, and the waste processor. Processes should be set up to ensure that there are cyclical flows between these four nodes, thus reducing their disruptive impact on external support systems.

Resource Flows

Applied industrial ecology studies the factors that influence the flows of selected materials between economic processes. The overall industrial ecology cycle can be divided into three stages:

(1) *Industrial Production of Materials:* This stage begins with virgin materials and proceeds through the processes of extraction, separation or refining, and physical and chemical preparation to produce the finished material. Both recycling and disposal of waste materials occur between some of these stages.

(2) *Industrial Manufacture of Products:* A number of finished materials will enter this stage of the manufacturing process, and then go through the forming, finished components, and fabrication stages to create finished products. Industrial physical designers are concerned with the

material flows within this process, i.e., waste flows, recycled material flows, and in-process recycle flows. Optimizing the industrial ecology implies increasing the recycle flows and reducing waste disposal. This optimization may involve trade-offs between the purity of the finished product on the one hand and reduction in the use of materials on the other.

(3) *Customer Product Cycle:* Customer decisions are made independently of the production of materials and the manufacture of products. Finished products are used by consumers, and they may then either be recycled or disposed of when they become obsolete. Industrial ecology moves toward optimization as recycling is favored over disposal.

Approaches to Industrial Ecology

Industrial ecology analysis can be material-specific or product-specific. Human institutions can promote or constrain desirable material flows, and both social pressures and private profit may be needed to develop a sound industrial ecology. Price incentives can be used in some cases to correct for externalities that may work against sound industrial ecology practices. In other cases, the desired results must be achieved by regulations such as the Clean Air Act.

In developing industrial ecology models, the industrial system should be viewed as part of a larger system. The problems must ultimately be posed in the framework of mathematical models. Input–output models and linear and nonlinear programming are all mathematical tools that can be used to model the industrial ecology cycle. The challenge, however, lies not in solving the mathematical model but in using appropriate insight and information in defining the magnitudes of the interactions among the components of the industrial ecology cycle.

Note

1. R.A. Frosch and N. Gallopoulos, "Towards an Industrial Ecology," paper presented to the Royal Society, London, February 21, 1990.

PART V

Accounting and Evaluation

Overview Essay

by Jonathan M. Harris

One of the known weaknesses in standard economic theory is its reliance on gross national product or gross domestic product accounts as a measure of income. Some of the limitations and inconsistencies in GNP/GDP have long been known to economists, including the failure to account for unpaid work, leisure time, and pollution damage. Ecological economists have expanded the critique of GNP and have started to propose alternative measures. The issue is potentially of enormous significance for policy. Growth in GNP is almost always a major economic policy goal, and GNP accounts provide the measure of success or failure in meeting this goal. If we change the yardstick of measurement, our policy priorities will undoubtedly change also.

GNP/GDP has not proved easy to displace, however. One reason for this is the strong attachment of statistical authorities to existing measurement categories. Another is the difficulty of achieving agreement among the critics on a clearly definable alternative standard—or even on whether such a standard should be sought. Efforts to grapple with this issue have given rise to an expanding literature on the subject, including a number of practical applications of revised national income analysis.

The case for new accounting techniques was first presented comprehensively in the UNEP/World Bank report *Environmental Accounting for Sustainable Development*, (1989) edited by Yusuf J. Ahmad, Salah El Serafy, and Ernst Lutz. The authors of original articles presented in this volume argue that a measure of *sustainable* income is needed, which standard GDP measures fail to provide. This argument is consistent with the widely accepted "Hicksian" definition of income, according to which current consumption can only be considered income if it does not reduce future welfare through depletion of assets. GDP fails to distinguish between income derived from production and income derived from depleting natural capital assets such as forests, soils, and mineral reserves. It also fails to identify *defensive expenditures,* such as costs of cleaning up pollution or restoring eroded soils. While these activities in themselves are productive, it is a form of *double counting* to add both the pollution-creating activities and the resulting cleanup activities into GDP.

The clear implication of these criticisms is that if natural resource depletion and pollution are significant factors, standard GDP may grossly overstate the well-being of an economy. The contributors to the UNEP/World Bank report suggest a systematic response to these problems—essentially offering methods to subtract the value of natural resource depreciation and defensive expenditures from standard GDP. This raises many questions of appropriate techniques for identifying and assigning a value to these factors. One set of issues in accounting and valuation concerns these questions of techniques for adjusting GDP figures. Another, broader discussion concerns whether it is appropriate to "adjust" an inherently flawed measure at all, with some authors suggesting that completely different, more ecologically based measures should be used, while others propose "pluralism," with no single measure dominating.

Prominent among those arguing for pluralism in national accounts is Richard Norgaard. In "Three Dilemmas of Environmental Accounting" he traces the environmental and resource depletion issues to more fundamental inconsistencies in the logic of GDP accounting, and in economic theory itself. This is a central point for ecological economics. The criticisms of the neoclassical paradigm raised by ecological economists have already been extensively discussed. In view of these sweeping criticisms, does it make any sense to accept a modified version of the neoclassical GDP construct as an adequate index of economic activity? Practical considerations may imply the need for a straightforward, single-value estimate of "modified" GDP to compete with standard GDP for the attention of policy makers. But in Norgaard's view there cannot be a theoretical justification for the use of such a measure. Rather, we must seek to measure different dimensions of economic and ecological reality, and oppose any single standardized system of accounts.

From the opposite, systematizing point of view there have been numerous efforts to offer, in Roefie Hueting's words, "a practical solution for a theoretical dilemma." Hueting's own proposal is to define a standard of sustainability, then adjust present GDP figures based on the estimated cost of achieving this standard. Jan Tinbergen and Roefie Hueting point out the paradox that environmental improvement may imply *lower* GNP but *higher* welfare (as when bicycles substitute for cars, or agricultural land is fallowed to rebuild soils). The use of an environmental standard system corrects for this inherent bias in GDP accounts. Henry Peskin advocates a similar system, using neoclassical techniques to measure the "services" provided by the environment as well as natural capital depreciation.[1] This system has been applied in a U.S. Environmental Protection Agency pilot study of the Chesapeake Bay region.

The article by Peskin and Lutz summarized here provides an overview of accounting techniques appropriate for environmentally adjusted national income accounts, but it offers no single recommended system. Peskin and Lutz also draw attention to the differences between industrialized and developing nations in this area; developing nations tend to be more resource-based and have more glaring environmental problems, but statistical data to account for this is often lacking. For the United States, Herman Daly and John Cobb have presented a systematic "Index of Sustainable Economic Welfare" which deconstructs national income analysis by sector to impose standards of sustainability (and equity) on all elements of the national income accounts.[2] No such measure has yet been derived for developing nations. The United Nations Development Programme's *Human Development Report* offers a GDP alternative based primarily on social factors, though they have recently introduced some environmental categories into their calculations of a "Human Development Index."[3]

During the period since the 1989 World Bank volume, considerable empirical work has been done to apply natural resource accounting techniques to specific countries. Robert Repetto and his associates at the World Resources Institute have published a number of natural resource accounting studies for developing nations, including Indonesia, the Philippines, and Costa Rica.[4] The studies can be summarized graphically as modified GDP time series, showing quite dramatically the difference made by an accounting for such factors as petroleum depletion, forest loss, and soil erosion in the growth trend of GDP. When investment trends are presented graphically in a similar fashion, the results are even more striking, with adjusted net investment becoming negative during years when gross investment appears high and rising.

Salah El Serafy has revised the results of Repetto's study of Indonesia to make the figures more compatible with standard accounting techniques. In his rendition, the series are less volatile but show equally dramatic differences in the interpretation of net investment. Kirk Hamilton has applied similar techniques to calculation of net savings, arriving at the startling conclusion that for most of the developing world, net savings have been negative since the mid-1970s when resource and environmental factors are included.[5]

The United Nations has performed similar resource accounting studies for Mexico, Papua New Guinea, and Thailand.[6] While this expanding list of country studies does not offer a systematic substitute for standard GDP, it does offer a detailed array of more environmentally sensitive measures for the consideration of development policy makers.

Another, more radical, approach to a systematic revision of national accounts would be to use a completely different basis for measuring economic activity. Malcolm Slesser, following the logic of the energetic school discussed in Part IV, proposes the use of an energy/embodied energy *numéraire*. Together with Jane King, he has developed a simulation model based on embodied energy which is offered as an alternative to standard GNP analysis. The model is used to study development options, with a special focus on the potential for transition to a solar-based economy.[7] Slesser uses the term *natural capital accounting* to distinguish this methodology from the more conservative approaches which have been developed by economists for resource accounting.

Georgescu-Roegen, as we have already seen, criticizes energetic models on the ground that "matter matters too," and cannot be subsumed in a single energy measure. A measure such as Slesser and King's undoubtedly focuses attention on the essential role of energy supplies in expanding carrying capacity; but perhaps we should bear in mind the criticisms of energetics, as well as Norgaard's call for pluralism, and regard such work as providing one measure, rather than the best or only measure, of economic activity.

Glenn-Marie Lange and Faye Duchin are skeptical about the value of environmentally adjusted national income measures for different reasons. In their view, there are too many methodological barriers to the construction of a single "alternative" measure, and the one-dimensionality of any such measure fails to capture the complex requirements of true sustainability. They propose instead the use of *satellite accounts* covering environment and resource data for different economic sectors. There is already practical experience with the compilation of such accounts in a number of countries. Lange and Duchin feel that they are better suited to policy analysis and development planning than any single measure. This is likely to prove true; but one criticism of the satellite approach might be that it leaves GDP measures, with all their distortions and internal contradictions, unaffected.

The longest and most successful experience with satellite national resource accounts has been that of Norway. Lange and Duchin cite the use of the Norwegian accounts in formulating energy, environmental, and land use policies. However, when we move to developing nations, data limitations are a major constraint on the construction and use of such accounts. For Botswana, preliminary accounts for important natural resource sectors have been compiled, but they are not yet available for other African countries. In general, the urgency of the need to address a particular policy problem, such as rangeland degradation, must be balanced against the costs of data collection. This is no small issue for a poor nation like Botswana. Unless significant resources are made available internationally for this specific purpose, policy formulation in developing nations will likely be severely hampered by lack of the necessary resource accounts.

Several of the articles summarized here address more specific problems of valuation and discounting in areas involving resource and environmental policy. Markandya and Pearce deal with the issue of discounting, pointing out the (probably insuperable) theoretical problems in selecting a single discount rate. They acknowledge that present social discount rates undervalue the interests of future generations and undercut environmental sustainability. Similarly, the standard economic approaches to risk and uncertainty (adding a risk premium to discount rates) may be inappropriate in evaluating the possibility of irreversible and catastrophic environmental damage. But rather than attempting to adjust discount rates, Markandya and Pearce favor imposing a sustainability constraint while continuing to use standard discounting for analysis of resource allocation.

Norgaard's article "Economic Indicators of Resource Scarcity: A Critical Essay" makes the point that market prices do not reflect real resource scarcity but rather the subjective judgments of resource allocators as to the existence of scarcity. This can be related to the discounting controversy. Current market participants typically give insufficient weight to damages inflicted on future generations; present known profits from resource exploitation are more attractive than uncertain future profits from resource conservation. Most economists, however, assume that current market prices accurately reflect resource values, and they regard any modification of market prices as the imposition of a value judgment. In fact, the value judgment that consumption today takes precedence over sustainability has already been imposed by resource allocators, and it is embodied in market price structures, as well as discount rates.

The standard economic techniques of cost–benefit analysis and contingent valuation are reviewed in Per-Olov Johansson's article and are subjected to a sweeping critique in the articles by Sagoff and by Funtowicz and Ravetz. No doubt the money-value measurement of environmental damage has its place, and the methods devised by economists for valuation (survey research, travel costs, hedonic prices, etc.) are better than assigning an implicit value of zero to "intangible" environmental factors. But as Sagoff points out, there are serious pitfalls in assuming that market valuation can be applied to the environment. Market valuation is based, in economic theory, on individual utility. But utility is a notoriously slippery concept, not susceptible to direct observation or measurement. If individuals can be induced to state a valuation for an environmental "amenity," it is questionable whether they would really be happier if paid that dollar sum in return for destruction of the amenity. Sagoff cites the results of a Wyoming study in which participants simply refused to place a dollar valuation on the environment.

In a similar vein, Funtowicz and Ravetz argue that there are epistemological assumptions embodied in economic valuation which are simply inappropriate for dealing with the complex ecosystems and ethical values at the center of many environmental policy issues. Their prescription of a "post-normal" scientific methodology is quite similar to Norgaard's methodological pluralism. The problem with standard economic methods, in this view, is not any technical deficiency but rather the underlying assumption that environmental considerations can be "scientifically" measured as money equivalents. If we adopt this view, then any numerically precise measure of GNP/GDP looks suspect.

A different perspective on income accounting has been proposed by Bruce Hannon. Rather than revising or substituting for GNP measures, he suggests a contrasting measure of ecosystem health—the "gross ecosystem product" or GEP.[8] The GEP is distinguished from GNP in that it can grow only up to an inherent limit. Further, GEP competes with GNP in the sense that increased economic output (at least using present fossil-fuel–based techniques) tends to *lower* GEP. The suggested goal, therefore, is to reform production techniques to make GNP and GEP more compatible—a process which clearly implies an upper limit to GNP growth as well. Hannon's approach, based as it is in ecological rather than economic analysis, will doubtless be uncongenial to economists, but it clearly harks back to the fundamental proposition of ecological economics presented by Robert Goodland in Part I—that ecological limits must govern the future course of economic development.

Here we return to the essential theme of ecological economics: we cannot separate economic activity from its relation to the biosphere. A "purely economic" measure turns out to be inconsistent even on its own terms (specifically in the treatment of depreciation and defensive expenditures). Yet once we try to correct for these deficiencies, we are drawn into an expanding set of measurement and valuation problems and normative judgments. All the authors summarized here are grappling with aspects of this problem. Perhaps the most significant implication of this discussion, as Salah El Serafy has pointed out,[9] is for macroeconomic policy making. Fiscal and monetary policy, public finance, and trade policy will all be affected by our measurement and perception of GNP/GDP and national investment. For this reason, it seems imperative to press on with the development of alternative measures of "green" GDP despite the methodological problems.

One general conclusion can certainly be drawn: the widely accepted focus on GNP growth as a goal of economic policy must be questioned. Instead, perhaps we should be asking the question of how full employment and ful- filling lives for a nation's people can be achieved *without* GNP growth, or with a modified and "lower" growth rate. This formulation of the issue has very different implications for developed and developing nations; we deal with aspects of this dichotomy in Part VI.

Notes

1. Henry M. Peskin, "Alternative Environmental and Resource Accounting Approaches," in *Ecological Economics: The Science and Management of Sustainabil- ity,* ed. Robert Costanza (New York: Columbia University Press, 1991), 176–193.

2. Herman E. Daly and John B. Cobb Jr., "Appendix: The Index of Sustainable Economic Welfare," in *For the Common Good: Redirecting the Economy Toward Community, the Environment, and a Sustainable Future* (Boston: Beacon Press, 1989), 443–507.

3. United Nations Development Programme, *Human Development Report 1993* (New York and Oxford: Oxford University Press, 1993).

4. Robert Repetto, William Magrath, Michael Wells, Christine Beer, and Fab- rizio Rossini, in *Wasting Assets: Natural Resources in the National Income Accounts* (World Resources Institute, 1989); Wilfrido Cruz and Robert Repetto, in *The Environmental Effects of Stabilization and Structural Adjustment Programs: The Philippines Case* (World Resources Institute, September 1992) Maria Conception Cruz, Carrie A. Meyer, Robert Repetto, and Richard Woodward, in *Population Growth, Poverty and Environmental Stress: Frontier Migration in the Philippines and Costa Rica,* (World Resources Institute, October 1992).

5. Kirk Hamilton, "Monitoring Environmental Progress" and "Green Adjust- ments to GDP," World Bank Environment Department discussion papers, 1994.

6. United Nations, *Integrated Environmental and Economic Accounting: A UN Handbook of National Accounting,* 1993.

7. Jane King and Malcolm Slesser, "The Natural Philosophy of Natural Capital: Can Solar Energy Substitute?" in *Toward Sustainable Development: Concepts, Meth- ods, and Policy,* eds. Jeroen C.J.M. van den Bergh and Jan van der Straaten (Wash- ington, D.C.: Island Press, 1994), 139–164.

8. Bruce Hannon, "Measures of Economic and Ecological Health," Chapter 12 in *Ecosystem Health: New Goals for Environmental Management,* eds. Robert Costanza, Brian Norton, and Benjamin Haskell (Island Press, 1992).

9. Salah El Serafy, *Country Macroeconomic Work and Natural Resources,* World Bank Environment Department Working Paper No. 58, March 1993.

Summary of

Environmental and Resource Accounting: An Overview

by Salah El Serafy and Ernst Lutz

(published in *Environmental Accounting for Sustainable Development*,
eds. Yusuf J. Ahmad, Salah El Serafy, and Ernst Lutz
(Washington, D.C.: The World Bank, 1989), 1–7.[1])

*(This summary is based primarily on the overview chapter of a volume of papers
selected from a series of workshops sponsored jointly by the World Bank and the
United Nations Environmental Programme, although it also draws on some
of the individual papers in the volume to clarify particular issues.)*

Present levels of population and economic growth put increasing pressure on the environment and natural resource base. Under these circumstances, there is little justification for economists' neglect of the role of the environment as a resource base and a sink for wastes. Economists have been treating the side effects of production and consumption activities on the environment as externalities. However, since someone must pay the costs of these externalities, the true costs of all activities should be internalized, and income generation should be clearly differentiated from the depletion and degradation of natural resources.

Shortcomings of the Current National Income Measures

Income accounting measures such as GNP, GDP, and net national product (NNP) are useful to economists and development planners as indicators of short- to medium-term changes in the level of economic activity and as tools for stabilization and demand management policy. However, these measures fail as indicators of long-term sustainable growth or welfare, and policies based on these figures could be faulty. While a number of shortcomings of national income accounting have been pointed out in the past, this volume addresses shortcomings with respect to environmental and natural resource issues as they relate to the proper measurement of income and variation in assets.

The Necessity of Measuring Sustainable Income

Income is sustainable by definition: if it cannot be sustained, then it is wrongly estimated. Sustainable income may be perceived as the amount that can be consumed in a given period without reducing possible consumption in a future period. "Sustainable" income is analogous to Hicks' concept of income: "we ought to define a man's income as the maximum value which he can consume during a week, and still expect to be as well off at the end of the week as he was at the beginning."[2]

To arrive at "sustainable" income, two adjustments need to be made to the conventionally calculated NNP. These are subtractions for defensive expenditures (DE) and for depletion and degradation of natural capital (DNC). These adjustments would yield the sustainable social net national product (SSNNP), i.e., SSNNP = NNP − DE − DNC.

Defensive Expenditures

Production and consumption result in unwanted side effects such as pollution, thus necessitating clean-up activities to counter these effects. These activities are called defensive expenditures. At present, the costs of defending the environment are treated as income generating, i.e., as final expenditures, but such outlays should instead be counted as intermediate expenditures. There are many proposals as to how this accounting can be done.[3] Two problems encountered in adopting some of these proposals are the lack of consensus on how natural capital should be treated conceptually, and the problem of actually measuring the level of environmental services and damages.

The Depletion and Degradation of Natural Resources

The present system of national accounts[4] treats human-made assets differently from natural resource assets. The former are valued as productive assets and their depreciation is written off against the value of production. The depletion of natural resource assets may or may not be similarly treated as depreciation in existing accounting systems. If privately owned, they may be depreciated, but in a large number of cases the loss of natural assets shows up as income in the accounts as they are being used for productive or consumptive activities.

The underlying logic of treating the depletion of natural resource assets as income and not depreciation is based on the implicit, though inappropriate, assumption that natural resources are abundant and have no marginal value with resource depletion and sale being treated as a means of promoting economic growth. However, such growth can be illusory if it is not recognized that the apparent increase in income is obtained at the cost of a permanent reduction in wealth. One way to mitigate the wealth-reducing aspects of natural resource depletion is to direct part of the receipts from the sale of natural resources into new productive investments. Proper income accounting would aid policy makers in bringing about this redirection.

Two approaches have been proposed to deal with the depletion of natural resources: the depreciation approach and the user cost approach. The depreciation approach is straightforward and similar to the method of depreciating human-made capital. The effects of the depreciation approach on the present System of National Accounts (SNA) would be to leave GDP unchanged but to eliminate the entire proceeds from the sale of natural resources from the NNP. In effect, the depreciation approach does not capture the income advantage that accrues to the possessor of a natural resource compared to those who have no such possession. This outcome is unsatisfactory, so the user cost approach has been proposed.

The user cost approach splits the revenue from the sales of a depletable resource into a capital element (the user cost) and a value-added element. The user cost represents asset erosion, which should be hypothetically or actually reinvested in alternate assets so that it generates income after the

$$\frac{X}{R} = 1 - \frac{1}{(1 + r)^{n+1}}$$

depletable resource has been totally exhausted. The ratio of true income (X) to receipts net of extraction costs (R) is given by the formula where n is the number of years over which the resource will be depleted, and r is the discount rate, both of which are exogenous and should be determined independently. $R - X$ would be the user cost that should be set aside for capital investment and excluded from GDP. The formula does not indicate an optimal rate of depletion.

Other Issues

The present SNA does not contain an explicit environmental dimension, so some economists and environmentalists advocate a system of environmental accounts independent of the present SNA. It is argued that accounts should be in physical (as opposed to monetized) terms. The advantage of accounts in physical terms is that one will get a sense of the direction and rate of change in the quantity and quality of resources. These physical accounts can be constructed as satellite accounts around the present SNA. To the extent possible, these satellite accounts should be "monetized" and combined with standard GDP and NDP measures to provide an estimate of sustainable GDP/NDP. It is hoped that eventually empirical and conceptual work will lead to an SNA that can be constructed without the intermediate step of satellite accounts.

Notes

1. The findings, interpretations, and conclusions expressed in this study are entirely those of the authors and should not be attributed in any manner to the World Bank, to its affiliated organizations, or to members of its Board of Executive Directors or the countries they represent.

2. John R. Hicks, *Value and Capital*, 2nd ed. (Oxford: Oxford University Press, 1946), 172.

3. Chapters 4, 5, 6, 9, and 10 of the volume address this question in detail.

4. That is, the system that has been in use since 1968. The new SNA, issued in December 1993, goes some way in the direction of the proposals contained here.

Summary of

Three Dilemmas of Environmental Accounting

by Richard B. Norgaard

[Published in *Ecological Economics* 1 (December 1989): 303–314. Reprinted with kind permission from Elsevier Science, B.V., Amsterdam, The Netherlands.]

The present system of national accounts (SNA) is an inconsistent measure of the values of environmental systems and their role in the economy. This article argues that it is not possible to rectify these inconsistencies by strictly rational arguments because of three logically irresolvable dilemmas.

Background

For over three-and-a-half decades it has been recognized that national income accounts do not capture the services of the environment and its resources. Over the years, many international organizations have attempted to build environmental data bases and to incorporate environmental variables into their analyses along with information provided by SNAs. Two broad groups emerged from this exercise. Economists (Keynesians and neoclassicists) argued that SNAs were basically sound and only needed to be improved. Others argued that economic and environmental accounting should be independent, with linkages to account for economic–environmental interactions. The former were interested in developing a measure of how economies perform, while the latter were interested in redirecting economies toward sustainable development.

Inconsistent SNA Dilemma

If SNAs were rationally designed from an understanding of a logically consistent economic theory, and the variables excluded from SNAs were independent from those that were included, then adding the excluded environmental variables to the present SNAs would solve the problem. However, two dilemmas can be identified with respect to this approach.

The first barrier is that SNAs are not consistent with economic theory, and this is true for two reasons. First, there is no consistent theory of economics applicable to SNA development; present SNAs are only a product of historical necessities to meet the tax collectors' needs. Aggregation of data is based on neoclassical market theory, while key indicators have been based on the Keynesian macro-model. A consistent set of extensions from this inconsistent basis is impossible. Second, neoclassical theory suggests rules rather than measures of welfare by adopting an "if-then" set of procedures. Such procedures are used in aggregation and in making adjustments for price changes. However, in reality the "ifs" are rarely met and often forgotten by SNA users. Environmental accounting issues challenge many of the conventions adopted by SNA design.

Value–Aggregation Dilemma

The second barrier arises from the fact that the present aggregation of heterogeneous economic products is achieved by summing their market values in monetary terms. Economists have developed techniques for estimating the monetary value of resources and environmental services, and they argue that these values can be obtained by knowing peoples' willingness to pay for environmental services; if people are not willing to pay, then the service has a low value. Environmentalists counter that ethical issues (e.g., the need to protect other species) should be considered; sustainability should therefore be a constraint, or at least an objective, in the development process. Thus two different philosophical views are in opposition—one contending that social values are the sum of individual values only, and the other claiming that society has its own values. Current economic indicators are based on the first view, and to a considerable extent public policy is based on the second. The problem is that if public policy seeks a more sustainable development framework, it cannot use environmental valuations based on choices of individuals within an economy that is less sustainable than desired. It has been argued that the difference in valuation with and without policy change will be very small, but if significant departure from the current path is called for this will not be true. The issue, therefore, is whether the required policy changes are small or significant. A similar problem exists with respect to using market values to estimate the value of non-market goods and services. If non-market goods and services are only a small portion of the total economy, then market valuations would suffice, but if not, market valuations would be inappropriate.

The problem of selecting weights for valuation and aggregation is called the value–aggregation dilemma. The point is that weights must be used regardless of which system of value aggregation is selected, so the dilemma cannot be avoided.

Bounded Knowledge–Synthesis Dilemma

Policy makers want to know how an economy has performed, where it is headed, and how it can be improved, and for this they need a model of cause and effect. However, SNAs only give current indications, they do not indicate where economies are headed. Moreover, the selection of indicators is based on the economic models being used. This selection should be based on models of economic–environmental interaction.

The third dilemma arises, however, from the fact that there is not and can not be one single model of economic–environmental interactions to provide planners with a consistent set of indicators. Each specific model simplifies reality by bounding the field of inquiry, and science does not have a single "meta" model for synthesizing the many bounded-knowledge models that exist. Moreover, the preferred methodology for synthesizing will often depend on one's understanding of a particular problem or familiarity with a particular methodology. Thus, while a synthesis is necessary to provide consistent, useful information to planners, we must conclude that, based on the bounded knowledge–synthesis dilemma, there can be no single correct way to improve SNAs.

Positively Reinterpreting the Three Dilemmas

The above dilemmas suggest that something must be done to make economic and environmental systems compatible. It is best that economists and environmentalists acknowledge, rather than ignore, the differences in their models and lay out as many scenarios as possible for policy makers.

From these differences, theory and measurement must co-evolve. A pluralistic approach using multiple methodologies is more likely to represent differing interests and indicate Pareto optimal solutions. By a process of learning by doing and sharing experiences, best methods—which themselves will change over time—can be obtained.

Summary of

Correcting National Income for Environmental Losses: A Practical Solution for a Theoretical Dilemma
by Roefie Hueting

[Published in *Ecological Economics: The Science and Management of Sustainability*, ed.
Robert Costanza (New York: Columbia University Press, 1991), 194–213.]

The Interaction between the Environment and Production: The Urgency of Correction

With some exceptions, economists and policy makers the world over regard the expansion of physical output—i.e., production growth—as *the* measure of economic progress and success, and as an indicator of increasing welfare as well. Growth is therefore at the top of economic policy makers' agendas. However, growth is accompanied by the destruction of the most fundamental, scarce, and valuable resource at mankind's disposal, and the very resource upon which growth depends: the environment. Yet the role of scarce environmental resources is virtually ignored in economics, and the systems of national accounts (SNAs) focus on growth alone, failing to account for the often irretrievable use of these resources in production processes. Three conclusions can be drawn from these observations:

(1) society is sailing by the wrong compass at the expense of the environment;

(2) this error is covered up by using terms incorrectly; and

(3) the belief in continuous exponential growth, as measured in national income, is at the heart of the environmental problem.

This article examines the sorts of information that ought to be incorporated into SNAs to properly account for environmental losses due to damage or use, and it discusses the practical problems associated with efforts aimed at valuation of environmental functions.

The current terminology regarding the concepts of growth and welfare reflects the strong belief that society is in good shape economically only when real production, as measured in GNP accounts, is increasing. The notion that growth is necessary to create support for financing the conservation of the environment—highly popular among economic and environmental policy makers—stems from this belief. This proposition is dubious, however, because environmental deterioration is in fact a consequence of the expansion of output. The growth that has occurred in the North has required a loss of scarce environmental goods that has not been taken into account. The minimum growth rate of 3% per annum globally advocated in official development policy is harmful to the environment in terms of both the resources it depletes and the waste it generates.

Reducing these burdens on society could be achieved in two ways: by introducing environment-saving measures into our current patterns of production and consumption, or by directly changing those patterns. The first method, which would involve changing the processes of production, results in higher prices and thus reduces the growth of national income. However, technological measures often will not solve the problem, either because increases in total production override the beneficial effects of the measure, or because, due to the cumulative character of the burden, the measure may succeed only in slowing down the rate of deterioration. Thus technology alone will not be sufficient to address these problems; a shift in behavior patterns is needed as well. Like process changes, changes in production and consumption patterns will also result in slower GNP growth. For example, purchasing a bicycle instead of an automobile, or reducing one's energy use, will result in a decline in GNP. However, assuming that we value bicycles, etc., and the ensuing environmental quality and a sustainable future, more than cars, etc., and the subsequent destruction and depletion of environment and resources, such shifts in the patterns of production and consumption would increase our welfare.

Two conclusions can be drawn from the foregoing discussion:

(1) stimulating GNP growth in industrialized countries will not solve the problems of the developing countries; and

(2) GNP growth and safeguarding the environment and resources are conflicting ends.

The extent of the environmental crisis we confront mandates a shift in our priorities from promoting growth to saving the environment. This reality does not necessitate a cessation of all growth; rather, it mandates a shift to patterns of production and consumption that are sustainable, which may still allow for increases in production.

The Unsolvable Problem of Shadow Prices for Environmental Functions

It follows from the above discussion that the environment is constantly put at risk by these misperceptions regarding growth and welfare, which lead to economic policies that stress increasing production as measured in the SNA. Therefore a correction in the national accounting system to include resource use and environmental destruction is necessary; but two problems make this correction difficult. First, the environment needs to be defined in a manageable way, with the link explicitly made between the environment and economics. In an economic approach, the environment can best be described as the physical surroundings of humans on which they are entirely dependent for all economic activities. The environment serves a number of economic functions, and these functions may come into conflict with one another if the use of one function inhibits the use of another. The environment takes on an economic aspect when competition arises for the use of functions, since competing functions are then scarce goods, and losses of function are costs, irrespective of whether they are expressed in money terms or whether actual markets exist. Qualitative competition arises when additions (wastes) and subtractions (species and habitat extinction) occur that compromise other potential uses of the environmental resource. Quantitative or spatial competition arises when the quantity of matter or space fall short of satisfying existing wants.

The second problem concerns the construction of shadow prices for environmental functions. To address the problems of environmental losses, it is necessary to construct these shadow prices in terms that are comparable to the market prices used in national income accounts. For this, demand and supply curves must be constructed. The supply curve can, in principle, be constructed by estimating the costs of the measures necessary to prevent environmental damage; this curve is referred to as the elimination cost curve. However, constructing a complete demand curve is difficult because the intensity of individual preferences for environmental functions cannot be expressed in market behavior or translated into market terms. This is further complicated by the fact that the consequences of today's actions will often only be manifest in future damage. Some efforts to resolve this difficulty have included asking people to estimate how much they would be willing to pay to conserve environmental functions, or how much function they are willing to lose over time. However, it is doubtful that this method will enable researchers to derive a complete demand curve. Therefore, the construction of theoretically sound shadow prices, necessary for the correction of national income accounts, is not really possible.

What Can Be Done Immediately?

There are a number of objections to equating levels of production with measures of social welfare. One category of objections has to do with a series of technical and theoretical difficulties with estimating and identifying the variables used in the accounting process. A second category relates to a number of expenditures currently treated as final goods and services which are, in fact, intermediate costs. Simon Kuznets emphasizes three particular classes of such expenditures:

(1) the numerous services designed to offset the disadvantages of intense urbanization;

(2) the myriad services associated with living in a technologically and financially complex civilization (e.g., banks, unions, brokerage houses, etc.); and

(3) a major part of government activity, including legislative, legal, and defense activities designed to facilitate the functioning of the system.

A fourth class can also be added that includes expenditures designed to offset the losses of environmental functions. All of these should be made intermediate entries in the SNAs; doing so would lower estimates of GNP.

A third category of objections relates to those elements of our welfare that are not directly related to production, such as leisure, employment, working conditions, income distribution, the quality of the general environment, and future environmental security. All of these factors play a part in economic actions and must be weighed against one another when one comes at the expense of one or more of the others. Thus, there is no single common denominator for evaluating social welfare. From this perspective, policies that result in less output may actually enhance social welfare if, at the margin, the environment is given greater weight than output.

A Practical Solution

While correcting for double-counting of intermediate services is conceptually straightforward, indicating environmental costs in monetary terms is more problematic. A practical solution depends on defining a physical standard for sustainable use of resources and identifying the measures necessary to meet it. Estimates can then be made of both the deviation from this standard at current GNP levels and of the cost of achieving the standard through either remedial activity or direct shifts from burdening to environmentally benign activities. For example, soil erosion above replacement rates can be measured, and the cost of soil restoration efforts can be estimated. This gives a monetary figure for the necessary GNP adjustment. For nonrenewable resources, the appropriate figure would be an estimate of the costs of introducing an alternative source, such as solar energy. For irreversible losses such as extinctions, an arbitrary value must be assigned.

Summary of

GNP and Market Prices:
Wrong Signals for Sustainable Economic Success That Mask Environmental Destruction
by Jan Tinbergen and Roefie Hueting

[Published in *Population, Technology, and Lifestyle: The Transition to Sustainability*, eds. Robert Goodland, Herman E. Daly, and Salah El Serafy (Washington, D.C. and Covelo, California: Island Press, 1992), 52–62. © 1992 The International Bank for Reconstruction and Development and UNESCO]

Consumer preferences dictate the goods and services that are generated in a market system. The market works efficiently and stimulates productivity, enhancing the quantity, quality, and diversity of goods available to the consumer. The national income accounts were devised in the 1930s to measure the level of production and its change from year to year. While economic policy over the last forty-five years has been directed toward increasing the growth of national income, there are a number of problems with this measure as an indicator of human welfare. The increase in production of human-made goods and services has resulted in widespread environmental destruction, leading to a number of natural disasters that threaten the living conditions of future generations.

The Relationship between Growth and Environmental Destruction

The three factors that determine the burden of increasing production on the environment are the population level, the per capita activity, and the nature of the activity. An analysis of the Dutch national accounts shows that the more burdensome an activity is for the environment, the greater is its contribution to GNP. This result is probably true for all industrialized countries. Thirty percent of activities account for 70% of the growth, and production and consumption in these activities harm the environment the most. These activities include oil, petrochemical, and metal industries, agriculture, public utilities, road building, transport, and mining.

The adoption of all available technical measures, including end-of-pipe treatment, process-integrated changes, recycling, increasing energy efficiency, terracing agricultural slopes and sustainably managing forests, is necessary to save the environment and maintain current lifestyles as much as possible. These measures require an increase in labor input and will therefore result in a decrease in labor productivity and an increase in product prices. However, although these measures will check the growth of GNP, unemployed workers will be absorbed into the economy.

Due to price changes, the adoption of these technical measures may result in changes in consumption activities toward environmentally benign activities, but in some cases additional changes may be required. For example, in a number of cases technical measures will not solve the problem but rather will only help retard the rate of deterioration. In other cases no technical measure may be available. Therefore, in addition to technical measures, behavior patterns must be influenced by rules, incentives, and taxes. A shift in production and consumption activities toward environmentally benign activities (e.g., cycling instead of using cars) will check the growth of GNP. Saving the environment will therefore lead to lower levels of national income, but this reduction in GNP should not upset policy makers, since present GNP estimates do not account for environmental losses that result from production and consumption.

Correction of National Income Based on Sustainable Use of the Environment

Humans are dependent on the environment, which provides a number of functions. Loss of function occurs when the use of one function by an activity is at the expense of the use of a function by another activity. When the use of one function comes wholly or partially at the sacrifice of another function, then environmental functions are scarce goods.

Shadow prices for environmental functions must be estimated to make them comparable to the prices of human-made, marketed goods; this can be done by constructing supply and demand curves for environmental goods. Supply curves can be constructed by estimating the costs of measures that eliminate the burdens on the environment, arranged in order of increasing costs per unit of burden avoided. Constructing demand curves is more difficult, since preferences for environmental functions are rarely manifested via market behavior. However, since the publication of the Brundtland Report in 1987, preferences have been voiced by society in favor of sustainable environments, which opens the possibility of using standards for the sustainable use of environmental functions as a basis for these demand curve calculations.

Therefore, one way to correct GNP for environmental losses is to start by defining the physical standards needed to maintain the sustainable use of environmental functions, and then to identify measures for meeting these standards. The difference in GNP between systems that do and those that do not apply these measures will indicate, in monetary terms, how far society has drifted from sustainable use of the environment. This method can also be used to do cost–benefit analyses of projects with long-term environmental effects.

Our Debt to Future Generations

Based on energy use and the resulting CO_2 emissions, we can calculate a rough estimate of the debt owed to future generations and how it can be paid off. One approach to sustainability could be to keep the rate of consumption of fuels, expressed as a percentage of known reserves, equal to the rate of increase in the efficiency of energy use. This implies that sustainable use of fuels requires that goods be produced and consumed with ever smaller amounts of energy. For example, calculations show that in 315 years, today's output must be produced with only 0.5% of today's energy use if we are to achieve sustainability. It is therefore important that new technologies such as flow (solar) energy be developed. In addition, to avoid greenhouse effects world output should be reduced by half. Resources should be directed toward the generation of substitutes and the development of technologies to improve recycling, and population growth should be reversed.

Summary of

A Survey of Resource and Environmental Accounting in Industrialized Countries
by Henry M. Peskin with Ernst Lutz

[Published as *Toward Improved Accounting for the Environment*, ed. Ernst Lutz (Washington, D.C.: World Bank, 1993).]

Current systems of national accounts (SNAs) reflect environmental and natural resource changes either poorly or not at all. The existing framework thus generates estimates of growth, income, and well-being that may be neither accurate nor sustainable. Developing countries' economies tend to be more resource based and to have more severe environmental problems.

As a consequence, traditional SNA methods will provide an even less accurate reflection of environmental realities than is the case in the industrialized countries. A number of industrialized countries are exploring various methods to incorporate environmental and natural resource data into their SNAs. This article surveys some of the proposals and problems of these efforts, in the hopes that they may contain lessons for similar efforts in the developing countries. Indications are given of which countries currently use each method.

Modifying the Accounts to Include Resources and the Environment: Alternative Approaches

In approaching the problem of altering SNAs, we must bear in mind the fact that these accounts serve the dual purpose of providing both a framework for compiling macroeconomic data and a measure of economic well-being and performance. Attempts to incorporate environmental and natural resource data are complicated by the fact that no standard definition of national environmental and resource accounting exists. In addition, many of the methodologies surveyed here have not been adopted as standard practice by their respective countries. The following systems are ordered progressively from those that require relatively modest adjustments in SNAs to those that would involve major restructuring of these accounts.

(1) *Identification and Reclassification of Environmental Expenditures:* This approach proposes reclassification of expenditures on pollution abatement—currently accounted as final demands—to treat them as intermediate inputs, thereby subtracting them from GNP. Closely related to this suggestion is the idea of identifying all "defensive" consumption expenditures whose sole purpose is to ameliorate the ill effects of pollution—for example, water filters, face masks used in Tokyo, etc.—and deducting them from GNP as well. These data on both environmental damage and defensive outlays can be useful even if they are not used to adjust the final aggregates. (France, Japan, Netherlands, Germany, and the United States)

(2) *Physical Resource Accounting Approaches:* In this approach there are a set of satellite accounts (prepared utilizing an input–output format) that describe the flows of resources, materials (including pollutants), and energy that underlie any economic activity. These accounts could show depletions of resource stocks, additions to the resource base (through growth or discovery), contribution of resources to output, and the flow of pollutants from various industries. There are two types of physical accounts: a "stock account" indicates initial stocks, any

additions and subtractions, and the final stocks of key natural resources; and a "pollutant account" typically describes air and water pollution generation by polluting source. However, since these types of accounts avoid valuation of stocks in monetary terms, it is difficult to use them to adjust the economic indicators found in most SNAs. Moreover, if they are to be comprehensive, the data can be very unwieldy and difficult to aggregate. (France and Norway)

(3) *Depreciation of Marketed Natural Resources:* The focus here is on the failure of SNAs to depreciate environmental and natural resource assets as the economy expands. This approach generally emphasizes "material resources," in particular those resources that contribute directly to GNP (e.g., timber or oil) or that closely contribute to the making of a marketed product (e.g., topsoil). This approach is particularly relevant for resource-based developing economies where resource problems may be more important than environmental problems. (Indonesia, Costa Rica, China, and the Repetto framework)

(4) *Full Environmental and Natural Resource Accounts with Valuation:* This approach is the most ambitious, since its intent is to incorporate all of the elements of physical resource accounting and to assign monetary values to all physical entries. Thus an attempt is made to assign market values both for environmental and resource contributions to economic activity as well as for losses in welfare due to environmental and natural resource degradation. The Dutch and the United Nations Statistical Office (UNSO) estimate the losses by calculating the cost to repair the damage, but this approach does not provide for evaluation of the efficiency of the policy. Peskin adopts a neoclassical framework in which benefit–cost calculations are based on estimates of willingness-to-pay to gain environmental benefits or to avoid costs. In practice, these estimates are derived from several environmental benefit–cost approximation methods. (Netherlands, UNSO, and the Peskin framework)

Implementation Considerations

All of these approaches encounter implementation problems.

(1) *Difficulties in Estimating Pollution-Control Expenditures:* Costs may be difficult to identify because either they are not discrete or they are not identified as such in corporate accounts. Since this information is acquired through surveys, nonresponsiveness is also a problem.

Reliance upon theoretical engineering estimates of pollution abatement costs may also present problems of accuracy.

(2) *Difficulties with Physical Accounting:* There are enormous practical problems in assembling data on stocks and flows of resources, and on their contributions to output and environmental degradation. The lack of a common monetary unit creates aggregation problems, as does the difficulty in identifying a single appropriate alternative (non-monetary) unit of measurement.

(3) *Difficulties in Estimating Natural Resource and Environmental Depreciation:* Most criticisms of this approach have centered on the depreciation calculation, which is derived from multiplying the reduction in the resource stock by the difference between the market price of a good and the cost of extraction. The resulting figure is only an approximation of depreciation and does not, for example, take into consideration profits that are reinvested in welfare enhancing ways. We must distinguish carefully between the depletion of a natural asset and its loss of economic value. Over-reliance on market valuation may underestimate the value of an asset; for example, a forest may be worth more than the sum of its trees.

(4) *Difficulties with Valuation in Estimating Environmental and Natural Resource Accounts:* In addition to the problems with assessing physical stocks and flows and assigning value to them as cited above, there are also difficulties in estimating monetary values for services generated by environmental assets and for damages arising from consumption of these services. In particular, the willingness-to-pay concept is subjective and tends to favor the rich over the poor.

Implications for Developing Countries

It is difficult to deduce clear lessons for the developing countries, as most of these accounting programs are in the early stages of development. Those that have been in use for some time are also the least ambitious. We do not conclude from this, however, that simpler is better. A simple, inexpensive data system that fails to facilitate the policy process is no bargain. On the other hand, a system that exceeds the collection capacity of a developing country is not effective either. The particular system developed in each instance must reflect the policy goals and the resources a nation is willing to devote to the process. Thus a system that succeeds or fails in an industrialized country may or may not inform the efforts to transform SNAs in a given developing country. The logistical problems encountered in implementation do provide lessons to assist developing countries in their own research efforts. Given the severity of environmental and natural resource problems in these countries, a productive strategy for them would be to initiate their own low-cost pilot programs now.

Summary of

Toward an Exact Human Ecology
by Malcolm Slesser

[Published in *Toward A More Exact Ecology*, eds. P.J. Grubb and J.B. Whittaker (Oxford, England and Cambridge, Massachusetts: Blackwell Books, 1989), 423–436. Summarized by permission of Blackwell Scientific Publications, Inc.]

The science of ecology entails an examination of nature in all its interconnected complexity. Human ecology, on the other hand, has a strong anthropocentric emphasis and is concerned more directly with mankind's interaction with the natural system. It is an integrative approach for looking at the world's economic system and the natural environment upon which it depends in the context of sustainability. Human ecology holds that one cannot understand either the economy or the environment without assessing the impact of each upon the other. A problem for analyses that link resource-based economic, environmental, and ecological considerations is the absence of a common numeraire. However, a procedure called natural capital accounting (NCA)[1] has been used to model an economy using an embodied energy numeraire.

Finding a Numeraire

In everyday life, our activities are quantified and interrelated in monetary terms; this has given rise to a set of conventions called "accounting practice" and is the numeraire of economics. In both of these, the monetary numeraire is used as a measure of value and as a reflection of preferences. In those spheres where a clear monetary valuation may be absent, such as many environmental resources or the value of goods and resources in the future, the standard response of the economics profession has been to utilize cost–benefit analysis. This is a sophisticated but highly subjective process whose outcome relies upon setting a discount rate and attaching value to those goods for which no market exists.

Development planning calls for estimates of how future choices will be made and valued. Thus forecasts based on cost–benefit analyses face considerable uncertainty, and they have been notoriously inaccurate. One consequence of this is a growing distrust of economic models as a guide to development planning, leading to a trend away from their use. This shift is serious, since it implies the replacement of an explicit statement of one's assumptions with hunches, prejudice, and guesswork.

A means is needed for considering both the set of feasible options that are determined by the physical aspects of the system and how each interacts with the environment. This requires a common numeraire, and it is proposed here that embodied energy be used rather than money. All transformations require energy, which must be available at the moment of use; there is no possibility of credit, and there is no substitute for energy. It is therefore desirable to make a model of the economy in which the flows of capital and conversions of raw materials are expressed in terms of their embodied energy.

Resource Accounting

The distinction between NCA and economic analysis is essentially one of numeraire. Money as a reflection of value subsumes all human inputs to production. NCA, which reflects energy, subsumes only the work (in a thermodynamic sense) done. With few exceptions, physical resources are so abundant in the earth's crust as to be virtually inexhaustible, provided energy and capital are available. Resources may be used, but they are never used up. However, access to them may become increasingly costly in energy terms. It is therefore clear that a flow of energy must be sustained if a given standard of living is to be maintained.

It is possible to network back all of the inputs to a production process and show that each is traceable to the twin actions of prior energy and labor use. These two inputs are in turn the only inputs that are irretrievably dissipated in production processes. Capital inputs are themselves the product of a previous process of manufacture and of dissipated energy. Similar reasoning can apply to all other inputs, including the life support systems for labor, with the result that energy is the only resource that is irretrievably dissipated. Economists contend that this argument amounts to an energy theory of value, but it is not exactly that. It is an embodied energy theory of production. Thus the dissipation of energy in the production process is a measure of the nonrenewable resource consumption of all economic activities, and it enables us to compare any action or policy that has a physical resource implication. Every economic activity thus becomes a sink for energy, and energy drives the economy rather than circulating the way money does. The procedures for evaluating economic activities in these terms are well established and are known as "energy analysis."

Application of NCA

Since all economic activity subsumes energy and is quantifiable, one may choose to model the development of an economic system in embodied energy terms. A common objection to this is that energy cannot be used as an allocation system since people do not make their decisions based on the differing energy inputs of economic alternatives. However, that is not its purpose, which is instead to quantify the long-term consequences of present-day decisions. On the other hand, NCA has less to offer in short-term decision making.

In NCA, a set of wants (demands) incur a demand for resources and human-made (manufactured) capital. The evolution of the system is set by the rate at which resources can be turned into human-made capital and thus provide for wants and liberate additional physical resources. This is not to say that wants or needs cannot be stipulated, or that there exists an inevitable future. It merely expresses a set of constraints—for example, natural laws, resource endowments, climate, sociocultural attributes—that will determine relationships and changes within the system. This is a more realistic view than the open-ended one implied by a purely economic approach, and it enables planners to probe for an acceptable future.

The approach of using energy resources as a starting point makes NCA suitable for studies of carrying capacity. Economic carrying capacity refers to the number of people who can share a given territory and be supported on a sustainable basis. Sustainability in the context of NCA can be defined very precisely: "Economic growth depends on the growth of capital stock (= embodied energy) to enable labor to provide enhanced output (= dissipation of energy). If this is to be sustainable, then the rate of energy flow (more precisely, flux) must always be maintained."[433] Economic sustainability, then, is a state in which the rate of growth of energy flow into the economy is sufficient to harness the resources necessary to indefinitely maintain or improve the standard of living of those within the system.

Assessment of these issues is carried out through simulation rather than optimization models. NCA has been put to work through a dynamic simulation model called enhancement of carrying-capacity options (ECCO). This model has been tested in a number of contexts, first in Kenya, and subsequently in several Asian countries.[2] In a validation modeling of the United Kingdom from 1974–1984, ECCO was eight times better than other conventional models in key areas. Among the uses of ECCO are studies to explore the consequences of policies for food and energy self-sufficiency, as well as assessments of the impact of population growth on the carrying capacity of an area and the resulting welfare of future generations. Many other policy options remain to be tested, and the potential for incorporating environmental factors has yet to be fully exploited.

Notes

1. In the original text the term used is "resource accounting." This term is used in an entirely different context by economists, and in later and current publications, the term used is "natural capital accounting."

2. Author's note: Since this article was written, the model has also been tested in the United Kingdom, European Community, Netherlands, and New Zealand.

Summary of

Energy Analysis and Economic Valuation
by Nicholas Georgescu-Roegen
[Published in *Southern Economic Journal* 45 (April 1979): 1023–1058.]

The "energetic" dogma refers to the view that only energy matters, and the energy crisis of the 1970s has revived this view. This article argues that it is not only energy that is important but that "matter matters, too."

The Energetic Dogma

There are different justifications for the energetic dogma. Fred Cottrell[1] argues that net energy is all that mankind needs. Following Cottrell, H.T. Odum[2] defines efficiency in terms of net energy extraction: the greater the net energy extracted, the more efficient the process. However, the question should be extended to ask why efficiency should not be related to net matter as well? For example, copper is used in the production of copper, resulting in a positive amount of net copper. Moreover, copper mining results in negative net energy, while energy production results in negative net matter. The bias of energetics is in looking only at positive net energy as a criterion of efficiency.

Another justification for the energetics view is made in the 1957 book *The Next Hundred Years*, by Harrison Brown, James Bonner, and John Weir. They claim that any material can be obtained by increasing the energy inflows to a system. This view has been extended by a number of writers who argue that, with adequate energy, the complete recycling of matter is possible.

The energetic view of the economic process in relation to the environment can be represented by a multiprocess matrix of flows and funds. This economic process can be divided into five parts:

(1) producing "controlled" energy from *in situ* energy;

(2) producing capital goods;

(3) producing consumer goods;

(4) recycling material wastes from all processes into recycled matter; and

(5) supporting the population.

To test the energetic dogma, a stationary state must be considered in which the only inflow to the economic process from the environment is energy, i.e., there is no inflow of matter. The only outflow from the economic process into the environment is dissipated (unavailable) energy. The system reproduces itself, including the material funds that are a part of it: capital, people, and land. The energetic model of the economic process must therefore be a closed system, since only a closed system can exchange only energy with its surroundings. The energetic view suggests that the economic system can provide internal *mechanical* work at a constant rate as long as there is a constant inflow of energy. However, this is impossible as a result of the inevitable degradation of matter over time (a principle that may be regarded as the Fourth Law of Thermodynamics).

The energetic view does not take into account that matter also continuously degrades into unavailable forms. For example, friction leads to the dissipation of both matter and energy. The energetic dogma instead claims that the dissipation of matter can be reversed completely given enough available energy.

Matter Matters, Too

Since complete recycling is impossible even in a steady state, there must be an input of available matter into the economic process from the environment to compensate for matter that dissipates and becomes unavailable. For example, if all of the iron produced in the United States between 1870 and

1950 were still in use in 1950, there would have been 13.5 tons per capita in use. However, in fact there was only half of this amount, the rest having been dissipated due to oxidation, corrosion, and general wear. This dissipation occurs for all forms of matter, and the flow of dissipated matter increases with the size of the material stock.

Two separate accounts must therefore be maintained in accounting for environmental transactions: one for matter and the other for energy. The relationship between the economic process and the environment described earlier must then be modified to include:

(1) an additional process that transforms matter *in situ* into controlled matter;

(2) a new set of flows to account for dissipated matter that will be passed into the environment; and

(3) a set of flows to account for "refuse" that flows into the environment.

Energy Analysis and Economics

The entropy law is the reason for economic scarcity; all commodities that have any usefulness must consist of low entropy. However, all commodities with low entropy are not necessarily useful. In spite of the role that entropy plays in the economic process, it is wrong to think of this process as a set of thermodynamic equations. There is no quantitative law that links the amount of pleasure to the amount of low entropy consumed.

A number of writers have argued in favor of an energy theory of value. This is surprising, as there is no consensus on how to measure energy values. An examination of either net energy or gross energy methods of economic valuation shows that "in *absolutely* no situation is it possible for the energy equivalents to represent economic valuations." [1048]

Global Analysis and Economic Choice

The delivery of goods to the consumer requires both energy *in situ* and matter *in situ*, so we must pay attention to the depletion of available matter. Given our present industrial system, in the long run matter will become a greater constraint than energy. Furthermore, natural resource economic choices cannot be reduced to physicochemical reactions, since matter and energy cannot be transformed from one to the other. All economic choices should therefore not be based on energy calculations alone. For example, if there are two technologies, one that results in more net energy and the other in more net matter, then the appropriate choice is an economic, not a technical, problem. If both the technologies result in the same net energy, then the technology that results in more net matter should prevail.

Global Analysis and Technology Assessment

Solar energy is considered "free," and this point is used to argue for technologies based on this source. However, one must be careful before accepting such a claim. There is a difference between feasible technologies and viable technologies. At present, solar energy is feasible, but not viable, due to the material and energy requirements of producing solar collectors. Clearly, attempts must be made to find viable solar energy techniques, but solar energy should not be viewed as a panacea that can overcome the problems of resource limitations.

Notes

1. Fred Cotrell, *Energy and Society* (New York, McGraw-Hill, 1953).
2. Howard T. Odum, "Energy, Ecology, and Economics," in *Ambio* 6, 220–227 (1973).

Summary of

Integrated Environmental–Economic Accounting, Natural Resource Accounts, and Natural Resource Management in Africa

by Glenn-Marie Lange and Faye Duchin

[Prepared as Technical Report No. 13 of Winrock International Environmental Alliance for USAID Bureau for Africa, (May 1993): 1–73. Contact author at the Institute for Economic Analysis at New York University for reprints.]

In the traditional approach to national income accounting, net domestic product (NDP), which is defined as gross domestic product (GDP) minus the value of produced capital used up in the course of production, has been interpreted as a measure of sustainable income. However, because NDP does not consider the maintenance of natural capital, it overestimates sustainable income. Many aspects of natural capital are omitted from the traditional accounts since they are not subject to market transactions. Natural resource accounts (NRAs) are designed to rectify this problem. The design of NRAs is still in a nascent stage and no conventional format has been agreed upon, though the United Nation's recently published handbook on NRAs helps to rectify this situation. Nevertheless, two major categories can be identified: summary NRA and management-oriented NRA. This article discusses the conceptual and methodological problems associated with these two categories of NRA and their application to policy issues. It argues that management-oriented NRAs are more appropriate than summary NRAs for the analysis of economic–environment interactions.

Summary National Resource Accounts

Summary NRAs attempt to calculate a single monetary value for all natural resource use and environmental deterioration and then to subtract this number from NDP to arrive at environmentally adjusted domestic product (EDP). Among the measures included in calculating the deterioration of natural capital are defensive expenditures (expenditures on pollution prevention and cleanup) and the value of depletion and degradation of marketed and nonmarketed natural resources.

There are three conceptual problems with EDP as a measure of sustainable income:

(1) In calculating EDP, it is assumed that produced and natural capital are near-perfect substitutes for each other. However, as natural capital is depleted, the scope for substitution of one for the other decreases. A single index that blurs the distinction between produced and natural capital is not useful from a policy perspective.

(2) The lack of markets for a number of environmental resources requires imputing values for these resources when calculating EDP, but there are two serious problems with these values. First, because of the wide variety of valuation techniques and assumptions on which they are based, EDP can take on almost any value—an unacceptable outcome for national accounts. More fundamentally, imputed values are by definition hypothetical. If these costs were actually incurred, all economic transactions would change. It has been argued that this is more appropriately treated as a modeling exercise, not an accounting exercise, since EDP would require estimation of the new economic transactions.

(3) Two important omissions in traditional national accounts also affect EDP estimates: the accumulation of human capital, and the informal sector. Both of these factors are important in understanding and for-

mulating sustainable development policies, especially in developing countries.

How good is EDP as a measure of sustainable income and how useful is it for policy makers? The above discussion indicates that NRAs are not a comprehensive measure of sustainable income. While proponents of summary NRAs would agree, they would also claim that summary NRAs are better than traditional income accounts, and therefore are a step in the right direction. However, differences in methods and assumptions adopted to calculate EDP in each country can result in very different measures of sustainable income, but there is no basis for standardizing these methods and assumptions for use in all countries. Moreover, even if EDPs could be estimated in a meaningful manner, their usefulness for policy is questionable because the implications of the numbers are unclear. In addition, summary NRAs do not provide the sectoral detail required for most policy analysis.

Management-Oriented Natural Resource Accounts

Management-oriented NRAs record the extraction of resources and their use in production, as well as the discharge of waste materials associated with each economic sector and with households. The UN has recommended that the NRA be linked to the input–output table of the system of national accounts (SNA) to bring out the interconnections between the environmental and economic activities. Management-oriented NRA are based on a physical approach to accounting. The physical data are then interpreted in policy terms through the use of physical indicators (like sustainable yields) and economic valuation. They can also be used to calculate EDP, subject to the weaknesses identified above.

The compilation of data at the sectoral level poses a considerable challenge, especially for developing countries with limited financial and human resources. This is one of the serious drawbacks of management-oriented NRAs. However, a large amount of data has already been collected or can be estimated from technical parameters calculated in other countries for similar problems. In these circumstances, the challenge of constructing NRAs becomes the difficult but less daunting one of integrating diverse data sets. In order to assure the usefulness of the NRA, it is essential that this undertaking be guided by a country's development problems and strategies. The article describes how a country could simultaneously pursue identification of sustainable development strategies and compilation of NRAs.

Use of Management-Oriented Natural Resource Accounts in Developing Countries

Management-oriented NRAs can be and already are being used for policy analysis and decision making in both developed and developing countries. They can be used to monitor resource use and environmental degradation at both the sectoral and economy-wide levels. They can also be used for policy analysis and planning, especially when linked to an input–output or related (Social Accounting Matrix, Computable General Equilibrium) model which brings out the direct and indirect effects of possible changes in the economic and environmental sectors. This is critical at the economy-wide and regional levels, where coordination among sectoral policies is necessary and spillovers or trade-offs must be identified.

While developing countries can learn from the experience with management-oriented NRAs of developed countries like Norway, France, and the Netherlands, developing countries may benefit from different emphases— for example, the importance of including both formal and informal sectors, creating NRAs for distinct geographical regions, and concentrating on different environmental issues such as biodiversity.

Management-oriented NRAs are already being used in developing countries like Indonesia and the Philippines to address issues such as the feasibility of continued food self-sufficiency as income growth changes the average diet of an increasing population, and the environmental impact of establishing a large pulp and paper industry or liberalizing trade.

In Africa, only Botswana has begun to construct NRAs, but a number of other African countries are planning to do so, including the Gambia, Zimbabwe, Namibia, and Ghana. Construction and effective utilization of NRAs require that a number of obstacles be overcome. In addition to the data issues mentioned above, and the need to coordinate development policy with NRA construction, NRAs pose institutional challenges. The compilation and use of NRAs cuts across ministries and professional disciplines and cannot be handled by one agency alone. Leadership is needed that can coordinate ministries, international donors, and university and professional research organizations, and which can link data collection with policy analysis.

Summary of

Development, the Environment, and the Social Rate of Discount

by Anil Markandya and David W. Pearce

[Published in *The World Bank Research Observer* 6 (July 1991): 137–152.]

Many environmentalists have questioned the use of the discount rate in formulating economic policies related to natural resource use. This article examines and evaluates the use of the discount rate in environmental decision making. It argues that rather than trying to "do something" about the discount rate for environmental reasons, the problem might be better addressed by developing the concept of sustainability as a policy instrument.

The Rationale for Discounting and the Choice of the Discount Rate

Sixty-one cents invested today at a 5% compound interest rate will be worth $1 in 10 years; $0.61 is called the present value factor when the discount rate is 5%. The higher the discount rate or the longer the time horizon, the lower the present value factor. Discounting is used because less weight is attached to future benefits or costs than to those in the present. This is either because people are impatient or because a dollar's worth of resources now will generate more than a dollar's worth of goods and services in the future, and an entrepreneur will therefore be willing to pay more than a dollar in the future to acquire a dollar's worth of those resources now.

The two main criteria used to determine the discount rate are the social rate of time preference and the opportunity cost of capital. Time preference rates tend to be lower than the opportunity cost of capital. The impact of costs and benefits on levels of consumption relative to savings are crucial in determining the discount rate. Both in theory and in practice, there is disagreement about the choice of discount rates.

Discounting and the Environment

There is no unique relationship between high discount rates and environmental degradation. While high discount rates may shift the cost burden to future generations, they also reduce the level of investment, and lower investments reduce the use of natural resources. For example, high discount rates discourage development projects with large capital needs, such as dams, and may therefore help preserve large areas in their existing state. We can consider five discounting methods and their implications for environmental problems.

Pure Individual Time Preference

There are three arguments as to why social discount rates should not be influenced by individual time preference rates. First, it is not necessarily true that an individual's welfare will be maximized if the individual acts on the impatience principle (which is the basis for the pure individual time preference rate). Second, individual wants carry no necessary implications for public policy. Finally, there are problems with the expression of the basic value judgment involved. Societies that seek to satisfy wants should be concerned with satisfying wants as they arise, and thus actually achieving tomorrow's satisfaction, rather than trying to achieve today's assessment of tomorrow's satisfaction.

These objections are debatable. Overturning the fundamental value judgment of the liberal economic tradition—i.e., that individual preferences should count in social decisions—requires more compelling reasons. While the third objection is philosophically persuasive, the discount rate should be retained on pragmatic grounds to deal with serious environmental problems in developing countries.

Social Rate of Time Preference

The social rate of time preference measures the rate at which the utility of consumption decreases over time. The social rate of time preference can be expressed thus:

$$i = ng + z$$

where i is the social rate of time preference, z is the rate of pure time preference, g is the rate of growth of real consumption per capita, and n is the percentage decrease in marginal utility for each percentage point increase in consumption.

The first concern that environmentalists have with this formulation is the presumption that the growth of real consumption per capita, g, will always be positive. They argue that there are limits to growth based on natural resource and environmental sink constraints. For example, in low-income sub-Saharan Africa, real per capita consumption fell by 1.9% between 1973 and 1983, yielding a negative g. While this might imply a negative i as well, these regions have individual time preference rates, z, as high as 10–15% that may result in positive social rates of time preference. However, the high individual time preference rates themselves can be questioned. One argument for high individual time preference rates in situations of poverty is that the need for immediate food is more urgent than the need for assurance of food in the future, but this argument is problematic in the context of environmental degradation; high discount rates may lead to environmental degradation, which may result in further poverty. Thus a vicious cycle is operating in which poverty calls for high discount rates, which themselves cause poverty. As a result, a social time preference rate based on the above equation may not be useful when real consumption per capita is negative or falling, because the value of z may not be relevant. A better method for determining a social rate of time preference is needed.

Opportunity Cost of Capital

The opportunity cost of capital is the rate of return on the best alternative investment of similar risk that is foregone as a result of undertaking a particular project. Basing the discount rate on the opportunity cost of capital is justified on the grounds that it is reasonable to expect a return on a project that is at least as high as the return on the best alternative use of funds. Environmentalists have objected to opportunity cost discounting on two grounds. The first objection is that opportunity cost discounting implies that the benefits of the investment will be reinvested at opportunity cost rates. If, however, the benefits of the investment are consumed rather than reinvested, then the consumption flows have no opportunity cost, and opportunity cost discounting becomes irrelevant. This problem has led to the development of weighted discount rate procedures, whereby the underlying discount rates are modified according to the levels of consumption and reinvestment.

Another problem with opportunity cost discounting relates to compensation across generations. If an investment today will cause x dollars worth of environmental damage T years from now, the damage will be valued today at much less than x dollars. The actual amount of the present value will depend on the discount rate and the length of time, T. The logic is that if this lower value is invested today, it will amount to x in T years, and it could therefore be used to compensate for the environmental damage when it occurs. Environmentalists have argued that the lower discounted value for the environmental damage is legitimate only if the compensation will actually be paid, but this argument confuses potential and actual compensations. Efficiency only requires that a sum for compensation be generated, not that it be distributed.

Risk and Uncertainty

As the uncertainty of an occurrence increases, the value of associated benefits or costs should decrease. Three kinds of uncertainty are relevant to discounting. First, the risk-of-death argument (i.e., will an individual be alive or dead in the future) is used to justify consumption today rather than in the future. The objection to this argument is that while individuals are mortal, society is not. A second type is the uncertainty about individual preferences in the future. This uncertainty may be relevant for some goods, but the future preferences for goods such as food, shelter, water, and energy are not uncertain. The third source is uncertainty about the size of benefits or costs in the future. It is often assumed that the further away in time benefits or costs will occur, the greater the uncertainty of their occurrence. However, there is no reason why this must be true. Economists accept this objection in theory, but use of risk-adjusted discount rates is still common in policy analysis. Rather than add risk premiums to discount rates, uncertainty can instead be dealt with by calculating certainty equivalents. However, these calculations are complex and the methodology is unclear.

Interests of Future Generations

A matter of debate and concern is whether the use of positive discount rates actually safeguards the interests of future generations. Models have been constructed in which the utility of the present generation depends on the utility of future generations, but these models reflect what the present generation thinks future generations will want, rather than what future generations actually want. Also, the results of these models depend on the extent and nature of the way present generations think about the future. There are a number of arguments suggesting that, for reasons relating to future generations' interests, social discount rates may be below market rates. However, there is no practical procedure to determine a social discount rate that accurately reflects future generations' interests, so using discount rates to account for these interests is a complex and probably untenable approach.

Discount Rates and Specific Environmental Issues

Two specific environmental issues—irreversible damage and the management of natural resources—can be analyzed to see how they are affected by the discounting process.

Irreversible Damage

Krutilla and Fisher[1] developed a cost–benefit methodology for analyzing projects that have irreversible outcomes, such as the flooding of a valley or the loss of tropical forests. For this analysis, all of the costs and benefits must be expressed in present value terms to determine whether or not the project should be undertaken. The lower the discount rate is, the larger will be the benefits of preservation and the lower the benefits of the project. In their analysis, Krutilla and Fisher do not adjust the discount rate. Instead they claim that the value of the wilderness will increase over time because the supply of such areas is shrinking and the demand for their services is increasing. The advantage of their approach is that it has the benefits of using a lower discount rate without the disadvantage of distorting resource allocations in the economy by using variable discount rates. They also argue that the value of the benefits from the project will decrease over time because better technologies will be available in the future. The basis for this argument is unclear, but it has the effect of lowering the discounted value of the benefits of development without altering the discount rates.

Management of Natural Resources

In general, the relationship between the discount rate and the pattern of exploitation of natural resources is complex, but the fundamental point is that higher discount rates lead to faster exploitation of resources. Discount rates also have important effects on the time profiles of costs and benefits. For example, in comparing two projects, one that would exhaust a resource in 10 years and another that would exhaust it in 25 years, a high discount rate will favor the shorter term project. Overexploitation will also occur if the resource is held by the private sector and the private rate of discount is higher than the social rate of discount. High discount rates may exist due to anti-inflationary monetary policies or capital rationing, and they may be justified within these contexts; but at the same time they can have undesirable consequences with respect to natural resource management. However, while high discount rates can lead to overexploitation of resources in several ways, overexploitation can be more effectively controlled by the imposition of taxes than by trying to change discount rates, due both to the practical difficulties of controlling the rates and to the need to use them as tools to control other problems within economies.

Sustainability

Environmentalists' objections notwithstanding, the discount rate should not be tampered with. The paramount concern of environmentalists is to protect the interests of future generations. This can be accomplished without rejecting discounting by pursuing a policy that recognizes the constraints imposed by the need for sustainability. The central idea behind sustainability is the protection of the natural resource base for future generations. While it would be absurd to require that no individual project harm the environment, it is possible to require that a portfolio of projects not cause harm, implying that some projects should improve the environment. Such a policy would permit the discount rate to function as a mechanism for resource allocation while protecting the environment.

Note
1. John V. Krutilla and Anthony C. Fisher, *The Economics of Natural Environments* (Washington, D.C.: Resources for the Future, 1975).

Summary of

Economic Indicators of Resource Scarcity: A Critical Essay
by Richard B. Norgaard

[Published in *Journal of Environmental Economics and Management* 19 (July 1990): 19–25.]

The theoretical and empirical literature in economics has discussed alternative indicators of long-run resource scarcity. This article criticizes the use of economic indicators to determine whether resources are scarce.

A Review of the Literature

The literature on economic indicators of long-run natural resource scarcity can be divided into empirical and theoretical parts. In the empirical literature, Barnett and Morse (1963) analyzed the changes in the amount of labor and capital needed to extract a unit of resource, finding that extraction costs declined by a factor of four between the latter part of the nineteenth century and the middle of the twentieth century. This finding formed the basis for the argument that natural resource scarcity could not be determined by simply looking at physical quality and availability of resources; past effects and the future potential of technological change and substitution must be considered as well. Other economic indicators of natural resource scarcity have subsequently been developed and thoroughly analyzed. Despite doubts raised by the effects of the energy crisis, the superiority of these economic indicators as measures of resource scarcity has become a basic premise of the empirical literature.

Starting with Hotelling's (1931) model, and considering the quality of information available to resource allocators, the theoretical literature has explored the paths of several indicators, including costs, royalties and prices. The results indicate that prices and royalties, may follow various paths, depending on a number of factors, including the size of the resource stock, interest rates, market structure, taxation policies, and substitute technologies. Moreover, changes in any of these factors will reset the paths. However, despite these theoretical findings, the empiricists have ignored these factors and continue to focus only on their economic indicators to identify scarce resources. But the superiority of this focus only on the indicators must be questioned, given the difficulty both of determining all of the effects of the other factors on the economic indicators and of distinguishing these effects from those actually caused by scarcity.

The Logical Fallacy

The theoretical models of Ricardo and Hotelling can be reduced to the following simple syllogism:

Major Premise: If resources are scarce, and
Minor Premise: If resource allocators are informed of resource scarcity,
Conclusion: Then economic indicators will reflect this scarcity.[22]

The empirical literature has looked at resource indicators (the conclusion) to deduce whether resources are scarce (the major premise), and empirical work has ignored the minor premise. In the theoretical literature there are no connections made between the nature of information possessed by resource allocators and the interpretations of the cost or price paths of resources.

In commenting on this critique, many economists have suggested that a true contribution to economics should help correct the problems, not simply point them out. A proper analysis would entail looking at economic indicators of resource scarcity while controlling for whether resource allocators are informed. However, to find out whether resource allocators are informed about scarcity, it is necessary to know whether resources are scarce, and this is the very question under investigation. Thus there is a logical fallacy. If allocators are well informed, then we should get information from them directly rather than analyzing indicators that are based on their actions.

How Did We Go Wrong?

The empirical analyses of the 1970s that were based on Hotelling's model did not clearly reveal the implications of the model because they suppressed both the stringent assumptions of the model and the sensitivity of the results to a number of factors. Moreover, despite the fact that both the Ricardian model and Hotelling's model do not fit the historical record of the United States, they were still used in the difficult empirical analysis of natural resource scarcity.

Conclusion

While there have been changes in views about what constitutes science, two tenets have remained unchanged:

(1) science feeds on the tension between theory and reality; and

(2) individual scientific arguments must be logical.

The use of economic indicators to determine whether resources are scarce over the long run does not meet either of these two criteria of a scientific approach.

Summary of

Valuing Environmental Damage

by Per-Olov Johansson

[Published in *Oxford Review of Economic Policy* 6 (Spring 1990): 34–50. By permission of Oxford University Press.]

Policy changes result in benefits for some groups and costs for others; often the costs of a project are costs to society, not to the individual or firm undertaking the project. Social cost–benefit analysis entails transformation of costs and benefits into monetary units to assess the desirability of a project. This article reviews several ways in which economic theory accounts for environmental damage.

Money Measures: An Example

The *willingness-to-pay* concept measures the maximum amount of money that individuals are willing to pay so as to undertake a project. The total that all individuals are willing to pay is a measure of the benefits of the project. This is compared to the costs of the project to determine its profitability. An alternative monetary measure is the concept of *monetary compensation,* which measures the minimum amount of money that individuals must be paid to agree that the project not be undertaken. Two other related concepts are *compensating variation* and *equivalent variation*. In the former, the individual is kept at a pre-project level of satisfaction, and the willingness-to-pay for environmental improvements or the required compensation for environmental degradation resulting from the project are calculated. To calculate equivalent variation, the individual is held at the level of satisfaction that would be attained if the project were carried out. In this case, we measure the willingness-to-pay to avoid environmental deterioration or the compensation required to accept that environmental improvements are not carried out.

A useful alternative interpretation of the willingness-to-pay approach is the referendum. Voters can be asked to vote on whether they are willing to pay a certain amount for a project, say £1000 per individual. If the majority vote yes, then it is fair to assume that the average voter is actually willing to pay more than £1000.

On the Total Value of a Resource

Four values can be attributed to environmental resources:
(1) consumptive use values, e.g., fishing and hunting;
(2) nonconsumptive use values, e.g., bird-watching;
(3) indirect services, e.g., services provided through books, movies, etc.; and
(4) existence values, e.g., satisfaction derived simply because a resource exists.

The total value of a resource is the sum of the four values, where all are expressed in monetary terms. Environmental damage affects the total value of a resource. Nonconsumptive uses and indirect uses can be thought of as public goods, and reductions in their supply cause reductions in welfare across a number of individuals. Existence values depend on both the stock and quality of a resource, so environmental degradation could affect the existence value of a resource by decreasing its quality, even if the stock remains the same. Environmental damage can affect the price of a resource and of commodities related to it, causing a loss in consumer surplus.

Valuation Under Certainty: Option Value

The discussion of changes in consumer surplus can be extended over many time periods. However, economic agents do not have perfect information about the future, and this uncertainty about the future value of resources gives rise to the concept of *option value*. There are two interpretations of the precise definition of an option value. The first sees option value as a risk premium arising from uncertainty. In this case, the option value is the difference between the option price and the expected consumer surplus. The expected consumer surplus is obtained by multiplying the consumer surplus by the probability that the resource will be destroyed, while the option price is the maximum the consumer is willing to pay to ensure that the resource is available. In some cases, the calculation of option values may be more complicated.

The second interpretation of the option value concept has been labeled the quasi-option value. For example, the decision on whether to develop a tract of land may lead to the destruction of plant and animal populations that may have economic uses in the future. Furthermore, the destruction of any one species may lead to the destruction of some ecosystems. The quasi-option value, then, is the increase in expected benefits of preserving rather than developing an area until the uncertainty is resolved. It can be calculated based on appropriate biological, engineering, and economic data.

Some Practical Methodologies

There are a number of methods used to estimate the willingness-to-pay for public goods, three of which are described briefly:

(1) *Survey Data:* This method entails asking individuals how much they will be willing to pay for a change in the provision of a public good, or how much they should be paid not to undertake a change. The problem with this method is that there is an incentive for some people to understate their willingness-to-pay if they believe they will be asked to pay the stated amount. On the other hand, some people may overstate their willingness-to-pay if they believe that the amount they claim will not affect what they must actually pay.

(2) *Travel Cost Method:* While a number of services (e.g., fishing or recreational services) are free or priced very low, the travel cost that individuals pay to undertake these activities can be recorded. The service will be used less by those from regions with greater travel costs. This information can be used to derive a demand curve for the service, and consumer surpluses can be calculated for different groups. One problem with the travel cost method is that it does not capture the existence value for those people who do not travel to use the service.

(3) *Hedonic Prices:* This method attempts to calculate the willingness-to-

pay for environmental services by comparing property values across regions. For example, if there are two similar houses in two different areas and the only difference is the air quality, then the difference in their values is assumed to be due to the difference in air quality. The main drawback with this method is that public goods such as parks and endangered species do not have prices attached to them, so this method cannot be used in these cases.

General Remarks and Problems

In theory, the same monetary measure should result regardless of the method used for valuing environmental damage. However, in practice this does not happen. Work therefore needs to be done to compare the relative reliability of different methods. In addition, in many studies there is a large difference between the willingness-to-pay and the willingness-to-accept measures. In this case the problem is not with the existence of differences but with their magnitude. A third problem in social cost–benefit analysis is that even if the benefits are greater than the costs, those who gain may not be able to compensate the losers. Fourth, in expressing their willingness-to-pay, respondents may not understand all of the consequences of a complicated policy change.

Summary of

Some Problems with Environmental Economics
by Mark Sagoff
[Published in *Environmental Ethics* 10 (Spring 1988): 55–74.]

Economists are increasingly using contingent valuation methods "to assess the economic value of recreation, scenic beauty, air quality, water quality, species preservation, and bequests to future generations."[1] These methods attempt to determine individuals' willingness-to-pay to preserve natural environments (preservation or existence values), to maintain the option of using natural environments (option values), and to bequeath natural environments to future generations (bequest values). This article argues against the defense of the contingent valuation method put forward by Steven Edwards in his article "In Defense of Environmental Economics," and then describes the outcome of an experiment conducted in Wyoming.

Edwards' Defense of Environmental Economics

Edwards' first point in defense of the contingent valuation method is that a relationship exists between an individual's willingness-to-pay and personal utility. His argument is that as people's incomes increase, so will their level of happiness, as they can procure more things that provide satisfaction. However, there is no empirical evidence that supports this claim. Albert Hirschman has pointed out that consumption can lead to both satisfaction and disappointment, and, according to Frank Knight, it is the education of desire, not necessarily its satisfaction, that leads to happiness. It is therefore wrong to argue that willingness-to-pay reflects the level of happiness that individuals will obtain if the purchase is actually made. In fact, resource economists define *personal utility* as that which willingness-to-pay measures; the two terms are interchangeable, and the relationship between them is purely tautological.

Edwards' second point is that the economic analysis that is applied to traditional markets (i.e., markets in which buyers and sellers transfer property voluntarily at agreed upon prices) can be extended to contingent markets. In effect, Edwards is arguing that the kind of economic analysis that is used to assess private markets can be extended to publicly owned resources, and that public resources should be auctioned off to the highest bidder. The problem with this line of reasoning is that in private markets individuals do not have to sell to the highest bidder. In technical terms, property rights in traditional markets are backed by property rules that allow the owner the right to exclude or not to transfer. When property rights are instead backed by liability rules, then the property must be sold to the highest bidder. The nature of property rights is therefore important in determining the nature and rules of transactions in markets. The economic analysis that Edwards defends creates an abstraction of the marketplace, without the ideals of exclusivity and consent, to justify the auctioning of public resources to the highest bidder. If, on the other hand, property rights are taken seriously, then the public may prefer not to sell at any price.

In many cases, respondents in contingent valuation surveys refuse to indicate the price at which they are willing to buy or sell environmental goods and resources. Why is this so? Edwards argues that respondents are indulging in strategic behavior in order to influence the final outcome, and he claims that they are misrepresenting their actual thoughts. However, it may be that respondents are motivated not by an attempt to deceive but by the belief that environmental policy—with its ethical, cultural, and aesthetic aspects—should be discussed and debated before decisions are made. In other words, respondents may be suggesting that the democratic process, not prices at the margin, should determine the moral and political questions involved in environmental policy. Or respondents may be aware that a number of publicly owned environmental resources are not marketable by statute, and they may therefore be unwilling to assist in a "backdoor" cost–benefit analysis of these resources. Finally, respondents may see through the circular definitions of utility used in these surveys. Whatever the actual reason, Edwards' claim that it is simply strategic behavior shows his unwillingness to take liberty and consent seriously.

Tangible and Intangible Values

The Clean Air Act and the Endangered Species Act dictate certain environmental regulations and standards on aesthetic and ethical grounds. Even the most ardent environmental idealist will acknowledge that at some point these regulations impede economic growth. We must then ask how much regulation is appropriate? This question is made more difficult by the fact that a number of these aesthetic and ethical considerations are intangible and unmarketable, and therefore they do not have market prices.

Two Approaches to Rationality

There are two senses in which the economic approach to environmental policy can be described as "rational" and "scientific." In the first, a decision is rational if it uses mathematical criteria and methodologies that are laid down in advance to arrive at conclusions based on exogenous preferences. Economists approach rational decisions in this framework by collecting data on prices and consumer preferences to determine the trade-off between environmental protection and economic development.

The second sense in which a decision can be seen as rational or scientific is if it is reasonable or sane according to a set of moral virtues: tolerance, respect for others' views, willingness to listen, and reliance on persuasion rather than force. This second notion of a rational decision depends on an open decision-making process that takes legal, ethical, technical, economic, and other realities into account. The conflict between these two methods arises when determining how much information should be presented, or how much discussion, deliberation, and education should be allowed in a survey. For the decision to be scientific in the first sense no discussion should be allowed, as it may influence people's views, i.e., the exogenous variables. However, without deliberations and discussions the decision will not be rational and scientific in the second sense.

The Wyoming Experiment

Adopting the economic notion of rational and scientific, three economists at the University of Wyoming undertook a study to determine the value of an intangible good: atmospheric visibility.[2] Atmospheric visibility is one of the requirements of the Clean Air Act. The economists showed photographs with different degrees of visibility to a variety of people and asked two questions:

(1) How much would you be willing to pay to prevent a given deterioration in visibility (as demonstrated by comparing two of the photographs) that would be caused by a power plant?

(2) How much should you be compensated if a loss of visibility does occur?

The economists had to decide whether they should explain to their subjects why the change in visibility would occur, since respondents' opinions might vary depending on whether the change would be caused by nature (e.g., an approaching storm) or by emissions from the smokestacks of a coal-fired utility plant. When the respondents were informed that pollution from a power plant would be the cause of the visibility loss, a majority of them refused to cooperate in the survey. They rejected a cost–benefit framework for the trading of pollution rights.

Information plays a key role in determining how people feel about environmental resources and contingent markets. Rather than pretending that respondents are being strategic when they do not cooperate in contingent valuation surveys, we should realize that they are thinking, political beings who are, in fact, rejecting the methodology of the surveys.

Notes

1. Steven Edwards, "In Defense of Environmental Economics," *Environmental Ethics* 9 (1987): 80; cited by Sagoff, 55.

2. R. Rowe, R. D'Arge, and D. Brookshire, "An Experiment on the Economic Value of Visibility," *Journal of Environmental Economics and Management* (1980).

Summary of

The Worth of a Songbird: Ecological Economics as a Post-Normal Science

by Silvio O. Funtowicz and Jerome R. Ravetz

[Published in *Ecological Economics* 10 (August 1994): 197–207. Reprinted with kind permission from Elsevier Science B.V., Amsterdam, The Netherlands.]

Economics has traditionally neglected uncertainties both in knowledge and in ethical issues. The economic paradigm is modeled on classical physics, and it is a "normal" science in the sense articulated by Thomas Kuhn.[1] The scientific enigmas and policy riddles of global environmental policies call for a "post-normal science." Central to this concept of a post-normal science is the organizing principle of quality, which requires a new methodology and social organization of work. The irreducible uncertainties and ethical complexities inherent in some issues can thus be managed as knowledge is democratized and the peer group is broadened to include a number of different perspectives and norms of evidence and discourse. This article lays out the framework for valuation techniques in a post-normal science.

Valuations

The "songbird" in the article title refers to species and ecosystems that are irreplaceable, whose market value does not represent their true worth. Valuation issues of this kind force us to focus on what value is, what is being valued, and how valuation is done.

In the case of the songbird, valuation cannot be divorced either from the methodology used or from ethical issues. While some people argue that rational policy debates require that valuations only be done in monetary terms, others object strongly when dollar values are assigned to species. In the middle lie those who reluctantly accept monetary valuation on pragmatic grounds but are against this method in principle. At present, the burden is on those who favor preservation of a wetland or a species to demonstrate—with a monetary yardstick—that the benefits of preservation are greater than the benefits of exploitation. The current convention of using money as the language of valuation constrains all valuation processes, so its adoption and use by all stakeholders in any environmental issue therefore seems appropriate.

With the development of ecological economics and a clear vision of what a sustainable future is, different conceptions of value and how it is measured will arise, and monetary values expressed through the commercial market will become only one of many forms of valuation. Operational definitions of value will reflect what is important and real, as well as the level of commitment of different stakeholders. Based on a number of legitimate perspectives, a new common language that is not dominated by any single group will evolve when negotiators recognize the irreducible complexity of the issues at stake. The problem with the present system is not only that the market is expected to determine value, but also that all valuation must be reduced to a one-dimensional standard. New forms of valuation will not and should not be unidimensional, and they will be the products of negotiations and mediations in the institutionalized political process. The task is to develop a set of concepts and practices whereby all of the complementary perspectives contribute to a rational dialogue in which ethical commitments are articulated.

Elements of a Post-Normal Science

This section sketches the elements of a post-normal science that can be used in the development of an ecological economics. An article by W.D. Nordhaus (1991)[2] is used as an example to demonstrate that mainstream economists are adopting the rhetoric of an ecologically sensitive approach, although not in a selfconscious and disciplined manner. These elements are discussed in the following subsections.

Appropriate Management of Uncertainty

The many uncertainties associated with ecological problems force economists to be more cautious with quantitative arguments than they usually are in regard to other issues. The article by Nordhaus is full of caveats, reflecting the fact that economics applied to environmental issues does not possess the same degree of control of uncertainties as, for example, analytical chemistry. The task is to manage the uncertainties so as to get the best quality of information from them.

Managing imperfectly understood uncertainties requires explicit guidelines. A set of guidelines called NUSAP—standing for "numeral, unit, spread, assessment, and pedigree"—have been developed. The first two categories of NUSAP are easily understood, but spread, assessment, and pedigree describe three distinct kinds of uncertainty. Spread refers to the precision or "random error" of data; assessment refers to the degree of accuracy or "systemic error;" and pedigree describes model uncertainties, i.e., the border with ignorance or the boundaries of knowledge about the information being expressed. An analogy with target shooting can clarify these terms: we have precision if the shots cluster closely, accuracy if they are near the bull's-eye, and pedigree determines whether there is a target at all.

The article by Nordhaus contains all three forms of uncertainty. However, despite clearly acknowledging uncertainty, the problems associated with it have not been well managed. Some of his entries have large intervals, some are unquantified, and others are based on adjustments that are ad hoc or derived from hunches. These problems notwithstanding, the final results are calculated with hyper-precision. The hyper-precision of final numbers represents an attempt to establish objective facts from intuitive fuzz. This defect of hyper-precision is not peculiar to the Nordhaus article but in fact is widespread in economic analysis. NUSAP provides frameworks to deal with uncertainty, to critique information offered in discussions of ecological economics, and to evaluate information as a basis for policy recommendations.

Appropriate Management of Quality

The Nordhaus article demonstrates inappropriate management of the quality of information in relation both to its inherent uncertainties and to its function as a basis for policy. Definite policy recommendations are based on less certain conclusions. Very different policy recommendations would emerge if the author had different hunches. The hunches themselves are buried in mathematical sophistication, giving the analysis an image of quantitative science, as opposed to what it really is: doctrine reinforced by guesswork. The important point is that it is wrong to manipulate uncertainties in information and conclusions in such a way that recommendations appear to be far more certain than can be scientifically justified.

Another problem is that value commitments, i.e., the different weights attached to the various risks and benefits, are masked in Nordhaus' arguments. Ecological economics must acknowledge the importance and legitimacy of value commitments and should take ethical stances. It should be explicit about where it believes the burden of proof must lie in debates on environmental policy. Forensic advocacy and scientific research both have their place in post-normal science, but it is illegitimate to claim to use one form of discourse when actually employing the other. Quality of discussion can best be maintained by expanding the peer group to involve a multiplicity of participants and perspectives. This will require both an explicit statement of ethical principles and development of appropriate modes of discourse, norms, and institutional arrangements, all based on the organizing principle of quality of dialogue rather than on abstract truth.

Plurality of Commitments and Perspectives

The organizing principle of post-normal science is quality, which is comprised of ethics and morality. The old ideal of scientific truth is no longer attainable or relevant for policy; no single perspective can claim a monopoly on wisdom. A number of different groups, including consumers, NIM-

BYs, representatives of the disadvantaged, champions of the natural environment, spokespersons for industries and governments, and academics, should all be part of the decision-making process. Negotiations and mediations based on principled advocacy rather than the pretense of uncommitted scholarship should also be part of the process. An honest recognition of conflicting interests and power relationships will prevent any single group from co-opting others.

Intellectual Structures

Traditional research in science has been motivated by curiosity, and there it is reasonable to attempt to define "foundations" that can serve as the basis for unity among researchers. More recently, mission-oriented research is based on producing "corporate know-how" rather than "public knowledge," and the traditional conceptual basis of scientific research has been eliminated. In an issue-driven post-normal science, searching for foundations can be the cause of confusion. Common commitment to certain approaches, rather than shared knowledge, is the most important factor in problem solving. Commitment to a resolution of the problem will give rise to appropriate problem-solving activity and dialogue.

Social Structures

Mission-oriented scientific research is carried out in bureaucratic institutions and is directed by managers based on the needs of the institution rather than on publicly defined issues. Moreover, many aspects of this kind of research are unknown to the public. Issue-driven post-normal science should be opened up to make research transdisciplinary and accessible to the public. Institutional changes will be needed to make this transition.

Conclusions

The worth of a songbird goes beyond questions of valuation in monetary terms; we must move beyond the commodification of all resources for the determination of their worth. The management of scientific uncertainties and value commitments is at the core of establishing an effective post-normal science.

Notes

1. Thomas S. Kuhn, *The Structure of Scientific Revolutions* (University of Chicago Press, 1962).

2. W.D. Nordhaus, "To Slow or Not to Slow: The Economics of the Greenhouse Effect," *The Economic Journal*, 101(1991): 920–937.

PART VI

International Economic Relations, Development, and the Environment

Overview Essay

by Rajaram Krishnan

Introduction

Global environmental problems demand global solutions because irrespective of the root of any particular problem the consequences are felt by many. In our present political system no single nation or group of nations can impose direct penalties on perpetrators of environmental degradation. Even if we assume that such penalties might be imposed, in a number of cases (where the causes of environmental degradation are indirect and complex) we cannot point to a single actor or source as the cause of the problem.

This part of the book deals with issues related to international economic relations, development, and the environment. The articles selected for inclusion in this part attempt to bring into focus perspectives which run counter to the dominant attitudes—"free trade is best" and "let the markets work"—in international economic relations. These philosophical underpinnings and dominant attitudes, long advocated by the World Bank and the International Monetary Fund, have been strengthened by the recent collapse of planned economies and the apparent triumph of the free market alternative in Eastern Europe. However, a reconsideration of these views is imperative given the disastrous results with respect to poverty alleviation in an absolute sense, widening income inequality in a relative sense, and the direct relationship between global environmental degradation and the dominant policy regimes.

This essay lays out the major issues related to how international economic and policy relations have been thought of in the development literature, and how they should be modified in the context of the ecological crisis that affects the globe. Such a discussion must be informed by, and must take into account, the very different perspectives which people hold depending

285

on their class and national origins. The differing groups do not lend them-selves to simple dichotomies such as North and South, rich and poor, urban and rural, or anthropocentric and biocentric. This is not to suggest that these differences are unimportant, but that no simple stereotypes can be formed. A history of the nature, costs, and benefits of international eco-nomic relations in the post-colonial world would be very different depend-ing on who was the narrator. There will be no consensus on the causes of environmental problems or on an ideal international policy package to address the environmental crisis that we all face. The differences arise because of varying interpretations of history, differences in where environ-mental problems fall in the larger scheme of problems, the perceived bene-fits and opportunity costs of meeting the environmental challenges, and the varied cultural and social backgrounds that people bring to the problem.

The complexity of such dichotomies notwithstanding, where issues regarding the environment are concerned there is one essential difference between the rich countries of the world and the poor ones. To the rich, the environmental problem stands as a constraint to ensuring for the future the affluence that is today taken for granted. Arguably, the environmental problem is the most serious threat and should be the primary policy con-cern of these countries. For the poor countries of the world, on the other hand, the environmental problem, while serious, is secondary to the prob-lem of poverty. Even though poverty and environmental degradation feed on each other in a vicious cycle of cause and effect, if asked which one prob-lem they would rather have solved first, political reality if nothing else will point toward poverty. This fundamental difference is bound to result in dif-ferences in policy prescriptions between the rich and the poor.

The rest of this essay is divided into three subsections. The first of these discusses what Wilber and Jameson[1] label the "orthodox" paradigm in development. Given its widespread influence in the practice of development policy it could well be called the mainstream or dominant paradigm. The second subsection discusses a critique of the orthodox paradigm—the dependency school—which was influential in the 1960s and 1970s. The third subsection is a guide to the articles included in this part of the book. The conclusion outlines the need for a reformulation of development the-ory and international economic relations in the context of global environ-mental problems.

International Economic Order—the "Orthodox" Paradigm

Until recently, international economic relations were governed by the realpolitik of the Cold War. The race between the East and the West dictated political and economic realities. Both sides were determined to establish that their respective ideologies and methods were not only better than those of the other side but that they were the best path for humankind. However, the common thread in the policy prescriptions of the East and the West was the propagation of economic growth. The desire for growth, so dominant in directing domestic economic policies of the East and the West, has also been central to the organizational structure of international economic relations. This section will analyze the philosophical underpinnings of the international economic order influenced by the ideology of the West. The primary intellectual foundations for this perspective can be traced back to European liberalism of the late eighteenth and nineteenth centuries.

The international economic order, with its emphasis on "free" trade and "open" markets, works on the premise that goods and services should be produced on the basis of comparative advantage for worldwide consumption. While there is widespread disagreement in the theoretical literature on the "free trade is best" doctrine,[2] its hold as a working concept ideologically and in policy is strong. Influential institutions, especially the World Bank and the IMF, have by and large advocated a rather doctrinaire line of getting the prices right and opening up markets to integrate the global economy. These policies are aimed at improving the global economic system based on the efficiency criterion.

A history of development economics since the 1950s reveals this bias toward a growth-oriented strategy. In the 1950s, surplus labor models associated with Sir Arthur Lewis and the "vicious cycle of poverty" concept suggested that investment shortfalls were the bane of developing countries. The argument was that developing countries were caught in a vicious cycle in which low investment led to low output and employment (read as low growth) which led to low savings which led to low investment, etc. The relevant policy was therefore to boost investment and encourage growth. Investment in developing countries was to be made available in the form of aid and favorable loans, and by the transfer of technology from the West. On the international front it was argued that open markets were best for development.

The evidence in support of these policies was seen in the success of Western Europe after the end of World War II and in the success of the "Gang of Four" (Hong Kong, Singapore, South Korea, and Taiwan) economies. Unfortunately such evidence is misleading. At the domestic level it was naive to believe that what was right for Western Europe was right for the newly independent countries of the Third World. The success of the "Gang of Four," while remarkable, cannot be attributed to a policy of open and free markets but rather to a planned policy of export-led growth. Furthermore, doubts have been expressed as to whether the success of these countries can be universally replicated.[3]

In the 1960s and 1970s, a realization that the policies pursued had a very small effect on poverty alleviation led to a modification of development theory and strategy. "Growth with equity" and "basic needs" put direct poverty alleviation at the center of development strategy. Growth was not abandoned, but poverty alleviation was added. The problem with these policies was that the processes that accompanied growth worked against poverty alleviation. Put simply, the policies were schizophrenic. Also the power of forces, both domestic and international, that work against redistributional policies was underestimated.

International Economic Order—the Dependency School

An important school of development thought whose influence has waned, but whose relevance has not, is the dependency school. The dependency school rejected the theories of linear progress from underdevelopment to development as espoused by W.W. Rostow. It had its origins in Latin America and is best expressed in the words of one of its leading proponents:

> Studies of dependency continue a live tradition of Latin American thought, reinvigorated in the 1960s by the proposition of themes and problems defined in a theoretical–methodological field not only distinct from what inspired Keynesian and structuralist–functionalist analyses (the theory of modernization, and of the stages of development that would repeat the history of industrialized countries), but radically distinct with respect to its inherent critical component.[4]

The dependency school attempted to explain the process of development of some nations and underdevelopment of others as part of the same process. Development and underdevelopment are two sides of the same coin, one responsible for the other. The processes that caused these dual outcomes were a result of the international economic system and the arrangements within it which are cultivated to ensure the spread of capitalism worldwide.

The term *dependency* is used to suggest that the nature of international economic relations is configured in a manner such that "most important decisions about development strategies—decisions about prices, investment patterns, government macroeconomic policies, etc.—are made by individuals, firms and institutions external to the country."[5] The dependent economy becomes integrated into a larger trading system and plays to the demands of the world economy, especially those of the developed economies. The developed countries of the world constitute the center and the developing countries constitute the periphery. The development of the periphery is dependent on the center, and the center "exploits" the periphery in its development.

As can be expected, there has been strong criticism, and indeed a dismissal, of dependency theory by the proponents of the orthodox school. Marxian analysts have also objected to the dependency school on a number of fronts. They see it as emphasizing nationalistic issues at the cost of class issues in explaining international exploitation.[6] While there is validity to a number of the critiques of the dependency school, there is an important aspect of the dependency analysis that bears on an analysis of environmental issues in the context of international economic relations. The nature of international economic relations has had an adverse impact on ecological systems, which has benefited some nations and classes while simultaneously hurting others. Domestic and international economic arrangements patterned after nineteenth century liberalism can in some circumstances be seen as zero-sum games, with some participants gaining at the cost of others because of impacts on the environment, rather than as arrangements which benefit all participants. However, unlike the dependency school argument, the gains and losses from environmental degradation do not cut across national lines but are instead a function of nation–class lines.

Introducing the Environment—Guide to Selected Articles

The above two sections have outlined the major themes which the economic development literature has put forth to understand the positive and normative aspects of international economic relations. Interesting from today's perspective is an absence of any direct discussion of environmental consequences and feedback effects. This is understandable since environmental problems were not on the radar screen when the theories were initially formulated. The articles in this part of the book attempt to fill in this gap. The selected articles do not have any single message but rather they represent different perspectives which are important for a reassessment of international economic relations given global economic concerns.

A reformulation of the nature of international economic relations must begin at the top. The article by Robert Goodland and Herman Daly, "Ten Reasons Why Northern Income Growth Is Not the Solution to Southern Poverty," argues that the present set of arrangements wherein the growth of the North is seen as important for markets of the South is fallacious. They argue that Northern growth and its offshoot, consumption, result in the North appropriating a disproportionate share of natural resources, and squeezing the South. It is interesting that the opposite argument, that the South should develop so as to create markets for Northern goods, has also been made by proponents of the "grow to consume, consume to grow school." While Goodland and Daly do not make the argument explicitly in this article, the end of economic activity cannot be growth and consumption, but must be development. Growth can in fact retard development due to its impact on the environment. An important empirical question is "How extensive are the environmental costs of growth and who pays for them?"

One way in which the rich have attempted to help the poor grow is through aid. The article by David C. Korten calls into question the underlying growth-oriented philosophy on which these aid programs are premised. Korten argues that the policies pursued result in environmental degradation and an extraction of ecological surplus, and that they perpetuate poverty in the South. Aid as it is presently construed is thus counterproductive, benefiting the North and the rich in the South, and hurting the environment and therefore the poor who depend on the environment.

The two articles discussed above clearly have elements of the dependency analysis in them. The general themes are that while the welfare of the rich depends on the use of environmental resources, exploitation of these resources makes matters worse for the poor, who depend on them for their livelihood. The dual nature of the process, described in the dependency argument as resulting in simultaneous development and underdevelopment, corresponds to an analysis of the environment aiding in the creation of wealth, while environmental degradation perpetuates poverty. Future research should concentrate on further analysis of this dual process at the micro level and attempts to establish such effects empirically. Otherwise this line of analysis risks being dismissed on the grounds that it lacks analytical and empirical rigor.

The most powerful "instrument" in the ideology of the orthodox school at the international level is the doctrine of free trade. There is a voluminous debate between the proponents and opponents of free trade. However, it is only now that connections between trade and the environment are being analyzed. While a lot of work remains to be done, the articles by Jagdish Bhagwati (a distinguished and renowned proponent of the free trade doctrine) and Herman Daly (one of the founders of the subdiscipline of ecological economics) ably present the two sides of the trade and environment debate. One major difference between the two perspectives is the nature of the question that is posed. While Bhagwati dismisses the notion that growth can have a detrimental effect on the environment, to Daly trade and increased growth may be inherently wealth reducing rather than wealth enhancing in a global sense. In addition, the ecological economics perspective is interested in the distributional aspects of trade, because such effects have an impact on levels of poverty, the deepening of which has an adverse impact on the environment.

A systematic overview of trade theory and its application to social and environmental issues is provided by Paul Ekins. He stresses that the ecological critique of the standard trade model is not a recent development but in fact has significant roots in the development of trade theory. A number of mainstream economists, from Samuelson to Krugman, have pointed out that the optimistic conclusions of free trade advocates are strongly dependent on unrealistic assumptions. In many instances, expanding trade can have negative effects both on resource-dependent developing economies and on the environment. Ekins argues that the goal of environmentally sustainable trade may be significantly different from the goal of free trade, and that GATT agreements or the new World Trade Organization rules must reflect this.

The next three articles we consider are by Jayanta Bandyopadhyay and Vandana Shiva, Martin W. Lewis, and Ramachandra Guha. They address the issue of alternatives to the present structure of international economic relations. The article by Bandyopadhyay and Shiva discusses the development of ecology movements which have micro foundations but which result in macro changes. It describes how the dominant ideology, with growth as its centerpiece, has destroyed the economy of nature upon which a vast number of the poor depend, and it stresses that trade-offs between development and the environment are false. Since the poor depend upon the environment, an important element of poverty alleviation is to protect the environment. A point made by Bandyopadhyay and Shiva, in common with radical environmentalists in the North, is that market capitalism works against both poverty alleviation and environmental sustainability and should be rejected in the process of development.

Martin Lewis critiques this position in his article, arguing that it is not modernization and industrialization that is the problem, but how these are pursued. In addition, Lewis introduces the population growth variable into the analysis. The vicious cycle of poverty and population worsens the existing vicious cycle of poverty and environmental problems. He argues that urbanization and industrialization can be achieved in environmentally positive ways and that population growth is one of the problems but not the primary problem for development policy. A policy response to these three problems simultaneously calls for a thorough understanding of the interrelated causes and feedback effects.

Ramachandra Guha, like Lewis, critiques the radical deep ecology position, calling it irrelevant for an understanding of environmental policy in Third World countries. However, he finds common ground with Bandyopadhyay and Shiva in suggesting that environmental protection policy must emphasize issues of equity and social justice. The task before us is to figure out how this should be achieved. Equity and social justice are important elements in the call for "sustainable development" strategies. Effort should be concentrated on making the good intentions associated with this call into a coherent and workable strategy. If not, it will prove to be another fad in the development literature, like so many before it.

In their article "Environmental Conflict and Violent Change," Homer-Dixon et al. add a political dimension to the economic and environmental interrelations. Garnering evidence from a number of different case studies, they demonstrate the connections between resource scarcities and inequities and violent conflicts at the local and international level. This is an important point to make when dealing with global environmental policy. In a purely economic sense, to say nothing of other aspects of human suffering, the prevention of such conflicts in many cases would be cheaper than their expected costs. Economic policy analysts have often made recommendations on the grounds that they can do very little with the political aspect. Such a limited perspective is inadequate given the interdisciplinary nature of the issues at hand.

The final article in this part deals with the international nature of responses to global environmental problems. Neva Goodwin's "Introduction to the Global Commons" discusses the prospects and possibilities for the creation of a humanitarian third sector to deal with the public goods aspects of problems facing the world. The nation-state as the main unit of analysis and policy prescriptions is inadequate given the global nature of many of the problems that we face. When everybody's business is nobody's business within the nation-state, governments step in. Who steps in and how do they do so when everybody's business is nobody's business at the global level? It is with these questions in mind that Goodwin presents a new vision of a "civic corps" working toward the solution of global problems. I anticipate that many bred on the philosophy of self-interest cast in its narrow dimensions will dismiss Goodwin's third sector as "pie in the sky." However, without working toward such a sector we may have neither pie nor sky to worry about. Clearly Goodwin's vision is only the first word, not the last, in developing a framework which can be truly international in its solutions.

Conclusion

Environmental concerns call for a change in the nature of international economic relations. The reason environmental problems are different from other problems associated with traditional development issues is that every-body is affected by them simultaneously. While the poor in Third World countries were a concern for all, they did not directly affect the lives of the well to do. Macro environmental problems, such as global warming and the depletion of the ozone layer, have a public goods quality in that none of us can escape their effects. Even micro environmental problems, such as soil erosion and destruction of forests, adversely impact all, though at different levels.

The intimate interconnections between economic growth, population growth, environmental problems, poverty perpetuation, and wealth cre-ation call for a interdisciplinary, holistic paradigm shift in international eco-nomic analysis. Richard Norgaard's call for "methodological pluralism" is especially relevant in issues regarding trade, development, and the environ-ment. Here we must break through well-entrenched stereotypes and dichotomies. For example, criticizing growth is not the same thing as rejecting the marketplace. However, not rejecting the marketplace does not mean accepting market solutions for all places at all times. Similarly, we should consider issues of *power* and *intentions* in understanding interna-tional economic relations. The underlying philosophical spirit of the depen-dency paradigm will be a useful starting point. A simultaneous endorse-ment of the "market perspective" along with an endorsement of the "dependency school" may seem rather contradictory. I contend that there can be a useful synthesis of these apparently exclusive perspectives. We should focus on theoretical and causal explanations of poverty, rather than simply attempting to figure out how people can be made rich. The default position that people are poor because they did not do the things that make them rich is inadequate.

The articles in this part do not offer definitive answers for the serious issues that face humankind. Rather, they introduce the reader to different strands of thought which are relevant but do not find an expression in the mainstream discussions of trade, development, and the environment.

Notes

1. Charles K. Wilber and Kenneth P. Jameson, "Paradigms of Economic Devel-opment and Beyond," in *Directions in Economic Development*, eds. Kenneth Jame-son and Charles K. Wilber (Notre Dame, Indiana: University of Notre Dame Press, 1979), 1–41.

2. For a detailed discussion of this point see Paul Ekins, Carl Folke, and Robert Costanza, "Trade, Environment and Development: The Issues in Perspective," *Eco-logical Economics* 9 (January 1994): 1–12.

3. See W. Cline, "Can the East Asian Model of Development Be Generalized?" *World Development* 10 (1982).

4. Fernando Henrique Cardoso, "The Consumption of Dependency Theory in the United States," *Latin American Research Review* 12 (1977): 7–24.

5. Wilber and Jameson, 17–18.

6. James H. Weaver and Marguerite Berger, "The Marxist Critique of Dependency Theory: An Introduction," in *The Political Economy of Development and Underdevelopment*, 3rd edition, ed. Charles K. Wilber (New York: Random House, 1984), 45–64.

Summary of

Ten Reasons Why Northern Income Growth Is Not the Solution to Southern Poverty

by Robert Goodland and Herman E. Daly

[Published in from *Population, Technology and Lifestyle*, eds. Robert Goodland, Herman E. Daly, and Salah El Serafy (Washington, D.C. and Covelo, California: Island Press, 1992): 128–145. © 1992 The International Bank for Reconstruction and Development and UNESCO]

There are two views on how poverty in Southern countries can be decreased. The traditional view argues that rich Northern countries should consume more in order to provide markets to support Southern growth. The alternative view argues that Northern countries should stabilize their resource consumption. This article discusses these two views and provides ten reasons why income growth in the North is not a solution to poverty in the South. It then makes recommendations on how the North can help the South.

Two Views: the Traditional and the Alternative

The traditional view argues that Northern income growth, resulting in Northern consumerism, is necessary to ensure that the South will not stagnate. The export of natural resources from the South to the North is seen as a source of income and growth for the South. It is suggested that the import earnings of rich elites in the South will then trickle down to the poor. In addition, the South can use the foreign exchange earned from these exports to import the latest consumer goods. This view assumes that the South is incapable of transforming these resources into necessities for its own people and therefore must remain dependent on the North. One problem with this approach is that, because both environmental sink capacities and stocks of natural resources are finite, growth and use of these capacities in the North implies less room for growth in the South.

The alternative view argues that, in the context of a finite, inexpandible ecosystem, the North should stabilize its consumption patterns to free up resources and ecological space for the South. The North has overused both the source and the sink capacities of the global commons, thus limiting the options of the South. The solution to Southern poverty therefore lies in the North reducing its throughput, while the South directs its efforts toward producing necessities for the many poor, rather than luxuries for the few rich.

Ten Reasons

There are ten reasons why the alternative view rather than the traditional view is the solution to Southern poverty. They are:

(1) *GNP: A Flawed Measure of Human Well-Being:* GNP is a poor measure of human welfare and a poor guide for prudent economic development and environmental management. Despite this, economic development takes GNP maximization seriously. Environmentally benign activities have a substantially smaller impact on GNP than environmentally harmful activities. For example, the clean-up costs in the aftermath of the *Exxon Valdez* oil spill increased GNP, but walking, biking, and use of mass transit contribute less to GNP than the use of automobiles. Preventive methods of environmental protection need not be an expensive choice that only the rich can afford, as is often suggested. However, cleanup of the detrimental environmental consequences of growth is expensive. In the case of the health of the environment, inexpensive prevention is better than expensive cure.

(2) *Importance of Relative Incomes:* The proponents of the traditional view who advocate global income growth must acknowledge that one unwanted side effect of this growth is an increasing income disparity between the North and the South. The gains from income growth accrue much more to the North than to the South. Since relative income is more influential than absolute income when competing for finite resources, the poor will increasingly be excluded from domestic and international market economies.

(3) *Differential Utility of Needs and Wants:* The utility gained from increases in income and consumption is much less in the North than in the South. Because levels of consumption are already high in the North, further increases are subject to sharply declining marginal utilities. In the South, on the other hand, increasing income still meets basic human needs with high marginal utilities. In addition, there are environmental costs associated with increasing incomes. Further income increases in the North could therefore actually result in decreasing welfare in absolute terms. If instead the North consumes less and saves more, while transferring resources to poverty alleviation in the South, then utility in the South will increase with relatively low environmental costs.

(4) *Misplaced Technological Optimism:* New technology is adopted to improve productivity and increase the material standard of living.

However, considering population growth and the disparity in incomes between the poor countries and the United States, it will be exceedingly difficult for poor countries to catch up with the rich despite any technological improvements, even over the next forty years.

(5) *The Value of Economic Self-Reliance:* Poverty alleviation in the South will be more readily achieved by promoting employment and self-reliance strategies in the South than by pursuing the traditional trickle-down approach. While obsolete technology in developing countries may initially result in waste, this problem can be solved by the export to the South of up-to-date technologies and industrial ecology strategies.

(6) *Throughput Growth as a Source of Both Income Growth and Environmental Damage:* Measured in terms of labor volume, one-quarter of all economic activities account for 65% of GNP, and it is these same activities that are most detrimental to the environment. In addition, these activities increase the real income of the other 75% of the economy's labor volume, thus causing additional consumption. A small part of the economy in terms of labor volume is responsible for a large part both of GNP and of environmental degradation.

(7) *Subsidized Resource Pricing:* The undervaluation of raw material exports from the South to the North means that the South is subsidizing the North through both government subsidies and the costs due to environmental externalities. International organizations should promote full-cost pricing that reflects the true economic costs.

(8) *Inequitable Trading Systems:* At present, the world trading system favors the North at the expense of the South. Much Northern growth is based on depleting Southern resources at prices below the cost of sustainable exploitation. Individual countries must take world prices as given. However, a number of goods exported from the South face low elasticities of demand in world markets, so world prices may fall as all of these countries attempt to reach their production targets. This results in declining export revenue, adversely affecting imports to these poor countries.

(9) *Dysfunctions of Imbalanced Trade:* The virtues of free trade have been overestimated, and this goal can conflict with the goal of "getting the prices right." Tariffs imposed to internalize costs should not be labeled "protectionism." In fact, ignoring the environmental costs associated with liquidating natural resources should be seen as a type of subsidy similar to "dumping." In addition, the environmental costs

of repaying debts through raw material exports and natural resource liquidation should be recognized.

(10) *The Insecurity of Inequality:* Increasing Northern incomes at the cost of Southern sustainability will lead to global insecurity. It will result in an increase in "environmental refugees" fleeing human-made disasters, poisoned water, air, and soils, soil erosion, and desertification. It is in the interest of the North to intervene to reduce income inequalities with the South and to work toward poverty alleviation.

Recommendations

The North and South should work together to achieve the goal of sustainability. The primary recommendations for how the North can help the South are:

(1) The North should reduce its consumption to more sustainable levels. Most importantly, there should be a transition toward the use of renewable energy sources. This can be achieved with a combination of carbon or nonrenewable energy taxes and tradable pollution permits.

(2) Northern countries should internalize the costs of disposal of toxics and other wastes, rather than passing them on to low-income countries.

(3) The North should change current policies that harm the South, such as underpricing of Southern exports.

(4) The North should review the debts of the South and conditionally write them off based on environmental progress. Loans and grants made for unsustainable purposes should be stopped. In addition, socially and ecologically beneficial technologies should be made more available to the South.

(5) Grants should be provided through the World Bank and other international organizations to encourage environmental investments in the South, including grants to support investments that promote maintenance of the biophysical infrastructure.

(6) The North should be directly involved in alleviating Southern poverty, rather than relying on the trickle-down approach.

(7) The South should be encouraged to pursue policies of population stabilization, transition to renewable energy, human capital formation, job creation, and direct poverty alleviation.

Summary of

International Assistance:
A Problem Posing as a Solution
by David C. Korten

[Published in *Development* 3/4 (1991): 87–94.]

A common measure for assessing the aid performance of high-income countries is the total aid given as a proportion of GNP. The accepted target among international agencies is currently 0.7%, although in 1988 the actual average for OECD countries was only 0.36%. The prevailing assumption is that more is better. However, despite total aid levels reaching $60 billion in 1988, as we enter the fourth official United Nations Development Decade we are confronted with several harsh realities: more people live in desperate poverty now than ever before; environmental destruction has reached crisis proportions; the number of economic and environmental refugees is increasing; and many southern economies are saddled with debilitating debts. Something is terribly wrong, and official assistance is not fixing it.

Growth—Solution or Problem?

Most development strategies are driven by the underlying premise that the central task of development is to increase output. Growth is viewed as the key to creating jobs for the poor and generating surplus to clean up the environment and control crime and violence. Unfortunately this logic seems flawed. The Worldwatch Institute calculates that global production has increased four-fold since 1950, with no measurable impact in terms of reducing poverty, stabilizing the environment, or eliminating the causes of violence. The reasons for this can be readily identified:

(1) increased output increases strains on the environment;

(2) when economic and political power are already concentrated, increases in wealth tend to flow to the already wealthy; and

(3) treating labor as a commodity forces people to place impersonal employment above all else, with negative implications for family, community, and culture.

In the 1980s we have begun to confront the ecological limitations on this approach, not so much in terms of oil or mineral resources supplies as in terms of the limits on both the demands we can place on water and soil systems and on the disposal of wastes in the air, water, and soils. We have completed the transition from an open, frontier system to a closed, zero-sum system; we can no longer treat the earth's ecological system as an expanding pie. Today, one person's increase in wealth comes at the expense of another's impoverishment. To complicate matters further, at this same time a new institutional force has been created: the transnationalization of capital. This force transcends the state and threatens the ability of people to control their own affairs and to demand accountability from the state.

Many of the official international development agencies have been instrumental in bringing about these processes of change, steadfastly promoting growth as the solution to global problems. They continue to fund large projects that displace the poor and destroy the ecosystem in order to enable the more privileged to expand their consumption, and they perpetuate the South's ecological subsidies to support the North's unsustainable overconsumption. Created to serve such a growth-centered development vision, these institutions have been reluctant to challenge the basic premises of that vision, because to do so would challenge their legitimacy and acknowledge that their very existence may be part of the problem.

Sustaining Overconsumption

The industrial nations, with roughly 20% of the world's population, consume two-thirds of the world's important metals and three-fourths of the world's energy. Their economies are overwhelmingly responsible for the pollutants that are depleting the ozone, causing acid rain, producing greenhouse warming, and otherwise threatening the global ecosystem. Northern lifestyles depend upon the South both for extraction of a disproportionate share of its mineral and ecological resources and for absorption of a disproportionate share of the wastes. This North–South expropriation is a component of many development projects subsidized and managed by development assistance. As the poor are evicted to make room for industrial parks, power plants, and commercial agricultural, timber, or fishery projects, their welfare is sacrificed to benefit those already better off. Furthermore, the debt taken on by the South to finance these projects allows the North to dictate economic policies to the South. Southern poverty is therefore not the consequence of inadequate charity from the North but a result of the North's expropriation of its ecological surplus.

The market is a powerful force of both technological and economic progress, and of political pluralism. However, when unrestrained, market forces can become destructive and oppressive; they must be balanced by the power of the state and of civil society. Unfortunately, the fall of the communist regimes has strengthened the position of the ideological extremists who advocate all power to the market, and the international institutions have followed this trend. In addition, the market itself is changing, as firms become increasingly remote from the communities in which they function, and transnational corporations move ever further beyond the reach of national governments and civil power. These trends erode the legitimacy of *laissez-faire* capitalism.

Even those few nations that have experienced a degree of success in achieving economic development by pursuing export-oriented strategies— specifically Japan, South Korea, and Taiwan—are not the free market miracles that they are often touted as. In fact, they all began by implementing radical land reform, while accepting substantial government guidance and protection to shape their economic growth trajectories. Even so, they are confronting real difficulties today with respect to the sustainabilty of their economies. The international assistance agencies continue to push free market strategies on developing nations, emphasizing production for global markets and dismantling trade barriers. However, this is not the path traveled by the Asian examples cited above; rather, in pursuing these policies, the agencies are aggressively aligning themselves with the interests of transnational capital.

Whether or not international assistance contributes to self-sufficiency depends in large part upon the discipline with which it is used by the recipient. Assistance applied appropriately can boost productivity in ways that enhance local control and self-reliance. Where discipline is lacking, however, assistance is more likely to produce profits for suppliers and contractors, subsidize the expropriation of resources, aid capital flight, mask economic mismanagement, and make governments dependent on foreign interests. Under these conditions, aid is often counterproductive.

International Cooperation: Agenda for the 1990s

The days of international assistance via capital transfers have passed. We cannot buy our way out of the current global crisis. Most of the conventional assistance organizations have become a problem posing as a solution, actively blocking more constructive approaches to these problems. It is time to sharply reduce their roles and to consider the possibility that many of them ought to be eliminated. We must come to terms with global realities and learn to live in constructive balance with the earth's ecology, achieving a semblance of economic justice and bringing the forces of transnational capital under human control.

The essential task is to reduce the flow of environmental resources from the South to the North so that they may be used to improve the South's quality of life. To accomplish this, Northern lifestyles must be brought into line with ecological realities. This effort must be accompanied by negotiations to substantially reduce the current debt burden and to begin holding transnational capital accountable. This is no small task, and it will require an enormous investment of intelligence and personal energy to make it happen. One of the major challenges of the current decade will be creating, strengthening, and shaping appropriate institutions to become a support system for global development and cooperation.

Summary of

The Case for Free Trade
by Jagdish Bhagwati

[Published in *Scientific American* 269 (November 1993): 42–49. Summarized with permission from Jagdish Bhagwati, "The Case for Free Trade."
© 1993 by Scientific American, Inc. All rights reserved.]

Economists are disconcerted by the opposition—at times illogical and disregarding the facts—expressed by environmentalists to both free trade and the General Agreement on Tariffs and Trade (GATT). The disagreements between economists and environmentalists on the issue of free trade are perhaps inevitable, as there are clearly times when seeking maximum gains from trade conflicts with environmental protection objectives. Conflicts also arise because trade typically functions through open markets without government intervention, but for environmental protection to occur governments must often intervene to create special markets. An underlying philosophical difference also arises because environmentalists assert nature's autonomy, while most economists see nature in the service of humankind.

While some of the concerns of environmentalists are valid, others are baseless. For example, the fear that free trade must increase growth and growth harms the environment is baseless. In reality, growth enables governments to raise the taxes needed to support many government activities, including protection of the environment. Growth can increase both the demand for a good environment and the level of pollution. The net environmental effects therefore depend on the kind of growth. Gene M. Grossman and Alan B. Krueger[1] found that sulfur dioxide pollution fell as per capita income rose in cities around the world, except in areas where per capita income was less than $5,000. In addition, rising incomes and freer trade enable countries to import pollution-fighting technologies available elsewhere.

The genuine conflicts between economists and environmentalists are divided into two categories of environmental issues by economists: problems that are intrinsically domestic, and those that are transnational. The first category includes environmental problems for which the causes and effects arise wholly within a country, while transnational environmental problems occur when the causes or effects cross national boundaries. Some of the most important examples of transnational problems include acid rain and global warming.

Domestic environmental problems create international concern because differences in environmental standards can affect competitiveness. Business and labor unions worry that countries with lower environmental standards may gain a competitive edge, and so they insist that these standards must be raised. Environmentalists fear that if countries with lower standards do not increase them, then standards may be lowered in high-standard countries so that they can remain competitive. Environmentalists also view lower environmental standards in other countries as unfair subsidies, or "social dumping," and call for import duties to be levied on goods from these countries.

Environmentalists should realize, however, that even if two countries have the same environmental objectives they might attack different specific types of pollution. Different countries may also value environmental goods differently. The main consequence of different environmental standards and values is that each country will have less of those industries whose pollution it does not like. Since these are legitimate differences, trying to correct for different standards through import duties is not a logical or desirable approach. One step that might be taken, however, is for high-standard countries to insist that their industries maintain these standards even when they relocate abroad.

Environmentalists also oppose free trade because they wish to impose their values on other countries. For example, they have demanded that the United States impose sanctions on Mexico based on Mexico's use of purse-seine nets (which kill dolphins) for tuna fishing. Such sanctions put the interests of dolphins ahead of those of the Mexican people. Also, once value systems start to intrude on free trade, there will be a never-ending stream of similar demands. The militant environmentalism being imposed on the South has led to accusations there that the North is indulging in "eco-imperialism," when in fact the North has the most adverse impacts on the environment. Rather than attempting to restrict free trade, environmentalists should use other methods, such as lobbying countries with inadequate environmental standards or organizing private boycotts of commodities from these countries.

Transnational problems require cooperative, multinational solutions that are both efficient and equitable. Any nation that is unwilling to join a multilateral environmental protocol must be given a chance to air their objections before trade sanctions are imposed. Promoting free trade and a protected environment simultaneously does pose problems, but none that are beyond resolution with goodwill and imaginative institutional innovation.

Note

1. Gene M. Grossman and Alan B. Krueger, "Environmental Impacts of a North American Free Trade Agreement," in *The Mexico–U.S. Free Trade Agreement,* ed. Peter M. Garber (The MIT Press, 1993).

Summary of

The Perils of Free Trade

by Herman E. Daly

[Published in *Scientific American* 269 (November 1993): 50–57. Summarized with permission of Herman E. Daly, "The Perils of Free Trade."
© 1993 by Scientific American, Inc. All rights reserved.]

The consensus among economists is that free trade based on international specialization is good, unless proven otherwise in specific cases. This article questions this consensus and argues that, as a general rule, countries should favor domestic production for domestic markets. Trade can be used when convenient, but not at the risk of environmental and societal disaster.

Economists are sometimes represented as being for free trade and environmentalists as being against it, but this characterization does a disservice to the issue. The real question is what regulations and goals are legitimate. Free traders favor maximizing output and profits, without considering the hidden social and environmental costs. They argue that the damage that results from growth can be dealt with using the wealth it generates. Environmentalists and some economists, on the other hand, believe that the environmental costs of growth are increasing at a faster rate than the benefits, thus making us poorer when growth occurs, not richer.

The rationale for free trade rests on the notion of comparative advantage that was formulated in the nineteenth century by British economist David

Ricardo. Ricardo argues that different countries with different technologies, customs, and resources will have different costs to produce the same product. Therefore, if each country produces goods for which it has comparatively lower costs and trades with others, then all parties will benefit. Ricardo assumed that capital was immobile across countries, but this is no longer true. In fact, free traders encourage a policy of capital mobility as a development strategy, but their argument is based on a theory that assumes that capital is not mobile.

When countries specialize, they no longer have the option not to trade, so they become locked in to free trade. This loss of independence can be a liability. Specialization also leads to a reduction in the occupational choices available in a country. Therefore, while diversity does lead to some reduction in efficiency, it is necessary for strong communities and nationhood. Proponents of free trade completely ignore the community dimensions of welfare. In addition, if high subsidies for the energy-intensive transportation costs associated with international trade are factored in, then the gains from trade are even lower.

However, there are arguments against the free trade approach that are even more fundamental than those described above, including problems with respect to efficient allocation of resources, fair distribution of resources, and maintenance of a sustainable scale of resource use. Trade leads to inefficient allocation of resources on a global scale because it encourages trade with nations that do not internalize their costs. For example, competition can lower costs by lowering standards rather than by increasing efficiency, as when companies move into nations with lower pollution control standards, lower worker safety standards, etc. One solution to this problem is for nations that do internalize their costs to impose tariffs on those that do not.

Problems of resource distribution arise because when capital moves from high-income to low-income countries it reduces wage levels in the high-income countries and increases income inequality there. Meanwhile, the tendency for wages to increase in the low-income countries due to capital inflows is thwarted by overpopulation and rapid population growth. Other groups in low-income countries may also suffer due to the effects of trade; for example, Mexican peasants will be the losers when low-price corn enters Mexico from the United States as a result of NAFTA.

The third fundamental problem with the free trade argument has to do with the goal of a sustainable scale of total resource use. The steady-state economic paradigm suggests that the economy is an open subsystem in a finite, nongrowing ecosystem. There is thus an optimal level of throughput for the economy, or in other words, there must be limits to economic growth. Free trade increases the growth of the economy, and therefore throughput increases as well. Moreover, free trade allows a country to exceed the regenerative and absorptive capacities of its ecosystem by "importing" these capacities, and it also makes comparisons of the costs and benefits of environmental exploitation difficult because they will be spatially separated. This will result in economies overshooting their optimal scales and postponing the day when they must face ecological limits.

For all of these reasons, the stance in favor of free trade should be reversed. If it is not, then we are headed for national disintegration.

Summary of

Trading Off the Future: Making World Trade Environmentally Sustainable[1]

by Paul Ekins

[Published as a pamphlet of the *New Economics Foundation*, London, United Kingdom, September 1993.]

"Globalization" is one of the most significant trends of our times and can be seen in almost every facet of human life. Perhaps this trend is most clearly visible with regard to the economy. World trade increased eleven-fold between 1950 and 1990. This increase is twice as fast as world product, which increased only five-fold during the same period. A principal actor in world trade is the large transnational corporation. The turnover of the world's 100 largest corporations now exceeds the GDP of almost half of the countries in the world. No less significant has been the trend of the degradation of the global environment, which is a result of much of this economic activity. In the context of these changing conditions, international trade is currently being rethought and restructured. Paramount in this thinking should be the relationship between trade, environment, and development.

Basic Trade Theory

In most recent discussions of international trade, free trade has been incorrectly assumed to be an unequivocally superior choice, regardless of the circumstances involved. A reexamination of basic trade theory, however, reveals that current discussions of the superiority of free trade are more dogmatic then scientific.

The theory of trade originated with the nineteenth century classical economist David Ricardo. The principal tenets of his theory were based on the distinct notions of specialization and comparative advantage. Individuals, firms, and nations all have the choice to produce smaller quantities of a diverse array of goods, or to *specialize* in the production of greater quantities of a few goods that they produce well (because of talent, geographic location, economies of scale, historical circumstances, etc.). With specialization, surpluses of the goods can be traded for those goods that either cannot be produced or that are not produced because of specialization. Thus, specialization tends to increase the number, variety, and value of goods and services. Lower overall costs of production in some area may be said to give a country an *absolute advantage* in that area; however, it is not necessary for a country to have an absolute advantage in any area for it to benefit from trade. The theory of *comparative advantage* suggests that, in a situation with two countries and two goods, if each country chooses to specialize in the production of that good which has the greatest relative cost advantage compared to another country, then both countries will gain from trade between them. This conclusion is held to be valid for multigood, multi-country situations.

The theory of comparative advantage rests on assumptions which include:

(1) *No externalities:* If costs of production are externalized, a product will be underpriced and appear to have more of a comparative advantage then it really does.

(2) *Stable prices:* Several countries may assume that they have a comparative advantage in a certain good and increase its supply substantially. However, if demand for these goods is inelastic, the market could be "flooded" and prices would fall, changing the distribution of comparative advantages.

(3) *Equally dynamic comparative advantages:* Some types of production have more dynamic comparative advantages than others, for example, production of chemicals versus bananas. Countries with less dynamic comparative advantages (banana producers) may not be able to exercise much range in innovation and could become "locked into economic stagnation" and inequality.

(4) *International immobility of factors of production:* Inherent in Ricardo's theory is the assumption that a country's capital and labor will stay within its borders to produce according to the country's comparative advantage. If they become mobile, trade will increasingly be based on absolute rather than comparative advantage. In the effort to remain competitive, countries will experience pressure on wages, environmental laws, and working conditions.

What Gains from Trade?

The gains from trade occur because countries specialize in production and trade according to their comparative advantage, which increases the total volume of goods to be consumed. However, several qualifications are necessary with regard to this extra product and the benefit it yields. To begin with, in less-industrialized countries a large amount of subsistence production and consumption occurs. When subsistence production, which is not accounted for in economic accounts, is shifted to production for trade, which *is* included in these accounts, a false amount of gain is perceived; "the actual gain is the traded product less the subsistence product it replaced."[3] Second, increased consumption does not necessarily improve social welfare. Gains from trade should be related to social welfare functions before any welfare determinations are made. Third, the gains from trade are unequally divided. It cannot be assumed that those who lose will be compensated; the stronger trading partner may set the terms of the exchange, leaving the weaker with few gains from trade. Lastly, specialization can lead to dependency. For example, the demand for a specialized exported product could decrease, but a shift to domestic production may be costly. Moreover, production for export is often dependent on external financing. Repaying the high foreign debt that results often requires structural adjustment programs, which in turn require more export-led activity. Rather than exporting to meet domestic needs, countries may be forced to export in order to repay debt, making it even harder to shift production to meet domestic needs should this become desirable.

The Reality of Trade

It is clear than many of the assumptions underlying the theory of comparative advantage currently do not hold. The level of unaccounted environmental degradation indicates that externalities abound. With regard to the second and third assumptions, i.e., stable prices and equally dynamic comparative advantage, the UNCTAD Secretariat has reported that:

> The price index of principal non-fuel commodities exported by developing countries fell by a staggering 50% in real terms between 1979/81 and 1988/90. . . . The main reason for these price declines is over-supply of almost all commodities due to productivity improvements and export subsidization especially in developed countries, and to increased production in developing countries prompted by debt-service obligations and structural adjustment efforts. There has also been a fall in demand for some

commodities as consumers move to synthetics or technologies that need fewer commodity inputs.[2]

Concerning the last assumption, the international mobility of factors of production, although labor has not been very mobile, capital mobility has never been greater than today.

Trade in the real world is increasingly based on competitive advantage in the market, with results which diverge significantly from the classical theory of comparative advantage, whereby the strong get stronger at the expense of the weak. Instead of prosperity, the weak's experience of increased trade has often been low commodity prices, poor terms of trade, high debt service, protected Northern markets, and an increasingly degraded environment. The North is also affected as unemployment and underemployment in the South put pressure on wages worldwide. There is a danger that trade will increasingly become a "zero sum game" rather than the "positive sum game" of traditional trade theory.

Trade and Environment

Trade institutions have long ignored the linkages between trade and the environment. Recently this linkage has been recognized, but trade proponents tend now simply to claim that free trade will cause more economic growth, which will in turn increase the demand for environmental protection and provide more resources to fund such protection. This benign outcome is, however, unlikely, for several reasons. First, economic growth creates more absolute environmental damage. Second, in many cases the additional resources that *could be* allocated for environmental protection *are not* in fact so allocated. Third, much environmental degradation cannot be repaired. Fourth, countries with comprehensive environmental protection will experience increasing pressure to reduce this in the name of competitiveness.

David Pearce has argued that externalizing the cost of environmental damage is actually a subsidy that is as economically distorting as any financial subsidy.[3] But for environmental externalities to be treated as such would require major changes in GATT's trading rules. In addition, trade is dependent upon transportation for its existence. It has been estimated that trade accounts for nearly one-eighth of world oil consumption, which is a major cause of environmental degradation. Again, if this degradation were internalized, trade—and indeed entire systems of production and consumption—could look radically different. Finally, changes in property rights due to trade may be among its most important environmental effects. For example, when land is primarily used for subsistence crops, small farmers and indigenous people are usually left undisturbed. However, when land can be used for export production to generate cash, pressure to expropriate it increases. The original owners may then migrate to and cultivate marginal land, causing enormous environmental degradation.

Trade can also contribute to improving the environment in some cases. If consumers demand products that are environmentally benign, some countries will produce or import such goods for competitive reasons. More empirical research is needed to reveal how trade actually affects the environment in the long run. Without this understanding, uncritical support for trade is as dangerous as its uncritical rejection.

Toward Sustainable Trade

The notion that the global environment is at risk is an almost undisputed fact. If the international trade regime were to suddenly collapse, much hardship would certainly result, but a collapse of the world's environmental systems would be much worse. It is in this context that policies should be devised to make trade (and economic activity in general) environmentally sustainable.

Many trade theorists and the GATT Secretariat have argued that the best way to address domestic environmental degradation is through domestic policy. This is correct in principle; however, such policies may not be politically feasible given the increased pressures of international competition. Comprehensive environmental protection may only be politically feasible if trade policies protect domestic industries from foreign competitors with lower environmental standards. It has also been argued that international treaties are the best way to approach global environmental problems, but such treaties are very difficult to ratify and enforce. Trade policies have an important role in overcoming these difficulties.

It will not be easy to adapt the world's trading rules to promote sustainable development. In any negotiations to do so, other North/South issues will play a large role. Many Southern countries fear that measures in the area of sustainable development in GATT negotiations are yet another avenue for trade discrimination against the South, where many of the worst effects of environmental degradation occur. In addition, environmental protection regulations could impose higher short-term costs which many Southern countries cannot absorb. With these considerations in mind,

Arden-Clarke has advocated recycling revenue from environmental tariffs on goods from developing countries back to those countries to provide funds for improving the environmental sustainability of their economies.[4]

Finally, it should be realized that the present highly integrated world economy dominated by transnational corporations bears little relation to the world economy of the 1960s, in which GATT's rules originated. Models of perfect competition have even less relevance now than then. The world needs to create a trading system that is predicated on civil, political, economic, and social human rights, as well as social justice and environmental sustainability.

Notes

1. This article is adapted from the introductory article to a special issue: Paul Ekins, Carl Folke, and Robert Costanza, "Trade, Environment and Development: The Issues in Perspective," in *Ecological Economics* 9 (January 1994): 1–12.

2. UNCTAD, "Commodities: A Struggle to Survive," paper UNCTAD/PSM/CAS/380/ADD.12, UNCTAD, Geneva, 1992, 1; cited by Ekins, 4.

3. David Pearce, "Should the GATT be Reformed for Environmental Reasons?" CSERGE Working Paper GEC 92-06, CSERGE, University of East Anglia/University College London, 1992, 21 and 29–30.

4. C. Arden-Clark, *International Trade, GATT and the Environment* (Gland, Switzerland: World Wide Fund for Nature, 1992).

Summary of

Development, Poverty and the Growth of the Green Movement In India

by Jayanta Bandyopadhyay and Vandana Shiva

[Published in *The Ecologist* 19 (May/June 1989): 111–117.]

In precolonial times economic processes in India did not cause serious environmental problems. The arrival of the British, however, resulted in major changes in natural resource use, as resources were increasingly used to meet demands in Western Europe. Resources such as water, forests, and minerals, which had traditionally been part of the commons, now came under the control of the British; peasants were forced to cultivate indigo and cotton, forests were felled to promote ship building and to meet the requirements of the expanding railway network, and control over water resources was monopolized. These changes resulted in new forms of poverty and deprivation, and in local protests as people sought to regain control over their resources.

Gandhi: Exploding the Myth of Resource-Intensive Development

The end of colonial rule saw the control of natural resources transferred to the new, politically independent state. However, the institutions set up under the colonial system to control natural resources did not change as the state pursued the goal of "economic development" in the name of meeting the basic needs of local people. That the nature of these institutions and their ideological underpinnings made them unsuitable for meeting this new goal was not seriously considered. Gandhi warned, however, that if India followed a Western industrial pattern of economic exploitation of natural resources, the consequences could be disastrous. He advocated a resource-prudent development strategy to meet the basic needs of the Indian people. However, his call was ignored, due in part to pressure on the newly independent nation to develop, and in part to the fact that natural resource parameters were not included in the framework of conventional economics.

The educated elite have been the main beneficiaries of economic development, while the mass of people have experienced increasing poverty. The natural resource base has been exploited and degraded to support the urban enclaves where commodity production is concentrated. For example, the revenues of commercial forestry companies have increased through expanded production of timber and pulpwood, but this has had detrimental effects on those people who are dependent on other forest products such as leaves, twigs, fruits, nuts, medicines, oils, etc. Destruction of the forests has also affected climate patterns, with adverse impacts on agricultural production. One response to this ecological destruction and environmental deprivation has been the initiation of a new politics by ecology movements to protect the interests of minorities, including women, tribals, and poor peasants.

Ecology Movements and the Development Process

The number of ecology movements in India has increased both as a response to threats to the survival of local people, and in order to demand the conservation of vital life-support systems, including clean air, water, forests, and land. These movements are present throughout the country, and they have opposed the exploitation of forests and mineral resources and the construction of dams that have detrimental ecological consequences. Though these movements are of local origin, their impacts are both national and global. This micro–macro connection results from the existence of "two Indias"—one that is poor and less powerful, and the other rich and powerful—competing for limited quantities of natural resources. The ecology movements are bringing the inherent injustice in the present process of development to the forefront, and they are attempting to redirect the development process in favor of those demanding a right to survive. This new process seeks to ensure justice with sustainability and equity with ecological stability. These movements question not only the impacts of individual projects, but the very foundations—political, economic, scientific, and technological—of the existing development paradigm as well, as they seek to create a new economics for a new civilization.

A linear view of progress, with origins in the eighteenth and nineteenth centuries, underlies the dominant development paradigm. This view, best articulated in Rostow's "stages of economic growth," equates development with economic growth, market economies, modernity, and consumerism, while non-market economies are equated with backwardness. However, productivity—in the sense in which it is used in the dominant paradigm—comes at the cost of environmental deterioration and declining resource productivity. In Rostow's framework, the first stage of economic development consists of traditional society, while the second stage is seen as a temporary coexistence of the "dynamic and progressive" modern sector and the "stagnant and backward" traditional sector. Rostow's third "take-off" stage envisions a breaking down of "old blocks and resistances" and the spread of the modern sector throughout society. The problem with this view of development is that inherent in it is an internal dynamic by which the impoverishment of the traditional sector is necessary to pay for the material basis of the modern sector. The underdeveloped sectors are not those that are yet to be affected by economic growth but rather those that pay the economic and ecological costs of growth, while others benefit.

The dominant paradigm has paid attention to the use of natural resources for commodity production and capital accumulation, while neglecting the processes responsible for regenerating natural resources. The neglect of two vital economies—the economy of natural resources and natural processes, and the economy of survival—has resulted in ecological destruction and threats to human survival. Ecology movements in the Third World are a reaction to these threats, which have been caused by expansion of the market economy.

It is naive to view the critique of the market economy as a critique of all forms of intervention in nature, but neither can the solutions to current ecological and environmental crises be found either by following the same strategies of growth that gave rise to the crises in the first place, or by simply adding an environmental aspect to the old development process. Ecological and economic crisis should not be seen as separate. The emerging ecology movements are set on a path of improving living standards without undermining ecological stability; implementing a new holistic development process will be their major task.

Summary of

Third World Development and Population
by Martin W. Lewis

[Published in Martin W. Lewis, *Green Delusions: An Environmentalist Critique of Radical Environmentalism* (Durham, North Carolina: Duke University Press, 1992): 191–241.]

Economic development and population growth are of essential concern to environmentalists. In those areas of the Third World where countries are experiencing rapid industrial expansion, there is evidence that air- and water-borne toxins are being generated at enormous rates, and that they are being disposed of far more carelessly than in the North. Meanwhile, in the least developed countries, population growth is exerting dangerous pressure on the carrying capacity of the ecosystems and producing widespread desertification and deforestation. In both cases the ecological problems are severe. There is a crucial paradox in that the very development deemed necessary to alleviate misery and poverty in the Third World by elevating consumption levels to those enjoyed in the North simultaneously has appalling ecological consequences. As a result, radical greens argue that the pattern of development in the South today must be quite different from that which occurred in the First World.

For and Against Development

The most extreme eco-radicals casually dismiss the very concept of development as one that constitutes an enormous threat to the environment and to society at large. The majority of eco-radicals, however, realize that a return to tribal subsistence is impossible. Moreover, much overgrazing and deforestation occurs precisely because so many in the Third World are so poor. The most common eco-radical position is therefore that Third World environments can only be preserved if poverty is alleviated through particular kinds of development initiatives. The challenge, then, is to develop environmentally benign methods of improving living standards, i.e., to pursue the path of eco-development.

The tenets of eco-development follow directly from the propositions of deep ecology: development should be based on small-scale projects, administered locally, and governed through participatory democracy. Communities would be better off in every sense if they simply bypass modern industrialization, focusing instead on local crafts and manufacturing using locally appropriate technology. Production should be for subsistence rather than for global exchange, and it should be aimed at achieving bioregional self-sufficiency and severing links with the global economy.

The eco-development approach has roots in dependency theory. It is based in part on the idea that the development of the North was a direct product of the colonial imperialist exploitation of the Third World, a process that simultaneously underdeveloped these colonized areas. The economies of the First and Third Worlds are therefore systemically linked in such a way that the ongoing prosperity of one is structurally dependent upon the impoverishment of the other. From this perspective, the industrialized economies are doubly objectionable, as they are based upon both the rapacious and unsustainable consumption of natural resources and upon the unconscionable exploitation of the land and peoples of the Third World. Development in the Third World along these traditional lines is therefore impossible. Investments in agricultural and industrial schemes will fail to generate a take-off into independent development even as they strain the environment.

Different perspectives on population growth also divide environmentalists into several camps. To many, it is the most troubling problem. Every gain in pollution control or habitat protection may be outweighed by the effects of population growth, and the earth is in danger of being suffused in a Malthusian nightmare. Writers who share this view tend to advocate relatively coercive population control measures as the solution, although radical greens of a more leftist bent tend to discount these sorts of arguments. However, the focus on population as the source of poverty and environmental degradation obscures the true underlying systemic causes; the real culprits are market production, Northern exploitation of the South, and overconsumption by the North.

From Eco-Development to Sustainable Development

Though many ecologists continue to cling to the views discussed above, they have increasingly come to question the feasibility or desirability of the eco-development approach. They recognize that such severe tactics will neither produce genuine development nor be politically feasible. The approach promotes unrealistic eco-panaceas amidst the very real and immediate grinding poverty of billions in the Third World. Moreover the single-minded, anti-industrial focus on small-scale development will not necessarily ease environmental pressures.

The concept of sustainable development has therefore emerged as a means to unite the concerns of both ecologists and Third World developers. The basic premise of sustainable development is that economic growth must never undercut the productivity of the natural ecosystem. From this perspective, rapid economic growth is possible provided it is accompanied by a rapid reduction of energy and raw material inputs per unit of production.

Most writings by sustainable development advocates tend to focus on rural problems and small-scale programs targeted at the needs of rural peasants. As a consequence, crucial urban issues have been systematically neglected. This neglect arises from the mistaken impression that cities can only be treated as part of the problem, because they are seen as both uninhabitable hells for those that must reside in them and as threats to the environment due to the wastes of millions of people and numerous industries that befoul their air and water. Ironically this view ignores one central environmental benefit of cities, especially given the critical population pressures that confront many Third World countries: urbanization can ease land pressures in the countryside, thus reducing rates of deforestation and desertification while helping to preserve habitats and biodiversity. This is not to say that urban environments are not appalling and dangerous in many developing nations but these problems are not insuperable; the city of London was once an environmental disaster but development and planning have rendered it a pleasant urban habitat. Urban problems may result more from underdevelopment than from overurbanization per se.

Once it is acknowledged that cities have their place, then industrialization must be given its due as well. The anti-industrial bias of many eco-radicals is a legacy of the earlier dependency theory perspective. However, they have clung to the early simplistic arguments of dependency theory, evidently unaware that substantial revision and reformulation of ideas has occurred even within that school. There is now a more broad-ranging discussion and debate about issues of development and progress. While exploitative relations between the North and South undoubtedly exist, it is now recognized that the dependency model, particularly in its simplest version, fails to describe reality. The emergence of the NICs testifies to the possibility of industrial development in the Third World and the fact that this development can alleviate poverty. Industrial development is therefore a necessary part of the transformation process. This is not, however, to minimize the environmental problems of industrial production. Both industrialized and industrializing nations confront monumental problems of resource use and waste generation. One of the tasks of sustainable development, then, must be to address these legitimate concerns.

While population growth clearly does not threaten us with the immediate Malthusian catastrophe envisioned by many, it remains a serious problem. A rapidly growing population clearly poses staggering strains on any economy. With population growth rates approaching 3–4% in many developing countries, economic growth must also achieve at least this pace just to maintain current standards of living. The infrastructure and educational needs of a burgeoning population can exceed the capacity of a developing economy to service them. Population stabilization is also essential to maintain biotic diversity. Population control therefore remains a crucial part of sustainable development programs, but population growth is not the primary cause of today's problems. Pollution and resource depletion are still primarily attributable to the wealthy societies, not to developing countries, even with their high birth rates.

Most radical greens are on shaky ground when they enter the Third World. They desperately desire to solve the devastating problems of poverty in the Third World, yet they advocate programs and policies that preclude genuine development.

Summary of

Radical American Environmentalism and Wilderness Preservation: A Third World Critique
by Ramachandra Guha
[Published in *Environmental Ethics* 11 (Spring 1989): 71–83.]

This article critiques the deep ecology movement and argues that, despite its claim to universality, it is a uniquely American phenomenon.

The Tenets of Deep Ecology

While there are political and philosophical differences among deep ecologists, there are four defining characteristics of the movement:

(1) Deep ecology argues that the environmental movement needs to shift from an "anthropocentric" to a "biocentric" perspective. Anthropo-

centrism is thought to be at the core of Western society and many of our current environmental problems, and others such as "shallow ecologists" are criticized for continuing to frame arguments in human-centered terms. There is also a belief in the intrinsic value of preserving nature quite apart from the benefits it would bestow on humans.

(2) Deep ecology focuses on "the preservation of unspoilt wilderness— and the restoration of degraded areas to a more pristine condition."[73] This obsession with wilderness follows logically from the biocentric world view described above. Scientifically, preservation of wilderness is supported on the grounds that it maintains a gene pool for future generations.

(3) Eastern spiritual traditions are invoked as the forerunners of the deep ecology movement, helping to strengthen its claims of universality.

(4) Deep ecologists see themselves as the spiritual, philosophical, and political vanguard of American and world environmentalism.

Toward a Critique

Some critiques of the deep ecology approach include the following:

(1) The call by deep ecologists for a shift from an anthropocentric to a biocentric perspective should be welcomed. However, the radical conclusions that they draw from this shift are unacceptable. Deep ecologists argue that preserving biotic integrity should be the guiding principle of intervention in nature, rather than human needs. However, focusing on the anthropocentric–biocentric dichotomy sheds little light on the true dynamics of environmental degradation, since the two major ecological problems facing the world are overconsumption (by the industrial economies of the West and Third World elites) and growing militarization. These two problems are consequences of the interactions between economic and political forces as well as individual lifestyle choices; they cannot be explained in terms of the anthropocentric–biocentric dichotomy. Blaming environmental problems on anthropocentrism is therefore "at best irrelevant and at worse a dangerous obfuscation."[74]

(2) While the anthropocentric–biocentric dichotomy may be merely irrelevant, the focus on preservation of wilderness is actually harmful to the Third World. For example, setting aside wilderness in India results in a redistribution of resources from the poor to the rich. Project Tiger, an internationally acclaimed program, displaced poor peasants who

had been living in the areas around the new reserves. The initial impetus for programs like Project Tiger came from members of the Indian feudal elite and from organizations like the World Wildlife Fund, which wanted to transplant the American system of national parks into India. Until recently, environmentalism has been equated with wildland preservation, ignoring the environmental problems that affect the poor, such as shortages of fuel, fodder and water resources, soil erosion, pollution, etc. The deep ecology approach provides a justification for such inequitable conservation practices.

(3) In invoking Eastern traditions to buttress their position, the deep ecologists lump together a number of complex and different traditions: Hinduism, Buddhism, and Taoism. The philosophers of these traditions are identified as the forerunners of modern deep ecology. However, while it is true that thinkers in these traditions such as Lao Tzu did reflect on the interactions between man and nature, the development of their philosophies must be understood within the context of the communities and societies of which they were a part. Their reflections were based on the active relationship between man and nature within these communities, rather than "on a mystical affinity with nature of a deep ecological kind."[77]

(4) Deep ecology should be seen as a radical movement within the wilderness preservation movement in America, but its radicalism is limited. The movement for preservation of wilderness in America is an outgrowth of economic expansion; having met the earlier goals of attaining necessities and conveniences, the national parks have been developed as the avenue for meeting newer aesthetic goals. In this sense, the deep ecology movement parallels the consumer society and reflects the coexistence of wilderness and civilization in America. By concentrating on the preservation of wilderness, however, the deep ecologists do not question the ecological and sociopolitical basis of the consumer society. Equating environmental protection with the protection of wildlife is a uniquely American phenomenon.

In contrast, the environmental movement in Germany (particularly the Greens) finds the roots of the problem in industrial societies themselves, and calls for limits to growth. Their prescription for ecological problems is a change in cultural values, arguing for an ethic of renunciation and self-limitation, with spiritual and communal values playing a bigger role in social life. This view has a strong resonance in countries like India, where industrial development has benefited only a small elite. The environmental traditions in both Germany and India therefore emphasize equity and social justice.

A Homily

Concerns about overconsumption, efforts to develop ecologically benign technologies, and opposition to a permanent war economy are all missing from the deep ecology perspective. By highlighting the anthropo-centric–biocentric dichotomy rather than concentrating on a synthesis of appropriate technologies, alternate lifestyles, and peace movements, the deep ecologists are doing American and world environmentalism a disservice.

Summary of

Environmental Change and Violent Conflict

by Thomas F. Homer-Dixon, Jeffrey H. Boutwell, and George W. Rathjens

[Published in *Scientific American* 268 (February 1993): 38–45. Summarized with permission from Thomas F. Homer–Dixon, "Environmental Change and Violent Conflict." © 1993 by Scientific American, Inc. All rights reserved.]

Over the next fifty years, growth of both population and world output will result in a sharp increase in the scarcity of renewable resources and a degradation of natural and environmental resources. The University of Toronto and the American Academy of Arts and Sciences commissioned studies to collect data on the impact of environmental problems on civil, social, and international strife. The studies suggest that scarcities of renewable resources are already contributing to violent conflicts, and this trend will probably increase further in the coming decades.

Environmental problems can affect social stability both indirectly and directly. Resource scarcity can contribute to social strife by altering the politics and economics governing resource use. In the face of scarcity, powerful actors may appropriate an inequitable share of resources. In addition, when environmental degradation is irreversible, even enlightened social change that removes the original political, economic, and cultural causes of degradation may not help. Irreversible environmental degradation may thus be an independent variable contributing to social strife.

Some claim that conflicts arising out of resource scarcity are nothing new, as they have been occurring throughout history. However, the pace, complexity, and magnitude of renewable resource scarcities in the next several decades will be unprecedented. In addition, because of the complex, interdependent relationships and linkages of renewable resources within ecosystems, sudden and unexpected problems can occur when they are rapidly overexploited.

There are three principal ways in which human action can bring about scarcity of renewable resources: (1) by using up natural resources at a rate faster than they renew; (2) through population growth; and (3) through an inequitable distribution of resources within a society, resulting in scarcity for the many. Specific cases are described below in which these three factors—singly or in combination—have resulted in environmental scarcity and social strife.

Specific Cases

Bangladesh and India

Population growth in Bangladesh has caused social strife in some adjoining states of India, and it will continue to do so. The United Nations estimates that by the year 2025 the population of Bangladesh will nearly double to 235 million people. At present, the population density is 785 people per square kilometer, a number much higher than that in the adjoining Indian state of Assam. The tremendous pressure on land in Bangladesh has caused large migrations of people into Assam, changing the distribution of land and economic and political power between different religious and ethnic groups in Assam. These changes have generated serious social tensions in the state of Assam, including the violent massacre of 1700 Bengalis in one five-hour period. Similar tensions are felt in the Indian state of Tripura. While religion and politics have contributed to the tension and violence, a shortage of land due to the increasing population is at the root of the problems.

Senegal and Mauritania

The underlying causes of a conflict between Senegal and Mauritania can be traced to increases in population and reductions in the quantity and quality of renewable resources. These factors led to a large-scale development project that changed patterns of access to resources for the rich and poor, thus causing social tension. Senegal has relatively abundant agricultural land, but its quality has declined due to wind erosion, over-irrigation, and intensification of agriculture. Mauritania is primarily arid or semi-arid except for the Senegal River Valley (on the border with Senegal), which is suitable for agriculture. The UN Food and Agricultural Organization has projected that neither nation will be able to meet its population's food needs without large increases in agricultural inputs. The Manantali Dam project was designed to increase the agricultural and energy outputs in Senegal and Mauritania. In anticipation of the project, land values increased along the river, and the elite white Moors in Mauritania rewrote legislation to strip black Africans of the right to farm, herd, or fish along the Mauritanian riverbank. This struggle for resources resulted in tension between Senegal and Mauritania, culminating in loss of life, destruction of property, and deportations based on ethnic and racial considerations (blacks were deported from Mauritania).

Philippines and Similar Cases

In the Philippines, unequal access to resources combined with population growth has caused environmental degradation. Insurgency and rebellion have arisen due to economic deprivation caused by the environmental degradation. While improved agricultural techniques have increased the demand for labor, they have not kept up with population growth. There has been downward pressure on agricultural wages and increasing rural unemployment, resulting in mass migrations to urban centers, as well as ecologically detrimental movement onto the hillsides. The lack of resources for an increasing number of people has fueled a communist-led insurgency and increased violence. This marginalization of the poor is not unique to the Philippines; it can be seen all over the globe, including the Himalayas, the Sahel, Indonesia, Brazil, and Costa Rica. Similar circumstances were responsible for the "Soccer War" between Honduras and El Salvador, and the decade-long civil war in El Salvador.

China

The loss of renewable resources can make increasing numbers of people dependent on government assistance, thereby overwhelming the administrative capacities of the Chinese state. Violent challenges to the state may result as different factions seek to protect their interests and jockey for power. Vaclav Smil suggests that environmental problems have had detrimental effects on productivity in many sectors. Crop yields are falling due to the degradation of water, soil, and air that has been caused by erosion, construction, and deforestation. Smil estimates the current losses to be 15% of China's gross domestic product and predicts that they will rise further. He expects mass migrations from the northern and interior regions due to scarcity of water, fuelwood, and land. All of these factors could lead to conflicts between different regions as they compete for scarce resources, thus weakening the state.[1]

The Middle East

Political instability as a result of water shortages is imminent in the Middle East. Israel depends on aquifers in the West Bank to meet a substantial part of its water needs. To protect this source, the Israelis have limited the use of water on the West Bank. Israeli control of Arab water use, as well as the general water scarcity in the region, contributes to tensions there.

Conclusion

Some analysts have argued that problems arising due to environmental scarcities can be avoided if proper incentive structures and the necessary means are provided to alleviate them. They contend that it is not environmental problems per se that are important, but the responses to them. The research presented in this article neither supports nor opposes this viewpoint. The research does, however, point to a strong link between scarcities of renewable resources and violence.

Note

1. See Vaclav Smil, *China's Environmental Crisis: An Inquiry into the Limits of National Development* (M.E. Sharpe, 1993).

Summary of

Introduction—Global Commons: Site of Peril, Source of Hope[1]
by Neva R. Goodwin
[Published in *World Development* 19 (January 1991): 1–15.]

Since Garrett Hardin's *Tragedy of the Commons* appeared in 1968, the metaphor of the "commons" has been applied in a wide range of contexts. Today we think of natural resources that we feel do or should belong to the entire human race as the "global commons." The global commons includes the earth's atmosphere, its oceans, frozen poles, forests, and the entire genetic reserve. Humankind did not make these biophysical structures but inherited them, and they may be referred to as the "global natural commons." The global natural commons are increasingly threatened by human action that is based on self-interest. To help counter these problems within the natural commons, we should turn to the "global human commons" for solutions.

The global human commons refers to behaviors and motivations tending toward "cooperation and sharing in the interest of pan-human, or even biosphere-wide, welfare."[2] The global human commons can be observed in institutions built and shared by all humans, including the world's universities, the different branches of the United Nations, nongovernmental organizations such as Oxfam America and the International Committee of the Red Cross, and international financial organizations like the World Bank and the International Monetary Fund. The global human commons also includes international treaties for the benefit of all humankind, such as the Law of the Sea, the Montreal Protocol, and the General Agreement on Tariffs and Trade. The role of the global human commons is to regulate access to the global natural commons in such a manner as to minimize conflicts between nations and interest groups, to increase equity of access among different groups, and to ensure sustainable resource use so as to balance the needs and wishes of present and future generations.

The issue of goals or intentions is central to the question of what entities are considered part of the global human commons; their main intention should be to serve pan-human welfare. These organizations belong to the "third sector;" they are designed to serve needs for which neither national governments nor the profit-oriented business sector are sufficient. Different people have different views about what constitutes the common good, and these views change over time. The third sector offers the best hope for providing a constant reassessment of what the common good is, in the context of a variety of often competing interests.

In the individualistic Anglo-Saxon tradition, national governments are viewed as institutions needed to solve problems arising out of market failures—for example, public goods, free rider problems, and externalities. However, some problems that exhibit characteristics of market failures transcend national jurisdictions and are of global concern, such as environmental problems, the spread and effects of science, technology and research, military conflicts, diseases and their cures, and human rights. National governments, markets, or a combination of both cannot solve these problems. The global human commons, working through the third sector, must transcend national interests in seeking solutions that serve the good of all of humankind in such cases. Whether the third sector works with or against governments will depend on whether both share a common ethic about what is right and assume the responsibility to follow through. Trust and responsibility are important if globalism is to succeed. The third sector needs to earn the trust of all concerned by acting in a responsible manner for the welfare of the whole of mankind. A "civic corps" comprised of volunteers working in a spirit of *pro bono publico* toward global goals must form the basis of the third sector.

What are the prospects for the significant development of the third sector in the future? A number of contemporary trends and processes give reason for optimism. First, the world is quickly coming to understand the economic and ecological interdependence between all people and nations, and it is recognizing the need for international institutions and regulations in the light of this interdependence. Second, communications technology is fostering a shared global culture and a commitment to solve global problems. Third, as affluence becomes more widespread, the meaning of work is being redefined. In the past, when people worked to pay for the necessities of life, work was meaningful by definition. A number of factors, including increased affluence and the welfare state, have weakened this nexus between work and providing the necessities for survival, contributing to a new spirit of redirecting work for the welfare of humankind.

Increasing global problems necessitate giving some institutions overarching powers to undertake long-term global planning. This planning could help coordinate and regulate a number of factors that are critical to human and ecosystem welfare. With the fall of the planned economies of Eastern Europe, there is skepticism about planning at the global level. It is important to emphasize, however, that there are different approaches to planning. Rather than the inhumane central planning experienced in Eastern Europe, the search must begin to put into place "decentralized, bottom-up, democratic, pluralistic planning."

"The promotion of 'global thinking,' as the final flowering of 'civic virtue,' may be seen as continuing, through education, the historical civilizing process: of expanding the way we define and understand our 'self-interest.'"[12]

Note

1. This article is an introductory article to a special volume of the journal *World Development* focusing on global issues that may require response on a global scale. Parts of this article that discuss the origins of this special issue and the other articles appearing in it have been omitted from the summary.

PART VII

Ethical and Institutional Issues in Ecological Economics

Overview Essay

by Neva R. Goodwin

The ethical and institutional issues discussed in the articles summarized in this part raise a number of recurrent themes. These include the future (and how people of the present do and should relate to it); questions about how to mitigate the effects of the pressures of human population and human technology upon our natural environment; and the combined tendencies toward globalism in some aspects of human affairs and toward localism in others.

These are, of course, among the major themes that have given rise to the environmental movement itself, as well as to the discipline of ecological economics. The environmental movement has generated, by now, a fair amount of knowledge about some of the practical things (such as recycling and reduced packaging, improved public transportation, and more rational pricing of energy and natural resources) that should be done to alleviate the dangerous stresses now being placed by humanity upon our environment. The questions remain, however: how much does "society" care about alleviating these stresses? What costs will be accepted by "society"—and how should those costs be allocated?

Here we come to what has always been at the heart of economics: the issue of motivation. The entire edifice of neoclassical economics is formally supposed to be derived from a single statement about human motivation—the "rationality postulate"—which says that "rational economic man maximizes his (perceived) utility." The logical objections to this axiom emphasize, in particular, the tautological way in which each of the critical concepts it contains ("rationality," "maximization," and "utility") is defined in relation to the others. While such a tautological character establishes an excessive degree of internal consistency, so that it becomes impossible to break out of this tight logical loop to say anything about the real world, another set of problems (of inconsistencies between the theory and the real world, or "external inconsistency") arises when the critical concepts are defined separately. Then (as observed by Nobel Laureate Herbert Simon) it turns out that maximization is usually not a feasible behavior; utility is unobservable and immeasurable; and rationality, in the neoclassical definition, has an inadequate ethical grounding.

This last problem is the one which is most critical for the big issues tackled in this part. A rationality that is poorly matched with the ethical system to which it looks[1] can neither generate nor support the final principles, or goals, that must be brought into play if we are to bring genuine, and widely valued, human concerns to bear on questions about the future, about the impact of humanity upon our natural environment, or on the tensions between globalism and localism.

In fact, neoclassical economics does not have a monopoly on ways of understanding rationality (although, during much of the twentieth century, it has come close to achieving such a monopoly position in Western, industrialized cultures). One alternative will be considered in the following discussion, which will contrast precautionary rationality with neoclassical rationality. The latter stems from the rationality postulate, cited above; its implications will be spelled out further below. The first is named after one of the most powerful propositions of the environmental movement, the precautionary principle. That principle says, in effect: "since we do not know everything about the natural systems on which we are dependent, it is only rational to be extremely careful; where we cannot predict the ecological effects of our actions, we should assume that they are dangerous until proved otherwise." (For more on the precautionary principle, see Perrings, 1991, summarized in Part III of this volume.) Evidently this kind of rationality is, to begin with, closely related to the primary goal—of species survival—that has been bred into all living beings through the process of evolution.

The simplest way to see the contrast between these two approaches is to consider what each would consider *irrational*:

(1) "It is irrational to do something that will harm you."

(2) "It is irrational not to do what you want."

Both of these appear to be simple, obvious statements that are not hard to agree with. However, they lead in what ultimately turn out to be dramatically different directions. Precautionary rationality, in pointing to actions that perhaps should not be taken, is open to such concepts as responsibility, and even sacrifice. Neoclassical rationality is all too easily translated into the dominant commercialized value of modern societies: "doing what you want" very often is assumed to mean, simply, "having fun."

How can it be that two apparently simple and compatible statements about rationality can lead in such different directions as *responsibility* versus *fun?* One explanation for this bifurcation comes from the verb tenses of the contrasting statements about what is irrational. The first includes attention to the future—"something that *will* harm you;" the second speaks only to the present.

Neoclassical rationality is not supposed to be especially shortsighted, any more than it is supposed to be purely local or selfish. Indeed, in formal writings about rationality, this postulate, like everything else that is formally admitted as a part of the structure of the theoretical system of neoclassical economics, is put forth as value-neutral.[2] Neoclassical rationality is about maximizing utility: utility can be whatever you wish; if you feel better when you do right, then ethics can enter your utility function.

That is the theory. However, ethics are, most often, politely ignored by neoclassical economists,[3] in a context that, by default, leaves ethics to be dominated by preferences; as Talbot Page (summarized in this part) says: "within the utilitarian framework used by neoclassical economics, 'preferences are all.' They soak up and explain all forms of choice and behavior at the individual level."[page 49 of Page's original article] Thus, mainstream economic modeling implies that ethics only affect economic behavior when they enter individual utility functions; and they only enter individual utility functions because they are chosen on the basis of preferences.

Ecological economics, by contrast, has apparently accepted some additional assumptions. Although these have not been explicitly laid out in the form in which they will appear here, it is easy—and useful—to infer these assumptions, in the form of one interpretation of facts and two psychological postulates:

(1) *We are facing a serious environmental crisis* (whether already arrived or just impending; the article by Goodland, summarized in Part I, is a good expression of this belief).

(2) *It is natural and normal for human beings to care about the crisis and its opposite (healthy survival):* That is, we assume that it matters—from a broader, longer term perspective than that of a single individual. (The perspective may be that of the human species; it may be that of the biosphere; or some, rather radical views may even attempt to represent the perspective of a portion of the natural world that does not include our species—seen, in this radical view, as a dangerous and destructive cancer upon the rest.)

(3) *It is natural and normal for human beings to adopt the position of precautionary rationality,* which says that it is foolish not to bend our efforts to avert or alleviate this crisis.

Thus, by contrast to the neoclassical position which claims value-neutrality, we see ecological economics as coming from a world view wherein a belief in ecological crisis is related to overt basic values that are assumed to be widely shared among normal, sane members of our species. These assumptions are not, however, sufficient to determine what kinds of responses, including institutions, are required to deal with the crisis. Such a determination requires a more formally worked out ethical system.

There are a number of ethical systems that are potentially compatible with the ecological economics world view. The articles summarized in this part have been selected, in part, because they help to clarify the options among several more or less formal ethical positions that are relevant to the issues of ecological economics. The following are some of the leading candidates:

(1) *Utilitarianism* is the ethical system that has informed the neoclassical value system. It is described by Talbot Page, especially with a view to what the classical and neoclassical versions of utilitarianism permit and/or require as ways of achieving intergenerational justice.

(2) *"Justice as Opportunity"* is proposed by Page as an alternative approach—one that includes a more realistic theory of mind and of human motivation than the utilitarian, and that emphasizes the resource base as a special concern of both inter- and intragenerational justice.

(3) J. Ronald Engel claims that there is an *ethic of sustainable development* (in the introduction to a book by that name). This ethic was characterized at the Ottawa Conference on Conservation and Development as resting upon five criteria: integration of conservation and development; satisfaction of basic human needs; achievement of equity and social justice; provision for self-determination and cultural diversity; and maintenance of ecological integrity. [Engel, pages 8–9] Engel adds that "the key to a normative understanding of sustainable development is to be found in the idea of 'individuals-in-community;' " this idea is held up as a leading fact about life by ecologists in general and may therefore also be expected to play an important role in the world view of ecological economists. Hence, "one task on the agenda of the ethics of sustainable development is to reconceptualize our inherited moral ideas so that they can do justice to the full complexity of interactions within and between biological and social communities." [Engel, page 19]

(4) *Religious Traditions* have been called upon by various authors, some claiming that religions are the cause of the faulty value systems which have brought about the environmental crisis; others finding in the same or other religious traditions the ethical system that is needed as a basis for institutional and other solutions. E.F. Schumacher describes an ethical system based on the Christian beliefs that man was created in order to "save his soul," and that "all the other things were created

in order to aid him."[Schumacher, page 129] Such an anthropocentric view has been criticized by Lynn White, Jr. and others as the problem, not the solution (see the summary of White's famous article in Part I); however, Schumacher derives from it his favorite four criteria of smallness, simplicity, capital saving, and nonviolence. (He derives rather similar criteria from Buddhism, in an article on "Buddhist Economics."[4])

Other religious traditions, associated with the native peoples of the Americas, the Orient, or other parts of the world, are also often cited as sources for ecological values, and sometimes for ethical systems. This approach also has its critics. A particular strain of environmentalism, called eco-radicalism by Martin Lewis, is described by him as using an often uninformed or misinformed idealism of native religions as a contrast to modernity, in which the West is singled out as "the sole source of environmental degradation, and indeed, in the most extreme examples, as the single repository of human evil."[5]

(5) J. Baird Callicott has written a long article which examines a number of different ethical systems that can serve as the basis for an environmental ethic. In addition to deep ecology and two versions of the Judeo-Christian tradition ("stewardship" and "citizenship," as expressed in various parts of Genesis), he also considers *traditional humanism*, which he finds problematical on account of its anthropocentrism, and *ecofeminism*, which he sees as suffering from a "theoryless pluralism" that, in refusing to choose between different, culturally based moral traditions, ironically leaves might as the ultimate arbiter of right.

In the portion of his article which has been summarized for this part, Callicott proposes another alternative, based upon Aldo Leopold's land ethic; he calls it *ecocentrism*. This term may be misleading, as it implies an emphasis upon ecosystem *rather than* on humanity. In fact, "the land ethic makes explicit provision for individual members, both human and non-human, of the biotic community as well as for the community as a whole. . . . instead of overriding familiar social ethics, the land ethic creates additional, less urgent obligations to additional, less closely related beings. . . . The land ethic obliges us to look out for the health and integrity, the diversity and stability, of nature in a way that is consonant with these prior duties to human beings and human aspirations."[Callicott, pages 375–76]

The first four articles summarized in this part have been selected as especially well-argued representatives of positions that are important for ecological economists to take into account. The remaining summaries are of articles which take more or less for granted the importance of these ethical issues and pose the institutional question: How should we organize our society to take such ethical issues into account?

Thus, the debate between Stone and Elder, on whether we should understand trees as having rights, starts with some fairly similar beliefs about the goals; it is the question of how to reach the goals that is most at issue. In debates such as this it often appears that there is most agreement upon the long run, where the requirements for a healthy economy seem to converge with those for a healthy ecosystem. The greatest divergence seems to be in the medium run—after we will have presumably taken the obvious "win/win" first steps, but while short-term self-interest still asserts itself in opposition to long-run convergence. An underlying tension is the assumption accompanying neoclassical rationality, that people are *only* motivated by self-interest (which is usually assumed, in practice if not in principle, to operate in a short-term, narrow way), as opposed to the assumptions made outside of the neoclassical social sciences that there is a broader range of motivations to take into account.

Brian Barry's article centers on the issue of fairness—a subject about which we find the comment, in an introductory economics textbook: "the concept of fairness is indeed a difficult one for an economist to treat. There is no economic definition of fairness, to be sure."[6] Barry asks "What happens when the principles for justice between generations are combined with moral principles governing distribution among people who are contemporaries, whether they live now or in the future?" [Barry, page 25][7] The challenge is thrown down for ecological economists to go beyond the neoclassical approach, in which it is commonly recognized that the emphasis upon efficiency leaves out questions of equity.

The last two articles summarized in this part provide especially good examples of the ethical and institutional issues that ecological economists must take into account when thinking about sustainable development. Miguel Altieri and Omar Masera make interesting and important connections among three ways of approaching these issues: sustainable development; the activities of NGOs (especially in Latin America), and a bottom-up, grassroots approach. They propose practical steps to enhance the effectiveness of each approach, stressing, in particular, two emerging evaluation procedures: participatory rural appraisal and natural resource accounting. (This emphasis is a good start toward addressing the problem mentioned earlier of naive expectations about simple translations from values to prices.)

The final summary, of an article by Jonathan Harris, takes a more global look at some of the issues of sustainable development, considering who (or what institutions) can be entrusted to implement a sustainable development strategy for the benefit of the people who most need it, now and in the future. Harris stresses that the first line of answers economists have given to these conflicts are not in themselves sufficient. Specifically, markets and prices alone will not create the appropriate incentive structures to address the diverse goals simultaneously, for they do not amount to feedback systems which are sufficiently sensitive, forward looking, or intelligent to convey all of the critical information. Similarly, local internalizing of externalities does not necessarily solve global problems.

Like Altieri and Masera, Harris urges a reassessment of the Keynesian perspective that has been out of fashion for the past decade and a half. He proposes a sweeping reassessment of global institutions (i.e., the World Bank, the IMF, and GATT) and the establishment of new institutions that will promote Keynesian tools for needs-focused (as opposed to wants-focused) development simultaneously with "the new functions of resource conservation, waste management, environmental protection, and planning for ecological sustainability."[Harris, page 119]

Harris notes that the efforts and costs involved in creating such new institutions, oriented especially toward the protection and enhancement of entities that now lack legal rights and of people who are without economic power, "would require the replacement of the 'yuppie' ethic with a revitalized 'Peace Corps' ethic."[Harris, page 121] In other words, the need is to replace neoclassical rationality with precautionary rationality.

Is this likely to happen in the world? What is being proposed here is a shift in ways of thinking—specifically, to understand our rationality in precautionary rather than neoclassical terms. Such a shift is proposed as the pivotal connection between how we (intentionally) act and how we (instinctively) *re*act. Where the need is for a change in ways of thinking, it is appropriate to look to thinkers (for example, academics and other writers) to lead the way. Ecological economics is a valuable force fostering the new ways of thinking that are essential for the kinds of ethical and institutional change required to respond to present and looming ecological crises.

Notes

1. While utilitarianism is the ethical system cited by neoclassical economists when their ethical grounding is challenged, there is, in fact, a serious discontinuity between that ethic (which assumes altruism, both in those who adopt "the greatest good for the greatest number" as their goal, and in those whose actions are determined by this goal) and neoclassical rationality (which formally permits altruism, but certainly does not assume it, and in some ways actually works to discourage it). Unfortunately, neoclassical economics' claim to value-neutrality has obscured this discontinuity, so that the limitations of utilitarianism as a basis for any

economic theory (as spelled out, for example, in Talbot Page's article) have not been confronted or dealt with in much of the theory that supposedly relies upon this ethic. The exceptional economist who has done the most to overcome this philosophical lacuna is Amartya Sen.

2. Here the *structure* of the system of neoclassical theory is contrasted with its *subject matter*. The latter does not, of course, have to be value-neutral, since it importantly includes the value-laden preferences of all economic actors.

3. There are, of course, exceptions. Again (as in note 1), the most obvious modern one is Amartya Sen. We have to go back to Alfred Marshall (1842–1924) to find an economist who was a leader in the field and who considered ethics to be of central concern. Marshall, however, did not attempt to model ethics; he continued to resist (even as he helped, ironically, to foster) the trend toward accepting the false syllogism: everything of importance to economics must be represented through formal models; whatever cannot be included in a formal model must not be of economic importance.

4. E.F. Schumacher, "Buddhist Economics," *Resurgence* 1 (January–February 1968); reprinted in *Economics, Ecology, Ethics: Essays Toward a Steady-State Economy,* ed. Herman E. Daly (New York and San Francisco: W.H. Freeman and Company, 1980), 138–145.

5. Martin Lewis, *Green Delusions* (Durham, NC: Duke University Press, 1992), 244.

6. Roger LeRoy Miller and Robert W. Pulsinelli, *Understanding Economics* (St. Paul, Minnesota: West Publishing Company, 1983), 48.

7. In relation both to Berry's article and to Stone's, the reader might wish to be aware of the classic essay on the legal rights of future generations: Edith Brown Weiss, "The Planetary Trust: Conservation and Intergenerational Equity," *Ecology Law Quarterly* ii (1984): 495–581.

Summary of

Intergenerational Justice as Opportunity

by Talbot Page

[Published in *Energy and the Future*, eds. Douglas MacLean and Peter G. Brown
(Totowa, New Jersey: Rowman and Littlefield, 1983), 38–58.
© 1983 by Rowman and Littlefield]

Resource use can potentially result in long-term costs, and how we view these costs can determine how much emphasis we put on conservation and other alternative courses of action. This article distinguishes between two views and considers each in the context of a utilitarian framework (the classical and neoclassical versions). The first, a global approach, discounts future costs, thus assigning weights to present and future costs. A positive discount rate implies that future costs count less than present costs. The second view argues that if costs are potentially large and very long term, the resource base should be preserved intact. Notions of justice between generations are central to this view; it is referred to as the specialized approach.

Global Versus Special Views of Long-Term Energy Costs

The central argument for discounting future costs (at a rate equal to the opportunity cost of capital) is that intergenerational efficiency will result. The criterion used for efficiency is that of Pareto optimality, i.e., a system is said to be efficient in an intergenerational sense if no single generation can be made better off without making another generation worse off. The problem with this criterion is that efficient allocations may not be fair or just. In contrast, the specialized approach is better suited to deal with issues of intergenerational justice.

Defining Neoclassical Utilitarianism

The notion of maximizing behavior is central to the economists' definition of utilitarianism. In fact, maximization is a universal process in the utilitarian framework. The following principles help define utilitarianism and clear away distinctions that can interfere with the maximization process:

(1) *Only preferences matter:* Decisions can be made on a number of different bases, including morality, religion, habit, or the maximization calculus. If these different bases for decision making are recognized, then to explain a decision we must explain the process used and the inter-

action with other processes. Utilitarians do away with these differences and their accompanying complexities by assuming that each individual has only one preference ordering.

(2) *All states are comparable:* According to this principle, an individual is always able to judge whether he prefers one complete description of reality to another, or whether he is indifferent between the two states.

(3) *Future and present states are directly comparable:* This principle extends the second principle, suggesting that individuals can compare different future paths as well. One can think of different present states as different snapshots, and different paths in the future as different movies. The second principle argues that individuals can compare snapshots, and the third principle argues that individuals can compare different movies.

(4) *Utilities of different individuals are not directly comparable:* Neoclassical utilitarians argue that because utility is not observable, it is not comparable across individuals, nor can it be summed across individuals. Therefore, while classical utilitarians want to maximize the sum of utilities, neoclassical utilitarians believe that individuals maximize their own utilities, and we should therefore aim for Pareto optimality in decision making.

(5) *Property rights must be well specified:* Since the best way of revealing preferences is through the market system, the only important rights for neoclassical utilitarians are property rights.

Discounting within Both Utilitarian Systems

There are a number of arguments that use the principles described above to argue in favor of discounting. Four of these arguments are discussed in this section: two in the classical utilitarian tradition and two in the neoclassical utilitarian tradition. A counterexample is also offered to show that discounting does not inevitably follow from the principles outlined above.

The first argument for discounting involves an unselfish planner (a classical utilitarian) who weights each generation's utility by the probability that the generation will not exist. Thus, while the planner attaches equal importance to the utility of each generation, he accounts for the possibility that future generations may not exist, and therefore discounts their utilities. The problem with this approach is that if a constant probability of extinction in each year is assumed in order to yield a constant discount rate, then the probability of a future generation existing is independent of the actions of the present generation.

The second argument involves a selfish planner in the tradition of a neo-classical utilitarian. He wants to maximize only his own generation's welfare, but he is also blocked by a veil of ignorance from knowing which generation he belongs to. Being selfish, this planner weighs the utility of any generation by the probability that he will belong to it. As in the first case, the declining probability of the existence of future generations leads to an argument in favor of discounting.

The third argument involves a classical egalitarian utilitarian who is concerned about productivity. In models that allow for capital productivity, discounting at a rate of zero results in present generations sacrificing to invest more in favor of future generations. To achieve an egalitarian solution when generations achieve equal utilities across time, the discount rate must be equal to the marginal productivity of capital.

The fourth argument, based on a theorem by Tjalling Koopmans, argues that an intergenerational planner who is fair because he adopts a set of axioms that are neutral, innocuous, and fair will select a social choice rule that discounts the utilities of future generations.

While these four arguments are all examples that start from a utilitarian tradition and favor discounting, discounting does not inevitably follow from the utilitarian framework. For example, when Kenneth Arrow's axioms are combined with crucial axioms of Koopmans', discounting does not follow. It is also interesting that in these variations on the fourth argument, Pareto optimality is always satisfied, whether or not discounting is favored. Therefore Pareto optimality cannot be the determinant of whether or not discounting should be adopted.

Outside the Neoclassical System

It is important to move outside of the neoclassical system to develop a common sense concept of justice that does not depend on preferences or utility. One reason for this is that the neoclassical framework is too narrow to reflect the normative issues that go into decision making. The following four distinctions are made with respect to the neoclassical principles outlined above:

(1) *All ownership rights are not on par:* This distinction is based on the Lockean notion of "just acquisition," in which ownership is a relative rather than an absolute concept. According to this notion, the larger the role one plays in the creation of a work, the larger is one's claim over the work. The present generation therefore does not have the right to run down the resource base that it did not help to create, when it is possible to treat it in a sustainable way.

(2) *Not all states or goods are completely substitutable:* This distinction argues that some commodities are more essential than others, so equating the resource base with this generation's capital stock accumulation may be invalid. For example, energy and primary materials are embodied in capital, and thus capital cannot completely substitute for those ingredients.

(3) *Offsetting harms with benefits:* Utilitarians believe that avoiding harm and doing good are really the same thing, and therefore they look for net benefits. However, in some cases this may not be in keeping with common sense notions of justice. For example, while killing one individual to save two renal disease sufferers may result in a net gain, common sense suggests that this is unjust. Similarly, in the intergenerational context, depleting the resource base and increasing the level of pollutants may be unjust even if there is a corresponding increase in the capital stock.

(4) *Opportunity versus utility:* Since it is easier to control the opportunities available to the next generation than to control future utility, it seems sensible to focus on passing on opportunities in the form of the cultural and natural resource bases.

The Inefficiency Issue

The main objection of neoclassical economics to special treatment of the resource base is that this could result in large inefficiencies. For example, a great deal of effort could be spent preserving things that future generations may not want. This proposition deserves empirical and conceptual consideration.

From an empirical perspective, it seems unlikely that future generations will not want essential goods like health, alternative energy resources, water, soil, etc. Second, the increases in human-made capital are increasing our dependence on the resource base. Until this trend reverses, we must assume that future generations will value preserved resources. Third, switching from the current system of subsidizing depletion to taxing it will impose few, if any, costs today, while producing benefits in the future. Thus preserving the resource stock based on a notion of justice as equal opportunity may also increase intergenerational efficiency.

Finally, at a conceptual level, we must consider compensating investments. It is important to note that, in some cases, if compensating investments to protect future generations are not made in the present, then the compensation option is lost, since the investments must be made now in order to grow over time and actually become available in later years. In addition, the argument for discounting suggests that a project that harms the future is acceptable provided that enough benefits will accrue to compensate the future, whether or not compensation will actually be made. However, when the harm done to the future is grave, the argument that only the possibility of compensation is important—not actual compensation—loses its appeal.

Summary of

Introduction: The Ethics of Sustainable Development
by J. Ronald Engel

[Published in *Ethics of Environment and Development: Global Challenge, International Response*, eds. J. Ronald Engel and Joan Gibb Engel (London: Belhaven Press, 1990): 1–23, and (Tucson: University of Arizona Press). Reprinted by permission of John Wiley & Sons, Ltd.]

(This is a summary of the introductory chapter of the book.)

In its 1987 report *Our Common Future*, the United Nations Commission on Environment and Development, under the leadership of Gro Harlem Brundtland, concludes that global well-being may depend on raising sustainable development to a global ethic. Exactly what this statement implies needs to be carefully examined. For example, we must ask what ecological, social, political, and personal functions sustainable development serves, and how human aspirations can be reconciled with our moral obligations to other species and to the ecosystem. We must also know on what grounds sustainable development can be called a *true* ethic for humans.

The Growing Concern for Ethics

Human attitudes toward development have changed fundamentally over time. The addition of a moral component, motivated by environmental concerns, is a relatively recent occurrence. However, not everyone shares the view that ethics are essential to solving the problems of the environment and poverty. Specialists, businessmen, and politicians argue that economic and scientific solutions are adequate to deal with environmental and material concerns. Past experiences with moral claims invoked in the public arena have also led to skepticism with respect to any approach based on ethics. Those in charge of policy must remember, however, that in the end all political and economic arrangements must be ethically legitimate in order to survive.

The Contribution of Ethics

Ethics can be defined as reflections on moral ideas and ideals. There are at least five practical reasons for the new interest in this topic; the fifth—defining a new paradigm for sustainable development—incorporates and builds on the other four.

(1) There has been growing awareness of the important role that the moral values and beliefs of a culture play in determining human behavior, and so the assumption that science and policy formulation can be neutral and value free is being rejected. A study of ethics is necessary to understand and evaluate the moral codes of cultures.

(2) There is a recognition that moral ideals can motivate people to act even when the costs are high. A number of environmental movements—including green consumerism, ethical investments, and voluntary simplicity—provide evidence of this.

(3) Ethics can have a role in clarifying the values at stake in policy decisions, and offer moral reasons for pursuing different policies. Lack of a clear understanding of the moral issues involved leads to policy formulations based only on custom, personal preference, or political and technical feasibility.

(4) Ethics can help resolve value conflicts that arise in development activities by redefining the issues so that the values in each position can be identified and reconciled. For example, the conflict between "ecocentrists" and "anthropocentrists" can be recast as an issue between values of ecological integrity and social justice, both of which are worthwhile ends that may potentially be mutually enhancing.

(5) Ethics has an important role both as a basis for critiquing the existing dominant paradigm of global development and in shaping the emerging paradigm of sustainable development. This paradigm shift is a product of the growing consensus in the international conservation and development communities that there are serious problems with modern industrial development and its emphasis on competition, consumption, and unlimited growth. The long-standing need to think in terms of dichotomies such as conservation versus development or humanity versus nature is being questioned. Many factors have motivated this shift, but the most important one seems to be the failure of modern societies to provide a good and sustainable way of life for all.

The Moral Challenge of Sustainable Development[1]

The primary problem for thinking in terms of a new moral paradigm and the ethics of sustainable development at a global level is that there is no common moral language for discussion and deliberation among the different cultures and religions. A common, cross-cultural set of moral principles needs to be developed as an alternative to both the resurgence of absolutism on the one hand and widespread relativism on the other. In fact, cultural diversity can best be preserved through adoption of inclusive moral principles that promote mutual respect among all peoples and cultures. This common moral language and set of principles can be developed by drawing on the resources of each culture and religion.

A second problem is that the term *sustainable development* is itself ambiguous, and it is important to differentiate between two common but irreconcilable interpretations. Some people understand sustainable development to imply a genuinely new mode of development rooted in ethics, but others understand it to simply support continued growth, with no ethical content. The authors in this volume hold the first view, extending the meaning of sustainable development beyond the concepts of growth with equity or development with conservation, and developing the moral dimensions implied by the term. In its broadest sense, sustainable development can be defined as "the kind of human activity that nourishes and perpetuates the historical fulfillment of the whole community of life on Earth."[10–11]

A third difficulty facing the emergence of a new ethical paradigm is the fact that the two main groups challenging the currently dominant development paradigm—advocates of alternative development and advocates of ecological integrity—are also at odds with each other. Thus, another challenge of the new paradigm of sustainable development is to bring these two groups together by merging environmental concerns into the normative discourse on development.

Religion, Science, and Sustainable Development

The development of modern societies has led in many cases to a growing dichotomy between religious value systems and secular scientific ones. While environmental and development issues were historically the concern of the secular system, recently there has been a surge of reaction among religious traditions to the environmental and development crises that have beset modern societies. This interest arises from the spiritual failures of human beings in modern materialistic societies, evident in the levels of greed, lust, and pursuit of pleasure and power that are observed. A path of sustainable development will require a fundamental change in humans with the help of spiritual disciplines. The mechanistic science that has dominated modern Western societies is seen by some as a primary cause of our present crisis. A new paradigm of sustainable development is needed that transforms scientific and religious systems and develops a greater mutuality between them.

Unity and Diversity in International Response

There is consensus that the concept of "individuals-in-community" is key to an understanding of sustainable development. This implies that rather than focusing on individuals or species as separate entities, they must be viewed as part of a larger whole. Our choice of world view is therefore not between the individual and the community, or between the environment and people, but between different kinds of "mixed" communities. However, ethicists from different parts of the world and different cultures still have different visions of what sustainable development means and what the emerging ecological world view should be.

An Agenda for Ethics

Despite differences based on culture and social contexts, ethicists from around the world are elevating sustainable development to a global ethic. The first task on the agenda is to reconceptualize inherited moral ideas in such a way that they do justice to the complexity of interactions within and between biological and social communities. Simultaneously promoting social and ecological values in a moral framework is a difficult task that is too big for any individual or even a single group. It must therefore involve the input of ecofeminists, ecophilosophers, religious leaders, and many others. Ethicists should work with grassroots organizers so that the principles of sustainable development can be developed from the ground up. In addition, the second issue on the agenda is to determine how moral principles can be effectively implemented. Voluntary organizations and individuals working in cross-cultural, cross-disciplinary, and cross-sectional coalitions can be effective in promoting moral principles and an ethical approach.

Note
1. The sections that follow are an analysis of articles in the book. In this summary we discuss the issues raised in these articles, but not the authors associated with the ideas.

Summary of

The Age of Plenty: A Christian View

by E.F. Schumacher

[Published in *Economics, Ecology, Ethics: Essays Towards A Steady State Economy*, ed. Herman E. Daly (New York and San Francisco: W.H. Freeman and Company, 1980), 126–137. Reprinted in *Valuing the Earth: Economics, Ecology, Ethics*, eds. Herman E. Daly and Kenneth Townsend (Cambridge, Massachusetts and London, The MIT Press, 1993) 159–172.]

The optimism that modern science and technology could provide for all is being questioned on all fronts. Environmental degradation, resource scarcity, and the limits to growth are responsible for a reconsideration of the efficacy of an industrial society. This article evaluates the future of industrial society from a Christian perspective. The Christian perspective flows from "The Fountainhead" of the St. Ignatius of Loyola which suggests that man should use the goods of the earth only so far as they help him attain a higher goal, and should withdraw when the material hinders the attainment of the higher goal.

If this premise is accepted, then quantitative concepts like economic growth and the gross national product become meaningless. Whether a good or service is good or bad need not determine the amount it adds to such quantitative measures. Rather than quantitative measures, qualitative concepts should be developed. The nature of income distribution is such that about one-quarter of the world is immensely rich and about three-quarters are immensely poor, with very few in between. This duality is abnormal and unhealthy for both groups, since one has too much and the other too little. What exacerbates the problem is that rich societies are perceived as the model which poor societies must follow and aspire to be like. The rich nations have used exorbitant resources in pursuit of their wealth. To suggest that modern science and technology has solved the production problem is fallacious, since modern production has required nonrenewable energy resources. From a physical perspective it is impossible for poor nations to follow the path of the rich. Furthermore, modern societies are facing a crisis of values which manifests itself in social unrest, rising drug addiction, and crime. There should be a reassessment of our aims and objectives so as to redirect the system. Two important questions are how this can be done and who should do it?

In the modern world the technical and social methods of production are chosen and developed from the perspective of efficiency. But the economic concept of efficiency is unrelated to the people involved in the production process and is defined in terms of the material aspects of production and profits. Organizing the production process with efficiency of materials as the criteria leads to a division of labor and specialization of tasks. The society that set up the production system in turn becomes molded by the logic of the production process. Thus a change of the aims and objectives of society necessitates a change of the production process, the prevailing technology, and the existing organizational framework. The technological change required should move us away from the giantism, infinite complexity, vast expensiveness, and violence to a system which is small, simple, cheap, and nonviolent.

Smallness implies bringing production units to a human scale and gives people independence in their activities. If production units are small, they use few resources, a distinct advantage when large resources are becoming scarce. Their levels of pollution are less and they are ecologically better than bigger units. They lead to a more even distribution of income and cause less congestion. Simplicity is to be favored for a number of reasons. The reason production processes should be simple is that then there will be time and energy for man to pursue other interests beyond making a living. This is important if the higher goals are to be achieved. If production processes are not cheap, only the rich and powerful gain access to them. Cheap technologies can make the poor self-reliant and help create employment. Nonviolence refers to humankind respecting the place of all animate and inanimate objects when dealing with them. The concept of nonviolence may take many directions, but a good example is respect for and preservation of the integrity of the ecosystem. In this case it would mean undertaking recycling of all organic materials and reducing our dependence on chemicals, reducing pollution, etc.

The required move should be gradual. It requires change in small units and that we put people and not material consumption first. Change is possible if we keep in mind the message of "the Fountainhead."

Summary of

The Search for an Environmental Ethic

by J. Baird Callicott

[Published in *Matters of Life and Death: New Introductory Essays in Moral Philosophy*, 3rd edition, ed. Tom Regan (New York: McGraw-Hill, 1993), 322–382. Summarized with permission of McGraw-Hill, Inc.]

Since the 1960s there has been a growing recognition that there is an environmental crisis. The solution to this problem cannot be purely technical or engineering based. A new environmental ethic is needed that promotes an ecocentric approach to the environment. However, there are some schools of thought which argue that existing ethics are adequate to deal with environmental problems. This article first considers and critiques some of these views and points out why they fall short. It then develops the basis and broad outlines of an ecocentric environmental ethic.[1]

Some Schools of Thought

Three schools of thought that reject the need for a new environmental ethic are considered here:

(1) *Traditional Humanism:* Traditional humanists treat the environment as a pool of natural resources that are to be utilized to increase human welfare. They acknowledge that some human beings indirectly have an adverse impact on others due to the negative effects of their actions on the environment. However, they argue that the solution to this problem can still be found in the old ethics based on moral consideration of all human beings. The problem with this approach is that, by focusing on humans alone, it does not take into account the adverse impact of human behavior on non-human members of the biotic community.

(2) *Deep Ecology:* The deep ecology movement, founded by Arne Naess, argues that humans are part of a larger ecological system, and it is the realization of this interconnectedness, not ethics, that is vital for maintaining the health and integrity of ecosystems. According to deep ecologists, "ethics" implies separate groups that must respect one another, an approach that results in a narrow conception of the self. However, these metaphysical views of the deep ecologists have no basis in scientific ecology. Scientific ecology reveals a differentiated oneness of nature, rather than the homogenous unity proclaimed by the deep ecologists.

(3) *Ecofeminism:* Ecofeminists argue that the ideology that leads to men dominating nature is the same one that is responsible for men dominating women. The solution to environmental problems is therefore the same as the solution that the feminist movement has been urging with respect to women's liberation: the overthrow of the patriarchy. Ecofeminists argue that the cause of environmental problems is not anthropocentrism (human-centered thought), but androcentrism (male-centered thought). Furthermore, ecofeminists object to any ethical theorizing (and therefore to a theory of environmental ethics) because theories are inherently male biased and serve to rationalize power. Instead, ecofeminists favor contextual analysis based on each situation. The problem with this anti-ethics position is that if power and not truth determines outcomes, then there is no reason for those who exercise power today (males) to give it up. The solution to the

exclusive hold on power by any one group, then, lies in a rational, honest, open-minded dialogue between all groups with a commitment to truth and reason.

The Ecocentric Approach to Environmental Ethics

An environmental ethic rooted in evolutionary and ecological theory is needed. From the perspective of scientific ecology, every living being is embedded in a matrix of relationships with other beings, and organisms develop their special characteristics through interactive adaptations within this matrix. Individual organisms that are independent of this web of interactive relationships are inconceivable. This matrix of relationships results in a biotic community in which each organism carries out specific functions. Environmental degradation occurs when organisms and functions begin to disappear.

An environmental ethic should therefore have both holistic and individualistic dimensions. Within this framework, right and wrong would be based on the structure and organization of the biotic community, rather than simply on the imposition onto the entire biotic community of ethics relevant only to interactions among humans. Aldo Leopold's "land ethic" can form the basis for such a development. Critics of Leopold are wrong when they suggest that the land ethic emphasizes the holistic aspects at the expense of individuals.

According to Leopold, "an ethic, ecologically, is a limitation on freedom of action in the struggle for existence."[2] This view of ethics raises an evolutionary paradox: how can the practice of self-limitation have evolved given the continuous struggle for existence? Would such an ethic not compromise an organism's struggle to survive and reproduce? Charles Darwin looked into this question from the perspective of natural history in *The Descent of Man*. He argued that since human beings can survive and successfully reproduce only as members of society, social instincts such as love, affection, and sympathy were naturally selected—because they were essential for communities to flourish. From the perspective of Leopold's land ethic, it is also important to consider the whole of the *biotic* community, rather than concentrating on any specific individual organism. This ethic fosters the belief that all organisms on earth are members of an extended family and implies respect for fellow members of the community as well as the community as a whole.

Some philosophers have objected to the implications of Leopold's land ethic. If the integrity, stability, and beauty of the biotic community is harmed by the overly large human population, wouldn't it then be our duty to eliminate a whole lot of people? This solution for protecting the welfare of the biotic community is not implied by the Leopold land ethic which would supplement, not replace, traditional human morality. Nevertheless, the human population should be scaled down over time in humanitarian ways.

An ecocentric land ethic should therefore be one in which human beings use the environment in such a manner as to enhance the integrity, stability, and beauty of the entire biotic community. In addition, any use of the environment, including cutting trees and killing animals, should be done in a skillful, thoughtful, and humane manner without waste. This can be achieved by considering the welfare of the entire biotic community and of individual organisms.

Notes

1. This summary does not encompass Callicott's entire article. In particular, it does not cover the extensive discussions of the Judeo-Christian and extensionist approaches to environmental ethics that are found in the original article, although points from these sections that are relevant to the discussion of the ecocentric approach to environmental ethics are included.

2. Aldo Leopold, *A Sand County Almanac, with Essays on Conservation from Round River* (New York: Balantine, 1966): 288; cited by Callicott, 361.

Summary of

Should Trees Have Standing?— Toward Legal Rights for Natural Objects
by Christopher D. Stone

[Published in *Southern California Law Review* 45 (2nd Quarter, 1972): 450–501. Summarized with the permission of the *Southern California Law Review*. See also Christopher D. Stone, *Should Trees Have Standing?: Toward Legal Rights for Natural Objects* (Tahoe City, California: Tioja Press, 1988).]

In the past, the child was considered less than a person from a legal perspective, but legal rights for children are now recognized and are, in fact, expanding. Legal rights have similarly been bestowed at different times upon a number of different groups, including prisoners, aliens, and women. The legal system has even bestowed rights on inanimate entities such as trusts, corporations, and joint ventures. At one time, bestowing such rights on these groups was unthinkable; until rights are actually bestowed, the "rightless" are considered mere things for our use. The time has come to bestow rights on "natural objects" in the environment, including forests, oceans, rivers, etc., as well as on the natural environment as a whole. This is not to say, however, that the environment should have the same rights as those conferred on humans, or that each environmental entity should have the same rights as every other. There are two sides to the discussion about granting rights: the legal–operational aspect, and the psychic and socio-psychic aspect.

The Legal–Operational Aspects

What It Means to Be a Holder of Legal Rights

"An entity cannot be said to hold a legal right unless and until *some public authoritative body* is prepared to give *some amount of review* to actions that are colorably inconsistent with that 'right.'"[11] In addition, for a thing to count jurally three other criteria must be met:

(1) the thing should be able to institute legal action at its own behest;

(2) in granting legal relief, the court must take injury to the thing into account; and

(3) the relief must run to the benefit of the thing.

The Rightlessness of Natural Objects at Common Law

Consider the status under common law of a stream being polluted. The stream itself has no standing and does not have rights. The pollution can only be challenged by a human being who can show that polluting the stream challenges his rights. However, this may not happen for a number of reasons: the human may not care about the pollution; he may be economically dependent on the polluter; or it may not be economically worthwhile for him to pursue the action to prevent pollution.

A second sense in which natural objects are denied rights has to do with how cases are decided. The fact that they are decided based on the economic interests of identifiable humans further denies any "rights" to natural objects. Courts compare the costs to the polluter of pollution abatement and the costs of pollution to others to determine whether pollution is permissible. Damage to the stream and the life-forms it cultivates are not considered.

The third way in which the common law renders natural objects rightless is by conferring the benefits of a favorable ruling on the person who brings suit against the pollution, rather than on the natural object itself. For example, the damages awarded in a water pollution suit will go to the plaintiff, not toward the repair of the body of water.

Toward Having Standing in Its Own Right

The fact that streams and forests cannot speak is no reason for them not to have legal standing. Corporations, states, estates, infants, etc. do not speak, but they do have legal rights. A guardian (either a conservator or a committee) can be appointed to represent the legal interests of natural objects. A number of existing organizations could play the role of conservator, including the Sierra Club, the Environmental Defense Fund, and Friends of the Earth, among others. The law should also allow the conservator to protect the interest of the natural object without first having to prove that the rights of the conservator's members are being violated.

There are two possible objections to the guardianship approach outlined above. The first is that the guardian cannot judge the needs of the natural object in its charge. However, the counter argument to this objection is that natural objects do communicate their needs in rather unambiguous ways. We know, for example, when the lawn needs water. Moreover, every day we make decisions on behalf of "others," and the needs and wants of these others are often less clear and verifiable than the wants of rivers, trees, and land. The second objection is that the federal Department of the Interior and the states' attorney generals are already guardians. However, the Department of the Interior is only the guardian of federal public lands, not local public lands or private lands. Furthermore, the actions of the Department of the Interior are often questioned by environmentalists who consider them detrimental to the environment. In addition, the states' attorney generals are political and must attempt to meet a wide range of goals, so their actions may not be in the best interests of the environment.

Toward Recognition of Its Own Injuries

Suits involving the environment have been decided based on the economic hardships of human beings, but we must question why these decisions should be based on profits to humans, rather than on costs to the environment. While it is well recognized in economic analysis that ideally every individual should bear the full costs that his or her activities impose on society, the legal–economic system fails to impose these costs in the case of pollution. This may occur, for example, because the costs of pollution of a river may be spread out, making coordination and redress difficult. By conferring jural standing on natural objects, the natural object itself, through its guardian, can coordinate the fragmented groups and press claims against a polluter. The guardian can also go further and represent other interests that are not presently recognized, such as those of endangered species. The cost of cleaning up the damage done to the natural object could be used in the courts as a measure of monetary worth.

Toward Being a Beneficiary in Its Own Right

Another advantage of making the environment a jural entity is that this approach prevents private litigants from selling out the environment in negotiations by making natural objects the beneficiaries of monetary awards. These awards can be put into a trust fund that can be used for guardians' costs and legal fees. We must also recognize that if "rights" are granted to the environment, then it may also bear "liabilities." Money in trust funds can be used to meet liabilities, such as crop destruction due to floods, and damages can be paid to those affected.

Toward Rights in Substance

For the environment to have rights in a meaningful way, it must be granted a significant body of rights that it can invoke in a court of law. This implies that there must be a process of review to determine whether the rights have been violated. The government should also mandate a set of procedures that must be undertaken to protect the interests of the environment before a project can be executed by corporations or individuals. While some forms of damage to the environment may be permitted, irreparable damage could be banned.

The Psychic and Socio-Psychic Aspects

There have been changes in laws and procedures that are favorable to the environment, but they seem to result from the realization that a better environment is good for humankind, rather than from a fundamental change in consciousness. It is still humankind, not the environment, that is taken into account.

Conferring rights on the environment will have costs, leading many to question why such rights should be granted. But this question is odd, as "it asks for me to justify my position in the very anthropocentric hedonist terms that I am proposing we modify."[44] It is analogous to asking why whites compromised their preferred rights-status with respect to blacks, or why men compromised their preferred rights-status with respect to women. Yet many people assume that an appeal must be made to self-interest in order to persuade humans to act.

Scientists have been warning us that the earth will face a crisis if we do not change our ways. The solution to the problems confronting us will require a reduction both in our living standards and in the growth of the economy, and they will also necessitate a serious reconsideration of our consciousness toward the environment. We will have to identify what our present consciousness and its consequences are, how to change this consciousness (if at all), and what sort of institutional reforms will be required. A new relationship between man and nature is necessary. We must stop viewing nature as a set of useless objects and instead see ourselves as part of nature. This attitude will free us of the need for supportive illusions.

Summary of

Legal Rights for Nature:
The Wrong Answer to the Right(s) Question
By P.S. Elder

[Published in *Environmental Ethics: Volume II,* eds. Raymond Bradley and Stephen Duguid (Burnaby, British Columbia: Institute for the Humanities, Simon Fraser University, 1989): 103–119, and *Osgoode Hall Law Journal* 22 (1984).]

The argument put forth by Christopher Stone in his article "Should Trees Have Standing?"[1] is rejected. This article argues that the "deep" ecology view put forward by Stone does not go any further in solving environmental disputes than conventional ethics and law.[2]

Criticism of Stone

Stone argues that since we have improved morally by extending rights to blacks, women, children, and some animals, we can progress further by giving rights to natural objects. However, this is a nonsequitur, since people and plants belong to different categories. Natural objects do not have any of the characteristics that bestow moral importance on a thing, including "awareness, self-consciousness, the ability to formulate goals, act to attain them and to appreciate their attainment."[110] Nor does Stone give any reasons for why the environment should have a moral claim. There is no reason to believe that objects in the environment "want" to survive or to remain undisturbed; objects without sentience cannot care or suffer. Moreover, we cannot know what trees want, so guardians of the environment can only argue on behalf of natural objects by imposing their own values. Deep ecologists are themselves being anthropocentric when they claim that they know what is good for the environment. Finally, how are we to handle situations in which the government, industry, and public interest groups compete to be the guardians of the environment?

Even if Stone is correct that humans are a part of the biosphere, and not separate from it, conclusions radically different from his could be drawn. For example, we can claim that humans, as a part of nature, have an equal right to compete, even if we prove to be better suited for survival than other species and cause the extinction of some. The deep ecologists might then argue that humans have moral duties to natural objects, but these duties arise precisely because we are different. Thus, we are both a "part of nature" but at the same time different from it, and "it is the essence of being human which leads to respecting the rights of morally important beings."[111]

Ordinary Ethics Get Us There Too

This article simply argues that Stone has not made his case that we owe rights to natural objects. Who then does have rights? The following categories are suggested:

(1) Any self-conscious being who has hopes and wishes, and who can weigh and choose among alternatives, is an object of moral concern.

(2) Even if a creature does not fall into the first category, if it can feel pain then it has a right not to have unnecessary pain inflicted on it.

For example, if whales or dolphins meet the definition of the first category, then they should not be murdered or enslaved for any reason. On the other hand, if they can feel pain but cannot conceptualize, then they can be used for food and experiments as long as they are not made to suffer unduly. Deep ecologists may not be satisfied with this approach, but they should recognize that many shallow ecologists are also distressed by the destruction of the wilderness and are in favor of environmental protection. The shallow ecologists' position is based on human reasons, but it can still lead to rigorous environmental protection.

Conventional Law Can Do It

Since laws are a human construct, we can legislate about any concern that we choose. Thus, rather than create rights for non-humans, the environment can be protected by giving humans more rights. Stone calls for assessment procedures that give a greater weight to the environment in policy-making. However, a number of policy and legal techniques for doing this already exist, and these can be extended to deal with environmental concerns like energy conservation or the effects of industrial chemicals on health and the environment. Environmental protection reforms are not hampered by the existing anthropocentric theories of rights; the real problem is a lack of political will.

The degradation of the environment has led to serious problems, including toxic and carcinogenic pollutants, human starvation, and the threat of a nuclear holocaust, from which our present economic and political system has failed to protect us. In light of these serious problems, the deep ecology argument for rights for natural objects seems trivial.

Notes

1. See previous summary.
2. To avoid repetition, the discussion of Stone's position in this article has not been summarized.

Summary of

Intergenerational Justice in Energy Policy
by Brian Barry

[Published in *Energy and the Future*, eds. Douglas MacLean and Peter G. Brown (Totowa, New Jersey: Rowman and Littlefield, 1983), 15–30.
© 1983 by Rowman and Littlefield.]

This article proposes a criterion for compensation of future generations by the present generation for the consumption of exhaustible natural resources.

The Nature of the Problem

All mineral resources raise problems of intergenerational justice due to their finite quantities, but fossil fuels raise two special problems. First, unlike other mineral resources, fossil fuels cannot be reused. Second, much of the known stock of fossil fuels is difficult and expensive to obtain and deliver to the point of use, so we can expect steadily increasing costs. In addition, in spite of the limited information on oil reserves, it is reasonable to suggest that the world cannot continue its consumption of oil at present rates.

Problems of fairness do not arise if any generation can use as much of a resource as it feels is necessary and still pass on adequate quantities to succeeding generations. However, by definition the problem with nonrenewable resources is that the more one generation consumes, the less future generations will have. More importantly, they will have fewer options as well, other things being equal. Therefore, we need just criteria for the use of nonrenewable resources.

A Solution and Its Defense

One solution for the problem posed above is for the present generation to compensate future generations with improved technology and increased capital investments to offset the effects of resource depletion. This "offsetting" could either be in terms of utility—i.e., ensuring that future generations can attain the same utility level as they would have if resource depletion had not occurred—or in terms of the "replacement of the productive opportunities we have destroyed by the creation of alternative ones."[17] The second approach suggests that resource depletion reduces the productive potential of future generations, and they should be compensated for this loss.

This article argues that the opportunities criterion should be adopted rather than the utility criterion. The basis for this position is valid for all contexts in which questions of justice arise; its application to intergenerational issues is only a special case. To see this, we should first consider in more detail the case for using the utility criterion.

The argument for using utility as a criterion stems from the general belief that, in the final analysis, what really matters is the level of satisfaction, happiness, or utility that individuals experience. A generally recognized problem with this criterion is that it is difficult to define objectively a measure of happiness, that is suitable for public policy purposes. However, there are additional objections to using utility as a criterion even if an objective measure of happiness does exist. Consider the case of two people who do the same work, at the same level, equally well. Justice demands that they be paid the same amount, irrespective of the level of happiness that each derives from that income. The fact that one of them gets more satisfaction from the income than the other would not be justification for transferring income from one to the other. Based on their work, these individuals have a claim to resources, not to a utility level. When applied to future generations, this line of reasoning suggests that we should be concerned with the choices available to future generations—in terms of productive potential—rather than the level of happiness they will achieve. Thus the opportunities criterion is more relevant than the utility criterion.

This analysis leads to two questions:

(1) Why should future generations not be left worse off than they would be if we did not deplete natural resources?

(2) How do we establish what the opportunities of future generations would be if natural resources were not depleted?

The answer to the first question is simply that there is no powerful counter argument; there is no compelling justification for the present generation to claim a larger share of natural resources than future generations, so justice demands that every generation should get an equal share.

The answer to the second question is both important and difficult. It is important because if we want to compensate future generations for the loss of opportunities caused by our use of natural resources, then we must know what their opportunities would have been had we not used the resources. One extreme solution suggests that if we leave future generations with a few picks and shovels to compensate for the resources we have consumed, then we have increased their productive potential, since "they would then be in a better position to exploit natural resources than if they had to use their bare hands."[22] This extreme suggests that the capital stock bequeathed to future generations is compensation enough. The problem with this approach is that the present generation did not create all existing capital and technology, but inherited a large part of it from past generations. Inherited capital and technology are similar to natural resources in that all are passed down from previous generations. Therefore, in addressing the problem of natural resource depletion and compensation, we must consider how weights can be assigned both to the capital stock inherited by a generation, and to the capital stock it passes on. While these questions need further thought and investigation, the basic principle for determining compensation should be to maintain the productive potential of future generations.

Practical Problems

There are three practical problems associated with the abstract discussion outlined above:

(1) *How can the compensation criterion be made workable?* For some resources we can compensate directly for our use. For example, if we use 10% of oil reserves, then we can compensate future generations by developing technologies that make it possible to extract 10% more oil,

leaving them with as much exploitable oil as the present generation has. When direct compensation is not possible, other avenues for resource substitution must be developed.

(2) *Where do issues of intragenerational distribution fit in?* Some people have raised objections to worrying about future generations when there is widespread poverty in this generation. This objection would be valid if intergenerational and intragenerational justice were incompatible, but they are not. However, we are still left with the problem of how to deal with issues of intragenerational justice. If we apply the arguments made for intergenerational transfers to intragenerational issues, then it is clear that natural resources and technology inherited from the past are the "common heritage of mankind." Poor countries therefore have a claim on rich countries.

(3) *How does one deal with issues related to uncertainty in relation to policies which have results in the future?* In some cases, the risks and benefits for future generations associated with alternative actions in the present are uncertain. Standard techniques of decision making under uncertainty cannot be used to determine whether the actions should be undertaken, since the probabilities associated with different outcomes are unknown. The only just solution to this problem is not to undertake the actions if the risks might include widespread and disastrous consequences in the future.

Summary of

Sustainable Rural Development in Latin America: Building from the Bottom Up

by Miguel A. Altieri and Omar Masera

[Published in *Ecological Economics* 7 (April 1993): 93–121. Reprinted with kind permission from Elsevier Science B.V., Amsterdam, The Netherlands.]

In recent years, the debate on sustainable development (SD) has gained momentum rapidly within Latin America, but a gap remains between the rhetoric of SD and its reality. Institutional arrangements and market forces in the agricultural sector are biased against sustainable rural development. Creating new policies that reduce the resource costs of farming and promote social and ecological sustainability will be a major challenge for SD, in addition to addressing the principal development priorities of the region that include reducing poverty, enhancing food security and self-sufficiency, conserving natural resources, and encouraging the empowerment and participation of poor rural communities. Most top-down national and international development approaches have not met these goals, but grassroots, bottom-up approaches by nongovernment organizations (NGOs) have opened new roads to target the poor directly. Promoting policies that are not only ecologically sound but also economically profitable is a major challenge for those NGOs involved in the agricultural sector. The long-term success of these NGOs will depend upon creating the socioeconomic conditions necessary for widespread implementation of agroecological programs.

Environment and Development in the Last Two Decades

Conventional "top-down" development strategies have proven to be fundamentally limited in their ability to promote equitable and environmentally sustainable development in Latin America. As Latin American countries are drawn into the existing international economic order, their governments adopt policies to service their enormous debts, and they increasingly embrace neoliberal economic models that emphasize export-led growth. However, these approaches have resulted not only in growth but also in increased poverty, as well as deforestation, soil erosion, industrial pollution, pesticide contamination, and loss of biodiversity.

During the 1970s, Latin American countries adopted an import substitution industrialization strategy (ISI), emphasizing highly capital- and energy-intensive industrialization primarily centered on the manufacture of durable consumer goods. Agriculture was subordinated to industrial development, and agricultural surplus was diverted into the industrial sector. This strategy produced high rates of regional growth, and social indicators did improve in most countries as a consequence of government social programs, despite growing inequality in income and land distribution. However, this approach was not environmentally neutral. Programs such as large energy and infrastructure projects, colonization of tropical forests, subsidies to agrochemical companies, expansion of mechanization in agriculture, and rapid industrialization all vastly expanded the human impact on the region's ecosystems.

The region's economy stagnated in the 1980s, exacerbating environmental problems. The massive debt problem was a key cause of this crisis; debt service captured between 20 and 40% of the region's exports, diverting financial resources needed for internal investment. The structural adjustment programs required by the multilateral development banks as a condition for new loans have entailed downsizing the state, eliminating subsidies, controlling inflation, and adopting neoliberal trade policies. The social costs of these new policies have been high, especially for the poor.

The increasing marginalization of the poor and the deterioration of these economies have had further negative impacts on the environment. Budgetary cutbacks and the urgent need to generate foreign exchange have led both to cutbacks in environmental programs and to increasing pressure on natural resources. Social pressure for access to natural resources has also increased among the poor, transforming them into agents of overexploitation of fragile lands.

Challenges for Sustainable Rural Development: The Case of the Peasant Sector

The urgent need to combat rural poverty and to regenerate the deteriorated resource base of small farms has stimulated a number of NGOs to search for new strategies of bottom-up agricultural development and resource management. These are based on local participation, skills, and resources, and so they enhance productivity while conserving the resource base. The central idea of this approach is that development and research should start with what is already there: local people, their needs and aspirations, their farming knowledge, and their autochthonous natural resources. The goal has been to define a new agricultural approximation to the peasant production process based on agroecological principles.

NGOs throughout the region face diverse socioeconomic and agricultural constraints, ranging from lack of access to land and low income of peasant families to various physical limitations of the agroecosystems. Preliminary evaluations of NGO activities show that they have produced tangible benefits for the local populations such as enhanced food production, regeneration of natural resources bases, and higher use-efficiency of local resources. Nevertheless, in many cases these efforts have met with mixed results, primarily due to an environment in which poor peasants have limited access to political and economic resources, and in which institutional biases against peasant production prevail. A bottom-up approach requires the elimination of three systemic constraints: (1) anti-peasant biases in credit and extension institutions; (2) perennial underinvestment in peasant communities; and (3) subsidies to capital-intensive and agrochemical-based agriculture.

Making Sustainable Rural Development Operative

The design of new procedures and indices for evaluation of projects and technology is a key step in making sustainable rural development operative, because it is through these procedures that the final assessment of alternative projects occurs. Current evaluation procedures, especially cost–benefit techniques, give all the weight to the economic dimensions and have proven inadequate to fulfill the requirements of a broader process of technology evaluation.

Two emerging evaluation procedures are participatory rural appraisal (PRA) and natural resource accounting (NRA). NRA techniques incorporate environmental externalities in conventional cost–benefit analysis and can be used to evaluate the profitability of agricultural systems when natural resources are taken into account. One problem with these techniques, however, is that markets are often imperfect or nonexistent in peasant agricultural systems, so it can be difficult to compile data on resource depletion and to assign market values to resource losses. NRA techniques also perpetuate the traditional economic bias by reducing the whole evaluation process to a monetary indicator.

PRA techniques constitute an important step toward the design of alternative bottom-up evaluation procedures. This approach emphasizes the informal gathering and presentation of information to facilitate a participatory process involving both local residents and multidisciplinary teams of researchers. The goal is to mobilize communities to define their own priority problems and opportunities and to prepare site-specific plans of intervention. Data gathering and presentation is based on a rich array of procedures that include semi-structured individual and group interviews. Technologies are evaluated through very general criteria addressing the environmental, economic, and social concerns expressed by the local community. The evaluation schemes utilized in PRA often lack detail, however, and need to be complemented with more thorough analysis.

Elements of both PRA and NRA techniques could be brought into a sustainable development evaluation framework that does the following: (1) incorporates aggregate and quantifiable indices, but does not lay out qualitative criteria; (2) addresses concerns and trade-offs among long-term and short-term objectives, and micro and macro costs and benefits; and (3) contrasts local people's priorities and interests with "desirable" technology or project characteristics as stated by the dissemination agency. Researchers and local residents should remain aware of the elements of both traditional agricultural knowledge and modern agroecological principles and techniques that offer the potential to conserve and regenerate resources, optimize productive potential and resource use, and facilitate farmer-to-farmer communication and extension.

Latin American countries must realize that future patterns of growth and development must be radically different from those of the past. The immediate needs are to achieve a more equitable distribution of wealth, secure adequate living conditions for the poorest, broaden the bases of participation in decision-making processes, and conserve and enhance the region's natural resource base.

Summary of

Global Institutions And Ecological Crisis
by Jonathan M. Harris

[Published in *World Development* 19 (January 1991): 111–122.]

The rapidly escalating environmental problems of today share a common characteristic: their global nature. This is immediately obvious with respect to issues such as global warming and the depletion of the ozone layer, but environmentalists are increasingly recognizing that many other problems once thought of as purely local concerns have a global dimension as well. Erosion, the degradation of soil productivity, groundwater pollution and depletion, desertification, deforestation, toxic agricultural runoff, acid precipitation, and the exponential rise in toxic industrial wastes are all global issues in that, to one degree or another, every nation must contend with their specific consequences. In addition, they are global because the cumulative environmental impact of these crises is transnational. Reliance on market forces as a solution to these problems is not only an ineffective response to these threats, but one that can actually create incentives that militate against effective solutions. An institutional approach is required, and the requisite institutions must be global in scope in order to effectively confront the truly global scale of the crises.

The Obsolescence of Present International Institutions

The existing international institutions (the UN, IMF, World Bank, and GATT) are all firmly rooted in a particular historic era. They were shaped by the emerging post-war Keynesian consensus and represent an attempt to institutionalize this policy framework at an international level. In the Keynesian vision, economic growth requires government guidance and activist policies to circumvent the cyclical instabilities that plagued the pre-war economies. The task assigned to these international agencies was to promote global economic expansion and to avoid the protectionism and worldwide deflation of the 1930s. The remarkable expansion of growth and trade in the early post-war era, as well as the dramatic reconstruction of Europe and Japan, seemed to fulfill the Keynesian vision and justify the faith many had placed in these institutions.

However, with the growing international economic stresses of the 1970s and 1980s, theorists and policy makers have moved away from the Keynesian perspective. Recent theory has sought to minimize the role and effectiveness of government policy. Meanwhile, in practice the primary policy response of the IMF to the debt crisis has been deflationary and contractionary rather than expansionary. Turning the legacy of Keynes upside down is doubtless applauded by many economists today, as Keynesian policy prescriptions have been repeatedly blamed for the worldwide inflationary conditions of the 1970s. In this view, the harsh monetarist policies that produced the recession of the early 1980s were a necessary corrective, an approach that would be validated by the ensuing surge of vigorous supply-side growth. However, while growth did resume in some areas, it was driven by the unplanned burst of consumer demand in the United States, supported by its trillion dollar credit line. Not only did this growth do little to help the developing nations, but it led as well to major structural trade imbalances and stagnation or decline for many nations.

Under these conditions, the role of the World Bank, the IMF, and GATT has shifted from guiding and shaping world economic development to struggling to manage problems and alleviate the symptoms of stress. However, the policy tools of these institutions are inadequate for this new task. The IMF lacks the authority to impose the necessary macroeconomic fiscal and trade policies on the United States, Germany, and Japan. At the same time, it has imposed austerity programs on Latin America and Africa that have made the 1980s a lost decade for these debtor nations. The World Bank's long-term development goals are frustrated by the overwhelming debt burden, so the Bank too has adopted short-term policies. GATT negotiations have focused on limiting the trade-restricting and neomercantilist policies being adopted by nations as they try to pay off debt or gain market share. It is becoming increasingly clear that these existing economic institutions will not provide an adequate basis for sustainable world development into the twenty-first century. This reality becomes starker when we factor in the global ecological crisis.

A Revitalized Keynesian Vision

The failure of the world economic institutions is not the failure of the Keynesian vision that inspired them. Indeed, in terms of the goals set in 1944 they have been spectacularly successful. The new problems faced today arise in part from their very success in meeting their original goals of reconstruction and growth of the northern economies. They also stem from the imperfect inclusion of developing nations in world growth, and from environmental issues unforeseen by the original architects of the post-war world order. A renewed global Keynesianism is needed that both focuses on the unsolved problems of development and is integrated with an analysis of the ecological basis of economic activity.

Keynesian interventionism goes beyond the limited neoclassical post-Keynesian vision that was derived from Hicks and systematized by Samuelson. In addition to demand-side fiscal and monetary policies, a thorough Keynesian analysis would include policies for income redistribution, greater social management of investment, market stabilization, and managed trade. Resource management and environmental protection policies are also quite consistent with this framework. The present global crisis demands the use of this whole range of Keynesian policy tools, but with a special emphasis on environmental policies.

Ecology, Entropy, and Economic Theory

Environmental analysis is still undeveloped in economic theory. Traditional cost–benefit analysis, though useful in some specific instances, is an inadequate tool for conceptualizing ecosphere disruptions that threaten the very basis of life on earth. There is, however, a body of work—unfamiliar to most economists—that endeavors to place the economic system within the context of the earth's biological and geophysical systems. This work analyzes economic activity as subject to the fundamental physical laws of entropy. According to this theory, much of our modern economic production uses up stocks of low-entropy matter, thus irreversibly decreasing our wealth in terms of available resources, while generating high-entropy wastes. These effects cause an unacceptable strain on natural systems that may ultimately destroy their ecological stability. Traditional economists tend to assume that new technologies will overcome these problems and assure a continuous supply of resources for economic use. The entropy theory, in contrast, is based on the presumption that there are limits to growth. It asserts that economic systems must operate under the constraints of limited stocks of low-entropy resources, the limited capacity of biological systems to produce foods, and the limited capacity of the earth to absorb high-entropy waste products. "Ultimately the only sustainable world economic system is a steady state economy using the low entropy available from the solar flux."[118]

New Institutions for Global Development

If we take the conclusions of entropy analysis seriously, economic policy must shift its focus from promoting economic growth to managing growth and maintaining sustainable forms of economic activity. Global institutions must then fulfill two sets of functions: the traditional Keynesian functions of employment creation, redistribution, and stabilization; and the new functions of resource conservation, waste management, environmental protection, and planning for ecological sustainability. These institutions should include:

(1) an expanded International Financial Institution based on the present IMF but with greater powers of liquidity creation;

(2) an institution similar to the World Bank, but with a vastly expanded capacity to focus on sustainability and environmental reclamation;

(3) a Global Public Works Institution that would finance and operate health, education, literacy, waste management, population control, and environmental protection programs in developing nations;

(4) a Global EPA with a mandate to conduct environmental monitoring;

(5) a Global Resource Management Agency charged with the creation and management of world parks;

(6) an International Research and Technology Transfer Institution to promote and disseminate ecologically sound technologies;

(7) an International Trade Organization to deal with questions of managed trade; and

(8) an International Peacekeeping Institution with more extensive powers than the present UN forces.

Such a global institutional structure is as sweeping and "unthinkable" in today's international politics as many of the New Deal reforms would have been in the United States in the 1920s. It took the calamity of the Great Depression both to reveal that the existing status quo was inadequate and to produce the political conditions necessary for reform. Now we are again at a stage in history in which economic developments have overtaken the institutions that manage them. The historic precedent is the establishment of the present global institutions in the 1940s, with their strong Keynesian inspiration—a process that was facilitated by the hegemonic position of the United States. Is it possible to replicate this success in the more pluralistic and conflict ridden world of today? Given the urgency of the crisis, and the perils of delay, it is not impossible to imagine that the political leaders of the developed world may become willing to take the risks and confront the ecological crisis. Measured against the severity of the problem, the political and economic barriers may not be as insuperable as conventional analysis would lead us to believe

Subject Index

Name Index

ISLAND PRESS BOARD OF DIRECTORS

Chair
Susan E. Sechler
Executive Director, Pew Global Stewardship Initiative

Vice-chair
Henry Reath
President, Collector's Reprints, Inc.

Secretary
Drummond Pike
President, The Tides Foundation

Treasurer
Robert E. Baensch
Senior Consultant, Baensch International Group Ltd.

Peter R. Borrelli
President, Geographic Solutions

Catherine M. Conover

Lindy Hess
Director, Radcliffe Publishing Program

Gene E. Likens
Director, The Institute of Ecosystem Studies

Jean Richardson
Director, Environmental Programs in Communities (EPIC),
University of Vermont

Charles C. Savitt
President, Center for Resource Economics/Island Press

Peter R. Stein
Managing Partner, Lyme Timber Company

Richard Trudell
Executive Director, American Indian Resources Institute